Birdscapes

It would be interesting if some real authority investigated carefully the part which memory plays in painting. We look at the object with intent regard, then at the palette, and thirdly at the canvas. The canvas receives a message dispatched usually a few seconds before from the natural object. But it has come through a post office *en route*. It has been transmitted in code. It has been turned from light into paint. It reaches the canvas a cryptogram. Not until it has been placed in the correct relation to everything else that is on the canvas can it be deciphered, is its meaning apparent, is it translated once again from mere pigment into light. And the light this time is not of Nature but of Art.

Winston Churchill, amateur painter

The real voyage of discovery consists not in seeking new landscapes but in having new eyes.

Marcel Proust

Birdscapes

Birds in Our
Imagination and Experience

Jeremy Mynott

Princeton University Press

Princeton and Oxford

Published by Princeton University Press, 41 William Street, Princeton,
New Jersey 08540

In the United Kingdom: Princeton University Press, 6 Oxford Street, Woodstock,
Oxfordshire OX20 1TW

Library of Congress Cataloging-in-Publication Data
Mynott, Jeremy.
  Birdscapes : birds in our imagination and experience / Jeremy Mynott.
    p.   cm.
  Includes bibliographical references and index.
  ISBN 978-0-691-13539-7 (hardcover : alk. paper)   1. Bird watching.   2. Birds—
Psychological aspects.   3. Human-animal relationships.   I. Title.
  QL677.5.M96 2009
  598—dc22   2008036405

British Library Cataloging-in-Publication Data is available

This book has been composed in Minion family with Bossa Nova MVB Display
Modified

Printed on acid-free paper. ∞

press.princeton.edu

Printed in the United States of America

1 3 5 7 9 10 8 6 4 2

Contents

Illustrations

Preface

I end at the beginning, like most authors. Just as well too. Strategic plans—whether for books, businesses, wars, or lives—always look more convincing if they are written after the event rather than before it. This book, at any rate, has been in the nature of an exploration for me, a journey whose sights and sounds I did not fully foresee when I started and whose destination was unclear. I have, however, resisted the temptation to rewrite the beginning to plot the route in the full glare of hindsight, hoping thereby to involve the reader more fully in my own ruminations, surprises, and discoveries along the way. The journey's the thing, and the "conclusions," such as they are, don't make any sense without it.

There is, however, a deliberate structure it may be useful to mention briefly. The first two chapters start to define the questions to be explored in the later, more substantive ones, which are on such things as rarity value, the physical qualities of birds, sound and song, landscape and season, bird names and symbols. These initial questions are developed, and I hope enriched, by the many examples and experiences (mine and other people's) that I examine in the course of the enquiry, and the chapters tend to get longer and more detailed as the book goes on. Each chapter starts with a "diary note" of an actual encounter, and I try to use these anecdotes to show how the topics that chapter deals with can arise out of such experiences. The chapter then goes on to offer some analysis and muse on the results. I make a lot of use of quotation, some of it unconventional for a book about birds, both to vary the voices and to enlarge the frame of reference. There are notes of two kinds: footnotes (mainly for self-interruptions, titbits, and asides) and endnotes in the reference section (mainly for bibliographical sources and references). There are also four appendices for larger digressions. Certain themes recur throughout the book—the snares of sentimentality, the pros and cons of anthropomorphism, the interplay between what we perceive in birds and what we project onto them, and the power of metaphors, names, and symbols to express or distort our vision. But that is already to make sound abstract and remote what is best understood through particular live examples, which is what I try to offer. Each chapter is self-contained, but there is a sort of spiral progression through these ideas, with many wanderings and wonderings, like revisiting a landscape (or indeed a bird) from different directions and at different times and seasons to gain a fuller picture. This is not a systematic treatise of any kind, rather a series of linked reflections. The mode is conversational, the mood enquiring and sometimes playful.

I wrote this book quite quickly, in exactly a year after signing a contract for it. I realised while doing so, however, that I had really been contemplating it for quite some time. It has been a way of making conscious the reasons that have sustained my interest in birds over so many years. I have many people to thank for their company in doing this. First, my brother, Simon, who got me into all this and in particular taught me birdsong at a very early age—the best present he ever gave me. Then other friends and family—my nephews Philip and Graham, my longtime companions Malcolm Gibbons and David Jenner— who have all loyally accompanied me on trips to remote places where our objectives must have sometimes seemed puzzling to them. After all, why *would* one sit on a cliff in an uninhabited island beyond the Outer Hebrides, at two in the morning in the rain, and declare oneself so happy to have heard (though not really to have seen) some small dark petrels flying in off the sea? Philip Allin also has made many memorable trips with me in Europe, and Steve Edwards has for many years been a most agreeable and knowledgeable companion for "the Scilly season." I have enjoyed many relevant conversations with each of them, during both the birding and the après-birding, and both have read and commented in detail on my draft chapters. Tony Wilson has yet again amazed me with the acuity of his reading and has saved me from many errors, not for the first time in my career. Sarah Elliott has been a perceptive and entertaining guide over the years to all the inhabitants of Central Park, New York, and I have learned a lot from her about both birds and birders. Marek Borkowski shared both expertise and ideas with me on a memorable trip many years ago to the Polish marshes and forests, which I now realise got me thinking about some of these topics. Other experts have read parts of the text and made many detailed suggestions, as well as giving me important encouragement: Mark Cocker and Jonathan Elphick (several chapters), John Fanshawe (chapter 8), John Peter (chapter 9 and appendix 4), Geoff Sample, Chris Watson, and Andrew Whitehouse (all chapter 6), and Pat Easterling (chapter 10). Princeton University Press's two readers, Stephen Moss and Wally Goldfrank, have been a wonderful source of advice throughout the project: each has read the whole thing in draft and made many excellent suggestions, with Wally giving invaluable guidance on the North American and neotropical examples in particular. Caroline Dawnay and Ivon Asquith were also important advisors at the early stages, and Caroline has stayed loyally with the project and been a great friend to me and the book despite disruptions to her own professional life.

Ian Malcolm at Princeton University Press has been a model editor, giving timely advice and encouragement in just the right tone of voice. He has demonstrated that some editors do still edit, by reading the whole text and responding both promptly and shrewdly to my drafts. It has also been a pleasure to deal with all his other colleagues at Princeton, of whom I would like to mention in particular Kimberley Johnson, Eric Rohmann, Sara Lerner, Madeleine Adams, and Peter Dougherty. It was very generous and trusting of Princeton to give me direct access to all these people, given my background and the high probability that I would want to participate in more decisions than authors really should.

My most special thanks, however, must go to Geoffrey Hawthorn. The idea for this book arose from various conversations I had with him on seawalls in Suffolk, and the whole book has been a sort of conversation with him thereafter. He has read every chapter as I drafted it and has made the most remarkably detailed and interesting comments by way of reaction to them (usually the next day). I really can't thank him enough. His thoughts went far beyond the sort of "reader's report" anyone has the right to hope for and they have been a tremendous stimulus to me—as well as providing ample material, I hope, for more conversations on more seawalls.

Finally, there is my wife. Diane Speakman is herself a professional author and editor. She too has read all the drafts and we have discussed many aspects of the format, style, and text. She believed in this project right from the start and has given me every encouragement and support in it, sometimes in testing circumstances, for which I am truly grateful. In all our twenty-five or so years together, however, I have never yet succeeded in persuading her to take the slightest interest in birds. This is my best and last shot, and in that fond hope I dedicate the book to her.

27 May 2008

1

Wondering about Birds

Wonder is the first of all the passions.

Descartes

Shingle Street, 15 September 2006

I am watching swallows. They are passing just above me, as they move down the coast in the early stages of their long migration south. A familiar scene, common birds, but utterly absorbing. The swallows are wonderful to watch in flight, driving vigorously forward with quick thrusts from those swept-back wings, then spending some of their forward momentum with sudden swooping and looping excursions or sideways dartings after flying insects. So acrobatic—I feel like applauding and holding up little placards: 10 for tariff of difficulty, 10 for execution, and 10 for artistic impression. Gold medal! How far do they actually fly, I wonder, for each aeronautical mile forward on the journey? One of them comes straight along the line of the seawall towards me, skimming just above the ground, really fast, and then at the last moment he rolls, banks, and veers away. He is close enough for me to take in the steely blue sheen of his back and the blood-red face and throat (surprisingly difficult to see at any distance). I think it is a "he," by the way, from the long tail streamers—the females' tails are just a bit shorter. Did you know you can sex adult swallows in flight this way?

I can see them literally feathering the air, making continual smooth adjustments to vary their speed, direction, and angle of flight. I think of the images of swallows tumbling through the air in Leonardo da Vinci's sketches for his treatises on flight and of the lines by Andrew Young:

> The swallows twisting here and there
> Round unseen corners of the air

Is this why birds inspire such a sense of wonder? This freedom of the air, the buoyancy, the perfect ease of movement? The name "swallow" itself comes from an old Germanic word meaning "cleft stick," a reference to the forked

1. Leonardo da Vinci, *Swallows in Flight* (Codex *On the Flight of Birds*, Biblioteca Reale, Turin, ca. 1505)

tail, which gives it this perfect feather-tip control, and Leonardo took a special interest in the aerodynamics of fork-tailed birds like the swallow and the kite.

I may be wrong in my impression of their speed. Swallows feed closer to the ground than martins or swifts and may seem to be flying faster than they really are. They are closer to us, in this and in various other ways. "Barn swallow" is the official British name now—also in this case the American name—and it once used to be "house swallow" or "chimney swallow," all indicating an intimate sharing of living spaces.

I hear the snap of a passing swallow's bill, but I'm not sure if that means he has just caught something or has just missed something. He calls a few times, a quick and untranscribable sort of bleat. I think of it as *uiveet-uiveet* or perhaps a clipped *ouwhit-ouwhit*. I check the British field guides afterwards and they say *vit-vit* or *tsee-wit* (and that makes me want to check some foreign guides, which I'm sure would hear this differently).[1] Now and then one of the swallows breaks into a snatch of their cheerful twittering song interspersed with soft dry trills. I wonder why they should be singing now, on passage?

Looking back along the seawall into the distance I can see more loose groups of swallows coming my way, all instantly recognisable, even a long way off, from their characteristic flight and profile. There are also some house martins travelling with them, and I can pick those out at a glance from their stubbier outline and the little circling glides they make as they feed, usually in some higher corridor of airspace; they also have a more chirrupy call, harder and more penetrating. Sand martins fly differently again, more direct yet at the same time light and fluttery, almost batlike, and there are one or two of those passing by as well. Perhaps I should also be looking out for other strangers caught up in this mixed flock of hirundines, like a red-rumped swallow, a very rare visitor to the United Kingdom. That would be a different kind of thrill, and a local coup. Is there anything in the procession moving in an unusual way?

The swallows keep coming by in straggly groups for the next hour or so, hundreds of them in all; and then there is a pause in the passage. A change of weather, a different line of flight, the end of summer? I think of where they are heading. Strange that it will be just as natural and ordinary for them to be swooping around elephants and crocodiles in southern Africa for their "winter" as it is for them to be here in our gentler countryside. Are these just different seasonal homes or is our hemisphere the primary one because this is where they breed? Do they *belong* in the same way in both landscapes? And are they welcomed back at the other end the same way as they are here in spring? A closely related species of swallow in Australia is actually called the "welcome swallow," which seems a very happy choice of name—remember the scenes in the Minoan frescoes, which are surely welcoming spring and which catch the flight of the swallows beautifully (better than even Leonardo does, in fact; see plate 1a). There is also the nice illustration on a Greek vase where they are actually saying, "Look, a swallow. . . . It must be spring!"

I think how much swallows figure in our representations of the world: in sayings and proverbs, art and literature, myth and folklore. One swallow may

[1] I also check the authoritative *Birds of the Western Palearctic (BWP)*, which comes in with a whole range of variant calls (or are they really just different renderings?), including *witt-witt, wid-wid, wiet-wiet, wic, twic, chwic, huit,* and *kuit,* and then goes on to offer some wonderful versions of distress calls, including *chiir-chiir, dschrlit, zissit, splee-pink,* and *dschiddschid;* and the indefatigable correspondent Vietinghoff-Riesch reports a variety of rather muffled calls when the birds are in danger, for example *zibist, zetsch, tsätsätsa,* and "a quiet *dewihlik* of distress." I shall listen out for that quiet *dewihlik.*

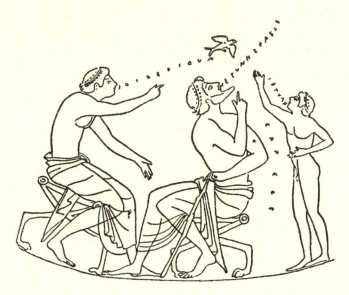

2. Greek vase painting, *The First Swallow of Spring* (in S. Reinach, *Répertoire des vases peints,* 1899)

not a summer make, but it's also true that it wouldn't be summer without the swallows. It is a fact, a semantic and psychological truth and not just a sentimental whimsy, to say that they are part of the meaning of summer for most of us. Suppose that with global warming they found that they could survive the winter here and stayed? Wouldn't "swallows" and "summer" mean something else then? Anyway, half an hour later the passage resumes and they are all around me again. Summer isn't quite ended yet.

• • • • •

I keep interrupting myself with all these questions, musings, and asides. But then, why should I move in straight lines, any more than the swallows do? This is how I experience birds—some combination on my part of sensation, perception, curiosity, playfulness, and imagination. These swallows make me wonder, in both senses of the word.

This book starts from such wonderings. It is about our experience of birds: the reasons why we are attracted to them, the ways we encounter and describe them, and the significance they have in our lives. I want to explore the sources of what is a widespread and for many people a very powerful interest, even a passion. I look at how this plays out in the different ways we perceive (or misperceive) birds, come to know and identify them, seek them out (in some cases obsessively), and find beauty, pleasure, and excitement in them. That will lead me to consider the dimensions in which we experience birds, in particular the seasonal cycle of time and the landscape of place. I hope by the end to understand better the ways we think and talk about birds: their names and classifications, their role in our imaginative and emotional lives, and their representations in myth, folklore, and culture. The book is therefore at least as much about ourselves as about birds.

Here are more examples of the sort of questions that interest me and on which I shall reflect within this framework.

- What are our favourite birds and why? Are there charismatic species (or just special experiences)?
- By what right and on what grounds do conservation bodies such as the RSPB (Royal Society for the Preservation of Birds) and the Audubon societies decide which species to privilege and "invest in"?
- Why are rare birds so important to birdwatchers when rarity is obviously just relative to time and place (gannets in London, tufted ducks in Central Park, swallows in December)?
- Why does the act of identification play such a large part in the experience? And why is that more about species than individuals?
- How much is what we see determined by what we know? And why do we make such bizarre mistakes (the cases of the Spanish crop-sprayer and the Scilly cowpat)?
- Does our concern with lists and counting indicate something we should worry about in ourselves? Is this acquisition or experience?
- How does the beauty of a bird differ from that of a butterfly, a tree, or a landscape?
- Can you enjoy a bird's song just as much if you don't know what it is? (Could anyone mistake a nightingale?)
- Why is it so satisfying to see the first swallow or swift of the year?
- Do birds "belong" in certain landscapes and help to define them?
- Do names matter, and are some bird names better or more "real" than others? (Why does the cuckoo seem to speak so many different European languages?)
- Why have birds been so important in augury, folklore, and literature? (And why particular birds such as eagles, owls, and cranes?)
- Is there some third realm between sentimentality and science in which we can relate to birds for what they are?

There are more ruminations than answers in what follows, I have to say. I do, however, summon help from a wide range of sources. Some of these will be familiar, like Gilbert White, John Clare, Keats, Thoreau, Darwin, Audubon,

Roger Tory Peterson, and E. O. Wilson; but others may be less so, at least in this context, like Aristophanes, Kant, Benjamin Franklin, Oscar Wilde, Freud, Lévi-Strauss, and Yogi Berra (talk about herding cats!). In fact, one principal purpose of the book will be to relate an interest in birds to other spheres of life, in both directions. That means a lot of the arguments and examples will be taken from work in literature, biography, philosophy, and science that is not usually thought of in this connection at all but can be brought to bear on the sorts of questions I ask. And it also means trying to use our experience of birds to take us outwards into other domains. The enrichment works in both directions. Some of the particular questions that occur to me watching these swallows can be answered or illuminated by relevant work in other areas, but the same questions can in turn also serve to enlarge and inform our curiosity about the world more generally and about our relation to it. This sort of reciprocity applies to many other activities, like gardening, sport, cooking, beekeeping, and mountaineering, but it may be ignored or resisted by the more introverted practitioners all these interests tend to attract. There is a sort of Gresham's Law of leisure pursuits, whereby the nerd drives out the good. But it need not be so, and my twin objective here is both to encourage some birders to look beyond the end of their telescopes, so to speak, and at the same time to draw in other people uncertain about their qualifications or embarrassed about the company they might be keeping. I want to show something of the range of different interests that can be taken in birds and the corresponding range of questions they provoke.

One large initial question all this may seem to raise, or even beg, is this. Granted that there are all these different kinds of interest and approach, are some more valid than others? Do some actually preclude others? Do we give an equal welcome to the sentimental and the scientific, the descriptive and the lyrical, the loopy and the learned, the acquisitive and the experiential? Do we say, in a generous democratic spirit, that these can all illuminate some aspects of the subject, or do we have to make distinctions and choices? Is there some new kind or combination of interests that may offer special insight and satisfaction? Could there be, in short, any one right way to talk about birds? There is a real question here, and an interesting one, but I think it is best asked towards the end of the book rather than at the beginning, by which time I suspect it may have dissolved or changed into something else. I hope at least that the intervening chapters will suggest some ways of approaching it. A good way to get our bearings at the outset, perhaps, is to look at some actual examples of the different ways people have responded to birds and the different ways they have expressed these responses. That sets up the discussion in a more direct way and demonstrates some of the options.

Witnesses and Prophets

I start with John Clare, who has been very happily described as "the finest poet of Britain's minor naturalists and the finest naturalist of Britain's major poets." He was especially drawn to seek out corncrakes and to write about them in both his poetry and his prose. Corncrakes are rare birds in Britain now, confined as breeding birds to the remote islands of the Hebrides in the far Northwest, and even if you are in the right place at the right time and the birds are "craking," they are so secretive and well-camouflaged that they are still extremely hard actually to see. But in the nineteenth century the landrail (as it was then called) was much more widespread in Britain and was a regular summer visitor to Helpston in Northamptonshire, where Clare lived much of his life. The bird was just as elusive then as now, though, and just as much a source of wonder (a word I notice Clare uses a good deal):

> They look in every tuft of grass
> That's in their rambles met,
> They peep in every bush they pass
> And none the wiser yet,
>
> And still they hear the craiking sound
> And still they wonder why—
> It surely can't be underground
> Nor is it in the sky,
>
> And yet 'tis heard in every vale,
> An undiscovered song,
> And makes a pleasant wonder tale
> For all the summer long.

As for the nest, that is even harder to find:

> A mystery still to men and boys
> Who know not where they lay
> And guess it but a summer noise
> Among the meadow hay.

Clare always pursued mysteries like this and seems to have had a special interest in finding birds' nests, not to rob them but for the sense of discovery this gave.[1] He enjoyed the hunt and the pleasure of knowing the ways of the

[1] He wrote one six-hundred-word poem in which he describes the nests of, among others, the blackcap, redcap (goldfinch), mavis (mistle thrush), blackbird, pettichaps (probably chiffchaff),

3. Corncrake
(Robert Gillmor)

bird well enough to find its nest—intimations here of ideas I shall be exploring further.

But a sense of discovery can take more than one form. The poets Clare and Keats were near contemporaries and their attitudes to nature have often been compared. Clare was a countryman and wrote from intimate knowledge and close observation. He expresses a delight in his findings, sometimes a simple delight but not a merely sentimental one. Indeed, Keats starchily complained that in Clare, "the Description too much prevailed over the Sentiment." Clare for his part thought that Keats had no firsthand knowledge of nature and so idealised it and made use of it for purely symbolic purposes: "his descriptions of scenery are often very fine but as is the case with other inhabitants of great cities he often described nature as she appeared to his fancies and not as he would have described her had he witnessed the things he described."

Here for comparison are extracts from their very different treatments of the nightingale. First Clare, who discovers another nest and gives it his close attention:

> How curious is the nest: no other bird
> Uses such loose materials or weaves

---

firetail (redstart), wren, wryneck, Egypt bird (spotted flycatcher), and swallow. He also devoted separate poems to the nests of the corncrake, nightingale, yellowhammer, skylark, bumbarrel (long-tailed tit), raven, moorhen, peewit (lapwing), and fern owl (nightjar). In addition to enjoying some of these old country names we may wistfully note the wider distribution then of the raven, nightjar, and wryneck, as well as of the corncrake.

Their dwellings in such spots—dead oaken leaves
Are placed without and velvet moss within
And little scraps of grass and, scant and spare,
Of what scarcely seem materials, down and hair.
For from man's haunts she nothing seems to win,
Yet nature is the builder and contrives
Homes for her children's comfort even here
Where solitude's disciples spend their lives
Unseen, save when a wanderer passes near
That loves such pleasant places. Deep adown
The nest is made, a hermit's mossy cell.
Snug lie her curious eggs in number five
Of deadened green or rather olive-brown,
And the old prickly thorn bush guards them well
And here we'll leave them, still unknown to wrong,
As the old woodland's legacy of song.

Then Keats, discovering himself. Here he is in his "Ode to a Nightingale," with all the stops out:

My heart aches, and a drowsy numbness pains
My sense, as though of hemlock I had drunk,
Or emptied some dull opiate to the drains
One minute past, and Lethe-wards had sunk:
'Tis not through envy of thy happy lot,
But being too happy in thine happiness—
That thou, light-winged Dryad of the trees
In some melodious plot
Of beechen green, and shadows numberless,
Singest of summer in full-throated ease.

And suffering a *petit mort* of passion:

Darkling I listen; and for many a time
I have been half in love with easeful death,
Called him soft names in many a mused rhyme,
To take into the air my quiet breath;
Now more than ever seems it rich to die,
To cease upon the midnight with no pain,
While thou art pouring forth thy soul abroad
In such an ecstasy!

4. Nightingale
(Thomas Bewick, 1797)

Some later authors have tried to combine the sentiment and the description in a way that is both moving and authentic. There is a line of natural history writing that runs from John Clare through figures such as W. H. Hudson and Richard Jeffries and reaches its furthest development, perhaps, in the work of the reclusive J. A. Baker, whose prose trembles constantly on the edge of excess. His most famous book is *The Peregrine,* an account of his obsessive quest to enter the peregrine's world and in a sense lose himself in it. Here is an extract from the introduction in which he explains the origins of his fascination and his mode of approach. He has just seen his first peregrine:

> This was my first peregrine. I have seen many since then, but none has excelled it for speed and fire of spirit. For ten years I spent all my winters searching for that restless brilliance, for the sudden passion and violence that peregrines flush from the sky. For ten years I have been looking upward for that cloud-biting anchor shape, that crossbow flinging through the air. The eye becomes insatiable for hawks. It clicks towards them with ecstatic fury, just as the hawk's eye swings and dilates to the luring food-shapes of gulls and pigeons.

By the end of the book the objective is accomplished, as he stalks a peregrine preparing to roost:

> I ran along the path beside the wall and saw him alighting on a fence-post on the inland side of the dyke. As I approached, he moved farther inland, flitting from post to post. When the fence ended, he flew across to a small thorn bush on the far side of the old sea-wall.
>
> Screened by the low green bank of the wall, I stumble along on my hands and knees towards the place where I think the hawk will be, hoping he will stay there till I come. The short grass is dry and brittle and sweet-smelling. It is spring grass, clean and sharp as salt water. I bury my

face in it, breathe in it, breathe in the spring. A snipe flies up, and a golden plover. I lie still till they have gone. Then I move forward again, very softly, because the hawk is listening. Slowly the dusk begins to uncoil. Not the short wild pang of winter dusk, but the long slow dusk of spring. Mist stirs in the dykes and furs the edges of the fields. I have to guess where I am in relation to the hawk. Three more yards, and I decide to take a chance. Very slowly I straighten up and look over the top of the wall. I am lucky. The hawk is only five yards away. He sees me at once. He does not fly, but his feet grip tightly on the thorny twigs of the bush, the ridged knuckles tense, and big with muscle. His wings loosen, and tremble at the edge of flight. I keep still, hoping he will relax, and accept my predatory shape that bulks against the sky. The long feathers of his breast are rippled by the wind. I cannot see his colour. In the falling gloom he looks much larger than he really is. The noble head lowers, but lifts again at once. Swiftly now he is resigning his savagery to the night that rises round us like dark water. The great eyes look into mine. When I move my arm before his face, they still look on, as though they see something beyond me from which they cannot look away. The last light flakes, and crumbles down. Distance moves through the dim lines of the inland elms, and comes closer, and gathers behind the darkness of the hawk. I know he will not fly now. I climb over the wall and stand before him. And he sleeps.

That is one kind of passion. Fanaticism is another, and today's twitchers have their own *sensations fortes*. Here is Richard Millington, a leading practitioner in the early days of serious twitching, who published a diary of his successful attempt in 1981 to find more than three hundred species in Britain in one year.[1] Note the combination of close description and euphoria when he encounters a real rarity, excited rather than moved:

11 October. St. Mary's, Isles of Scilly
One Red-eyed Vireo seen feeding in lower part of hedge above the quarry at Porthellick House. Watched in bright sunshine in this, just about the only, sheltered spot on the island! A totally hyperzonky megacrippler,

---

[1] A real feat then, before the advent of modern communications systems, and therefore seen as more outlandish. The RSPB hierarchy of the time considered *A Twitcher's Diary* so offensive to good taste and to the traditions of their "establishment" organisation that they tried to censor it and actually blacked out the title in a book club advertisement in their magazine *Birds*. The gentlemen versus the players. Three hundred was more species than most birdwatchers had seen in a lifetime then. When Baden-Powell published his *Scouting for Boys* in 1908, he wrote confidently, "There are 177 different kinds of birds in Great Britain," and he urged "the good scout" to discover as many of them as possible.

5. Red-eyed vireo, St. Mary's Isles, Isles of Scilly (October 1980) (Richard Millington)

perhaps reminiscent of a giant Firecrest. In size possibly a little larger than Garden Warbler, and often appearing pot-bellied with a broad, flat head. Upper-parts goldengreen, extending as a smudge on the "shoulders," with darker bronzy-olive wings and tail. Underparts silky-white with a clear lemon-yellow wash on the vent area and under-tail coverts. Head pattern most striking—bluey-grey crown bordered on either edge by a black stripe, long white supercilium (narrow at bill and flaring out behind eye) and black eye-stripe above green ear-coverts. Rather heavy dark-edged pale bill, strong grey legs and feet, and deep wine-red irises noted. Though moving very quickly between bushes, appeared rather lethargic while feeding, adopting Hippo-like actions to pick up caterpillars which were beaten on the branch before being swallowed. The clean, fresh plumage and yellow vent suggest a juvenile bird.

This sort of pursuit has the potential to generate competitive tensions, of course, especially when flamboyant characters are involved. D.I.M. Wallace pioneered many of the identification criteria that have since found their way into standard field guides and was also one of the small group of birdwatchers who in the 1960s "discovered" the Isles of Scilly as an outstanding place for rare migrants. Here he is reminiscing, with more than a hint of nostalgia, about the popularisation of birding and the eclipse of the officer class:

Coming back to St. Agnes in 1971 after a near three-year sojourn in Nigeria, I was astonished by the rise in the number of birdwatchers.

Where once a rarity might have been seen by a handful of veterans, any good bird would rapidly attract a boatload of 30 to 50 new faces and it was clear that an all-island search strategy was close to achievement. Thus while St. Agnes was still respected as something of an ornithological sanctum, any sense of its experienced observers exercising any real leadership over the archipelago had largely gone. This collapse in discipline was never more apparent than during the still-famous controversy over the identity of a smallish crake that haunted the Big Pool from 26th September to 9th October 1973.

Two bitterly opposed parties form, one claiming it as a spotted crake (a rare but fairly regular migrant in Scilly), the other as a sora rail (an extreme vagrant from North America). Wallace supports the minority (sora) party. The combatants very nearly come to blows in the Turk's Head Pub and eventually it is decided to trap the bird to settle the matter. The affair ends in farce.

> The Sora walked dutifully into the net, was there ignored by the net-minder ... and wriggling free of the mesh performed one last flight to the safety of the opposite rushes. Asked what on earth he thought that he was doing, the leader of the Spotted camp could only mutter abjectly, "Sorry, I thought it was a rat." Paul Dukes announced an imminent heart attack and the Big Pool echoed with guffaws of laughter. After its unneeded brush with man, the bird left overnight for places unknown and 14 days of rather bad behaviour went into birding history. Ornitho-politics had finally reached Scilly and muddied all our feet.

The ultimate prize in this domain is of course a "first for Britain," which generates exceptional levels of adrenaline, interest, and anxiety all round, now boosted by the speed of modern communications via mobile phones, the Internet, and personalised pagers. Returning to the hirundines, here is part of the report by Jeremy Hickman, the lucky finder of Britain's first tree swallow (a North American species) in June 1990, again in Scilly:

> On Wednesday 6th June 1990, having finished my shift behind the bar in the Mermaid Inn, I decided to go to Porth Hellick. I watched from the main hide for a while and could hardly believe how devoid of bird life it was. I could not even console myself by counting the Moorhens *Gallinula chloropus*.
>
> At about 19.00 BST, five hirundines approached low over the pool: one House Martin *Delichon urbicum*, three Barn Swallows *Hirundo rustica* and another bird. This fifth bird gave the impression of a martin, but with no white rump and a glossy blue-green mantle and crown, and pure

white underparts. My heart sank as the bird then flew to the back of the pool and began hawking around the pines and surrounding fields. I rushed to Sluice to obtain closer views and to note its plumage in detail.

It appeared slightly bigger and bulkier in the body than a House Martin, with broader-based wings and more powerful flight. Its underparts were all pure snowy white, from its chin to its undertail coverts, with only a very tiny extension of white from the flanks to the upperside of the body at the base of the wing. Its upperparts were the most amazing bright, glossy blue-green. The wings and tail were matt-black, and the underwing and undertail off-white to silvery grey. The colour of the crown extended well below the level of the eye and squared off into the ear-coverts. The shape of the tail was similar to that of House Martin, being short, but less forked when closed.

The next few minutes were total panic. Would it go? Would it stay? What was it? I was not calm! As it was June, there was no-one anywhere. At about 20.00 BST, I ran back to my car and drove to Old Town to phone the other resident birders on St. Mary's (all two of them). At this stage, I was still unsure of exactly what I had found. I was not expecting to see American birds in June, and I had no knowledge of any eastern species of this nature.

He checks it out in the books and excludes other remote possibilities like violet-green swallow and Bahama swallow and goes back to claim the tree swallow as a first for Britain, which a thousand desperate birders rush to Scilly to see over the next five days. The bird leaves again on 10 June with the same group of hirundines with which it had arrived.

But this is only a mild taste of the sort of extended taxonomic description the serious field ornithologist deploys. Here is a short extract from an article in *Birding World,* a popular rather than a scientific journal—light reading for the experts. The authors are making comparisons between various closely observed individual gulls, to identify the separate subspecies involved. I give three of the summary captions to illustrations, though in fact you scarcely need to read beyond the title of the article to get the general flavour:

Moult Variability in 3rd Calendar-Year Lesser Black-Backed Gulls

Larus fuscus graellsii. Commonly, all the primaries, secondaries and retrices are retained through the winter and spring, as on this bird. Note that few wing coverts and upper tertials have been renewed in the winter quarters. Some scapulars have also been retained but, in general, the brown wing covert panel contrasts with the grey saddle. This is typical 3cy *graellsii* with a black tip to the bill.

Which is clearly very different from:

> *Larus fuscus intermedius.* The moult on the wintering grounds included
> the whole tail, all the secondaries and at least P6–P7 (probably P1–P7),
> where the sequence was interrupted. The wing coverts are a mixture of
> new dark and retained brown feathers. The complete moult began with
> the innermost primary and has now arrived at P5, which has been
> dropped. The advanced winter/spring moult and blackish upperparts
> of this 3cy *intermedius* are features more typically associated with 3cy
> *fuscus.*

And hardly likely to be confused with:

> *Larus fuscus fuscus* undergoes an extensive moult in the winter quarters,
> which includes some or all of the primaries. "CIXE," a typical 3cy *fuscus,*
> has interrupted its moult at P8, with the inner primaries renewed and
> just the two outer primaries retained. The fresh primaries have small
> white tips and are glossy black, contrasting with the browner retained
> feathers. The mirror on P10 is exceptionally large. The worn scapulars
> and wing coverts show a mahogany hue characteristic of *fuscus.*

The text of the article goes into more detail, of course.

I could go on further in this direction, with examples of ever longer, denser, and more detailed accounts that treat the bird as a combination of physical parts to be analysed, studied, and minutely described. The great advantage of this more scientific approach is that it is demonstrably so *successful* in its objectives. It does produce definite, verifiable answers to at least the factual questions that amateurs ask about the characteristics, behaviour, distribution, and migration of different species. It is also *progressive,* in that it continuously extends and improves our knowledge in ways that eventually trickle down to the ordinary observer through better descriptions in the field guides and reference books.

Compare, for example, the following descriptions of the arctic tern in four different field guides, published respectively in 1927, 1937, 1954, and 1999 (see fig. 7). The first is Edmund Sandars's *A Bird Book for the Pocket* (1927), which was my very first birdbook and which I learnt almost by heart. The entry for the arctic tern is a brief one:

> Length 14½ ins. *Sexes* alike. *Summer migrant,* Apl.–Oct., in Scotland
> and Ireland, locally in England and Wales. Differs from Common Tern
> as follows: breeds later in June, preferring island sites. Its call is shorter,
> a harsh *Kleeah.* Sometimes eats earthworms.

6. Arctic tern from Edmund Sandars, *A Bird Book for the Pocket* (1927)

I'd forgotten about the earthworms (can it be true?). The illustrations in the book are quite appalling, or as the author modestly says in the introduction, "In my drawings a just general effect has been aimed at rather than feather accuracy."

The Observer's Book of British Birds was published ten years later and the illustrations are certainly more realistic, most of them being reproduced from the work of Thorburn and other serious bird artists. The book is compiled by a Miss S. Vere Benson, whose style on the title page is given as "Hon. Sec. of the Bird-Lovers' League" and who devotes most of the introduction to anecdotes about the "interesting and lovable bird personalities" she had encountered in her work of caring for injured birds. The main species accounts, however, are unsentimental and workmanlike and an improvement on those in Sandars:

> The Arctic Tern closely resembles the Common Tern, though the underparts have a distinctively grey tone, instead of only slightly so. The mantle is soft grey, the crown and nape black, and the bill and legs red. The immature plumage is mottled with buff. The Arctic Tern is a summer visitor. The breeding haunts are further north than those of the Common Tern, the terneries being most numerous in Scotland and Ireland.
>
> Haunt. The coast.
>
> Food. Small fish.
>
> Notes. Almost indistinguishable from those of Common Tern: *krik* or *kree-a.*

The third book is the famous Peterson *Field Guide to the Birds of Britain and Europe* (1954), which in its time revolutionised bird identification. The illustrations were both more accurate and more revealing, and included depictions of a greater variety of plumages (not just spring males). The text too was more closely based on observable field characters:

> Identification: 15″. Distinguished from Common Tern by *wholly blood-red bill* (wholly blackish in winter, and tip may still be black in spring);

(a)

(b)

Juvenile

Adult
Summer

(c)

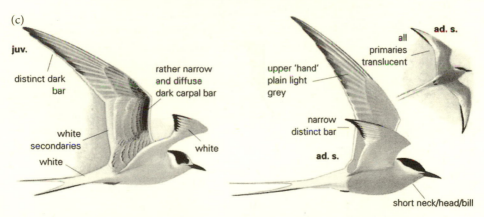

juv.

distinct dark
bar

rather narrow
and diffuse
dark carpal bar

white
secondaries

white

white

upper 'hand'
plain light
grey

narrow
distinct bar

ad. s.

all
primaries
translucent

ad. s.

short neck/head/bill

7. Arctic terns from (a) *The Observer's Book of British Birds* (1937); (b) Peterson, Mountfort, and Hollom, *A Field Guide to the Birds of Britain and Europe* (1954); (c) *The Collins Bird Guide* (1999)

when perched, usually by *shorter legs.* Under-parts and neck usually greyer than in Common and Roseate, often showing by contrast a *white streak below the black cap.* Tail streamers usually project *a little* beyond the wing-tips when perched, but never as far as in Roseate.

Voice. As Common Tern, but whistled *kee-kee,* with rising inflection, said to be characteristic.

Habitat. As Common Tern, but more maritime and more frequently on rocky off-shore islets.

And the fourth is the current market leader, the *Collins Bird Guide* (1999), which says of itself that it "provides all the information needed to identify any species at any time of the year, with detailed text on size, habitat, range, identification and voice. Accompanying every species entry is a distribution map and illustrations showing the species in all the major plumages (male, female, immature, in flight, at rest, feeding: whatever is important)." The account of the arctic tern now introduces several more differentia:

L 33–39 cm (incl. tail-streamers 7–11½ on ad.), WS 66–77 cm. Breeds in colonies (in N often very large and dense) or singly along coasts, on islands in sea-bays, locally at ponds in taiga or barren mountains, and on tundra near water. Summer visitor (end Apr–Oct), winters off S Africa and Antarctica. Probably has the longest migration of all birds.

Identification. Very similar to Common Tern; Arctic told by: slightly smaller size; shorter bill, head and neck and longer tail, making wings look ahead of centre of body; very short legs; slightly narrower wings. Flight often more elastic and gracefully bouncing than Common Tern's, but display flight of latter is just as elegant. Often dives with "stepped hover," dropping short distance and hovering again before final plunge; at times snatches prey from surface in Black Tern fashion. Adult summer: Bill dark red (blood-red) without black tip; lower throat, breast and belly washed grey, creating subtle contrast with white upper throat and cheeks, stronger than on most Common Terns; long tail-streamers extending beyond wing-tip when perched. Upperwing uniformly pale grey (lacking dark wedge or "notch" of Common), and all flight feathers near-white and translucent from below, outer primaries with neat black trailing edge (narrower than on Common). Juvenile: Carpal bar often fainter than on normal Common Tern, and secondaries are whitish, not shaded grey as on Common Tern; often a white triangular area on hindwing. Dark bill first red-based, from Aug/Sep all black. Forehead white (more clearly demarcated than on Common). Ist-summer (scarce in Europe): white forehead, dark bill, a faint dark carpal bar (thus resembles adult winter).

Voice. Recalls Common Tern; includes piping, clear *pi-pipi-pi, pyu pyu pyu,* and ringing *prree-eh,* and quarrelling, hard rattling *kt-kt-kt-krrr-kt;* alarm disyllabic *krri-errrrr* (variable, like Common's or harder, drier).

And if you want the full treatment you can turn to the comprehensive reference work *Birds of the Western Palearctic* (9 volumes, 1977–94), where the arctic tern gets about fifteen thousand words in a tight two-column setting, summarising every known fact about the species—including the very welcome information that in Iceland earthworms do indeed figure in its diet (but we read it first in your book, Mr. Sandars).

These are real advances, which not only help us see the significance of features we may have noticed but ignored before (like the "stepped hover") but are also enabling us actually to see things we did not see before (like the translucence in the wing). The same sort of thing has happened often in the history of art. The first European painters in Australia in the nineteenth century could not actually *see* the shapes or colours of the native eucalyptus trees except through European spectacles, and they drew them as if they were oaks or elms.

Moreover, this is the kind of progress in ornithology to which we can all, in principle, contribute; there still are many unanswered questions about bird behaviour, which intrigue amateurs at least as much as scientists and which amateurs can sometimes help answer, as they do also in the sciences of astronomy or archaeology (but scarcely at all in nuclear physics or neurology). After all, it is the observations and records of thousands of ordinary birdwatchers that provide so much of our knowledge about bird migration and distribution, for example the arrival and departure dates of migrants in different parts of the country. Scientists may call it phenology when they do it, but the data are largely supplied by amateurs. The famous evolutionary biologist Ernst Mayr, whose life (1904–2005) spanned almost the entire twentieth century, made this point very strongly in a presidential address to the American Ornithologists' Union in 1962:

> There is perhaps no other branch of biology, indeed of science as a whole, to which the amateur has made so many and such important contributions as ornithology. In a way, I do not like the word "amateur" because it suggests something dilettante, and this would surely be a misleading description of the work of so many of our leading ornithologists. The precision of their observations, the imaginative and highly original posing of problems, and the lucid and informative recording of their researches would dispel any notion of their work being that of dilettantes. . . . They differ or differed from professionals only in one

respect, by earning their living as doctors, lawyers, or businessmen and receiving no pay for their ornithological labors.

He might have added any number of other occupations, since birding is notoriously, and attractively, a classless interest. He might have particularly mentioned vicars. For the father of phenology in this sense, as well as the unofficial patron saint of natural history writers worldwide, is of course Gilbert White, the vicar of a small Hampshire village in the eighteenth century, whose *Natural History and Antiquities of Selborne* is one of the most famous books in the English language and a perennial comfort to booksellers and publishers.[1] I am duty bound to include an extract from Gilbert White in this initial sampling of "talk about birds," but he does in any case provide a paradigmatic example of a further genre of writing, the nature diary, which you might expect to be at least partly superseded by scientific progress in the way that the older field guides are. Gilbert White was a wonderfully painstaking and honest observer, but he has, not surprisingly, been proved wrong in some of his speculations, for example that swallows and martins might hibernate locally in the winter rather than migrate away from Britain. Why then does his work outlast and outsell the further and better accounts of such things that we now have? Here is an extract from his account of house martins, which he is comparing to the swallow and other similar species. Note the sensitivity to what we would call "jizz" (and what he called a bird's "air") and the final unsentimental observation.

> Martins are by far the least agile of the four species; their wings and tails are short, and therefore they are not capable of such surprising turns and quick and glancing evolutions as the swallow. Accordingly they make use of a placid easy motion in a middle region of the air, seldom mounting to any great height, and never sweeping long together over the surface of the ground or water. They do not wander far for food, but affect sheltered districts, over some lake, or under some hanging wood, or in some hollow vale, especially in windy weather. . . .
>
> House-martins are distinguished from their congeners by having their legs covered with soft downy feathers down to their toes. They are no songsters; but twitter in a pretty inward soft manner in their nests. During the time of breeding they are often greatly molested with fleas.

The hirundines were evidently White's favourite family and he was particularly fond of swallows. Here are the two words (and several exclamation

---

[1] *The Natural History of Selborne* is said to be the fourth "most published" book in English (presumably after the Bible, Shakespeare, and perhaps Izaac Walton or Bunyan), with more than two hundred separate editions.

marks) with which he greeted the arrival of the first swallow, in his diary entry for 13 April 1768. It was still possible in those days to be emotional in Latin.

Hirundo domestica!!!

A modern salutation of a different kind comes in Kathleen Jamie's *Findings*, in the chapter where she talks about corncrakes. As I explained, the population of corncrakes in Britain has declined dramatically since Clare's time, so keen birdwatchers make for known locations in places like Coll and then spend hours of anxious searching trying to catch sight of a corncrake to add to their lists. And not only young men:

> Birdwatchers come especially—Sarah tells of an old lady who sat quiet and demure on this very viewing bench for an hour, two hours . . . then there was a whoop, and Sarah turned to see the old lady leaping around, punching the air like a footballer, just for a glimpse of an elusive brown bird.

Jamie doesn't share this compulsion:

> When, later that day, I do see one, it's scuttering away from the wheels of the car. Like a miniature roadrunner, a slender upright hen with hunched shoulders and strong, long, pinkish legs, it squeezes under a wire fence, and with relief vanishes among the irises, even as I brake. It's the colour of slipware and looks, in that glimpse, like an elegant ceramic water jug suddenly come to life. That's that. I do not punch the air.

But she is attracted by another response, very different again:

> Another person arrives at the viewing bench, not an old lady but a man in young middle age, a holiday-maker. We fall into conversation—he obviously knows his stuff about birds. He has a young family with him on the island and, while they're on the beach, he has slunk off for an hour in the hope of spotting a corncrake. So here he is, an Englishman of higher education with a professional job, a family, a cagoule and good binoculars.
> "Can I ask why you like them? Corncrakes I mean."
> "Well," he said. "They're like . . . little gods of the field, aren't they."
> I could have punched the air. If corncrakes are rare, animism is rarer still. Anyone can clear his throat and talk about biodiversity, but "Corncrakes . . . little gods of the field" will not get you published in ornithologists' journals. That's how I picture them now, however: standing chins up, open-beaked, like votive statues hidden in the grass.

I end this section with a response to birds that is purely physical and per-
formative, a silent acknowledgement of affinity. Barry Lopez, in the preface to
Arctic Dreams, describes how on his first encounters with snowy owls and
other Arctic birds he found himself bowing:

> It was on that evening that I went on a walk for the first time among the
> tundra birds. They all build their nests on the ground, so their vulnera-
> bility is extreme. I gazed down at a single horned lark no bigger than my
> fist. She stared back resolute as iron. As I approached, golden plovers
> abandoned their nests in hysterical ploys, artfully feigning a broken
> wing to distract me from the woven grass cups that couched their pale,
> darkly speckled eggs. Their eggs glowed with a soft, pure light, like the
> window light in a Vermeer painting. I marvelled at this intense and con-
> centrated beauty on the vast table of the plain. I walked on to find Lap-
> land longspurs as still on their nests as stones, their dark eyes gleaming.
> At the nest of two snowy owls I stopped. These are more formidable
> animals than plovers. I stood motionless. The wild glare in their eyes
> receded. One owl settled back slowly over its three eggs, with an aura of
> primitive alertness. The other watched me, and immediately sought a
> bond with my eyes if I started to move.
>
> I took to bowing on these evening walks. I would bow slightly with
> my hands in my pockets, toward the birds and the evidence of life in
> their nests—because of their fecundity, unexpected in this remote re-
> gion, and because of the serene arctic light that came down over the
> land like breath, like breathing.

This can surely only be understood as an act of homage and of recognition.

Birds and Ourselves

These scrapbook cases of different kinds of reaction to birds do not, of course,
illustrate all the possible genres and subgenres. I have not, for example, yet
represented the hunter (of or with birds), the cook, the bird-fancier, the
farmer, or the gamekeeper, along with many others, and there is a whole tribe
of white-coated specialists at work on aspects of avian taxonomy, physiology,
and behaviour. But this first selection does already exhibit sufficient variety
both to alert us to the breadth of the spectrum and to locate a central issue
I want to explore. There is a tension, at times a conflict, in these sources and
in ourselves, between the wish to be open to all these interests and experiences and the equally strong wish not to be fooled or embarrassed by them.
We want to be both tough-minded and open-minded, to recognise the

constraints of science and hard fact but also the insights of literature, art, and the imagination. We want to be sensitive, that is, without being merely sentimental. The great bogey here is anthropomorphism. If sentimentality in this context is the sad vice of expressing towards animals emotions that are more properly directed towards people, then anthropomorphism is its scientific counterpart—ascribing to animals what are distinctively human emotions, purposes, and capacities. The emotional exchanges are devalued in the first case and misrepresented in the second. But what then are the *appropriate* emotions in these cases? What is an *authentic* experience? Do we have to choose?

Most writing on animals is undoubtedly marked (or, if you like, infected) with some degree of anthropomorphism. This is evident in its most obvious forms in the kinds of children's books where owls offer wise advice and female badgers are likely to be wearing aprons, but it also insinuates itself into quite sober and technical reference works. For example, the excellent *Collins Guide* I cited earlier says of the swallow's voice:

> Noisy, its loud calls enlivening farmsteads and small villages. In "itinerant flight" gives cheerful sharp *vit*, often repeated two or three times. Mates preen each other and entertain the barn livestock with cosy chatter almost like budgerigars. Cats are announced with sharp *siflitt* notes.

All that is vivid, helpful, and recognisable, but is it "true" in a more austere sense? In the same vein, robins are said to "curtsy," corncrakes "sneak away cleverly," and jackdaw pairs look "amorous." And we don't even notice the more subtle implications of the language when magpies are said to "walk confidently," herons "wait patiently" when fishing, and swifts produce a "chorus of screams" as they fly in a group around buildings. But what are we to do? Can the language of our descriptions and responses to birds be purified without being altogether drained? How are we to convey the meaning or significance certain encounters have for us without projecting something of our own experience into the description?

I hope to deal more fully with these issues later. My instinct now is to say that some degree of anthropomorphism is probably both unavoidable and positively desirable. I would argue this, partly by pointing to the benefits of a largely unnoticed *ornithomorphism* or *zoomorphism* in our lives. That is, there are similarities and continuities as well as differences between the human and the natural world and they work in both directions, from birds to ourselves as well as from us to them. And we can perhaps see this more easily if we travel the other way—seeing how we use the world of nature to illuminate our own world, which we do very regularly, if often unconsciously. For now, however,

I shall try at least to arrest this bogey long enough to prevent it from threatening the whole enterprise.

Scientists are taught to develop a deep disapproval of anthropomorphism, as the cardinal sin against objectivity. The sort of thing they are objecting to may be illustrated from the work of a nineteenth-century naturalist, the Reverend F. O. Morris. Here is his description of the dunnock as a model of Victorian family values:

> Unobtrusive, quiet and retiring, without being shy, humble and homely in its deportment and habits, sober and unpretending in its dress, while still neat and graceful, the Dunnock exhibits a pattern which many of higher grade might imitate, with advantage to themselves and benefit to others through an improved example.[1] (F. O. Morris, *A History of British Birds*, 1853)

No wonder, then, that scientists have sometimes thought of anthropomorphism as a kind of disease, which they are especially qualified to cure:

> In conclusion, I think we can be confident that anthropomorphism will be brought under control, even if it cannot be cured completely. Although it is probably programmed into us genetically as well as being inoculated culturally that does not mean the disease is untreatable. We human primates can defy the dictates of our genes. Anthropomorphism may be showing some resurgence just now but over the last two hundred centuries it has been retreating. This must be credited to the remarkable human invention called science. (J. S. Kennedy, *The New Anthropomorphism*, 1992)

But could that be just a little *too* confident, both about the human race in general and scientists in particular? Scientists can try their best to expunge any trace of human contamination from the language in which they describe other species, including of course birds. They rightly want to avoid importing into their studies any false assumptions or implications that could vitiate the results. At a certain point in this process of cleansing, however, the language they use almost ceases to describe in any real sense, or at least so limits its area of application that it fails to describe the whole phenomenon it is confronting. Eliot Howard was an amateur scientist, not now much remembered, who wrote about bird behaviour in the 1930s and 1940s and tried to grapple with

---

[1] This is both unctuous and inaccurate: the dunnock is now known to have a very lively and devious sex life. See N. Davies, *Dunnock Behaviour and Social Evolution* (1995).

this problem. He published a study of the moorhen in 1940 with the rather jolly title *A Waterhen's Worlds*. The book was issued in a large format, has some attractive illustrations, and gives every expectation that it will be a good read. That plural in the last word of the title may already have given a warning to the wary, however, and in any case the preface soon leaves us in no doubt about the difficulty of the enterprise:

> I divide the Waterhen's life into cycles, the cycles into parts, the parts into actions. I separate action from action, and part from part, and thus reduce everything to one. But no part has separate being or separate value. Each owes its being and its value to the whole, and therefore each has the nature of the whole. But the whole is never the same, for everything is always changing; and so it comes about that a waterhen lives in different worlds—territory, sexual, platform and family worlds.

By the end of the book the author has staggered with his moorhens through these metaphysical swamps. He emerges, breathing heavily, and announces his conclusions:

> So, in sum, it amounts to this:
>
> I start with the Waterhen as percipient, with power to refer.
>
> The becoming of a world depends upon the exercise of this power.
>
> For two months, day by day, or hourly, or even minute by minute, the Waterhen shifts from one world to another.
>
> The particular actions which belong to a particular world and express a particular feeling have, as their natural correlate, a particular object which is external to the bird's body.
>
> Mere vision abstracted from all mental stuff records no whole, but a succession of unrelated points.
>
> A whole is never seen as a whole, but is perceived as a whole.
>
> Perception, being a process which has in it something of the past as well as something to come, involves reference, memory, and expectation.
>
> Knowledge of the external world is therefore indirect.
>
> A particular feeling for a particular object has no abstract existence. Nor has the particular action, which belongs to the particular feeling and is directed to the particular object, any abstract existence.
>
> Feeling, action, and object are a whole or nothing.
>
> Having no language a bird has no power to abstract—no self, no past or future, or any other concept. The past is perceived as present, and lived in as present, and is the basis of expectation and seeking.

I take this to be an admission of defeat.

A corrective move is made, rather more attractively, by John Ruskin in his essay "The Relation of Wise Art to Wise Science" (1887). He has been admiring the intricate architecture of a bullfinch's nest:

> It was a bullfinch's nest, which had been set in the fork of sapling tree, where it needed an extended foundation. And the bird had built this first story of her nest with withered stalks of clematis blossom; and with nothing else. These twigs it had interwoven lightly, leaving the branched heads all at the outside, producing an intricate Gothic boss of extreme grace and quaintness, apparently arranged both with triumphant pleasure in the art of basket-making, and with definite purpose of obtaining ornamental form.
>
> I fear there is no occasion to tell you that the bird had no purpose of the kind. I say that I fear this, because I would much rather have to undeceive you in attributing too much intellect to the lower animals, than too little. But I suppose the only error which, in the present condition of natural history, you are likely to fall into, is that of supposing that a bullfinch is merely a mechanical arrangement of nervous fibre, covered with feathers by a chronic cutaneous eruption; and impelled by a galvanic stimulus to the collection of clematis.

If we reduce language to a system of symbols capable of describing a bird in terms only applicable to a bird, then almost by definition it is no longer a language we ourselves understand. Perfect accuracy is achieved only at the cost of total incomprehension. What we have to do instead is use the language we have to bridge this gap, knowing that it is systematically impure in this way and using it as sensitively and critically as we can. That is why we rely so much on analogy and metaphor in our ordinary descriptions and evocations of birds and why we need to be open to the larger imaginative frameworks of art and literature as well. Description involves language and the language is in the end a human language, which has its own history and is shot through with echoes and reverberations from that history and with meanings and metaphors drawn from human experience. The metaphors may be conscious or unconscious, dead or alive, but they are there at work.

This plays back also into the emotional tensions we feel, wanting to empathise in some way with birds without sentimentalising them. The author to quote here is Richard Jeffries. Few writers of natural history have conveyed so strongly the sense of affinity with nature that Jeffries enjoyed, but it was all the more painful for him to realise that his feelings could never be reciprocated:

I thought myself so much to the earliest leaf and the first meadow orchis—so important that I should note the first *zeezee* of the titlark—that I should pronounce it summer, because now the oaks were green; I must not miss a day nor an hour in the fields lest something should escape me. How beautiful the droop of the great brome-grass by the wood! But today I have to listen to the lark's song—not out of doors with him, but through the windowpane, and the bullfinch carries the rootlet fibre to his nest without me. They manage without me very well; they know their times and seasons—not only the civilized rooks, with their libraries of knowledge in their old nests of reference, but the stray things of the hedge and the chiffchaff from over sea in the ash wood. They go on without me. Orchis flower and cowslip—I cannot number them all—I hear, as it were, the patter of their feet—flower and bud and the beautiful clouds that go over, with the sweet rush of rain and burst of sun glory among the leafy trees. They go on, and I am no more than the least of the empty shells that strewed the sward of the hill. Nature sets no value upon life, neither of mine nor of the larks that sang years ago. The earth is all in all to me, but I am nothing to the earth: it is bitter to know this before you are dead. These delicious violets are sweet for themselves; they were not shaped and coloured and gifted with that exquisite proportion and adjustment of odour and hue for me. High up against the grey cloud I hear the lark through the window singing, and each note falls into my heart like a knife. (Richard Jeffries, "Hours of Spring," 1886).

We are less likely to be anthropomorphic in the wrong ways, that is, if we are also less anthropocentric, but it may be a painful recognition. This sort of reflection encourages a proper modesty, and even irony, in our attempts to come to terms with the natural world, see it as it is, and enjoy it in the ways we may. This is the sense in which a book like this on birds is really about ourselves or even, if you like, about our selves.

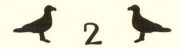

Amusive Birds: Attraction and Association

As I have regarded these amusive birds with no
small attention, if I should advance something new
and peculiar with respect to them, and different
from all other birds, I might perhaps be credited,
especially as my assertion is the result of many
years' exact observation.
Gilbert White, Letter to Daines Barrington,
28 September 1774

AMUSIVE. (1) Deceitful, illusive. (2) Fitted to afford
relaxation from graver concerns. Recreative.
Oxford English Dictionary

Horsey, Norfolk, 31 December 2005

I am in a remote marsh on the last day of the old year, looking and listening
for a very special bird. It has been a raw, wet, and dull day. I position myself
on a bank overlooking a huge area of reedbed, scrub, and rough grazing and
gaze out over the drowned landscape. The only buildings in sight are two distant windmills, and if there are any other human watchers out there they are
as silent and still (and no doubt as cold) as I am. I wait. By 3 PM it is already
getting gloomy and the only birds in evidence are some lapwings and a ghostly
barn owl that floats by. I am losing contact with my fingers and toes. By 4 PM
it is almost too dark to see and I am stiff with cold and about to call it a day,
when suddenly I hear this thrilling sound—at first a distant, muted bugling
and then a chorus of loud ringing cries as six huge birds glide in low over the
marsh and drop down to roost. The cranes have landed.

Cranes are special. In the first place, they are very impressive birds physically, standing more than four feet tall (much larger than a heron), with long,

elegant necks and legs to match. The plumage is basically a soft ashy grey, with a black-and-white pattern on the head and neck, topped off with a red patch on the back of the crown. On the ground they walk in stately fashion, carrying behind them the distinctive "bustle" of plumes that helps to give them their majestic bearing. In flight they propel themselves powerfully through the air with measured wingbeats, neck outstretched in front and legs trailing behind. They are most famous, of course, for their courtship displays when couples, or even whole flocks, leap into the air with wings and necks outstretched, then bow and flirt with each other and excitedly toss around small objects, trumpeting the while in chorus. This "crane dance" is one of the great wildlife spectacles. Is the source of the impulse one we share, or must we keep the quotation marks round "dance"?

Cranes are, however, very shy and wary, so it is a privilege to encounter them anywhere in the wild. In Britain they are extremely rare, but now one tiny colony has become established in the Norfolk Broads. They used to breed more widely in East Anglia in the Middle Ages but became extinct around 1600 as the vast wetlands on which they depend for food and security were being drained and diminished. Then to the amazement and delight of naturalists a pair came to these marshes in the early 1980s and stayed to breed. Since then the colony has built up, slowly and precariously, to reach double figures now. So this is a homecoming of a kind.

I have also watched cranes in the Russian steppe, in this case demoiselle cranes, a little smaller and even more lovely than the Northern European ones, with long white head plumes and black trailing breast feathers and with subtly different proportions in the head, neck, and tail. The story is that Marie Antoinette gave her pet crane the name "Demoiselle," in admiration of its demure elegance, and the unusual scientific name *Anthropoides virgo* ("of human form, like a young girl") has the same connotations. This is a bird of dry grasslands, which migrates over huge distances, some to winter quarters in North Africa but some right over the Himalayas to the flat plains of Western India. Its arrival is noted and welcomed everywhere, whether in summer or winter.

Cranes have always excited the human imagination. They appear in the very first works of European literature, when Homer likens the advance of the Trojan army to the clamour of cranes, and Hesiod defines the farmer's seasons by the appearance of cranes in the sky:

Take note when you hear the voice of the crane, who every year calls out from the clouds above. He gives the signal for ploughing and marks the season of rainy winter.

8. Demoiselle cranes in flight (photo: N. Stepkin)

They are equally powerful symbols in Oriental poetry and thought, for example in the work of Confucius, Basho, and the even pithier Zen master Dogen (thirteenth-century Japanese):

> The world?
> Moonlit water drops
> From the crane's bill.

Similar references can be found in the song and poetry of India, Africa, and Australia. Why do cranes feature so strongly in myth, folklore, and literature of almost every culture?

The author and naturalist Peter Matthiessen travelled the world for more than a decade to see all the fifteen remaining species of crane, many of which are threatened through loss of habitat or by human persecution. He wanted to raise consciousness about their endangered status, in support of international conservation efforts and ecological awareness generally, and he sees the cranes as "heralds and symbols of all that is being lost." He also conveys the intensity of his personal experiences in watching cranes and describes the sight of the Japanese crane dancing in the snows of Hokkaido as the "ultimate pilgrimage for ornithologists."

"Pilgrimage" is rather a strong word, surely? But then, what was I doing in such discomfort on the marsh that bleak day? How can a bird exert that sort of influence on us? Why do some birds affect us more than others? What's going on here?

In the first chapter I started looking at some of the different ways we respond subjectively to birds, ranging through various degrees of passion and different kinds of interest. I now want to turn that around and look at the objects of our attention, the birds themselves, and ask what it is we are responding to. This is still very much in exploratory mode, but by the end of this chapter I hope to have set out the main themes that I will develop in the subsequent chapters.

Favourites and Fancies

Gilbert White wrote of swifts as "amusive birds" in the letter quoted as an epigraph to this chapter.[1] The letter was in fact also presented as a paper to the Royal Society of London and was published in 1775 in the Society's *Philosophical Transactions,* a journal that had the splendid eighteenth-century style on the title page, "Giving some Account of the Present Undertakings, Studies and Labours of the Ingenious in many considerable Parts of the World." White was nothing if not ingenious, in this larger eighteenth-century sense of talented and discerning, and he had amply demonstrated that even the most parochial records could be of universal interest. His description of the swifts as "amusive" nicely combines two distinct meanings that term then had: "deceitful" and "appealing." I want to revive this happy ambiguity here and ask what is genuine and what imagined in our attraction to particular birds. What do we discover and what do we project?

In 1927, Viscount Grey of Fallodon published a book under the title *The Charm of Birds,* which was an immediate best seller and has become a much-loved, if not now actually much-read, classic. It is itself a work of great charm, and indeed innocence, written by the man who as Sir Edward Grey had been the long-serving British foreign secretary (1905–16) in the very troubled period just before World War I. In the preface he describes his book as a simple tribute to the pleasure, solace, and interest birds have given him over the years and he gives his reason for writing his feelings down:

> One who reviews pleasant experiences and puts them on record increases the value of them to himself; he gathers up his own feelings and

---

[1] He uses the expression again in a poem titled "The Naturalist's Summer Evening Walk" (he was an occasional, if undistinguished, poet as well as a diarist). He is musing here on the mysterious arrivals and departures of his favourite summer birds, especially the swift and swallow, and exclaims in affectionate exasperation, "Amusive birds!"

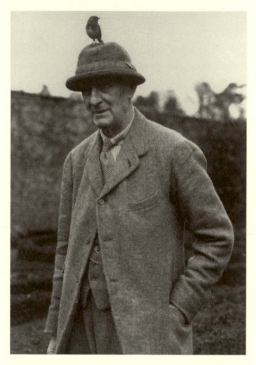

9. Edward Grey at Fallodon with robin on hat (1933)

reflections, and is thereby better able to understand and to measure the fullness of what he has enjoyed.

Unlike most authors, he sees that this is not in itself sufficient reason for *publishing* his reflections, but he does go on to offer a typically modest justification for that too:

> After all, it is not entirely to exchange information that lovers of birds converse together on this subject. An artist will paint the commonest object in order to bring out some aspect that has particularly struck him. So with watchers of birds, some are attracted by one aspect of a well-known species and some by another. Thus even those of us who have nothing new to tell, may have something that is fresh to say.

The book then takes the familiar form of a year's diary, with a particular (and still unusual) emphasis on birdsong. The birds whose "charm" he most celebrates are, as he says, quite common species, such as the robin, song thrush, skylark, nightingale, and blackcap, and he does succeed, often very perceptively, in helping us to see what it is that attracts him and us to them.

This would seem a natural starting point for this chapter. Why not just produce a list of the top ten national favourites of this kind and then see what the
common factors are? But this turns out not to be so simple. You will begin to
see the problem if you pause for a couple of minutes to jot down your own list
before reading on (one minute to write a list, and then another to start feeling
dissatisfied with it).

I will replicate the exercise. Here is a possible top ten, first presented as a
simple list and then with notes about my initial uncertainties, some of them
perhaps pedantic but some potentially more undermining.[1] We can start with
the five examples I gave from Grey:

Robin
Song thrush
Skylark
Nightingale
Blackcap

And then add another five plausible candidates:

Golden eagle
Kingfisher
Mute swan
Puffin
Barn owl

Your list of popular favourites will no doubt be somewhat different, but I'd
be surprised if there were no overlaps, and most people would agree that all
of these are possible choices. So what's the problem? Well, I want to suggest
that the only common factor here is a rather paradoxical one; and I will try
to show this by first questioning the claims of these birds to be on such a list
anyway.

Robin. This was voted Britain's national bird back in 1960 and has been a
perennial favourite: celebrated by poets from Chaucer to Ted Hughes, sharing
its name with such national heroes as Robin Goodfellow and Robin Hood,
and providing nicknames and branding opportunities to sundry wearers of
red uniforms, including one military regiment (the Fifth Royal Irish Lancers),
three professional soccer teams (Swindon Town, Bristol City, and Cheltenham

[1] This is just a British list, to simplify things at this stage. The geographical scale of America and
Australia affects the idea of "national favourites" there, though I do go on to discuss national and
state birds in these and other countries in chapter 10 (pp. 278–80), for those who want to jump
ahead.

Town), and one car (the Robin Reliant). Since the mid-nineteenth century robins have also been a near-compulsory motif on Christmas cards (see plate 7b) and indeed gave their name to the first messengers carrying such post, the "robin postmen," who originally wore red coats. The robin is widely loved for his plump and jolly shape, his trusting, friendly habits, his sweet, soulful song in the dark days of winter, and of course for that bright red breast. But things are not quite as they seem. Robins are in fact extremely aggressive and are ready to fight to the death other robins who trespass onto their territory. They are so tense that they will attack virtually anything red, supposedly even just a piece of red cloth if you hang one up. Nor is "he" the only one who sings—robins are unusual in that both sexes take up territories in winter and sing to scare off rivals, not to serenade them. And their friendliness towards our own species is the merest cupboard love. On the Continent, where robins are hunted and (can you bear it?) *eaten,* they are shy and wary birds of the deep forest. It's only in Britain that they have learned to charm the gardener, with clear ulterior motives. As for the red breast, that's real enough, but this is not just the cheerful red of Christmas cards and holly; in folklore at least, the robin's breast is stained red for darker and more sinister reasons to do with blood, sacrifice, and death.

I'm sorry about all this. I like robins too, but in a different way. Is this a case where more knowledge exposes a shallow sentimentality in the initial attraction and leads us to view the bird differently?

Song thrush. This seems an obvious candidate too. Edward Grey thought the thrush would top any league table of British songsters and he seems to be vindicated by the large number of poets who have been moved to celebrate it and find in it the very spirit of spring (Tennyson, "Summer is coming, summer is coming"), of hope (Hardy, "The Darkling Thrush"), or even of England (Browning, "Home Thoughts from Abroad"). Browning in particular captures the repetitions and variations on a simple theme that make the song so recognisable and popular:

> That's the wise thrush; he sings each song twice over
> Lest you think he never could recapture
> That first fine careless rapture!

But even here other poets have seen a darker side. For Ted Hughes thrushes are just killing machines:

> Terrifying are the attent sleek thrushes on the lawn,
> More coiled steel than living—a poised
> Dark deadly eye, those delicate legs

Triggered to stirrings beyond sense—with a start, a bounce, a stab
Overtake the instant and drag out some writhing thing.
No indolent procrastinations and no yawning stares,
No sighs or head-scratchings. Nothing but bounce and stab
And a ravening second.

In another thrush poem, Hughes deromanticises them even further, and perhaps more tellingly, by contrasting their everyday preoccupations with their performance as songsters:

O thrush,
Is that really you, behind the leaf-screen,
Who is this—

Worn-headed, on the lawn's grass, after sunset,
Humped, voiceless, turdus, imprisoned
As a long-distance lorry-driver, dazed

With the pop and static and unending
Of worms and wife and kids?

And the less suspicious Lord Grey undercuts his own rankings somewhat by conceding that the thrush is more to be admired for persistence and effort in his singing than for pure quality, where he actually scores the blackbird higher.[1] Moreover, even the poets' plaudits may be sometimes misplaced, since "thrush" (or "throstle") was once used interchangeably for both song and mistle thrushes; and indeed, many people who might vote for the song thrush in this little game could be unsure how to distinguish it from the mistle thrush, or even be unaware that there were two different and common species, both with a fine song. Things get even murkier when you learn that there are also at least two different races of song thrush in Britain—the Hebridean thrush is a distinct form, which may possibly one day be regarded as a separate species. More perplexing still, perhaps, is the fact that the thrushes in our gardens are not necessarily the same birds all the year round. Some of "our" thrushes migrate south in winter, when we in turn receive an influx of migrants from continental Europe. Mark Cocker records how people become so attached to their supposedly local blackbirds (and, I expect, thrushes) that they give them pet names like Billy, Blackie, and Beaky. How would these people feel if they discovered they were addressing foreigners, strangers, or imposters? Can you count as a "favourite" something you may have misidentified?

---

[1] As did President Theodore Roosevelt when Grey took him out on a birdwatching trip. "You as a nation do not make enough of the blackbird's song," he complained. Roosevelt's explanation was that the bird's *name* was what damaged its reputation.

Skylark. Another natural for the list, surely. Who cannot respond to the soaring song of the skylark as Shelley did?

> Hail to thee, blithe spirit!
> Bird thou never wert,
> That from heaven, or near it,
> Pourest thy full heart
> In profuse strains of unpremeditated art.

The skylark has an even longer citation list in poetry than the song thrush, with no dissenting voices that I am aware of. Even Ted Hughes feels nothing more menacing than a sense of relief when skylarks finally rest from their extreme labours and stop singing:

> So, it's a relief, a cool breeze
> When they've had enough, when they're burned out
> And the sun's sucked them empty
> And the earth gives them the OK

The bird is equally celebrated in music, most famously in Vaughan Williams's *Lark Ascending,* where the solo violin captures perfectly the ascending spirals of the lark's song flight in steadily rising cadenzas. The piece lasts almost fifteen minutes, which is about the time the lark too can sustain its song, and the score is prefaced by some equally mimetic lines from George Meredith, which begin:

> He rises and begins to round,
> He drops the silver chain of sound,
> Of many links without a break,
> In chirrup, whistle, slur and shake.

I have hesitations, however. First, although the skylark is a remarkable performer I actually prefer the woodlark's song myself. The standard reference work, *Birds of the Western Palearctic (BWP),* says quite accurately, if rather crushingly, at the start of its long entry on the skylark's voice, "Loud and melodious, but with fairly restricted range of sounds." The woodlark, by comparison, has a song that is complex, subtle, and piercingly beautiful, evoking a quite different kind and quality of emotional response (see pp. 173–74). The French composer Olivier Messiaen captures the musical possibilities of this fugitive sound beautifully in the *Catalogue d'oiseaux,* where a woodlark drifts in to duet briefly with a nightingale and then slowly departs.

The woodlark is now a scarce bird in Britain, however, restricted in both range and habitat, and therefore more of a birdwatchers' bird, a connoisseurs' choice rather than a popular one. Were its song better known, would it supplant the skylark?

Second, this is an interesting case of how our attitude towards a bird can change over time. The skylark has declined dramatically in numbers in Britain over recent years, mainly as a result of the effects of intensive farming and habitat loss, and is now the object not only of our devotion but of earnest conservation efforts too. Up to the end of the nineteenth century, however, it was mainly thought of as a delicacy for the table and the scale of the butchery was immense, with some four hundred thousand a year sent to the main London markets alone, including deliveries of up to thirty thousand on some single days. If the skylark was then in the top ten favourites, it was for rather different reasons. Even in the twentieth century opinions varied. When migration studies revealed that the skylarks that ate the winter corn in Norfolk came from the Continent, the local farmers in the 1930s decided they were not British enough to protect. "Skylarks that sing to Nazis will get no mercy here," a newspaper headline ran.

Last, is there not a possibility that our feelings for the skylark may derive more from the music and poetry it has inspired than from our direct responses to the bird itself? Does it have a sort of cultural status independent of our actual experience of it?

None of this may disqualify the skylark, but again our criteria begin to seem more complicated and insecure than we might at first have supposed.

Nightingale. Surely this is safe in its place, at any rate? The nightingale far outranks every other songster in popular estimation. The song is universally recognised and admired, in life as in literature, even above that of the lark. The special case of Romeo and Juliet only proves the rule. Juliet, you remember, begs him to stay on:

> Wilt thou be gone?
> It is not yet near day;
> It was the nightingale,
> Not the lark
> That pierced the fearful hollow
> Of thine ear . . .
> Believe me, love, it was the nightingale.

Romeo, however, is not to be deceived:

> It was the lark, the herald of the morn.
> No nightingale.

And we know he is right, as does Juliet of course. No one could mistake a nightingale.

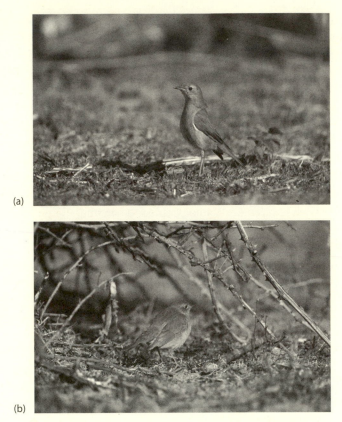

(a)

(b)

10. Two nightingales (photos: Robin Chittenden)

It seems heresy to object, but to be more precise, what we are really saying is that no one could mistake a nightingale's *song*. How many people who would put this on their list have actually *seen* a nightingale, or ever tried to? It is quite difficult, even by day, since the bird is a skulker and usually sings from deep cover. Is it OK, then, to have as a favourite bird one you have never actually seen but only heard? And would you recognise one even if you did see it? Look at figures 10a and 10b, which show the rare sight of nightingales out in the open—would you be able to identify them?

And is it even true that the song is universally recognised? "A nightingale sang in Berkeley Square" probably refers to a robin disturbed by the street lighting—in 1940 the nightingale would have been an extreme rarity in central London.[1] They can be and have been confused with species as various as

[1] To be fair, Keats's famous "Ode to a Nightingale" was inspired by a bird that did sing on Hampstead Heath in the spring of 1819 (and see p. 156n2). But for some deeper puzzles, see appendix 3.

blackbirds, blackcaps (the "Northern nightingale"), and sedge warblers (the "Irish nightingale"). Moreover, if you live north of a line between the Humber and the Severn you are unlikely ever to hear one near home in the wild anyway. They are common in Southern Europe, of course, but if you hear a nightingale in Northern or Eastern Europe it will be a quite different species, the thrush nightingale, *Luscinia luscinia,* which is very similar in appearance but which has a much poorer song and has nothing like the same iconic status in the countries in which it occurs. And even if you are in the right latitude and can correctly identify the common nightingale, *Luscinia megarhynchos,* you have only about six weeks each year in which to hear it, since they don't arrive here until late April and cease singing by the end of June. Is that a broad enough basis of experience for inclusion? I now reveal that figure 10a was of a common nightingale, while figure 10b was of a thrush nightingale, the quite different continental species. Did anyone notice?

Blackcap. This species may be somewhat less well-known to the general public, but it certainly ranks as a favourite for anyone with even an elementary interest in birdsong. Grey put it in the very first division, along with the blackbird and nightingale. Indeed an old country name is the "Northern nightingale" and it does sometimes imitate the real thing. There should in any case be at least one representative of the large and attractive warbler family in this top ten, and the blackcap is one of our commonest and most widely spread warblers, as well as being one of the best songsters; it is in fact also becoming increasingly familiar as a "garden bird," because of the trend in recent years for blackcaps to overwinter in the United Kingdom and make an appearance at the bird feeder. My only hesitation is that it represents one further category of possible confusion with another species. The song thrush may be sometimes confused with the mistle thrush through a general similarity in appearance, and the nightingale and thrush nightingale can be separated visually only by the most expert observers; but the difference with the blackcap is that it is commonly confused with one other species for precisely the thing for which it is most admired—its song. Many people find it hard to distinguish the songs of the blackcap and the garden warbler, and Grey himself describes the difficulty, while also setting out some of the differentia quite aptly:

> The garden warbler's song is very good: in one respect it surpasses that of the blackcap; it is more sustained; but the bird never seems absolutely to clear the throat and let out the sound so pure and free as the blackcap does. To my ear the opening notes of the blackcap's song and those of the garden warbler are so alike that I hear them with a doubt of which bird I am listening to; but the garden warbler goes on and on for a longer time

and yet never seems to liberate its voice upon the air so completely as the blackcap does. In other words, a garden warbler's song seems always on the point of achievement, to which only the blackcap attains.

But if it's as hard as that, even for an aficionado, can we confidently include the blackcap on the list of favourites? And, by the way, the garden warbler makes it difficult in other ways too. It overlaps with the blackcap in range and habitat, though it doesn't show itself much in "gardens," unless you happen to have an especially grand garden with its own shrubberies. Indeed it doesn't show itself much at all, being notoriously elusive and nondescript.[1] So you do have to rely on the songs for the most part and they can be tricky.

There are therefore problems about each of these five charming birds. Either they aren't quite what they seem, or they can be confused with something else, or may even be representing something else. That brings me to my second set of five.

Meanings and Masks

I select these further species not from *The Charm of Birds,* and certainly not on the grounds of their "songs," which are in these cases largely nonexistent. But they are undoubtedly all very popular birds, or at any rate very prominent in the general consciousness about birds in our society. In the five cases already considered I tried to show that what first seemed an automatic selection could become more contestable when you queried the criteria underlying the choice, and different objections emerged in each case. The next five illustrate some of the same points as well as introducing a few new problems. But what I mainly want to emphasise now is the paradox that seems to be emerging: the only thing these birds have in common is that they stand for something other than themselves.

Golden eagle. Eagles seems inevitably to attract the epithets "majestic" or "magnificent," and they have been of enormous symbolic importance over the ages and in many cultures across the world. They were the birds of augury for the Greeks; the emblem of empire and power for the Romans, Charlemagne, Napoleon, Hitler, and Saddam Hussein (not an altogether wonderful team, but the Royal Air Force uses it too); and an icon in many mythologies and religions (in Christianity, for example, an eagle is almost a standard fitting on church lecterns). More locally, the golden eagle is installed as the national bird

---

[1] The garden warbler was only "discovered," in the sense of being recognised as a separate species, in the late eighteenth century; and it continued to be confused with other warblers, to the extent of even sharing a vernacular name (the "pettychap") with the chiffchaff. Its main distinguishing feature is that it doesn't have one.

of Scotland, to celebrate the Highland landscape, where almost all the United Kingdom's breeding pairs live, though ironically enough when the Scottish RSPB conducted a poll of its members to discover their favourite bird the dratted robin came out top again! *The Scotsman* knew how to get the right answer, though. In its 2004 poll it specifically asked readers to nominate a national bird for Scotland, and the golden eagle was the runaway winner, despite a late surge by the red grouse, which on investigation turned out to have been prompted by an email campaign by the marketing department of Famous Grouse whisky. The top ten in that poll were, in descending order: golden eagle, red grouse, capercaillie, osprey, puffin, gannet, sea eagle, peregrine, crested tit, and lapwing. I would predict that sea eagle will move up this Scottish list—unless of course it is successfully reintroduced into England.[1]

No matter, by common agreement the eagle really is the king of birds, and therefore the ideal logo for all manner of commercial as well as political purposes worldwide. But with just one pair in England and the Scottish birds largely restricted to wilderness areas, how many people have ever seen one, except on TV? You would think a "favourite" bird would also have to be a familiar one, like a favourite chair or book? Could you have a favourite film you had never seen, or a favourite town you had never visited? Or does the eagle's mystique actually *depend* on its remoteness?

Kingfisher. This bird is at any rate much more widely distributed in England (though not in this case Scotland), and is instantly recognisable by everyone from its startling plumage. Mind you, recognition *has* to be instantaneous because you rarely get more than a glimpse of an electric blue flash rapidly disappearing round the bend of a river. I live in a Suffolk village with a "kingfisher river," but despite their eager efforts over many years most of the local inhabitants have yet to see one. However, the kingfisher is there on our village logo and Web site and is proudly referred to in communications with less well-endowed parishes. Most people could give a decent description of its colours, its stumpy shape, and its habits and skills as a fisherman. And we all seem to share a common sense of ownership in these conceptions. Think of how often the name itself is used for buildings, boats, roads, and houses, and think of all those images on tea-towels, mugs, fabrics, and wallpapers. Is it the *idea* of there being such an exotic jewel in our midst that we treasure? The hummingbird perhaps plays much the same part in the Americas, especially in the south. Is it the *bird* we are familiar with in these cases or something else?

---

[1] See further on the symbolism of the golden eagle chap. 10, pp. 273–79, and on the proposed reintroduction of the sea eagle chap. 8, pp. 227–28.

11. The Swan Inn at Clare (photo: Steve Bryant)

Mute swan. As eagles epitomise grandeur so swans seem to be inescapably "stately" and "beautiful"; and the swan, unlike the eagle and kingfisher, is a common and approachable bird, familiar at firsthand to everyone. There are also countless evocations of the swan both in high art and in popular culture, where it is represented so conspicuously, for example, in all those pubs with swan names.

There's a long and well-documented history of the relationship between swans and humans in Britain, based initially on their elite status as the royal dish of choice for ceremonial banquets and other exclusive occasions. Swans were regarded as the property of the crown and were protected by special "swan laws" overseen by a Royal Swan Master, and there are survivals of all the attendant customs and rituals in the Swannery at Abbotsbury and in the an-nual swan-upping expeditions led up the Thames each July by The Queen's Swan Marker and The Worshipful Companies of Dyers and of Vintners.[1] Is it now possible to strip away all these connotations and see the actual bird, even though we encounter it so closely and so often in our parks, rivers, lakes, and estuaries?

Isn't the swan in any case compromised as a "favourite" by two of its special characteristics? Because of its history it partly was, and still feels as though it is, a semidomestic species: tame, protected, managed, and supported. But we

---

[1] The British genius for rationalising traditions in order to prolong them has led to this now being described as a conservation exercise (see the contribution by Christopher Perrins in *BB*, p. 63).

wouldn't let a peacock or a budgerigar onto the list, would we? The robin's tameness is different—that gives us the thrill of a moment of contact with a truly wild bird. Isn't the swan, by contrast, just a bit too familiar, in the wrong sense? Moreover, doesn't the very size of the swan raise an issue, and possibly also its muteness (hissing doesn't really count as vocalisation, after all)? Do we even think of it as a *bird* in quite the same sense as we do robins and nightingales? Birders like to count everything, of course; but to take a more extreme case, doesn't even the hard-line lister have a twinge of doubt when he solemnly ticks "ostrich" on his world list after his African safari? Isn't that big game?

Puffin. Everybody loves puffins: the clown with the outrageous multicoloured beak and the sad eyes; the earnest bumbling walk in a formal dinner jacket; the soft, round, cuddly shape; the magic and make-believe of rocky island homes; the ultimate photogenic celebrity. It's hard to see a puffin except through these metaphorical spectacles, and hard to describe one, even with the most sober intentions, without lapsing into anthropomorphic shorthand. *BWP* refers to its "comical, endearing character," and even the scientific name *Fratercula arctica* is a give-away. "Little brother from the Arctic," indeed!

At the other end of the world there is of course a counterpart, the penguin, which might well have appeared on some "top ten" lists in the United Kingdom or the United States, though it's an Antarctic bird of course, only encountered by most of us in zoos or in the company of David Attenborough on TV; moreover, it is actually a family and not a species at all (there are seventeen different kinds of penguin). The penguin charms us in many of the same ways as the puffin: the "penguin suit," the funny walk, the body shape, the upright posture, and, perhaps particularly, the busy city life amid the wilderness of rocks and sea. What do they remind us of? Ourselves, of course. And in the case of penguins, the process of anthropomorphism is given a new twist. The documentary film *March of the Penguins,* which appeared in 2005, was an enormous box-office success, not because of an upsurge of popular interest in the breeding biology of *Aptenodytes forsteri,* the emperor penguin, but because the commentary presented it as a moral fable.[1] The film was duly hailed by the Christian Right in the United States as a demonstration of the truth of Intelligent Design and the importance of monogamy, fidelity, self-sacrifice, and family life. The opposition countered by pointing to Roy and Silo, the resident pair of gay penguins in New York's Central Park, and to the un-American behaviour of emperor penguins outside the breeding season. The premise all

---

[1] Not by the peerless David Attenborough in this case but by Morgan Freeman, whose tone was not one of wonder and enquiry but of syrupy, sentimental acclaim. Still, it could have been worse: in the original French version, actors were provided to give the penguins voices in which to plight their troths.

parties shared, though, was that penguins were somehow our moral arbiters. Human values were first projected onto a nonhuman species that did not share them, and then reflected back onto ourselves from this bogus source of validation. Once into Wonderland, and twice through the Looking-Glass.[1]

No wonder the entrepreneurial genius Allen Lane selected "Penguin" and "Puffin" as the names of his two most famous imprints. His biographer, Jeremy Lewis, tells the story of the brainstorming session in a "dark little office in Vigo Street" that first led to the adoption of the name "Penguin." Allen Lane knew the importance of promoting his new idea as a brand, with a corporate name and logo that tapped deep into the national psyche. They rehearsed and rejected various names like "Phoenix," "Dolphin," and "Albatross," and then Lane's secretary piped up from behind her partition and said "What about Penguins?" Lane decided on it immediately and despatched a designer with funds from the petty cash to go to London Zoo to sketch one for the covers. In justifying his decision Lane said the name had "a certain dignified flippancy," but he must have known instinctively that it went deeper than that.

Barn owl. Owls are very "other," and the barn owl in particular has a most striking physical presence. There is first the distinctive flight: a floppy gliding, wheeling, and dipping motion, powered by a few beats on stiff mothlike wings. The wingspan is that of quite a large bird—some three feet across—but the bird is gossamer light at just ten ounces. The feathers are specially fringed to ensure absolute silence in flight. The ears are exceptionally acute and are asymmetrical in size and position to offer precision guidance in hunting, and those huge facial discs amplify the minute noises of the owl's prey by acting as sound-dishes. The eyes are large, binocular, and designed (you see how easily you can slip into the metaphor) for night vision, set at the front of the large round head. And of course the plumage itself is a ghostly, sometimes an almost phosphorescent, white (see plate 3c, of a bird hunting over the Suffolk marshes). Many writers have described the striking effect these features have on the human observer and I select just two, by way of illustration. First, J. A. Baker on the purely physical impression made by an owl in flight:

> There is a sudden haunting whiteness to the south. It seems to hover on the shining surface of the sea. Then it descends and comes closer. It is a barn owl. He glows in the last sunlight, like burning snow, a white incandescence casting a black shadow. He flies quickly through the cooling dusk of the fields, and his whiteness is strangely difficult to follow.

[1] Interestingly, the film itself provided some of the scientific counterevidence. Penguins were shown to be monogamous only for one breeding cycle, and to be able to watch with insouciance while a proportion of their offspring were being eaten by petrels and skuas. But this was ignored, or not really seen.

Some of his owl-shape seems to ebb away into the ambient air. He turns in the darkness of an oak, and floats forward over the fading giraffe-skins of light and shade that still dapple the sunlit field. Over the wet grass, through the thorns of shadow, the owl advances, his wings waving softly in the damp green dusk. He flies a yard above the grass: ten high wing-beats and then a drowsy glide. His flight is fast and even, yet every wing-beat jolts him slightly, making his body rise and fall in a smooth undulation. The edges of his wings are constantly feeling the air. Their silky fringes, like antennae of thistledown, impose a white silence in which all sounds are magnified. The glides are sudden and brief, slow-moving, with the long white wings held upward and changing shape, like listening ears. The broad head looks down, hanging like the globe of a giant puff-ball below the moth-like fanning of the wings. The soft ear-coverts lift in a wind of sound, and the cavernous ears beneath them echo with the endless rustling of the running mice. The white facial disk of the barn owl is a corolla of shining feathers, a radiance of petals that beams the diminishing light down to the dark-channelled calyces of the owl's huge Lebanon eyes. (*The Hill of Summer*, pp. 156–57).

And then Richard Mabey, on the more unconscious associations, as he ponders the bird's decline:

Few birds are so dramatically beautiful, or can bring the exquisite delicacy of flight so close to us, or can look us so penetratingly, eye to eye. But they mean more than that. Ecologists look to the condition of "top predators" as a measure of how well the ecosystem on which they depend is working. The barn owl is a cultural indicator, too. We recognise, at a deep level, the meaning of that ritual crossing of the fields. It is a sacrament, a consecration of "good ground" and the boundaries between light and dark, of the proper order of things. Just as the summer migrants stand for renewal, so the barn owl stands for continuity, and its passing leaves us that bit less grounded. (*Nature Cure*, pp. 137).

Owls undoubtedly do present themselves to us with more associations, and therefore through more opaque filters, than perhaps any other family of birds. And then there is the final filter of darkness itself, which adds to the sense of mystique and omen. Moreover, this reaction to owls seems to be a universal phenomenon, across time and cultures. The barn owl is one of the most widely distributed of all land birds, found throughout the tropics and reaching its northern limit in about southern Scotland; and everywhere it figures in myth, folklore, and ritual. But in Britain at least the physical characteristics combine to produce a sense of affection as well as awe, and with the help of Bill Oddie and others the barn owl has become a cultural object and joins the puffin and the penguin in the soft toys department. The relevant characteristics here are the upright posture, the big round head, the cuddly size, and the soft dumpy shape. I suppose the much-loved Bill Oddie is the same somatotype?

What this second group of vignettes demonstrates, I think, even more clearly than the first group, is that all these species have acquired a special status that goes beyond our actual experience of them and is only partly derived from that experience. We fall in love with the idea of these birds and what they come to represent. The barn owl in particular seems to have this further dimension and so makes a natural link to my next section.

Charisma and Beyond

It may help now if we deliberately look at more extreme cases, which may highlight things we overlook or take for granted in our everyday perceptions. Madness may be easier to define than sanity, and may have some deeper insights too. Anyway, we do know that the outcome of polls depends on the questions you put and the samples you take, and if you asked keen birdwatchers rather than the general public for their top ten birds you would get a somewhat different list from the one I have just considered, especially if you asked them not for their list of "favourite" birds (which, as I have said, tends to elicit the familiar ones) but for the ones they found most "attractive." You might go even further and use the word "charismatic." It's quite common nowadays to hear birdwatchers talk about their quest for "charismatic" species. But what could "charismatic" mean when applied to birds? What are the criteria here and how do they relate to the criteria for our first list of favourites? Charismatic birds must surely have some extra "x" quality to transcend the category of the merely charming—something that gives them an additional mystique, something to quicken the pulse with a "wow" or an "ah" factor.

The word "charisma" comes from the Greek and literally means "grace"—a personal quality or gift that seems inspired and inspiring—something quite out of the ordinary and with a special kind of impact. Most people would say that Muhammad Ali, Nelson Mandela, and Mahatma Gandhi had charisma. Among American presidents, J. F. Kennedy and Bill Clinton had it, but not Jimmy Carter or Gerald Ford. Among actors Greta Garbo and Marilyn Monroe, but perhaps not Judi Dench or Laurence Olivier, however wonderful their professional talents.[1] But can the term be applied to things other than people?

---

[1] The National Portrait Gallery in London had an exhibition in 2005 of "The World's Most Photographed People," which isn't quite the same thing but has interesting overlaps in terms of

In the case of birds, what would it consist in? What produces this special emotional reaction in us?

Here is a personal list of ten candidates for charisma, to examine further:

Barn owl	Swift
Crane	Waxwing
Red kite	Firecrest
Lapwing	Capercaillie
Nightjar	Leach's petrel

I found it hard to make these choices and restrict myself to just ten. How could I leave out the swallow, raven, chough, woodcock, and wryneck, for example, all of which I respond to strongly? Bittern, avocet, osprey, peregrine, and corncrake will have their supporters, too. All birdwatchers will have their own preferences and their own reasons for them, but again I would expect some overlap, as well as some blurring with the first list of national favourites. (You'll see that the barn owl is on my list here, and the golden eagle and kingfisher might well appear on this second list too for some people.) What is it that makes these birds "charismatic"? Are there really special birds or only special experiences? And what about other parts of the natural world? If I think about special butterflies why do swallowtails, clouded yellows, and small coppers come immediately to mind, and in the case of trees why oak and black poplar?

Well, it clearly isn't just a question of rarity. Birdwatchers are by definition familiar with a wider range of species than the general public and may have a different sense of the exotic as well as a different kind of interest in it. But though several of these birds are quite unusual, some, like the swift and lapwing, are common enough and all of them except the waxwing breed in Britain. Of course, there are also genuine rarities (in British terms) that I would class as charismatic—harlequin duck, pallid harrier, Pallas's warbler, and wallcreeper—but I left those off my list deliberately in order to demonstrate that rarity isn't the main determinant. Moreover, plenty of rare birds seem quite *un*charismatic to me: if you didn't "need" them for your British list would you cross the street for a washed-out rosefinch or savannah sparrow? Anyway, rarity is clearly just a relative matter. The magpie is certainly a common bird for most of us (common in more than one sense perhaps), but in the Isles of Scilly it is rarer than an American bobolink or parula, so when one appeared

---

celebrity. Its top ten were: Elvis Presley, Muhammad Ali, Mahatma Gandhi, Adolf Hitler, Greta Garbo, Audrey Hepburn, James Dean, John F. Kennedy, Marilyn Monroe, and (a surprise) Queen Victoria.

there in 2001 it attracted hordes of twitchers desperate to get it on their Scilly list. There were two interesting aspects to this ludicrous spectacle. First, since the magpie was officially a Scilly rarity, observers had to submit "descriptions"[1] to the relevant rarities committee to have their records validated; and many of them realised they had never really looked at a magpie before and had to consult the reference books afterwards to discover what plumage features they had actually seen. Some of the records were actually rejected, I think, as inadequate evidence, which certainly shows a steely objectivity on the part of the committee (all of whom were well aware that it really *was* a magpie). Second, the magpie is of course a physically striking bird, but I don't think anyone found it especially charismatic, even in circumstances where it was also a rare bird. In the rush to find it, no one was breathing heavily for reasons other than unfitness.

How about beauty and appearance, then? Surely basic physical attraction must be one of the most powerful factors at work here? Several of these charismatics certainly have attractive plumages, but you wouldn't really say that of my swift or petrel, or indeed of the skylark and nightingale from the earlier list. And the categories don't fit neatly the other way round either. There are plenty of beautiful birds that are surely not charismatic (pheasant, Canada goose, and, if you like, magpie). Moreover, even within a single species beauty may vary according to the biological factors of season, sex, and age. The bird may be most arresting in just one form: the summer black-throated diver and grey plover, the male smew and hen harrier, and the adult long-tailed skua; or the ruff, only in the contingent combination of adult, male, and summer. But could you have charisma just on a temporary basis or in one aspect? That doesn't sound like a very constitutive characteristic. So it doesn't seem to depend solely on physical impressions either.

Could it then be something involving broader questions of behaviour, voice, and movement? Flight itself might seem a plausible candidate, as a prime source of our fascination with birds in general? We think of flight as a fundamental characteristic of birds, almost a defining one. "Winged birds," Homer calls them. This is their special gift—that buoyant passage through the air with perfect control. Are we drawn to birds because of their power of movement, their boundless freedom in the skies, grounded and clumsy as we are? That

---

[1] This has long been standard procedure for all rarity records, and the "descriptions" of a generation or so ago were often very superior pieces of prose (and perception). Technology has changed this, however, and digital photographs are now an almost mandatory requirement while the descriptions are reduced to a commentary on those and on the circumstances of the encounter. See further pp. 92–93 and 116–17.

ancient dream—the Icarus fantasy. And not just Icarus. Freud noted how common "flying dreams" were and drew his own conclusions about the kind of liberation involved—plausibly perhaps, when you think of the success of the airline slogan in which a smiling hostess invites you to "Fly me." The word "aviation" itself means "flying like birds," and Leonardo da Vinci based his pioneering designs for flying machines on an intensive study of the mechanics of bird flight, naming his flying ship the "ornithopter." More generally, it was on birds, and in particular on birds in flight, that the art of augury relied for special insight, and we still find our own kinds of significance in them. We may wonder, as I did at the start of this book, at the artistry of swallows in the air, or the aerial mastery of the red kite and the eagle; we thrill to the spectacular stoop of the peregrine and the dive of the gannet; and we are stirred in some deeply evocative way by the wafting flight of the barn owl. Sometimes it is the combination of sight and sound that moves us: the measured beat of a line of wild swans, the war whoop of a plunging lapwing, the clamour of a thousand geese rising as a flock, or the screams of swifts hurtling round houses. All these are powerful attractants, and perhaps contribute to charisma. As before with rarity and beauty, however, they can't quite define it, since they work only in some cases, not in all. Robins, firecrests, and capercaillies all have a characteristic flight but scarcely a moving one. Who has ever even *seen* a nightingale in flight? And penguins are actually flightless, unless you count underwater flying.

Should we then be looking for some combination of features rather than one uniquely defining characteristic? And should we be looking both more widely and more deeply at the contexts in which certain birds acquire a special meaning for us? Consider further the species on my list.

I start with what may be the most surprising one. Leach's petrel figures there not because of its beauty or scarcity. The plumage is mainly blackish and some fifty thousand pairs breed in the British Isles. The flight is certainly quite striking, a curious flitting and veering, unpredictable like a bat; but the bird is rarely ever seen since it is a truly pelagic species, feeding far out to sea by day and returning to its nesting burrows only in the small hours of the night. There is, it is true, a small passage down mainland coasts in autumn when the keenest sea-watchers will glimpse them briefly, and there are also occasional dramatic "wrecks" when the bird is driven inshore or even inland by violent storms out in its feeding grounds in midocean. But these sightings are untypical and have the excitement only of the abnormal, like seeing a whale in the Thames. Leach's petrel is in fact special precisely because of its inaccessibility. It dwells in the remotest parts of the kingdom, breeding on just a handful of island groups way out in the Atlantic beyond the Outer Hebrides, all of them very difficult to visit. And it is there on my list because I did in fact visit them. I spent a night alone on the Flannan Isles for this very purpose and heard for myself the extraordinary "devil's chorus" made by the birds returning to their burrows at 2 or 3 in the morning. They were there all around me, several hundred of them, floating in like moths and flopping down at my feet. The noise was over-whelming—weird, deafening, and of course wonderful partly because I knew I was the only one hearing it (and the only person within forty miles, in fact).

The other birds on my list qualify through some similar combination of special features and personal experience. The red kite is there because of its amazing aerial control and its gorgeous coloration, but also because of what I know about its history of persecution and recovery and because of my memo-ries of searching for it in wild Wales years ago when the U.K. population was down to some thirty pairs. I shall be interested to see if my feelings gradually change now that it has been "reintroduced" in so many places and is no longer threatened (you can see them any day from the M40). The capercaillie makes it on grounds of brute size and physical presence, its dawn displays and cork-popping song, and the ancient forests it inhabits. The crane scores on almost every count: an imposing presence on the ground, its beautiful plumage tones, the wild bugling cries of a distant party in flight, the famous courtship dance, and again what I know of its history and its secret homecoming to the marshes of East Anglia. And so on. In each case the reasons are somewhat different but there is some dynamic combination of attributes, and one to which we our-selves contribute.

So perhaps this is more like an Olympic decathlon, where one has to score well in several different events to succeed. Or, maybe a better analogy, like those skating events where contestants are judged both on technical and artis-tic merit. The waxwing, firecrest, and kite score high on beauty; the crane, capercaillie, and waxwing on scarcity; Leach's petrel on inaccessibility; the crane and caper on display; the nightjar, lapwing, and Leach's on dramatic voices; the kite and crane have resonances from history, as the swift and barn owl do from folklore; and the lapwing, swift, and kite excel in aerial acrobat-ics. There are then two other key determinants, perhaps the most important of all for me: the contexts of time and place. Some birds recall, or almost define, a season of the year or a moment in the cycle of the day. Here is Hughes again, on the arrival of the swifts in summer:

> Fifteenth of May. Cherry blossom. The swifts
> Materialise at the tip of a long scream
> Of needle. "Look! They're back! Look!"

Swallows in spring and the songs of the first chiffchaff and cuckoo produce the same charge, the same Proustian moments; while the barn owl and night-jar inescapably recall the time of dusk and the gloaming. It is the same with landscape and location. Some birds not only belong in certain distinctive habitats but also become a constitutive part of them. The caper and Leach's inhabit wild, dramatic places; the swift, barn owl, and lapwing usually tamer ones; but they all form part of our expectations about the place in question; indeed in the years of its occasional winter invasions the waxwing can produce a sense of excitement even about a visit to a supermarket, where they have their own feeding frenzies on the berried bushes in the customers' car parks.

Following this decathlon analogy, then, you perhaps have to do well in several categories really to catch the eye. If you want to press the analogy and schematise the game you could produce a little table to score your list of birds against criteria such as scarcity, remoteness, plumage, voice, display, flight, location, seasonality, history, folklore, and personal significance. (Crane comes out top in my league table.) By the same means you could demonstrate how and why some birds seem so decidedly *un*charismatic. I don't propose to produce yet another list of top ten (or bottom ten, in this case—a sad activity for wet Sundays), but it seems to follow logically that the existence of charisma would imply the possibility of its opposite (what is the word for a black-hole personality?) or at least its absence. Otherwise the whole thing threatens to break down and we have to say either that *all* birds are charismatic or that no birds are. In fact we can recognise the lack of charisma as easily as we can the presence of it, and there should be the same measure of agreement about what qualifies. There are distinctions and degrees, but I would put wood pigeon, pheasant, greenfinch, coot, Canada goose, and greylag, for example, on the wrong side of the dividing line because they just do not have that combination of qualities that give the fizz.[1] You might go further and argue that some species don't merely have an absence of charisma but actively repel—magpies, crows, gulls, and starlings would be examples for some people. Indeed, some people have a very real fear of the beaks, talons, and whirling feathers that are the nightmare images Alfred Hitchcock exploited so effectively in his film *The Birds* (see p. 265 note).

You might also travel further up the scale the other way. No doubt you could produce a list of international charismatics or supercharismatics, including,

---

[1] After writing this, I saw that Stephen Moss had listed his "five least favourite birds" in his *Guardian* column (republished as "The Hit List" in *This Birding Life*), in ascending order of *un*charisma: meadow pipit, greenfinch, wood pigeon, greylag, and Canada goose. I had in fact wondered about including the meadow pipit in my list of examples, but had reprieved it because of the "parachute song," so evocative of seawalls and uplands.

perhaps, ivory-billed woodpecker, greater roadrunner, hoatzin, resplendent quetzal, California condor, satyr tragopan, hyacinth macaw, superb lyrebird, emperor penguin, and wandering albatross. Some people do, after all, use more extreme terms even than "charisma." Peter Matthiessen talked of his "pilgrimage" in search of cranes; the American poet Leonard Nathan, in a running dispute with a determinedly scientific friend in his *Diary of a Left-Handed Birdwatcher*, longed for "epiphany" in the form of snow buntings; and for a generation of American scientists and birders the ivory-billed wood-pecker has been the "holy grail."[1] But these are more extreme forms of devo-tion than we need for present purposes, and the word "charismatic" has turned into a useful secular term, whatever its religious origins.

This is a sort of sideshow, however. I introduced charisma in the first place only to highlight what it was we were looking for. In the end the real point of any analysis comes in the subsequent reintegration of the parts, where we look again at the whole but perhaps now see it differently and with more under-standing. In actual fact all these birds are experienced just as *birds*. Scarcity, behaviour, habitat, seasonality, and history will all be connected to produce a unique personality and presence that cannot just be reduced to a series of sep-arate attributes. We may be reacting to an occasion as much as to a species. Some birds can excite when in flocks much more than as singletons, like a winter flock of snow buntings blowing along a shingle bank or the clamour of rooks returning to roost in the evening sky; and a party of long-eared owls at roost will thrill even when they are asleep, inert, and almost invisible, indeed *because* of this. And in the final analysis, birds are also individuals whom we encounter one-on-one, as well as members of a species that we comprehend, and may only see, generically.

There are some deep questions here about perception and association. Wil-liam Hazlitt, in his essay "On the Love of the Country," suggested that "the in-terest we feel in human nature is exclusive, and confined to the individual, the interest we feel in external nature is common, and transferable from one ob-ject to all others in the same class." That sharp contrast seems to me false in that form, though. We can respond to both humans and birds at every taxo-nomic level. For example, we may have attitudes to the human species as such, and to the French, Eskimos, immigrants, politicians, football teams, family groups, and members of the opposite sex as well as to individual people. In the same way we can react to birds as a class and also have separate responses

---

[1] So described by Dr. John Fitzpatrick, the director of Cornell University's Laboratory of Orni-thology, in announcing its "rediscovery" in April 2005; but as with that other grail, doubts about the ivory-bill's existence are now beginning to creep in, I see.

to families like gulls, owls, and waders as well as to genera and species like nightingales, bluebirds, greenfinches, and bald eagles; we can also respond to our own individual robin or cardinal in the garden. The more interesting question is what we do and don't perceive when we are thinking generically, whether about humans or about birds, and that I try to address in the next chapter.

We have now moved a long way from thinking of attraction as just a response to the static or physical "museum" appearance of a species towards some much larger idea of how a bird presents itself in the world, its context in landscape, season, and history, and the ways we experience it. This suggests a more complicated index of significance, which serves to connect this chapter to the last. We looked there at some of the different ways people respond to birds and we have now started exploring what it is they are responding to, which turns out in part to be themselves.

3
Seeing a Difference

You can observe a lot by just looking.
Yogi Berra, U.S. baseball manager

Isles of Scilly, 30 September 1986

I have been watching a group of assorted waders at the far end of Porthloo beach, about a hundred yards away. Mostly dunlin, though there are also some sanderling, turnstone, and ringed plover among them, and two more interesting-looking birds. One of them seems a shade larger than the other dunlin; it also seems to have a longer bill, faintly decurved; the patterning of the back looks different too, though it's hard to be sure at this distance in the dull light of an autumn afternoon. Isn't it also striding around with a rather different gait? Something clicks. This is surely a curlew sandpiper, so called because of that curved bill, which also indicates a different feeding habit. The curlew sandpiper is an uncommon migrant in Britain in the autumn, just passing through briefly from its breeding grounds in the Russian Arctic tundra to its wintering areas in Africa. A good sighting for Scilly in September. The other bird that stands out is noticeably smaller than the dunlin and is feeding rapidly with a light bobbing motion, something between a peck and a dab. The bill looks tiny. The underparts are a very clean white, the back dull brown with a faintly stripy pattern. The legs are blackish, as far as I can make out. This has got to be a little stint, the smallest of the waders that occur in Britain, also an unusual visitor and on much the same route as the curlew sandpiper. Come to think of it, they do often appear in the same places at the same time when on passage. Nice birds.

Another birdwatcher approaches me. I recognise him as one of the Scilly regulars who follow the rare birds here each autumn. In fact he is one of the "rare men," as they are called, the high priests of the British Birds Rarities Committee who adjudicate on all claims and records of species classified as national rarities; indeed he is the *pontifex maximus,* Peter Grant, the chairman of that committee, one of the greatest experts on identification in the Western

12. Semi-p on Scilly, 30 September 1986 (photo: Peter Wheeler)

world and one of the joint authors of what was to become the standard field guide to the birds of Britain and Europe. I knew Peter a bit and he nodded to me in a friendly way, with the gentle arch of the eyebrows that is the polite form of enquiry when one birder comes upon another who has been watching something ("what have you got?" is the less polite form). I felt quietly pleased to be able to point something out to an expert of this distinction. "Oh," I said, very low key, "just some dunlin and odds and bobs, but there's a curlew sand-piper and a little stint among them too." "Oh good," he said appreciatively, raising his own binoculars. Pause. "Yes, nice curlew sand . . ." Longer pause, a bit unnerving. " . . . but you know, I think your stint is a semi-palmated sand-piper." SEMI-PALMATED WHAT!? A semi-palmated sandpiper is a five-star rarity, even in Scilly. This is an American wader, one of the small "peeps," as they are known after their thin, piping calls. At this time (1986), only a hand-ful had ever been recorded in Britain, and only two ever in Scilly. I had never seen one in my life. They are very hard indeed to distinguish from the other small stints and peeps, even close up and even when you are forewarned and looking hard for the key features, the clincher being the partial webbing be-tween the toes that gives the species this slightly absurd name but is visible only at a range of a few yards, if at all. He was right, of course. That is what it turned out to be after all the watchers on the islands had assembled, as they very quickly did, scrutinised every feather (and the toes), watched it fly, heard it call, photographed it, and consulted the American reference books. We had made a real find.

But what had Peter noticed that I had missed? I had been looking at a semi-palmated sandpiper but I hadn't seen one. How on earth could this man begin to identify that species, which he couldn't at all have been expecting to find here, at such a range and with such unassuming confidence, in a matter of seconds? And why was there such a swell of excitement at the discovery? The bird in question was hardly a beauty, after all, just a dingy stranger on a dull day, a vagrant who had missed his way. The semi-p[1] stayed around a few days. Detumescence sets in quickly among birders in these situations, however, and as celebrity turned to familiarity and then to boredom, no one really bothered to look at it anymore; they would merely check out its presence in a confirmatory way and then search for novelties elsewhere. "Anything about?" "No, just the semi-p."

Distinctions and Differences

Birdwatching begins with noticing differences, and this is one of its first pleasures. The child who is discovering the world wants to recognise its contents and put a name to them, especially if they are colourful, noisy, animate, and mobile. Most people learn what a bird is very early on. Birds move. They respond when you put food out for them in the garden or chase them on the beach. They are little beings, like us in some ways and different in others, so very good for stories, play, and imaginings—very good, that is, for discovering ourselves as well as the world outside. And we soon notice differences among them, as well as between them and us. Many children in Britain must learn to distinguish a robin, gull, duck, and pigeon (probably also an owl and a penguin, though they may never actually see one) well before they know the different kinds of trees, cars, or fish that there are.[2] They do it by noticing differences, and are therefore becoming birdwatchers of a kind. And the more differences they observe the better birdwatchers they are likely to become.

This chapter is about making these distinctions—about our abilities to do so and the kinds of pleasure to be found in the activity. All pleasures have their extreme forms and perversions, of course, and I also look at those, both for the interest they have in themselves as human curiosities and for the light they throw back on more normal enthusiasms. I was present on another Scilly day in October 2006 when news broke of a Canada warbler found on the west coast of Ireland. Now, a Canada warbler is even rarer than a semi-p: it is a small North American warbler that should have been migrating from Canada or New England to South America; this was only the second record for Europe (the first was in Iceland in 1973) and the first ever for the British

[1] There is a birders' slang that consists largely of abbreviations of this kind (curlew sand, semi-p, and so on). For a longer list, see pp. 254–55. Use of the correct argot is a mark of membership in this community as in others.

[2] This will depend somewhat on parental interest and location, of course. Presumably the children of St. Kilda, when that was inhabited (up to 1930), learned at an early stage to distinguish the seabirds that furnished the staple diet—fulmar, gannet, and puffin—if only by taste.

Isles.[1] The bird was identified in the afternoon and by the evening that day the top listers on Scilly had made their plans. First thing next day a helicopter took them off the islands to Penzance on the mainland; they then drove up the coast to Newquay in Cornwall, where a light aircraft chartered from Blackpool met them and flew them to Shannon; there they hired a car and drove with the devil behind them to Loop Head in County Clare, where they made a brief contact with the bird. They then repeated all these stages in reverse and were most of them back in Scilly that evening for the log-call, just in case they had missed anything there. The cost-benefit analysis? I examine the pathology of such extreme behaviour in the next chapter, but first let us look at some more ordinary accomplishments.

The act of identification seems to be fundamental. It plays a part not only in the child's growing understanding of the world but also in all the different kinds of interest in birds I sketched in the first chapter. We can salute the birds, in person or in poetry; we can sentimentalise them, count them, list them, describe and study them; we may seek empathy with them, we may want to hunt, cook, breed, or conserve them; but for all these purposes we first need to know what they are. For birdwatchers this may represent a sort of lad-der of progress—the more acts of identification we can reliably perform the higher the level of skill; the more subtle the distinctions the more satisfying the discrimination; the larger the list the greater the success. You can see how that would work for the lister, but there is an inherent risk, and a paradox, in this. If the accumulation of identifications is sufficient in itself and is our only interest, it becomes a pleasure of acquisition not of experience. And then you may kick away the rungs of your own ladder. Think of the process of scanning a mixed flock of birds in a hedge in winter: yes, chaffinch, greenfinch, blue tit, black-bird, dunnock—is there going to be a yellowhammer or even a brambling? As each species is correctly identified it is checked off in the mind, as it were, and you pass quickly on to the next. At no point *after* the identification do you bother even to look at those birds again; they have been screened out to assist in isolating the less common species. And the consequence of that is that we may actually forget what some common birds look like in any detail that goes beyond the most obvious distinguishing features. You can test yourself on this:

- What colour is a house sparrow's bill?
- Can you sketch the face pattern of a blue tit?
- Where exactly does the white come on a magpie?

[1] Great Britain and Ireland are usually regarded by listers as one territory. Politics and history count for little in this sport, and I doubt if many people keep a strictly U.K. (i.e., Great Britain and Northern Ireland) list, whatever their passports may say.

13. Outlines of species: (a) house sparrow; (b) blue tit; (c) magpie; (d) chaffinch; (e) heron; (f) robin

- What is the shape of a chaffinch's wing bar(s)?
- What's the leg colour of a heron?
- How many distinct colours are there on a robin?

This impatience with the common can become self-defeating, since at all levels of expertise the ability to distinguish, or even notice, a less common species may depend crucially on an exact grasp of the features of a more common one: you must know a reed warbler very well indeed, for example, in order to recognise a marsh warbler by sight, and the same applies to common and arctic terns, and to black-headed and Mediterranean gulls; analogous examples in America are black-capped and Carolina chickadees, fall blackpoll and bay-breasted warblers, and song and savannah sparrows. Many rare birds are undoubtedly overlooked just because the common ones are underlooked.

Species and Individuals

But what is it that we are identifying or failing to identify anyway? For most purposes we seem to be more interested in the bird as a representative of a *species* rather than as an individual. That's what we name, count, admire, conserve, or eat. There are exceptions, of course. New Yorkers follow the courtship and family life of the red-tailed hawks in Central Park as eagerly as they do those of the characters in any TV soap, and Pale Male and Lola are familiar habitués of Fifth Avenue apartment roofs. In the United Kingdom, people often befriend a garden blackbird and give it a name. And the BBC *Springwatch* programmes with Bill Oddie and Kate Humble have encouraged people even to recognise and name individual blue tits in the nest. A long-staying rarity can become a celebrity, if it belongs to the right sort of species, like Sammy, the black-winged stilt that frequented Titchwell Nature Reserve in Norfolk for many years, or Albert, the black-browed albatross that returned each summer to his rock on Hermaness vainly seeking a mate.[1] But even in these cases we probably aren't really familiar with the individuals involved and don't always have quite the relationship with them that we imagine. When a bottlenose whale strayed up the Thames at the start of 2006 it quickly became a national hero, with tens of thousands lining the banks to cheer it back to safety and millions more following its fortunes through TV news bulletins and live feeds on the Internet. The public interest required that it have a name, so *The Sun* called it Wally, while *The Times* countered with Billy. The story ends badly. The whale failed to escape; it died; and in the postmortem examination that a grieving nation demanded it was found to be a female.

When we need to recognise individuals for scientific purposes we usually have to resort to colour-ringing or some form of marking, though occasionally if we work hard at it we can detect some of the physical differences the birds themselves must be relying on. For example, at the Slimbridge Wildfowl Trust Reserve in Gloucester, founded by Peter Scott, staff at the reserve have found a way of studying the behaviour of the wild Bewick's swans that arrive from Russia to winter there by noting the pattern of black and yellow on their bills; there are slight variations in these markings between different birds and these are recorded in little sketches that can then be used to identify the individuals.

Presumably there are similar variations within every species that its own members can immediately pick up but are largely invisible or inaudible to us. And this may be both a cause and a consequence of our fixation on the species itself. One wonders how easily birds themselves can distinguish individuals *across* species, since for most territorial and breeding purposes they are interested just in their own. The blackbird needs only a generic sense of a

---

[1] Size as well as ease of identification seem to be factors here—a rare bunting or pipit wouldn't qualify. On the political implications of this, see chapter 8, pp. 224–28.

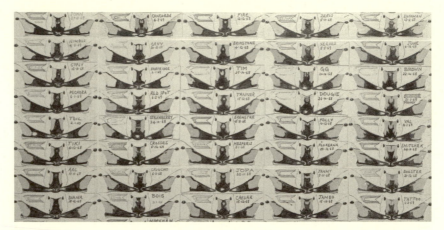

14. Detail from Bewick's swan: identification of individual birds by bill patterns (Peter Scott / Wildfowl and Wetlands Trust)

sparrowhawk to avoid the threat it poses by dashing for cover when it sees that profile; waiting to secure an individual ID might prove fatal. And in the reverse case the sparrowhawk has no *personal* interest in particular blackbirds—blackbird-as-prey is what it is pursuing. The evolutionary origin of our own concern with birds as sources of food is certainly related to species, not individuals, and that also suggests at least one of the deeper sources of our urge to discriminate and observe them. We needed to know which plants, animals, and birds were good to eat, where and when to find them, and, by extension, something of how they lived. Mind you, the surviving art and artefacts of our ancestors suggest that this wasn't by any means the only, or perhaps even the main, interest they took in birds, and I come to this later in chapter 10.

There are other practical considerations that make species rather than individuals the focus of our attention. Not only aren't we well equipped to distinguish individuals in most cases but there are also just too many of them to deal with. Species, on the other hand, are manageable as well as recognisable. You can have a response to a flight of brent geese across the Essex salt marshes (a powerful one, in my case), but you can't have a *relationship* with all five hundred birds in the group. You can maintain an intelligible and satisfying garden list, country list, or life list of species identified; and you can at least imagine there being some ten thousand species of birds in the world; but you couldn't make any sense of counting all the individuals you come across in any of these cases. You don't say, "Interesting day out today; I saw 251 birds." Insofar as we are interested in the actual numbers of individual birds it is as statistics in population studies of species.[1] It means something to have observed thirty wigeon, one hen harrier, two hundred lapwings, five common snipe, and fifteen redshanks at a particular marsh in Essex on a December day, but it doesn't mean anything to have seen 251 birds there. There are reasons for those species being there at that time, in those numbers, and behaving as they were. You can take an interest in species, study them, and generalise about them.

What about our emotional and aesthetic reactions, though? Surely they are related to particular experiences of particular individuals? The idea of a species is after all just an abstraction, isn't it, a convenient way of relating a lot of birds that share certain common properties? In fact, do we ever perceive a species directly? Do we ever see robin, rather than this or that robin? Beware! Here be dragons, mesmerizing philosophical dragons with whom Plato, Aristotle, and all their successors up to the present day have wrestled, and always lost. Don't go there. Philosophy can be wonderfully liberating, but it can also make you assert things you couldn't possibly believe and deny things you know perfectly well. For our present purposes, I think this objection presents more of a paradox than a problem. When Lopez bows to the snowy owl, when Keats suffers his *petit mort* of passion with the nightingale, when Shelley and Richard Jefferies thrill to the skylark, when you or I have a privileged moment of encounter with a barn owl or a swallow, we are all, it is true, responding to a particular moment of experience, prompted by a particular bird, in an unrepeatable instant. It is, as they say (so often as to blunt the point of the comment), a unique experience. But that doesn't mean that these are the only realities, especially since there seems to be no way of describing them except by reference to other levels of experience. Think of the analogy with music. We can only hear particular performances of Mozart's *Magic Flute* and can only have the experience we are having at the time; there is, however, also such a thing as the piece of music called *The Magic Flute*, which is not the same as any one of those performances but is just as real as they are.[2] We can and do have feelings about *The Magic Flute* as a species and can discuss how it ranks or compares with other favourite pieces of music. You couldn't even hear those particular performances unless Mozart had first created *The Magic Flute*, let alone describe them and have feelings about them. In the same way,

---

[1] Roger Tory Peterson, however, once made the heroic calculation that at some point in the 1950s there were precisely 7,612,866,560 individual birds in North America.

[2] Nor is it the same as the written score and libretto. That would be like saying a species just consists in its DNA specification.

we say, "did you hear that nightingale?" or "I saw a lovely barn owl," or "there's the curlew sandpiper," referring to a kind, not an instance, and making perfect sense, which we all understand.

Indeed, Dr. Johnson would argue that our most important feelings and thoughts operate at this level. We have to sense the general through the particular:

> The business of the poet . . . is to examine, not the individual, but the species; to remark general properties and large appearances: he does not number the streaks of the tulip, or describe the different shades in the verdure of the forest. He is to exhibit in his portraits of nature such prominent and striking features, as recall the original to every mind; and must neglect the minuter discriminations. . . . He must write as the interpreter of nature, and the legislator of mankind, and consider himself as presiding over the thoughts and manners of future generations; as a being superior to time and place. (*Rasselas,* chap. 10)

And Fielding, as a novelist, would agree:

> I describe not men, but manners; not an individual, but a species. Perhaps it will be answered, Are not the characters then taken from life? To which I answer in the affirmative; nay, I believe I might aver that I have writ little more than I have seen. The Lawyer is not only alive, but hath been so these 4,000 years. (*Joseph Andrews,* book 3, chap. 1)

The fact is we do care about species of birds. We know what they are, we can recognise them better than we can individuals, and we relate most of our human reactions to birds to that level of experience. We can relate to other levels too, though in a rather different way. We may have a liking for owls, waders, or warblers as such, and can usually recognise these categories too and see the family resemblances. But it would be unusual to have a taste for counting genera, say, rather than species, on a day's outing or in a life list. These are all different levels, kinds, and degrees of interest that reinforce my main point rather than contradict it.

Of course, the idea of a species is not itself an entirely hard-edged one, a fact that produces employment for scientists and may induce neuroses in listers. Species evolve by progressive and usually gradual divergence from common ancestors and at some point in that process, when the taxonomists judge that the differences are sufficiently significant and stable, they pronounce that a separate species has been formed. The maps of branching evolutionary trees illustrate the origins and family relationships that underlie this for any one species, and the Linnaean terminology of classes, families, genera, and species explains it all in words. So, for example, to follow the branches that lead to the species house sparrow *(Passer domesticus)*, we start from the class of birds *(Aves)* and go down through the order of passerines (perching birds, *Passeriformes*), to the suborder of song birds *(Oscines)*, to the family of weavers *(Ploceidae)*, to the subfamily of sparrow weavers *(Passerinae)*, to the genus of true sparrows *(Passer)*, until we reach the species *(Passer domesticus)*. Tracing these links can be very instructive: it demonstrates in this case, for example, that the house sparrow is more closely related to the weaver birds of the African savannah than it is to the finches and buntings you find it next to in the British field guides, which themselves are more closely related to the very different American sparrows.

Since species evolve and develop by random variation they don't by definition constitute fixed and god-given categories.[1] It is a matter of judgement when a separate species has been formed (assisted perhaps by geographical separation) and when separate species have merged (for example, through interbreeding and hybridisation). This is not an arbitrary matter—it is an issue for serious scientific enquiry and reflection; but neither is it an obvious and undisputed matter. Indeed, it arouses fierce debates between the splitters (egged on, you might say, by the listers) and the lumpers (a much more conservative body), who clash like Swift's big-enders and little-enders over matters of little practical consequence for most of us. The yellow wagtail *Motacilla flava*, for example, has various related forms and races that are certainly distinct in appearance in the cases of the blue-headed, black-headed, and grey-headed wagtails (and some authorities distinguish up to eight varieties, others up to eighteen—see plate 1b).

But are these different subspecies, which may one day diverge further and become full species in their own right? Are they different races of the same species, which are just geographically separated for the most part? Or are they already different species? Do you have four species or one on your European list? What about hybrids? And what about those species that seem to present an unbroken continuum of variations, like the European herring gull, *Larus argentatus*, and the lesser black-backed gull, *Larus fuscus* (see fig. 15 and pp. 14–15).

[1] Do creationists have a view on subspecies and hybrids, I wonder? Would they think the splitting of the herring gull and yellow-legged gull in 2005 was a discovery or an invention? To say with Genesis 1:21 that "God created every winged bird according to its kind" just begs the question. There is a partial answer in *The Design and Origin of Birds* (2006) by the wildlife illustrator Philip Snow, who is also a committed creationist and gives a fundamentalist account of the Bible creation story and the capacities of Noah's Ark. His basic argument seems to be that the biblical "kinds" refer to a higher taxonomic level than species.

15. Herring gull races from Snow, Perrins, and Gillmor,
Birds of the Western Palearctic, concise edition

Americans don't have this any easier. The familiar song sparrow (no relation to the European sparrows) can be subdivided into twenty-nine or more
named, regional subspecies based on plumage details and size; but they all interbreed freely and clearly recognize one another as song sparrows. And the
American glaucous-winged and western gulls raise just the same problems as
do the European herring gull group. Where do you make the divisions in a
spectrum? It's rather like the separation of colours in the rainbow, where we
say there are seven colours but know that in fact each colour merges imperceptibly into the next.[1]

There have been many attempts, of course, to define a "species" in some
very precise way, but there always seem to be exceptions and grey areas. The
main contenders for a suitably exclusive definition have been: (1) *biological organisms that interbreed*. But then you have interbreeding between mallards

---

[1] This arbitrary segmentation of the spectrum was no doubt based originally on the prestige of
the number seven in magical and religious thought. We could easily do without orange and indigo for most practical purposes if you didn't have to have seven colours in total.

and other ducks, for example, which are clearly different species, and hybrid offspring that interbreed further; and you soon run into the Catch-22 of taxonomy—you can't be sure how much they interbreed until you can distinguish them, but you can't distinguish them because they interbreed; (2) *organisms with a distinct form or appearance,* including differences of voice and behaviour. But then you get a continuum of variations, as in the case of the gulls and wagtails mentioned above, and you just have to decide what differences are significant enough to be "distinctions"; and (3) *organisms separable by DNA analysis.* This sounds promisingly "scientific" and definitive, but then turns out again to be a matter of degree rather than kind and produces results that contradict the other two criteria and common sense; it demonstrates, for example, that on this basis the two visually very similar forms of Bonelli's warbler, eastern and western, are as different from each other as they are from the wood warbler, while the very different-looking pied and white wagtails are the same species.

So we probably have to go back to what the great man who got us into all this had to say himself by way of evasive comment:

> Nor shall I here discuss the various definitions which have been given of the term species. No one definition has satisfied all naturalists; yet every naturalist knows vaguely what he means when he speaks of a species. (Darwin, *Origin of Species*)

"Vaguely" indeed. Darwin changed our view of the world and of ourselves, but the one thing he didn't do is tell us what a species was.

Anyway, this is just to say that the idea of a species, though "real" in itself and fundamental to our understanding and appreciation of birds, is still a softer notion than you might have thought, and one defined to some extent by our own purposes and decisions. The consequences of those decisions can in some cases be important, of course—in politics, law, or business. Would we put the same conservation effort into protecting the Scottish crossbill, for example, if we thought it was "only" a subspecies? Would the Famous Grouse whisky company want to name itself after a subspecies of the European willow grouse, *Lagopus lagopus lagopus,* rather than the endemic and unique-to-Scotland red grouse, *Lagopus lagopus scoticus?*[1] And what about the emotional and financial consequences for twitchers, unsure whether to make the long, nauseating, and

[1] Ironically, the red grouse was also the emblem originally chosen for the front cover of the very serious ornithological publication *British Birds* when it was founded in 1907. The design lasted ninety-seven years, by which time the red grouse had been downgraded into a subspecies, and the grouse motif now survives only as a small outline logo.

expensive voyage to St. Kilda to see the St. Kilda wren (currently a subspecies but certainly distinguishable)?

Observing and Perceiving

Granted that there are species, then, and that we know in a general way what they are and can in principle identify them, let us go back to the question I raised at the beginning of this chapter. How did Peter Grant perform that feat of identification on the Porthloo beach, and how do we do it ourselves in less testing circumstances? Is this a natural gift or a skill you can improve by training or experience? "Both" sounds like the right answer, but not a very helpful one. Let us start somewhere else, with Sherlock Holmes.

In the story of "The Greek Interpreter," Sherlock introduces his staunch but stolid companion, Watson, to his brother Mycroft, who, he has told Watson, has even greater powers of observation than he does himself. They meet in Mycroft's club, seat themselves in a bow window, and gaze out the window down the street:

> "To anyone who wishes to study mankind this is the spot," said Mycroft. "Look at the magnificent types! Look at these two men that are coming towards us, for example."
>
> "The billiard-marker and the other?"
>
> "Precisely. What do you make of the other?"
>
> The two men had stopped opposite the window. Some chalk marks over the waistcoat pocket were the only signs of billiards which I could see in one of them. The other was a very small dark fellow, with his hat pushed back and several packages under his arm.
>
> "An old soldier, I perceive," said Sherlock.
>
> "And very recently discharged," remarked the brother.
>
> "Served in India, I see."
>
> "And a non-commissioned officer."
>
> "Royal Artillery, I fancy," said Sherlock.
>
> "And a widower."
>
> "But with a child."
>
> "Children, my dear boy, children."

This is all too much for Watson, and Holmes has to explain:

> "Surely," answered Holmes, "it is not hard to say that a man with that bearing, expression of authority, and sun-baked skin is a soldier, is more than a private, and is not long from India."

"That he has not left the service long is shown by his still wearing his 'ammunition boots,' as they are called," observed Mycroft.

"He has not the cavalry stride, yet he wore his hat on one side, as is shown by the lighter skin on that side of his brow. His weight is against his being a sapper. He is in the artillery."

"Then, of course, his complete mourning shows that he has lost someone very dear. The fact that he is doing the shopping looks as though it were his wife. He has been buying things for children, you perceive. There is a rattle, which shows that one of them is very young. The wife probably died in child-bed. The fact that he has a picture-book under his arm shows that there is another child to be thought of."

Watson, we assume, is still staring out of the window with his mouth open. He only saw the dunlin.

Now, some birdwatchers certainly have great acuity of sight and hearing, and that can give them an advantage in certain situations, but it is not on the whole how they see and hear more than other people do. The much more important attributes, it seems to me, are (1) active attention, (2) informed expectation, and (3) ambition of imagination. These are the ways we maximise such powers of perception as we have and they are very powerful tools indeed.

Active attention is the means by which we concentrate in a selective way on specific features of the world. There is an almost infinite number of potential external stimuli, which would threaten to swamp our senses if we were just passively open to all of them. So we narrow our focus on those that interest us at any one time and make a positive effort to attend to them, like turning up the power of a searchlight and directing the beam. You listen instead of just hearing and look instead of just seeing. Or as the great detective chides the bewildered Watson in another of the Sherlock Holmes stories, "Scandal in Bohemia," "You see, but you do not observe." Detectives, artists, sportspeople, hunters, connoisseurs of all kinds, and psychotherapists refine this faculty of attention into a professional skill, and birdwatchers can do it too. You walk through a wood with a companion who does not share your interest and they just do not register the sights and sounds that are so evident to you—the quick movement at the top of a tree, the dark shape silhouetted in the hedge, the call from the distant copse. And when you point these out, they say, "you must have good eyesight," or "how on earth did you hear that?" But it isn't that at all. It's a matter of attention. It's all in the mind. (Though the ironic thing is that you are the one more likely to be called "absent-minded," since this heightened "presence" of mind comes at a cost, and you may well have missed important information your companion has to impart about world affairs or domestic obligations.)

Informed expectation makes you capable of what look like extraordinary feats of perception. On that woodland walk I can refine my focus even further on the basis of what I already know about the preferences and behaviour of certain species and can be actively looking out, or more likely listening out, for them. That plantation of conifers is just the place for coal tits and lisping gold-crests; those old oaks could well have a nuthatch trilling in the upper branches or a treecreeper crawling around the bark; be ready for the hoarse double-note of a grey wagtail down by the river where the stream runs fastest and for the high whistled call of a kingfisher flying off (you will only have a second to see it before it disappears); inspect that distant ridge for a soaring buzzard. Continuous assessment and anticipation of this kind will produce results. If you are on a familiar walk in your own patch you can of course perform even more impressive *coups de théâtre:* you will know in advance the bush the blackcap sings from, the favourite perch of the kestrel, the corner of the lake where the dabchick will be diving, the distant dead tree where the great spot-ted woodpecker drums. You can check all these out well before anyone else could possibly notice them. There is intense pleasure, and not just as a party trick, in enhancing one's powers in this way: you feel a knowing intimacy with your local landscape and more a part of the natural world around you.

The point about expectation applies more generally too, of course; for example in scientific discovery:

> Where observation is concerned, chance favours only the prepared mind. (Louis Pasteur)

and in sport:

> The more I practise the luckier I get. (Gary Player)

My third attribute is *ambition of imagination.* This is what distinguishes the great observers from the merely good ones. This is what marshals, integrates, and then finally transcends all the other skills. I mean by this the critical abil-ity always to question what has seemed accepted, established, or obvious. It means doubting those same informed expectations I was celebrating above. This is going that one creative step further, or more likely in the other direc-tion. It is the habit of looking at a little stint and wondering, when it would have occurred to no one else to wonder, whether it could possibly be a semi-palmated sandpiper, and then having the experience, knowledge, perception, and sheer *nerve* to answer the question "yes."

There are many examples of very rare birds that were only identified when someone asked such a question and saw the bird afresh, despite many experi-enced observers having approved an earlier identification. Britain's first, and extraordinary, record of a long-billed murrelet, which belongs thousands of miles away in the North Pacific, was only confirmed when someone looking at a photograph of it felt it "didn't look right" for the little auk it had been claimed as, and then had this unthinkable thought.[1] Similarly, the first Eurasian sky-lark *(Alauda arvensis)* ever to be recorded in California was misidentified for months by hundreds of good birders as the state's first Smith's longspur (*Calcarius pictus,* a sort of bunting)—understandable in a way, since both of these would have been unfamiliar species to most Californians, though they are in fact only superficially similar. Local observers had been expecting a Smith's longspur to show up there sometime, saw what they expected (and in the case of later observers saw what had then been "confirmed") and never considered the possibility of a skylark, which was a thought too far. We can only see what the mind is prepared to believe.

Illusion and Self-Deception

"Would you just describe exactly what you saw?" says the crime officer or the judge. It sounds like an easy question, but they know it isn't. We mix firsthand and secondhand knowledge, we elaborate or exaggerate for effect, we conceal, we misremember, we confuse different occasions, we try to please, we try to deceive. Bird recorders know about these human fallibilities too. I remember Mike Rogers, who was for many years the secretary of the British Birds Rarities Committee, telling me how useful his early training as a police detective had been in sifting truth from falsehood in the many claims the committee had to adjudicate. He knew the telltale signs of fabrication and he knew who had form. Doctors, teachers, parents, and barmen are performing similar acts of interpretation all the time in the course of their work, since not everything they are told is strictly true. We all know it's very hard to get at the truth, the whole truth, and nothing but the truth in any endeavour that relies on human reportage; but we do manage, more or less, and we do at least believe there is a truth that could be got at, if only everyone was truthful and could remember their actual perceptions clearly.

But the problem of accurate reportage gets even worse when the scientists studying human perception go to work on it, as Richard Gregory explains:

> Any retinal image is infinitely ambiguous. That is: it could correspond to, or represent, an *infinity* of possibilities of shapes and sizes and distances of objects. This is easily seen with an ellipse: it could be given by

[1] The fact of it being a *photograph* may be relevant here. It is interesting that in the same year (2006) Britain's first olive tree warbler and first black-eared kite were also identified from photographs, having originally been identified as, respectively, an olivaceous warbler and a black kite.

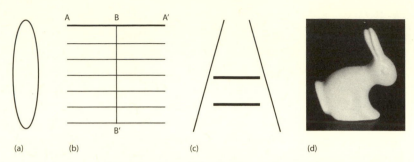

16. Classic illusions: (a) ellipsis; (b) bisection; (c) Ponzo; (d) duck-rabbit

a tilted circle, a small near circle (or ellipse), or a farther correspond-ingly larger circle or ellipse. . . . The possibilities are endless—yet amaz-ingly, we generally see just one of the infinite range of what might be out there. *(Eye and Brain)*

Human beings aren't just recording machines. Perception itself turns out to be an act of interpretation on the part of the brain, to try and give some initial meaning to the material that is reaching us through the channels of our five senses. This material may be partial or inconclusive, though, and that leads to various ambiguities, distortions, and mistakes. Here are some of the classic il-lusions. First, an example showing how context affects our perception even of a very simple figure (see the bisection illusion, 16b). Here the vertical and hori-zontal lines are really the same length, though the vertical one looks longer.

Our perception of size in relation to distance is also fallible, as in the Ponzo illusion (16c), where you could swear that the further line is the longer one (but it isn't).

Then there are ambiguous images like the famous duck-rabbit (16d). Which you see first depends partly on the angle of rotation and partly on what you think is more likely.

Finally an outright fiction, where you see something that isn't there at all. The Kanizsa triangle (16e) seems to have a brighter-than-background tri-angle, though it is not physically present. What is perhaps most disturbing about these cases is that we *continue* to misinterpret them even when we know the truth about the illusions.

In none of the cases are we deliberately misrepresenting or misreporting our perceptions, but we are ourselves deceived by them. The brain is doing its best to make sense of the world and construct something credible. Seeing is believing, but believing is also a part of seeing. Moreover, these are cases

16. Classic illusions: (e) Kanizsa triangle

where we couldn't have any emotional investment in the perception in question, as we may have where the identification of birds, and particularly rare birds, is involved. It doesn't matter to us which of the lines is longer in figure 16b, but it may matter a lot to some people if one bird has longer legs or wings than another. Look at the illustrations of juvenile European golden, American golden, and Pacific golden plovers in a field guide (fig. 17). The plumages are very similar but the structure does look slightly different. Can you be sure of not deceiving yourself about this when only one bird is present in the field?

All birdwatchers have made spectacular mistakes of identification based on misperception or wishful thinking, or some combination of these and the other human frailties listed earlier. My worst was in Extremadura in Spain, where a friend and I were scanning a plain to find a great bustard, one of the specialities of the region and an amazing sight when displaying, as I hoped one might be at this time, with its feathers all puffed up into a huge, fluffy white ball. I suddenly saw exactly this and called it triumphantly. We watched, and through the heat haze in the distance a man emerged slowly from below a ridge with a large white container of crop-sprayer strapped onto his back. There was also the famous case of the Scilly nighthawk. The nighthawk is an American species, very similar to the British nightjar, and an extreme and much sought-after rarity over here. An excited birder reported one on St. Agnes in Scilly, which he had spotted roosting on the ground, partly camouflaged by the bracken. He had a CB radio and was giving a running commentary to guide other birders in. "Yes, I can see it now. Showing well. I'm fifty yards away. It's just right of that grassy mound. I can see the primaries—very dark. I can see the face pattern. . . . I'm now twenty yards from it—it's got

17. Juvenile golden plovers: (a) American; (b) Pacific; (c) European (Alan Harris)

the white throat patch—must be an adult. It's lying very still. . . . I'm only ten yards away now—crippling views. . . . Wow. . . . [Long silence] . . . Oh, it's a cowpat."[1]

Alexander Pope knew what the problem was in these cases:

> To observations which ourselves we make,
> We grow more partial for the observer's sake.
> ("Epistle to Lord Cobham," 1734)

Some other mistakes are just ludicrous misreadings of size and distance, especially in extreme light conditions like those in the Arctic. In *My Life with the Eskimo* (1923), the explorer Vilhjalmus Stefansson recalls spending an hour stalking a tundra grizzly that turned out to be a marmot; another explorer had all but completed a full description in his notebook of a craggy headland with two unusually symmetrical valley glaciers, the whole of it part of a large island, when he realised that what he was looking at was a walrus;

[1] Or words to that effect. I have heard Bryan Bland tell this story in one of his excellent talks on problems of identification. He tells it in person, with the dramatic pauses, much better than I can on the page.

and Joseph Miertsching wrote of a polar bear that "rose in the air and flew off" as the hunting party approached—a snowy owl.

Patterns, Profiles, and All That Jizz

These comical mistakes are examples, perhaps, of how we are sometimes betrayed by the very skills and techniques that in normal circumstances make us so successful in interpreting the world and recognising features in it, sometimes on the basis of quite fragmentary information. They are cognitive shortcuts, an instantaneous assessment of the probabilities that underlie the feats of "informed expectation" I described earlier as well as causing these embarrassing failures. I now want to consider more closely just how this works. What is it we are looking at or for that enables us to jump to conclusions, wisely or otherwise?

In the first place, our attention has to be selective. There's just too much sensory information to take in otherwise and too many facts about the birds we might need to remember. In Britain alone there have been nearly six hundred separate species identified to date and many of these have different plumages for male and female, winter and summer, and adult and juvenile birds, as well as a huge range of calls and songs, which may also vary by situation and season. You need to home in on the key things to look and listen for. It was the simple but inspired use of little arrows to direct our attention to these "field marks" in the illustrations that helped to make the first Peterson *Guides* such an immediate and lasting success. (These pointers also had the less beneficial effect, however, of focussing everyone's attention on the visual clues to the exclusion of the auditory ones, and I come to that later.) It is relevant too that the most successful field guides use artists' illustrations to portray the birds rather than photographs, which you might have thought were necessarily more accurate. In fact it is these stylised versions that make comparisons between similar species much easier. They do it by suppressing irrelevant (for this purpose) individual variations and presenting the species itself in a standard format that highlights the key points of comparison. They are in this sense more accurate by being less truthful (or the other way round, if you like).

The larger reference books elaborate all this in much greater detail. In good viewing conditions and when the bird is within reasonable range and under observation for a lengthy period of time, these fine distinctions provide a very good way to analyse it and separate it from other species with which it is easily confused. Often we don't have that luxury, though, when we are actually in the field trying to detect such subtleties. You are looking against the light, in pouring rain, from a lurching boat, or in gathering darkness; the bird itself flashes across a clearing, dives into a bush, soars at great height in the sky, bobs about in heavy seas, or disappears behind a seawall; you are cold, wet, or blown about, your spectacles or binoculars mist up; a dog barks at you, the children want to go home, a tractor forces you off the path, someone stands in front of you, the landowner approaches. In these, actually more normal, situations you need to rely on other skills.

You therefore look for distinctive shapes and structures or characteristic habits of behaviour, the sorts of things that are not so easily distorted or obscured and can be grasped in an instant. Have you ever been to one of those school reunion parties where everyone is immediately recognisable even though you haven't met for twenty, thirty, or forty years? That nose, those ears, the set of the shoulders, the nervous laugh, the worried eyes, the gestures, that loping walk—dead giveaways, whatever the superficial changes over the years (usually localised and for the worse). And it isn't just the visual clues. You pick up the telephone and a voice at the other end says the one word, "hello." You often know straightaway who it is. You don't analyse it and decide by elimination: let's see—too high for a man's voice, not throaty enough for Michèle, too calm for Angela, wrong accent for Carolyn.... You just *know*. You can also perform these feats of recognition at great distances and in adverse conditions: you can be certain that it is your wife walking down the road half a mile away; you could pick out your own child's voice on a busy day in the Tower of Babel; and you would almost never make a mistake in distinguishing male and female faces at a glance (except, forgivably, during the Halloween Parade through Greenwich Village in New York), though you might find it difficult in any of these cases to give a full and explicit description of the differentia. We are all very good at this mode of recognition. It relies on what birdwatchers call *jizz*.[1]

Political cartoonists rely a lot on jizz. When a new president or prime minister comes into office it usually takes the cartoonists a little while to decide which features to select as field marks but they then stylise these in ways that make them instantly recognisable to the rest of us, even though they may be grossly exaggerated.

In this process we may have learned to notice something we had seen and had not quite registered before but which we cannot now *not* see. One can

[1] No one really knows the etymology of this word "jizz." The usual explanation is that it comes from U.S. World War II military slang, the acronym for "general impression of shape and size," but that is one of those clever derivations that comes after the fact, since it was certainly used by T. A. Coward in its current sense in 1922. One wordsmith (happily called Dot Wordsworth, writing in the *Spectator* magazine, 15 October 2005) speculates that it ultimately comes from the older slang homologue "jizz" or "jism," which means spunk, spirit, or energy, and one can imagine a possible shift from that to the "essence" or "set" of a bird or beast.

18. "The Harmony Boys" (David Low cartoon, 2 May 1940)

think of analogies in the history of art more generally. We now think of Constable as a supreme "representational" artist, copying "what was there" in realistic detail. That was not how he was viewed in his day, however. He sold only twenty paintings in England in his lifetime (1776–1837), though he was appreciated in France, winning the gold medal in the 1824 Paris Salon; it was only after the 1888 bequest of his paintings to the Victoria and Albert Museum that a new generation, now familiar with French impressionism, could appreciate his rendering of the effects of light on landscape and see what he saw. And now we can't unsee it. In the same way cubism, at first incomprehensible and repugnant to most people, has now become just a cliché of advertising. The creativity of such artists lies in forgetting or resisting what they have learned to see and in observing afresh.

The neuroscientist V. S. Ramachandran called this phenomenon "peak-shifting," the ability of art to highlight distinctive features of an image to make recognition easier, and related it to what birds do themselves in certain critical situations requiring instant recognition. David Lack in his classic monograph on the robin drew our attention to the propensity of robins defending territory literally to "see red" and attack any object, such as a bit of red cloth, that had the general appearance of the red breast of a rival. There are also famous experiments with herring gull chicks, in which a stylised representation of the mother's beak, consisting of a yellow stick with three red stripes on it, can provoke more frenzied feeding behaviour on the part of the chicks than the real thing does. The cuckoo chick does the reverse and secures the exclusive

*Roadside
Silhouettes*

1　Bee-Eater
2　House Sparrow
3　Starling
4　Chaffinch
5　House Martin
6　Swallow
7　Wood Pigeon
8　Jackdaw
9　Little Owl
10　Whinchat
11　Kestrel
12　Red-Backed Shrike
13　Magpie
14　Wagtail
15　Sky Lark
16　Lapwing
17　Pheasant
18　Blackbird
19　Partridge
20　Rook

19. Peterson "roadside silhouettes" *(A Field Guide to the Birds of Britain and Europe)*

attentions of its unfortunate foster-parents by presenting a larger and more colourful gape at the nest than their real offspring can. So, birds use jizz themselves, and are sometimes deceived by it just as we are. But presumably they are far more sensitive, by instinct and early learning, than we could ever be and have no difficulty with such visually difficult pairs as willow warbler and chiffchaff or marsh and willow tits. Perhaps there's an analogy with the learning of languages. Japanese speakers notoriously often confuse the "r" and "l" sounds in spoken English because in their own language they have not had to learn to hear them. Conversely, speakers of English as their first language cannot, I understand, detect the consonant in Thai that lies somewhere in the slide between "d" and "t"; even in the more familiar case of French, native English speakers do not easily hear the difference between *sans* and *son*. The native speakers in each case have no such difficulty.

The jizz of birds that human observers rely on consists of some or all of a combination of factors. The most basic purely physical factors are probably the structure and the proportions of bill, legs, and wings, which may only be seen in silhouette but which are relatively unchanging. The endpapers of the

20. Raptors and aircraft recognition: (a) R. S. Fitter and R.A.R. Richardson, *The Pocket Guide to British Birds* (1952); (b) T. Hamilton, *Identification: Friend or Foe* (1994)

Peterson *Guides* have a useful set of such silhouettes, which also convey posture and bearing to some degree (see fig. 19).

In the case of birds of prey, which are often seen only in outline high in the sky, this is crucial and there are some nice comparisons to be made between the illustrations in raptor guides and those in the early aeroplane spotters' handbooks of a similar period, as well as between the two groups of devotees.[1]

Other factors may include striking patterning, as between pale and dark areas and any particularly prominent physical features. But especially revealing, for birds as for schoolmates at a reunion, are their characteristic movements and habits. You see a small plump bird in the garden dropping to the ground from a low branch, straightening up smartly to attention, bobbing to pick up some tiny morsel with its beak, and then lightly flicking up to its perch again with a little flirt of the wings and tail. You can recognise a robin from this routine, even at dusk and at a distance. It doesn't depend on the fine

[1] Aircraft recognition became a mass pursuit in Britain in the 1940s and one of the first popular guides, *Aircraft Recognition* (1941) by R. A. Saville-Sneath, sold more than seven million copies. History is now repeating itself in the form of nostalgia, and Penguin successfully reissued the same book for the Christmas market in 2006.

perception of colour or plumage details, which can be much affected by light conditions and which in any case vary by age and season. All birds have their own routines in this way, whether of feeding habit, gait on the ground, or flight. A midsized bird flies out of a wood: does it have the floppy flight of a jay, is it bounding like a woodpecker with the wings held closed between forward thrusts, does it flap and glide like a cruising sparrowhawk, hover like a kestrel, or jink like a woodcock? Look at birds on the ground in your garden or in a park: compare the busy striding-about of the starling with the deadly concentration of the song thrush in his short marches and with the flighty pattering of a pied wagtail; in the shrubbery the shuffling gait of the dunnock is quite different from the quick dartings of the wren; and so on in the same way, for sanderlings chasing the wave edges on the shore with little twinkly steps, corncrakes sneaking through the grass, and grey plovers hunched plumply on a mud bank. You tend to reach for adverbs at these moments. Metaphors and poetic images may also sometimes help us grasp these traits better than plain descriptions can. Hughes's "bounce and stab" for the song thrush is perfect, and so is Baker's "ten high wing-beats and then a drowsy glide" for the barn owl.

These are behavioural constants and real signatures of identity.[1] We come to know them by acquaintance and experience, not by conscious analysis. The technical terms are "gestalt perception" or "holistic knowledge," a kind of knowing that is or becomes a grasp of the whole and prompts immediate recognition. We do this all the time with entities other than birds—with trees, buildings, cars, aircraft, and especially, as I have suggested, with other people. Something similar may even extend into as abstract a field as mathematics. There is an anecdote told about the Indian mathematician Ramanujan (1888–1920). He was a self-taught prodigy with no formal training in the subject, but his genius was recognised by the eminent Cambridge mathematician G. H. Hardy, who brought him over to England and befriended him. Years later, when Ramanujan was seriously ill in hospital Hardy went to visit him, having travelled to the hospital by taxi. Both were shy men with no small talk, and the exchange went as follows:

> He went into the room where Ramanujan was lying. Hardy, always inept about introducing a conversation, said, probably without a greeting, and

---

[1] Most field guides do in fact refer to these factors in their prelims, but people tend not to read the often very interesting introductions to reference books such as encyclopedias, dictionaries, and field guides, which are usually consulted in piecemeal fashion rather than read continuously. A pity, because the compilers may have distilled all their mature reflections on their long labours into these few pages, the most famous example being Dr. Johnson. Electronic access to such compilations tends to intensify this problem.

certainly as his first remark: "I thought the number of my taxi-cab was 1729. It seemed to me a rather dull number." To which Ramanujan replied: "No, Hardy! No, Hardy! It is a very interesting number. It is the smallest number expressible as the sum of two cubes in two different ways."[1]

I think Ramanujan *recognised* that number. The very best birdwatchers can do the same thing with a semi-palmated sandpiper, and then explain the slow way of working it out to the rest of us afterwards.

[1] C. P. Snow in the introduction to Hardy, *A Mathematician's Apology* (1973). For those interested in the calculations, what Ramanujan "saw" straightaway was that $1,729 = 1^3 + 12^3 = 10^3 + 9^3$.

4

Rarity Value

They are merely possessed for the sake of possession
itself, and the ownership of them with the
ensuing renown is the main source of their value.
Bronislaw Malinowski, *Argonauts of
the Western Pacific* (1922)

Central Park, New York, 10 May 1986

New York City has always been thought of as a concrete jungle, with Manhattan its citadel and symbol. But there are jungles within jungles even there, as Ogden Nash noted in 1964:

> If you should happen after dark
> To find yourself in Central Park
> Ignore the paths that beckon you
> And hurry, hurry to the zoo
> And creep into the tiger's lair.
> Frankly you'll be safer there.

That at any rate was its reputation then. Nowadays Central Park is wild only in a highly managed sense, but once it was a real wilderness, a sort of swamp inhabited by squatters with their herds of goats and pigs, well beyond the limits of civilised New York. "A wasteland, ugly and repulsive," William Cullen Bryant called it in 1850. His dream of a People's Park was put into effect by two landscape architects of genius, Frederick Law Olmsted (an American) and Calvert Vaux (an Englishman), who proceeded to recreate it completely, according to their manifesto that "the Park throughout should be a single work of art." They introduced lakes, hills, rocks, streams, meadows, gardens, and woodlands, all designed to serve their grand unifying vision. Every aspect of it was planned, manmade, and controlled. But there is still one area of what you might call permissive wilderness. That is the Ramble, where I am now, a thirty-seven-acre area of dense, mazy woodland on the lakeshore, designed specifically by Olmsted and Vaux to be a "natural" sanctuary. This is the best place in Central Park—and one of the best on the whole East Coast of the United States—to see a wide range of migrant birds (and birdwatchers).

Today is a "wave" day (U.S. birders' slang for a "fall" of migrants—both metaphors are good ones) and there is a frenzy of activity. Thousands of birds must have arrived overnight, pausing on their way north to rest and feed. New York is strategically situated right on the flyway from their winter quarters in the south to their summer homes in Canada and New England, and Central Park must look from the air like a kind of oasis in the desert of urban development. And here they are all round and above me. It's only 8 AM and I have so far seen five different kinds of thrushes, four sparrows, two tanagers, three vireos, and, best of all, seventeen different species of warbler. These warblers are the stars of the spring migration. Most European warblers are quite modest in appearance, mostly subtle shades of green, olive, and brown with just a few discreet distinguishing features like wing-bars and supercilia, but they then compensate with their very melodious and distinctive songs. With most American warblers it's just the reverse. Few of the American "wood" warblers (the big *Dendroica* family, quite unrelated to the European warblers) have much of a voice—the songs mostly consist of high-pitched *seeping* notes, varying only in pace, pitch, stress, and rhythm. But to look at they are just stunning (see plate 2), as their names suggest: magnolia, black and white, yellow-rumped, chestnut-sided, cerulean, bay-breasted, golden-crowned, orange-crowned, yellow, blue-winged, black-throated blue, black-throated green (following this line of nomenclature, the local wags call house sparrows "black-throated browns"); and there are other warblers of at least equal beauty but with less transparent names: the parula, the blackburnian, and my personal favourite, the prothonotary.[1] Well, "prospective favourite." I've seen all the above here except this one, though a few of them do pass through the park each year. The prothonotary is the "most wanted" species for my Central Park list.

Like most birders I keep a "local patch" list, and since I have been visiting New York regularly on business for some years this has become my "away patch." My Central Park list stands at present at 149 species, quite good for a visitor but of course very modest by the standards of the dedicated local

[1] The parula has a remote etymological connection with the European coal tit; the Blackburnian is named after an English biologist, Anna Blackburn(e), who was sent specimens of interesting American birds by her brother in the late 1700s; and a prothonotary is a religious official at the Vatican in Rome (i.e., a "protonotary"), though none of them ever had a cloak of quite this golden hue.

watchers who may see well over two hundred in the course of a year and will have a lifetime Central Park list of nearly three hundred.[1]

I allow myself to wonder a bit about my motivation here, as I peer through a swampy thicket for a glimpse of golden treasure. Do I really want to see a prothonotary or do I just want to find my 150th bird for Central Park? I tell myself I am trying to replicate here the deep satisfaction I feel in my real local patch back in West Suffolk in *knowing* the place so intimately in all its seasonal particularity and variety; and that means knowing the strangers and visitors as well as the residents; surely I am not just being competitive (with whom?) and acquisitive (of what?). Reassured, I look and listen harder, thinking about the best likely habitat, and trying to remember the calls and songs from the recordings I have studied. This is what I enjoy—the search, the exercise of a skill, the intense awareness of the physical world. An hour passes, very happily.

But then there's an unexpected development, which revives and complicates my earlier dilemma. The word spreads rapidly among the community of watchers in the park that morning that there's a strange unidentified duck on the reservoir a mile or so north of the Ramble, maybe a real rarity. Streams of birders hasten there and converge. I dislike these gatherings and try to avoid them; but it's hard not to feel the surge of excitement that communicates itself through the crowd, as it does at a football match or a political rally, hard to suppress the curiosity too and the sense of a lucky break, the chance of witnessing some extraordinary happening or spectacle that may never recur. Anyway, in the end I am spared the embarrassment of decision. I am enlisted because it's known that I am a Brit and it is thought the bird might be a tufted duck, a very common bird in Britain but a real rarity in the Eastern United States and a potential new bird for most of those present. I confirm its identification and am famous for five minutes. Well, there's my 150th bird anyway and a species I will probably never again see here. But I'd still rather have found a prothonotary.

In this chapter I want to look more deeply into these satisfactions and dilemmas as they emerge in the practices of keeping lists and pursuing rarities. Such activities seem to follow on naturally from our capacity to make the sort of distinctions I discussed in the last chapter, but they may also lead to extreme forms of behaviour. What kind of interest or obsession is this, and what are the rationales and rewards?

---

[1] For comparison, the analogous figures for Hyde Park/Kensington Gardens in London (which has a slightly smaller area of 635 acres against the 840 of Central Park) are 108 for a year list (Des McKenzie, 2006) and an all-time total of 188 (to the end of 2007).

The Listing Habit

The pleasure we first take in noticing differences and making identifications is usually soon accompanied by the further pleasure of making lists of our discoveries. Or rather, the second pleasure is the natural completion of the first. We may only feel that we have really made the identification when we have written it down and recorded it. In the same way diaries and private journals can for some people be both the expression and the natural realisation of a personal experience, and a way of transmuting it into a form that prolongs it in memory and recapitulation. This is an innocent pleasure, which is likely to become a habit, though then of course, like other habits, it may morph into a preoccupation, eccentricity, or obsession. And birdwatching is such a habit.

The making of lists has an ancient pedigree. Some of the earliest written texts in Western Europe are just lists. For example, the Linear B tablets of palace records in ancient Crete, which are dated to around 1700 BC and are written in an early form of Greek, are mostly inventories and records of transactions. There are Middle Eastern texts that go back even further, in particular the huge collection of Sumerian texts from Mesopotamia (now Iraq), which are also largely lists. In this case they are apparently lexical lists used for scribal training in the language—embryonic dictionaries and reference works of a prescientific kind, recording the names of various features of the natural world including trees, fish, animals, and, of course, . . . birds. This part of the corpus, which is surely the world's first surviving bird list, is so interesting that I have included a summary of it in appendix 1. The list of bird names that can be identified with some confidence runs to more than thirty species[1] and includes such exciting entries as ostrich (Syrian race, now extinct in Iraq), crane, bittern, black francolin, imperial eagle, and long-legged buzzard (but it was too much to hope for the Basra reed warbler). It is a fascinating exercise with this, as with all bird lists, not only to see what the list tells us about the bird life of the time but also to try and work backwards and see what it tells us about the observers and their world. We can sense even in these bare records the desert places and also the vast marshes which later travellers like Gavin Maxwell and Wilfred Thesiger celebrated but which Saddam Hussein was then to drain of life, human and avian. In addition to these lists of birds there is also a later

---

[1] For comparison, in *The Birds of Ancient Egypt* (1986), Patrick Houlihan lists seventy-two species that can be identified from the art of the ancient Egyptians from predynastic times (about 4500 BC) to the end of the Ptolemaic period (30 BC), and he has a further and very exotic list of fifty-four species that can be identified from mummified and bone remains in the tombs, including no fewer than thirty-two different raptors and also various ducks and geese that were mummified for the sole purpose of providing sustenance in the afterlife.

and more literary corpus of Sumerian writings, including a wonderful creation myth that tells the story of how the goddess Nanshe comes down to earth to create all the different species of birds and determine the fate of each.

The Bible, of course, records another Middle Eastern creation story and has its own lists. I don't know whether the Sumer scribe or Adam is the Ur-lister, so to speak, but Adam too names the world and its birds:

> And out of the ground the Lord God formed every beast of the field, and every fowl of the air; and brought them unto Adam to see what he would call them: and whatsoever Adam called every living creature, that was the name thereof. (Genesis 2:19)

And if Adam was the first lister then Noah must have been the first collector, perhaps the only one ever to achieve a perfect and complete set (with two of everything just to be on the safe side). Creation precedes classification, and classification precedes collection. We shall return to this connection between listing and collecting.

Lists can have many other functions that go well beyond the utilitarian, the scientific, or the devotional. They figure prominently in creative works of literature, for example. Starting at the top there is the great catalogue of ships in book 2 of Homer's *Iliad,* the very first work in Western literature proper and still one of the greatest. The somewhat hypnotic, repetitive quality of the recitation of the individual contingents, like the steady beating of a martial drum, serves to impress on us the scale and importance of the forces as a whole. The genealogies in the early books of the Bible, though rather tedious for straight reading (*x* begat *y,* etc.), may have an analogous function. In poetry and novels too the listing of particulars may have far more emotional and rhetorical force than would a more abstract generalisation, as for example in Dickens's *Bleak House,* where at least a metaphorical connection is made with our main subject:

> "Another secret, my dear. I have added to my collection of birds."
> "Really, Miss Flite?" said I, knowing how it pleased her to have her confidence received with an appearance of interest.
> She nodded several times, and her face became overcast and gloomy. "Two more. I call them the Wards in Jarndyce. They are caged up with all the others. With Hope, Joy, Youth, Peace, Rest, Life, Dust, Ashes, Waste, Want, Ruin, Despair, Madness, Death, Cunning, Folly, Words, Wigs, Rags, Sheepskin, Plunder, Precedent, Jargon, Gammon and Spinach."

Nor is this confined to literature: think of the impressive international list of Don Giovanni's conquests in the Mozart opera. In popular music too, Cole

Porter knew how to deploy a witty list, as he did in the famous song "You're the Top" and also in this less well-known composition about his pastime of "collecting country places":

> I've a shooting box in Scotland
> I've a chateau in Touraine
> I've a silly little chalet
> In the Interlaken Valley,
> I've a hacienda in Spain,
> I've a private fiord in Norway,
> I've a villa close to Rome,
> And in travelling
> It's really quite a comfort to know
> That you're never far from home!

Even a list of apparently unconnected items can have a point, in telling us something about the person who connects them:

> I like hourglasses, maps, eighteenth-century typography, etymologies, the taste of coffee, and Robert Louis Stevenson's prose. (Jorge Luis Borges)

Publishers have long recognised this appetite. The popular success of works such as *The Guinness Book of Records, The Book of Lists* by David Wallechinsky and Amy Wallace, and Schott's *Original Miscellany* have an unacknowledged ancestry in booktrade stalwarts such as *Pears Cyclopedia* and *Whitaker's Almanac,* which are full of lists. The Internet itself can be thought of as a gigantic list-maker, with all kinds of commercial, educational, and recreational possibilities; and Internet-dependent operations such as Amazon.com give this a clever twist by encouraging customers themselves to assist in their rankings. The hugely burgeoning reality TV shows do the same, using their audiences to give them an apparently democratic validation. The resulting "choices" in this case, however, have an artificial, media-driven character far removed from those based on any objective criteria or on spontaneous curiosity and pleasure.

We produce lists for all sorts of reasons: serious lists like inventories, catalogues, wills, and property holdings; lists for play and games, like fantasy armchair-lists of world Elevens (or Sevens, Eights, Thirteens, or Fifteens, depending on your location and sporting interest—here is another list in the making, you see); shopping lists, lists of jobs to do, books to read, and places to visit; lists to celebrate, memorialise, control, and record; and lists to organise, arrange, and make sense of the world by dividing it up. Lists, in short, are ways of marking similarities and differences. They are therefore ideally suited to the interests of birdwatchers.

The variety of possible bird lists is almost infinite. The commonest, I suppose, are either geographical lists (garden, local patch, county or state, national, and world lists) or chronological ones (day, trip, year, or life). These then lend themselves to all manner of possible subdivisions, extensions and permutations of a more or less rational kind. Some of these can yield information of general interest or even contribute in a limited way to scientific research in population studies or environmental change, and that may add a warm sense of justification to an exercise whose original motivation is likely to have been more personal. Others lists are *avowedly* more personal and arbitrary. People pass the time by making lists such as: birds seen on the way to work, from the M25, at airports, from bed, in films on TV, and even, in one curious case I knew, on Tuesdays. None of this is of any interest or use except to the lister and anyone inclined to compete with him (usually a him) in an exotic contest. The pointlessness of the enterprise in these cases guarantees the purity of the purposes, I suppose, as in any game played for its own sake, but a slippery slope to eccentricity and beyond soon beckons.

Just occasionally a bizarre list can serve a useful purpose, though. In 1886, Frank Chapman, then a bank official but later to become an eminent ornithologist at the American Museum of Natural History, took two afternoon walks through the uptown shopping district in New York to count birds. He identified some forty native species, including blackburnian warbler, scissor-tailed flycatcher, snow bunting, Virginia rail, and pine grosbeak. A remarkable assemblage in one location! These birds were not flying about, however. They had been killed and then variously disassembled to appear on women's hats, in fact on 542 of the 700 hats he counted on one of these walks.[1] This was the feather trade at its height and Chapman and other naturalists in the United States were pointing out its dire consequences; in the United Kingdom similar protests (mainly by women) led directly to the establishment in 1889 of the organisation that became the RSPB.

There have been many famous lists and listers of a more standard kind. Thomas Jefferson produced a Virginia list. Jefferson was a passionate and very well-informed naturalist. When he was at home in Virginia he kept a garden diary recording all his observations round his estates through the cycle of the seasons. The account for 1766, for example, marks the progress of spring locally and begins in a way that will be familiar to many nature diarists: "March 30: Purple hyacinth begins to bloom. April 6: Narcissus and puckoon open.

---

[1] I have included as appendix 2 the full text of Chapman's letter about this experience, published in the U.S. magazine *Forest and Stream* (25 February 1886). His figures are sometimes misquoted and there is a nice little social history statistic at the end.

21. "City Stroll": women's hats in turn-of-the-century New York (Getty Images)

April 13: Puckoon flowers fallen." He also kept rather obsessive notes about the planting dates of his own vegetables, and about meteorological phenomena and other useful facts: "May 6: Aurora Borealis at 9 PM. A quart of currant juice makes 2 blue teacups of jelly." So when in 1780 he was asked to give an account of the natural history and resources of Virginia, he threw himself into the project with the greatest enthusiasm and energy, and what began as the answer to a questionnaire was eventually published as a substantial monograph in 1787 under the title *Notes on the State of Virginia,* and this included a comprehensive list of birds. The main part records ninety-three species (including, without comment, the ivory-billed woodpecker) and then there is a supplementary list of a further thirty-two species, which has in it some very intriguing popular names like wethawk, water-witch, mow-bird, and squatting snipe, most of which are probably identifiable, but then runs out of invention with the final item "red bird, with black head, wings and tail." What could that be—rose-breasted grosbeak perhaps (the towhee and cardinal already appear in the main list)? The current West Virginia list, by the way, stands at 326 species and the current Virginia list at 427. I reproduce the main elements of Jefferson's list in appendix 1.

Thoreau had a Concord list. He was a wonderful observer of all natural phenomena and his *Journals* are full of the most detailed records of his findings. He sometimes felt ambivalent about this activity, though, because he thought of himself first and foremost as a writer, not a naturalist or a scientist of any kind: "Here I have been these forty years learning the language of these fields that I may better express myself" (20 November 1857). He also worried that observing nature so closely might in the end prevent him from enjoying it: "I feel that I am dissipated by so many observations" (23 March 1853). He sees risks in the kind of "active attention" I discussed in chapter 3 (p. 67), in which he excelled:

> I must walk more with free senses. . . . I have the habit of attention to such excess that my senses get no rest—but suffer from constant strain. Be not preoccupied with looking. Go not to the object, let it come to you. . . . What I need is not to look at all, but a true sauntering of the eye. (13 September 1852)

His "saunterings" were often walks of more than twenty miles in which he could indeed lose himself, and he wanted them to provide some antidote to the listing habit whereby "the walker does not too seriously observe particulars, but sees, hears, scents, tastes, and feels only himself" (30 March 1853). But whatever Thoreau told himself in such diary notes, the fact remains that he had a wonderful eye and ear and was for most of the time totally absorbed in observing and identifying different "particulars." He takes care, for example, to demonstrate that he can distinguish wood thrush, veery, and hermit thrush, and the *Journals* are full of nice points of this kind. His essay on "The Natural History of Massachusetts" (1842) demonstrates this tension in his work and suggests a way of resolving it. The essay was commissioned as a review of some official volumes on the biodiversity (as we should now put it) of the state of Massachusetts, and in it he regrets that the compilers of this work concentrate so much on mere facts. What he wants is something richer in context and more affirmative of the real value of these natural resources, but he recognises that even a fact can suggest a larger truth:

> The volumes deal much in measurements and minute descriptions, not interesting to the general reader, with only here and there a coloured sentence to allure him, like those plants growing in dark forests, which bear only leaves without blossoms. But the ground was comparatively unbroken, and we will not complain of the pioneer, if he raises no flowers with his first crop. Let us not underrate the value of a fact; it will one day flower in a truth.

In the course of the review he refers to the 280 species of birds then recorded within the state boundaries[1] and offers his own thickly textured account of the behaviour and appearance of many of them. Is this a compromise or having it both ways?

John Clare had a Northamptonshire list. He had been planning to write a *Natural History of Helpston* and produced various lists and "biographies of birds" in the mid-1820s in preparation for that. He never brought the project to publishable form, but the lists survive together with his vignettes of the species. He records 119 species that can be identified with some certainty, 4 more that may be one or the other of two closely related species (like willow or marsh tit), 22 that are unclear or unlikely (*most* unlikely in the case of the black guillemot), and 3 that are just literary fancies: a grand total of 145 species (the full list is included in appendix 1).[2] He also mentions one or two mysteries:

Saw four odd-looking birds like large swallows of a slate colour on their wings and back and their bellies white. They had forked tails and long wings and flew exactly in the manner of the swallow, but instead of skimming along the ground they rose to a great height. I frit them up from Swordy well, a pond so called by the roman bank, which is never dry and often haunted by water birds.

Pratincole, surely! Clare does make mistakes, of course—he attributes exaggerated lung control to the dabchick (said to stay ten minutes underwater), and confuses some features of swifts and swallows—but the overwhelming impression, from both his prose and his poetry, is of a very honest, acute, and careful observer.

The listing habit is a very old and honourable one, then, and can take many forms. Most of these need no defence or apology. They are pleasures in themselves, informative and instructive to a degree, and as Thoreau wisely noted, they can also lead to more serious forms of knowledge when the facts finally flower into truths. But listing can also feel like a form of collection or acquisition. Is that a covert part of its attraction and is that always so innocent?

Collection and Possession

If you visit the Louvre in Paris and make your way to the *Mona Lisa* you will encounter a sight of some ornithological interest. You will see a great crowd

---

[1] The Massachusetts state list now stands at 470 species.

[2] Gilbert White, writing some fifty years earlier, had claimed a list of 120 species for Selborne parish alone, which he proudly pointed out was more than half the total Swedish list at the time of 221 and nearly half the total British list (letter to Thomas Pennant of 2 September 1774).

22. The *Mona Lisa* twitch (photo: Ed Alcock)

clustered excitedly around the exhibit, all facing more or less towards it but many of them looking at it through the view-finders of their cameras and mobile phones, which they are holding up to capture an image. After inspecting the results they usually move on quite quickly to the next highlight on their itineraries. They are clearly all very keen to *have seen* the *Mona Lisa* but they don't actually want to look at it very much. What they want is a souvenir to confirm the occasion and add to their collection.

Some birdwatchers behave in a similar way at a major twitch, to use a technical expression.[1] They may desperately want to *have seen* some celebrated rarity like the Central Park tufted duck, the Scilly semi-p or the Irish Canada warbler and may travel miles to do so at great personal cost, but they may not want to examine it too closely or prolong the experience. The dimension of

---

[1] Another birders' term with uncertain origins, though the physical associations are suggestive (see Moss, *Social History*, p. 265, for a specific suggestion). "Twitchers" are birders whose principal or only interest is in the finding and identification of rare birds to maximise lists of species, and a "twitch" is the activity or the location (as in "the happy couple met at the grosbeak twitch"). The terminology for different kinds of practitioners has evolved over time: "twitcher" is fairly clear in its meaning; "birdwatcher" now has a faintly old-fashioned air but can still be useful in conveying a kind of attitude, while "birder" is the self-description of choice for most enthusiasts younger than fifty; "naturalist" suggests a broader interest in wildlife, while "ornithologist" has a more scientific, professional connotation. There is a corresponding hedonic scale: ornithologists aren't expected to enjoy themselves and twitchers have never discovered how to.

time is interesting here and may be illustrated with another analogy from the art world (museums are great laboratories of human behaviour too). When you visit the Sistine Chapel in Rome to see the famous Michelangelo frescoes you will hear as you enter the chapel a recorded message requesting absolute silence so that the work can be viewed with suitable attention. The milling crowd of tourists falls silent. After about half a minute the first whispers and murmurs begin; after a minute there are sporadic exchanges at ordinary voice levels; by two minutes there is general conversation; and at the three-minute mark the hubbub has reached its original volume. The preset message is replayed at precisely this point in the crescendo and the crowd falls silent again. The cycle is repeated. That is the attention span for many of the collectors of such experiences.

There is a parallel diminution of attention and interest among listers at a big twitch, though in this case the changes in noise levels are reversed: first, the big shot of adrenalin and the punchings of the air and attendant exclamations ("wow, what a crippler!"); then some mutual reassurance by reference to the key features ("those tertial fringes are really contrasting, aren't they?"); a little later some perfunctory aesthetic appreciation to give a veneer of justification to the excitement ("very well marked bird, that"); and then, really quite soon, the first fiddlings with the pagers and mobile phones to announce the triumph and see what else there is around, followed by abrupt and silent departures. Another need satisfied, another item collected. This is the tick-and-run syndrome.

What is the general psychology underlying such examples? We shouldn't make the snobbish mistake of thinking that these are just vulgar forms of behaviour. There are nerds in green velvet smoking jackets as well as in anoraks. The same compulsions are sometimes found in just as competitive a form (and certainly a more expensive one) among collectors of antiques and high art, and among connoisseurs and bibliophiles. Very often the point of any acquisition they make is to enlarge, or if possible complete, something seen as a *collection*. The individual item is not valued in itself but only as a part of a set. It is most keenly desired in its absence, not its presence. You may buy a book, that is, not to read it but because it is a member of a limited class you have chosen to collect, like Hemingway first editions or volumes in the original New Naturalist Series. Indeed, it has been suggested that a true bibliophile never *reads* his books at all. Personal possession in some form is what really matters, leading the social theorist Jean Baudrillard to remark darkly that what such people are really collecting is themselves: "Any collection comprises a succession of items, but the last in the set is the person of the collector." There are other dark eddies swirling around here: possession can generate possessiveness, greed, envy and spite. Consider the following story Baudrillard tells:

> A bibliophile has a magnificent set of books he believes to be unique; he learns one day that a bookseller in New York has placed on sale an item identical to one of the volumes he owns. He takes the plane, purchases the book, and then arranges to have a notary public present when he sets fire to the second copy. He slips the formal attestation inside the first volume and retires happily to bed.

This is "gripping-off" with a vengeance, to use another technical term,[1] and the ornithological equivalent would be killing the rare bird to deny it to others. Not even hard-core twitchers would do that, however. Indeed, earnest efforts are sometimes made to revive a failing bird so that it may remain animate and therefore countable, as in the case of the 2004 Scilly cream-coloured courser that was flown at great expense to a hospital on the mainland, where it unfortunately expired. Birders tend to be both competitive and collaborative in a complicated way. But the idea of an item collected not for its own qualities but because of its place in a larger aggregation does sound relevant to the more extreme forms of bird listing. The British birders who made the round trip in a day from Scilly to Ireland to see the Canada warbler didn't really want to see a *Canada warbler* as such; a black-throated blue would have been as good, a prothonotary even better.[2] They just needed something they didn't already have.

The Hunting Instinct

Hunting is another kind of collecting and this instinct is also ancient and deep. By evolution and culture we are hunters as well as gatherers. It should be remembered that the principal way of identifying and recording rare birds up to at least the early twentieth century was literally by "collecting" them, that is, shooting them. With the later improvements in optical equipment, field guides, and observer skills and with important changes in public concerns about animal cruelty and conservation, this physical form of collection was

---

[1] "Gripping-off" is birders' slang for getting one over a competitor by seeing a bird he or she has missed. I hesitate to explore the origins of the term: think of it as *schadenfreude* without the insincerity.

[2] The 2006 Canada warbler was the first record for the United Kingdom and Ireland but the second for the Western Palearctic (one was recorded in Iceland in 1973). Iceland also had a black-throated blue in 1988, but there has been no record of prothonotary as yet anywhere in the WP region.

largely replaced by virtual collections on paper (or on film—we talk of "cap-
turing an image"). And the extraordinary advances in photography bring us
full circle in a way. Whereas previously a "specimen" was required to authenti-
cate a difficult identification, now a digiscoped image is preferred to a field
description. There was an intervening "golden age" when both observational
and writing skills were more highly valued. Some of the underlying drives
have remained the same, however. It may be helpful here to look sideways, so
to speak, at how these passions are described by hunters and collectors of
some other forms of wildlife than birds, in particular wildflowers and butterflies, which have traditionally also been "collected" in both senses of the term.

Here is the nineteenth-century botanist Professor J. H. Balfour of Edinburgh celebrating the pleasures of field excursions, the companionship they
bring, and his favourite families of alpine plants:

> Excursions may be truly said to be the *life* of the botanist. They enable
> him to study the science practically, by the examination of plants in
> their living state, and in their native localities; they impress upon his
> mind the structural and physiological lessons he has received; they ex-
> hibit to him the geographical range of species, both as regards latitude
> and altitude; and with the pursuit of scientific knowledge, they combine
> that healthful and spirit-stirring recreation which tends materially to aid
> mental efforts. The companionship too of those who are prosecuting
> with zeal and enthusiasm the same path of science, is not the least de-
> lightful feature of such excursions. The various phases of character ex-
> hibited, the pleasing incidents that diversified the walk, the jokes that
> passed, and even the very mishaps or annoyances that occurred—all be-
> come objects of interest, and unite members of the party by ties of no
> ordinary kind. And the feelings thus excited are by no means of an eva-
> nescent or a fleeting nature; they last during life, and are always recalled
> by the sight of the specimens which were collected. These apparently
> insignificant remnants of vegetation recall many a tale of adventure, and
> are associated with the delightful recollection of many a friend. It is not
> indeed a matter of surprise that those who have lived and walked for
> weeks together in a Highland ramble, who have met in sunshine and in
> tempest, who have climbed together the misty summits, and have slept
> in the miserable sheiling—should have such scenes indelibly impressed
> on their memory. There is, moreover, something peculiarly attractive in
> the collecting of alpine plants. Their comparative rarity, the localities
> in which they grow, and frequently their beautiful hues, conspire in

shedding around them a halo of interest far exceeding that connected with lowland productions.

Orchids are another family that has always excited the collector. Peter Marren in his book *Britain's Rare Flowers* (1999) tells some wonderful stories about the discovery (and necessary concealment) of various orchid sites and explains his own attachment to the "lowland productions" of a chalky landscape through a defining boyhood discovery:

> It is hard to put into words why one wanted to find flowers at all (it still is). One could be technological about it: I wanted to take pictures of them with my new camera, but it was the flowers that had brought forth the camera, not the other way round. I was drawn to them in a visceral way that is beyond words. I did not want to pick them or grow them or even paint their portrait. . . . I just wanted to see them in their natural surrounding and learn a bit more about calcareous pastures, for it was the places as well as their plants that were part of the magic. I can see it in my mind's eye now, that first special place.

The place was St. Margaret's Bay in Kent and the species he sought was *Ophrys spheregodes,* the early spider orchid:

> There all of a sudden it was, a little group of Early Spiders perched near the cliff edge where white chalk had started to show through the turf. . . . I roared with delight, waved my arms about (or so it was claimed) and fell to my knees. They were both like and unlike the pictures in the books. The latter were accurate enough in their botanical details, but gave you no real idea of the *presence* of the plant in its setting of turf, rock and sea, nor its soldierly bearing, with military greeny-yellowy-browny colours and lead-grey markings glinting in the sunshine like wet enamel paint on an Airfix model. The flowers bulged in a way that did remind you of a garden spider which had somehow got its head stuck in a flower. In short, it was everything I had hoped for and more. In retrospect, at least, finding it was a transcendent moment in which wild flowers, chalk cliffs and the colours, sounds and scents of nature seemed to imprint themselves in my bones. I have never really got over it.

I have quoted these accounts at some length because they contain so many points of cross-reference, particularly in emphasising the importance of place. Indeed, birders in the United Kingdom sometimes switch to butterflies and dragonflies (or even orchids) in "quiet" times of year like mid-July to keep their listing instincts exercised and indulged. There are also some differences with birdwatching, of course. The wildflower hunters have it easier in one way, since their quarry is at least stationary when it does appear,[1] and their patterns of seasonal activity must be very different (birdwatching is very much an all-the-year-round outdoor interest). But the similarities in these accounts are more striking than the differences. Moreover, the number of wildflowers in Britain is quite convenient too—about 1,200 in all, 320 of them defined as "rare," which is enough to last a lifetime but not so many as to be unimaginable or unattainable. Marren describes elsewhere the quiet satisfaction of someone who had, remarkably, got to the end of the list (or what was then the end):

> Andrew Young once asked George Claridge Druce if he had seen all the British plants. He replied that he had, though the last ten had given him a hard struggle. "Are you the only botanist who has seen them all?" pursued Canon Young, but Druce merely smiled. When Young enquired about an orchid so very rare that it had only been seen a few times, Druce pointed out modestly that two of those times he had seen it himself. Working in the Druce herbarium in Oxford for this book, I sought out the specimen that, I had read somewhere, had completed Druce's tour of the British flora. It was a dim and very rare little flower confined to Guernsey and Herm, called Guernsey Centaury or *Exaculum pusillum*. Druce had attached a typewritten note to say that he had collected it on 31 July 1913. . . . And there were the proud words: "My last British species."

The butterfly hunters, by contrast, have only about seventy species to look for, though this too can take a lifetime of summers. One of the great British butterfly collectors was Ian Robert Penicuick Heslop (1904–70), a colonial administrator who spent most of his life abroad hunting big game but also maintained a much-prized British butterfly collection, as Matthew Oates describes.

> He collected an unrivalled 66 species of butterfly in Britain and pinned 185 specimens of that most elusive of our butterflies, the Purple Emperor, despite spending so much of his adult life abroad. In fact he could have taken 67 species; he remained haunted by his failure to seek out the Black-veined White *Aporia crataegi*, "while it was still possible to do so.

[1] Though it may of course go missing for many years, like the well-named "ghost orchid," which has not made an appearance since 1986, thus rivalling the "invisible rail" of the Indonesian island of Halmahera (not seen for years on end), the "inaccessible rail" of Tristan da Cunha (hard to get to), and the "cryptic warbler" of Madagascar (only discovered in 1996).

I suppose I thought I could wait. I was wrong, and this remains the one great hiatus and irremediable lacuna in my entomological activities."

Heslop was apparently known as the "Purple Emperor" in some circles.

The most famous butterfly hunter, however, is best known for different reasons. Vladimir Nabokov, the author of *Lolita* and other novels, was also a very serious lepidopterist who wrote some twenty scientific papers, discovered several new species, and worked for six years at the Harvard Museum of Comparative Zoology.[1] In his autobiography, *Speak, Memory* (1966), he explains that hunting butterflies was the ruling passion of his life from a very early age and he celebrates that passion as a kind of ineffable privilege. He describes the experience of standing among rare butterflies and their food plants:

> This is ecstasy, and behind the ecstasy is something else, which is hard to explain. It is like a momentary vacuum into which rushes all that I love. A sense of oneness with sun and stone. A thrill of gratitude to whom it may concern—to the contrapuntal genius of human fate or to tender ghosts humouring a lucky mortal.

It is interesting how difficult all these writers find it to *explain* just what the lure of the rare consists in, but the general sentiments seem to be common to most forms of hunting and there are similar, if less high-flown, passages in the literary writings of hunters of mammals (like Turgenev, for example). Reptiles and insects (other than butterflies and moths) may be different since most of them are actively repellent to many people and are less often pursued as a hobby. They tend to attract the more scientific collector, who may also have to suffer for his calling:

> The other day a member of the Lister Institute called to see me on a lousy matter, and presently drew some live lice from his waistcoat pocket for me to see. They were contained in pill boxes with little bits of muslin stretched across the open end through which the lice could thrust their hypodermic needles when placed near the skin. He feeds them by putting these boxes into a specially constructed belt and at night ties the belt around his waist. . . . In this fashion he has bred hundreds from the egg upwards and even hybridised the two different species. (W.N.P. Barbellion, *Journal of a Disappointed Man,* 16 August 1915)

He was not married.

---

[1] The museum still possesses his "genitalia cabinet," which stored his collection of the genitalia of male blues of the *Lycaenidae* family (his speciality). He based his identifications on the microscopic examination of these sad remains.

Fishing is a different sort of case in some ways, but an important one since it does attract a huge number of enthusiasts—more in the United Kingdom than for any other sport, apparently. One of the most striking features of fishing to an outsider is the relative immobility of the practitioners and the high proportion of time apparently available for reflection. Perhaps that is paralleled in some ways by hunting from hides and in the specialised form of birding called sea-watching, which involves enormous patience, skill, and, in most parts of the world, discomfort as you sit for hours on a wind-swept shore staring out to sea at impossibly distant and fast-moving dots. Where fishing and game hunting are certainly different from birding and from the pursuit of wildflowers or butterflies, however, is that success is measured not so much by the number of different species encountered but by their verifiable length, height, or weight. Is that what makes them sports? But fishing too has its rich hinterland of literature, and many of the skills and satisfactions described are very recognisable to birdwatchers: there are the "trophy" species, the need for an intimate knowledge of your quarry and its habits, the fieldcraft, the awareness of surroundings, the emotional roller coasters of hoping, watching, and waiting. Fishermen also emphasise the fact, common to all these activities, that something more than just getting your quarry is involved. When the legendary hunter Kenny "River Rat" Salway was asked about fishing, in the course of a film about his life on the Mississippi River, he chewed slowly on his pipe, stared into the hazy distance, and drawled, "If fishing was all about catching it would be called catching. It's about being out there."

Extreme Pursuits

Why do rarities matter so much to all these activities, whether listing, collecting, possessing, or hunting? Where does this sense of excitement and privilege when we find something special come from? I suggested in chapter 2 that the relative rarity of a bird is one criterion—but only one—that may make it attractive to us or in a more extreme case give it "charisma." We all thrill to an unusual bird whatever the level of our experience and knowledge and however we interpret "rarity." The ordinary garden watcher who sees their first nuthatch or blackcap on the bird feeder, the beginning birdwatcher further afield discovering their first kingfisher or barn owl, and so on up the scale to the semiprofessional twitcher after the Canada warbler—all are responding to something unusual or unique in their experiences, though the experiences are very different. So the first point to make is that rarity is a relative matter: relative to the observer, relative in degree, and relative in the emotions it provokes, which run all the way from harmless pleasure to certifiable obsession. It is the

upper half of this spectrum that most interests us in this section. Let me schematise this in a playful way by constructing a sort of Beaufort scale of reactions. The Beaufort scale is a guide to the relative strength of winds, from calm
to hurricane-strength.

Table 1. Beaufort Scale

No.	Wind conditions	Observable wind effects
0	Calm	Smoke rises vertically
1	Light air	Wind direction shown by smoke drift but not by wind vanes
2	Light breeze	Wind felt on face; leaves rustle; vanes moved by wind
3	Gentle breeze	Leaves and small twigs in constant motion; light flags extended
4	Moderate	Raises dust, loose paper; small branches moved
5	Fresh	Small trees begin to sway
6	Strong	Large branches in motion; difficult to use umbrellas
7	Near gale	Whole trees in motion; difficult to walk against wind
8	Gale	Breaks twigs off trees; impedes progress
9	Strong gale	Slight structural damage caused
10	Whole gale	Trees uprooted; considerable damage occurs
11	Violent storm	Widespread damage, seldom experienced in Britain
12+	Hurricane	Only encountered in tropical revolving storm

My birdwatchers' equivalent—let us call it the Linnaeus scale after the great
naturalist and classifier—is presented in table 2.[1] This is crude and exaggerated but recognisable, I suggest. Let us look at the clinical casebook.

One of the earliest and best accounts of a year list is the story of a thirty-
thousand-mile journey around the United States in 1953 by two very eminent
naturalists, one British and one American. They were James Fisher and Roger
Tory Peterson, and their adventures were published in their book *Wild America* (1955). They began in Thoreau's Concord in April and ended at Anchorage
in Alaska in July, by which time they had surpassed the previous record of 497
species in a year by a good margin. Fisher had reached 536 by the time he
went home and in fact pulled a fast one in Anchorage, because while Peterson
stayed in the hotel to work on a drawing Fisher went out with a guide and got

[1] British readers can make adjustments to the example species to suit their own locations in the
country but Americans and readers in other parts of the world will need to construct quite different examples. It might be instructive to build up an international dossier.

Table 2. Linnaeus Scale

No.	Status of bird	Species	Observable birder behaviour
0	No birds visible	none	Total calm (may be asleep or unconscious)
1	Common garden resident	robin, blackbird	Watches passively from chair
2	Less common garden visitor	coal tit, goldfinch	May stand up to see; points out to others in room
3	Local resident	jay, moorhen, kestrel	Sees on casual walks; not especially looked for; doesn't view through binoculars
4	Less common resident	nuthatch, marsh tit, little owl	Looks out for more actively; may make note in personal log
5	Seasonal migrant	nightingale, wheatear	Looks out eagerly for annual recurrence, notes in log; may report dates for county records
6	Scarce breeder	nightjar, bittern, hawfinch	Plans visit to special locations; may take partner; sense of frustration or satisfaction ensues
7	Unusual passage migrant	wryneck, water pipit, great grey shrike	Hurries to see; uses telescope; tells other birders around; reports to local recorder; suffers when dips out
8	Rare migrant or vagrant	night heron, Pallas's warbler, black kite	Changes plans to go and see; walks rapidly or runs to site; mood swings of anxiety, hope, and relief; phones in record with digital photos
9	National rarity	wallcreeper, harlequin duck, hawk owl	Very high anxiety levels; travels long distances at great expense; may deceive partner or employer on whereabouts; may lose sense of humour (or job or partner)
10	First for United Kingdom	willet, black woodpecker	Takes serious risks to health, livelihood, and marriage; massive adrenaline surges; uncontrollable twitching; incoherent speech
11	Rediscovery of extinct species	great auk, Eskimo curlew	Widely disbelieved; paranoid reaction: joins searchers after Elvis, Bigfoot, Nessie, and the Abominable Snowman; gibbers obscurely

Table 2. (*Cont.*)

No.	Status of bird	Species	Observable birder behaviour
12	New to science	Meinertzhagen's magpie?	Persistent delusions; full-blown Messiah complex; names species after self; may return to level 0 on scale, this time in padded cell

five new birds; so for a short time an Englishman held the record for the number of wild birds seen in a year in the United States (Peterson went on to get 572 that year, though).[1] These two men, both very serious ornithologists, gave themselves totally to the chase and relished each new tick with unaffected pleasure. None more so than for the legendary California condor. After a long search in the mountains, they are on the point of giving up when they see a distant speck in the sky, which slowly comes their way and turns out to be the very bird. It flies right over their heads:

> It was like a bomber, its flat-winged posture quite unlike the glider-dihedral of the turkey vulture. It was huge, black, pale-headed, and as it came over the big white bands forward on its underwing showed it to be an adult. For five minutes we watched its monstrous ten-foot span, its primaries spread like fingers. It made a couple of slow flaps, as if it had all the time in the world, caught a new thermal, and soared away to the southeast until it became a tiny speck and disappeared.

Fisher then makes two remarks which from an Englishman of his class and generation represent pretty strong language:

> "Tally most incredibly ho!" I said as I ticked it off on my checklist. "Worth seeing, actually."

Peterson, notoriously, rarely thought about anything other than birds, as Fisher describes:

> I've learned several things about Roger in the course of our acquaintance, and one of them is this: that Roger talks most of the time about

---

[1] There is a modern version of the same quest entertainingly told in Mark Obmascik's *The Big Year*, the story of a fierce three-way competition in which the winner records an extraordinary 745 species over the course of 1998 (no one would now think of starting the attempt as late as April and stopping in July, of course).

birds. When the subject switches, a faraway look comes into his eye. He just waits for a lull and steps in where he left off.

A famous example of this habit is when Peterson was accompanying a party of eminent statesmen and others on a bird trip to a U.K. estuary. Lord Alanbrooke, chief of the General Staff during the Second World War, was holding forth to an attentive audience on his relations with Winston Churchill when Peterson abruptly turned to the group and said ruminatively, "I guess oystercatchers will eat most any kind of mollusc." Mind you, Alanbrooke could let his own obsessions distract him from far more momentous conversations. He describes in his *War Diaries* the occasion on 30 January 1943 when he and Churchill had a top-secret meeting with the Turkish president and his own opposite number, Field Marshall Çakmak, in a remote railway siding in rural Turkey. In the middle of the very sensitive negotiations he sees out of the carriage window, over Çakmak's shoulder, a raptor quartering the fields. He wondered if it could possibly be a pallid harrier, a bird he had never seen but much wanted to—possible in this area, but not easy to distinguish from some other harriers:

> I was consequently very intent on looking out of that window, much to Çakmak's discomfiture, who kept looking round and possibly thought I had spotted someone getting ready to have a shot at him!

An early model of the year list in the United Kingdom was Richard Millington's *A Twitcher's Diary*, published in 1981. This came from a very expert but nonestablishment source, perhaps one could even say an antiestablishment source (see p. 11 note), and was expressed in a far more exuberant idiom than James Fisher would have ventured: "a totally hyperzonky megacrippler" was how he described a red-eyed vireo seen in the October of his Big Year.

The quest for a Big Year list is usually breathless, anxious, and very tiring. But the narrative of a Life list can be exhausting even to contemplate and is sometimes more poignant than exciting. In *To See Every Bird* (2005), Dan Koeppel tells the harrowing story of his father's determination to become a Big Lister, one of those birders who play out their obsession on the largest possible scale and have it as an unachievable objective to see all the birds in the world. There are about 9,600 species in all;[1] about 250 people have seen

---

[1] The number keeps shifting upwards as subspecies are promoted to species and new birds are discovered (as still happens surprisingly often: 128 new world species were added between 1980 and 1999, for example).

more than 5,000 of them, about one hundred more than 6,000, twelve more than 7,000, and two more than 8,000. Koeppel became a seven-thousand-plus man but in the course of doing so spent a fortune, ruined his health, destroyed his marriage, and alienated all his friends and family. His son records that as the addiction took hold it extended to other areas of his father's life as well, until in the end he was wholly occupied with making lists:

> At this point, Dad wasn't just counting birds. He was also checking off cheeses and beers, usually sampling new ones on his birding trips. And he was in the midst of an all-out attempt to read every single book that had won or been short-listed for the Booker Literary Prize. Many were out of print, but he eventually found them all, tallying 169 novels.

Koeppel clearly felt the devil behind him, as, with more justification, did the biggest lister of them all, Phoebe Snetsinger—yes, a woman. She became a Big Lister after receiving a cancer diagnosis at the age of forty-nine. She was given only six months to live but decided to forgo treatment and pursue birds instead. Her race against time lasted seventeen years in the end, through various remissions, and took her to the ends of the earth. She told Koeppel that birding was what kept her alive. She survived a shipwreck in Indonesia, an earthquake in Costa Rica, and a brutal rape in New Guinea, but then after sighting bird number 8,450 she was killed in a bus crash on a remote road in Madagascar.

The narrative of the year list or life list is now a flourishing subgenre of bird-watching literature as new records are attempted, fierce rivalries worked out, and scores set if not settled. The books tend to be pacy, lively accounts, a bit two-dimensional perhaps but not more so than most detective or adventure thrillers, which they resemble also in the stories of obstacles overcome, false starts and misinformation, personal sacrifices, broken relationships, and eventual success for the modest hero. Recent examples from the United Kingdom are Adrian Riley's *Arrival and Rivals* (2004) and James Hanlon's *UK 500: Birding in the Fast Lane* (2006); from the United States, Mark Obmascik's *The Big Year* (2004); and there is one Australian example, Sean Dooley's *The Big Twitch* (2006), where he sets a new Australian record of 703 for a calendar year.[1] The

---

[1] The total Australian all-time list was then 830 species. Statistics for the other accounts mentioned are: Riley, 380 species in Britain in 2002; Hanlon, 506 life list (Lee Evans taxonomy) from a total British list then of 572 (British Ornithologists' Union taxonomy); Obmascik, Sandy Komito's 1998 list of 745 species from a total North American list (American Birding Association area, excluding Hawaii but including Canada) of 932.

publisher's blurb for the Obmascik book gives the flavour of the thing, with a little saving irony:

> A captivating tour of human and avian nature, of courage and deceit, passion and paranoia, fear and loathing. *The Big Year* reveals the extremes to which man will go to pursue his dreams, to conquer and to categorize—no matter how low the stakes.

And Adrian Riley is equally confessional, describing his brief encounter with a buff-breasted sandpiper at Wheldrake Ings in Yorkshire:

> On arrival at the site, I jumped from the car, trained my binoculars on the bird, satisfied myself that it was indeed the one I wanted and sped off again. I left that beautiful bird without so much as "by your leave." I appreciated it not one iota; it was merely a "tick." I was more interested in getting the grey phalarope at Titchwell. I hope that all my readers never fall into this abyss of insensitivity.

One main difference between these and the earlier stories is in the technology now available to help the would-be record breakers. Information is disseminated at extraordinary speed and in enormous quantities and a fully teched-up birder will know from his computer screen, pager, or mobile phone exactly what has been seen where in the last week, day, or hour in any part of the country. It is therefore possible to amass a large total of species one could never have hoped to discover just on one's own or through one's immediate network of friends. The information itself tends to be anonymous in character and, initially at least, just raw data lacking any context or emotional colour. The authors cited above are clearly all very active and expert birders who use these technical advances without being limited by them, but the ready availability of such precise data can encourage a sort of uncritical passivity. When the observer arrives at the spot indicated by his GPS system for the rare bird he has been alerted to by email, he has only to get out of the car and walk over to the nearest of the many telescopes already fixed on the bird to enhance the virtual sighting he will already have inspected on his computer screen. This must in the end affect the quality of the experience. Far gone are the innocent days that Hilda Quick enjoyed when she walked out from her home on St. Agnes in Scilly:

> I know that seeing rarities is not the main business of bird-watching. The odd vagrant blown out of its course, or the young bird wandering beyond its range, add nothing to our knowledge, and it is of more use

and interest to study the habits or the movements of our own local birds. But it is undoubtedly FUN to see a new bird—jam on the daily bread of observation—and a bit of added knowledge for oneself, if for no one else! So I will tell a few tales of the birds that I have met here from time to time.

Her "tales" include finding Britain's first blue-cheeked bee-eater on a June day in 1951 when she went out down the lane in St. Agnes to collect the milk, and then in September 1955 finding on the same day both a lesser grey shrike and two nighthawks (the second record for Britain). Happy discoveries, in every sense.

Phoebe Snetsinger was exceptional in various ways, not least in being a woman in what is usually a male domain. Women, of course, have their addictions,[1] but it is a fact that most of those possessed by this particular compulsion are men. In its absolute, blinkered focus and urgency it sounds like a form of Asperger's syndrome, whose distinguishing symptoms are said to include:

- Obsessive interest in a single object or topic to the exclusion of any other
- High level of expertise in that area
- Repetitive rituals and routines
- Peculiarities in speech and language
- Socially and emotionally inappropriate behaviour. (Web site of the U.S. National Institutes of Health, Institute of Neurological Disorders)

The language in which twitchers describe their desiderata is certainly symptomatic of something unenviable. They seem to suffer a kind of psychological depletion that can only be satisfied by acquisition and possession. They talk of "needing" a certain species they haven't seen and having "had" it or having "got" it when they have been successful.[2] It sounds more like the temporary relief of a pain than an enduring or positive pleasure. The activity is also characterised by rule-governed behaviour of an extreme kind. The rules in question are required to quantify and validate the results because it is part of the psychology to demand order, control, and certainty. There are very precise

---

[1] One thinks of seriously acquisitive females like Imelda Marcos (shoes), Elizabeth Taylor (husbands), and Queen Victoria (subjects); and one of the greatest natural history collectors ever was Lady Margaret Cavendish Bentinck, who in the eighteenth century filled a museum with her immense acquisitions (see Allen, *The Naturalist in Britain*, p. 29).

[2] And this leads to some hilarious locutions. "I need a nighthawk" perhaps sounds intriguing; "I need a bobolink," "a grackle," or "a dickcissel" rather more suggestive; while other examples sound like minor perversions or statements of the obvious ("ostrich," "phalarope," "shag").

rules, therefore, determining what can and cannot be "counted" in this highly artificial activity and there are designated authorities to settle difficult cases. The rules are designed to ensure that the birds counted are wild, live, and free-flying, that they belong to full recognised species, that they are seen within the prescribed geographical and time limits, and that they are identified on the basis of sufficient criteria. This all sounds sensible enough and for most people on most occasions it is sufficient. But you are dealing here with messy real-life situations and with highly competitive individuals not always blessed with common sense and good judgement. Every one of these parameters gives rise to borderline cases and contested interpretations. The instinct then is to generate subsidiary rules, codicils, and so on in a desperate search for some kind of objective "certainty," which will never in fact be forthcoming since the activity itself is entirely artificial. God doesn't care and won't settle it. Nor will Nature.

It's easy to construct examples on the borderline:

- When exactly does a bird cease to be tame or introduced and become wild and self-sustaining? Egyptian geese have just about made it in the United Kingdom but black swans haven't yet. What about eagle owls, sakers, monk parakeets, and marbled ducks? What if they breed—is one generation enough, or two? What if they then cross-breed with other escapees? Can a species (or the same bird) be a countable resident one year when it was only an escapee or immigrant the last?
- When does a subspecies become a species and on whose say-so? Do you have to revise all your old lists when a change is made or has the world changed? Since different authorities use different lists and standards you can get the paradoxical situation whereby the same bird sighting counts on a world list, say, but not a U.S. list (a real example involves the two forms of black-billed magpie, which were split for one list but not the other).
- What about birds arriving on ships? What if they land on the ship halfway across, nine-tenths of the way across . . . ? What if they are fed on board? Is opening a hatch to let a raptor get at the rats an act of "feeding"?
- Is it OK to identify a bird by sound alone? What if its voice is more distinctive than its visual appearance? What about a bird you hear well but see poorly?
- What about a bird viewed distantly but identified by others on the basis of closer views, when it is clearly the same bird? What about two birds seen in flight where one of them is later identified as a rarity?

Did you "see" that bird or did you just see the bird that was that bird?
Is this a significant difference?

- What about a bird within a boundary but seen from outside it (looking back from the "wrong" side of a river, for example)? Or vice versa?
Or a bird seen on 31 December but not identified until 1 January?

- What about a roadkill where the bird hasn't quite expired? Or is later
revived in care? Does it make a difference if it was a deliberate roadkill to settle an identity question? Is this a matter for the ethics sub-
committee or the records one? And what if it was your brother who
was driving?

- How is this affected by the technology? What if a distant seabird is
visible only using a telescope and not with the naked eye? Most people would still say they'd seen it. But what about a Webcam beaming
images of a nesting osprey from the nearby Loch Garten hide? Most
people would say not. What's the difference in principle? What about
using a parabolic reflector for distant calls? What if we one day get
more powerful telescopes that work over a range of five miles, night
vision equipment for owls and kiwis, DNA bar-coders and sensors
for difficult splits? When is a perception a direct one?

You can construct further rules to answer all these questions, but I can then
find new questions and raise new doubts. Wherever you draw the line there
will be a borderline area. You can't finally satisfy a neurotic that there is nothing to worry about.

Discovery and Diversity

What authentic pleasure can we take in rare and unusual birds, then? We have
to accept straightaway that all rarity is relative and is not a primary quality of
the birds themselves (like wing-bars and red legs). A gannet is rare in London[1]
but sixty thousand pairs nest on St. Kilda. There are special pelagic charters to
see a Wilson's petrel off Cornwall, but it is one of the world's most numerous
birds with a population estimated at around sixteen million. A swallow is
noteworthy in London or New York in December, not in May. Being rare depends on being in a particular place at a particular time. This is obvious, but
rather deflating. Why should we be so excited by mere statistical anomalies?
Why would anyone rush to see a Canada warbler in Ireland but ignore one in
Central Park? We need some distinctions.

[1] There was actually one record "of an adult associating with mute swans on the Round Pond,
which stayed from about midday to early evening on 14 October 1952" (R. F. Sanderson in E. M.
Nicholson, *Bird-Watching in London: A Historical Perspective.*

First there is the notion of *inaccessibility*. It is exciting to see birds in some remote place that is their natural setting but is not easy to reach. The birds may be rare only in the sense of rarely seen, like the colonies of Leach's petrels on the Flannan Isles or North Rona, where they breed in their thousands safe from disturbance; and even if you make the long and uncomfortable journey there, you still have the difficulty that the birds emerge only in the hours of darkness and may still elude you.

Then there is *worldwide scarcity*. Some birds are born rare, into species that have only ever existed in tiny populations around the world. These would include the island endemics and the birds adapted to some very specialised environment (like several parrot and rail species). Others seem to achieve rarity by gradually failing in the Darwinian struggle and now survive only in relict, dwindling populations (like the slender-billed and Eskimo curlews and the Bachman's warbler). Some others have rarity thrust upon them by persecution or gross human interference with their environment (like some raptors). These Shakespearian categories are not sharply distinct, of course, and usually there is some combination of factors at work, but it will always feel like a privilege and a thrill, if occasionally a guilty thrill, to see one of these threatened species in its natural habitat.

Local scarcity can be at least as exciting, even when there is a thriving national or world population, and this too can take various forms. For example, most birdwatchers in the United Kingdom would take great pleasure, and in my view a very rich pleasure, in finding a local colony of tree sparrows, a wintering flock of hawfinches, elusive and declining species like willow tit or lesser spotted woodpecker, occasional breeders like Montagu's harrier, sporadic invaders like waxwing, nutcracker, and rough-legged buzzard, or species that are regular on migration but only in small numbers and specific locations like dotterel, long-tailed skua, and, to take a much rarer and more recently discovered case, white-billed divers (which are basically an Arctic species but seem to have a tiny but detectable migration through the Western isles each April). These may be species on the edge of their range (whether contracting like the corncrake or expanding like the little egret and Cetti's warbler), or birds brought here by difficulties in weather conditions (little auks) or shortages in their usual source of food (crossbills, short-eared owls). In all these different cases what we enjoy, I would suggest, is not just the pleasure of an unusual experience but an experience that has a context and a significance. We can make some broader sense of it and are no longer treating the birds themselves as just anonymous items on a list, each of equal value since none has any value in itself. Compare that with the rather blank experience of seeing the 2006 long-billed murrelet in Devon, an extreme vagrant that added one tick to the lists of all who saw it but was just in completely the wrong part of the world and for no interesting reason. Most extreme vagrants, whether borne here by ships, by hurricanes, or by dysfunctional internal guidance systems, are in any case usually abject and distressing objects likely to die soon, not pioneers to welcome and celebrate. I look more closely at the importance of time and place in chapter 7.

There are two other factors that may contribute to our legitimate feelings of pleasure in seeing rare birds. One is the sense of *discovery*. It makes all the difference whether you encounter and first identify the bird yourself rather than just rolling up to join the crowd (sometimes in a queue, possibly even a paying queue, where the space is confined and numbers have to be limited), in order to look briefly at some bird whose exact location has been announced on the Birdlines. In the first case there is the element of surprise as well as discovery. It can, however, also be a particular pleasure if you find the bird at a location you'd rather fancied for that species but which had never yet yielded it. For some years I've been watching an isolated little clump of trees and bushes on the East Anglian coast that I just know will produce a red-breasted flycatcher one October day, and the pleasure will eventually be all the greater for my having expected and waited for it.

And finally, there is the larger sense of celebrating *diversity*, of expanding our own range of experience of the natural world by seeing more of its members. That human instinct is very well described by the scientist Edward O. Wilson in his book *The Future of Life* (2002), which is in equal measures uplifting and depressing in its account of the riches of the planet and the pressures on them:

> It is not so difficult to love nonhuman life, if gifted with knowledge about it. The capacity, even the proneness to do so, may well be one of the human instincts. The phenomenon has been called biophilia, defined as the innate tendency to focus upon life and lifelike forms, and in some instances to affiliate with them emotionally. Human beings sharply distinguish the living from the inanimate. We esteem novelty and diversity in other organisms. We are thrilled by the prospect of unknown creatures, whether in the deep sea, the unbroken forest, or remote mountains. We are riveted by the idea of life on other planets. Dinosaurs are our icons of vanished biodiversity.

Birds are a key part of our present biodiversity—distributed unevenly across the world in nearly ten thousand species, all with their own special characteristics and attractive to us in all kinds of ways, not least in their variety. No wonder we want to see as many of them as possible.

5

Beauty and the Beholder

Remember that the most beautiful things in
the world are the most useless; peacocks
and lilies, for instance.
John Ruskin

Volga Delta, 25 May 2007

The Volga Delta is a vast wetland in southern Russia where the mighty Volga
River spreads out to become a water-wonderland of rivers, streams, brooks,
marshes, and oozing filaments as it drains into the Caspian Sea. We think we
have large reedbeds in East Anglia in Britain, at places like Hickling, Walberswick, Minsmere, Cley, and Titchwell, but this is a marsh so immense you could
fit the whole of East Anglia into one corner of it. It is a wildlife paradise for all
kinds of reedbed warblers, herons, bitterns, egrets, ibises, pelicans, cranes,
terns, waders, wildfowl, and several birds of prey (especially sea eagles); there
are also wild boar, raccoon dogs, and even a specially adapted marsh cat; and
by the sound of it just now, about ten million frogs, by far the noisiest inhabitants, which keep up a deafening background chorus all day and night.

I am in the tiny village of Obzhorovo, perched on an island of dry land in
the middle of this watery jungle, where the "garden birds" are themselves a
real thrill. They remind me of the time when I got my first serious bird book,
the famous Peterson *Field Guide to the Birds of Britain and Europe,* which was
first published in 1954. Peterson opened our eyes to all kinds of alluring species young birdwatchers like me had scarcely even heard of, and I remember
one colour plate that particularly captivated me. On a single page it featured
bee-eater, roller, and hoopoe, all spectacular birds to look at but all impossibly
exotic and remote.[1] I wondered then if I should ever see any of them.

---

[1] Plate 46 in the original edition of 1954. It is an index of the inflation of expectations in these
matters that the same page in the fifth edition of 1993 now includes also belted kingfisher (an extreme U.S. vagrant) and blue-cheeked bee-eater (still a great rarity in most parts of Europe but
present, as it happens, in the Volga Delta region).

23. Peterson "exotics" page (*A Field Guide to the Birds of Britain and Europe*, 1954)

And here they all are around the village I'm staying in, visible from my front door in fact, the common garden birds, which the locals scarcely look at twice. To me they are like some brilliant Russian circus troupe: the bee-eater with its suit of rainbow colours, trilling as it swoops and darts around catching bees on the wing, something between a flycatcher and a swallow in flight action; the hoopoe strutting around busily like a huge pink starling, flirting that outrageous crest and floating a few yards away on black-and-white butterfly wings when I get too near; then the roller, like a sort of overdressed gangster with startling blue and chestnut plumage, poised menacingly on the fence posts to drop down and stab snakes, beetles, or small mammals with its dagger bill. In the hot sun and the strong light they make a vision of dancing colours of almost tropical intensity in this otherwise drab and dusty village. Surely they represent the very essence of avian beauty? Or are there relativities

in beauty as well as in rarity? I realise I haven't seen a single robin, wren, dunnock, blackbird, or song thrush all week—they would be the rarities and celebrities down here. And I must have appeared a rare bird myself in a place
where they rarely see foreigners at all, let alone eccentric Englishmen with
beards, bushkit, and binoculars. A small girl shyly peeped at me from behind
her mother's skirts one day and said something to her mother I couldn't understand. I asked my Russian friend to translate and he gave me a look. "She
says 'Does he work in the circus, mummy?'"

I remembered that in Central Park, though I always got great delight from
the pageant of brilliantly coloured spring warblers, I did in the end feel almost
sated by the powerful visual stimuli and sometimes turned with relief to the
subtler pleasures of discrimination provided, for example, by the thrushes, flycatchers, vireos, and sparrows, where you have to look more carefully and the
differences in songs and calls become important. Is there an aesthetic parallel
here? Might I sometime come to feel that my troupe of Russian players were
too obvious in their charms, even garish or tarty? Would I long for the delicate
gradations of brown, grey, and black in the plumage of the domestic dunnock
or the cheerful modesty of the robin's red breast? It is said that the smell of violets is so overwhelming that after a short exposure the olfactory sense closes
down and for a minute or so you can no longer smell the violets or anything
else. And we all know the experience of temporarily losing the power of sight
when dazzled by very bright lights. Would I get roller-glare here in the Delta,
with similar effects? And what if a roller turned up on my home patch back in
Britain, where it really would be an exotic rarity: would its beauty then be enhanced or reduced in that very different range of light and landscape colours?
And what about the landscape itself, come to that? Does our perception of
beauty there depend to any degree on the spectacular effects of novelty and
extreme features? Is it the same with butterflies, flowers, and trees, and how
does the natural world in general compare in this respect with the world of
human art and artefacts? Do these comparisons tell us anything of interest
about our appreciation of birds?

These are the sorts of questions I explore in this chapter, following the programme I set out in chapter 2 of investigating in turn the different aspects of
birds that may be thought to explain the nature and strength of our attraction
to them. In chapter 4 I looked at the impulses to list, collect, and acquire that
may lie behind, or in some cases even constitute, the interest many serious
birders have in finding and identifying unusual birds. Relative rarity is the
main criterion for them. Physical appearance is surely another major factor in
attraction or "significance," and one that appeals more widely to the public at
large than does mere vagrancy. I have seen bumper stickers saying, "Birds are

beautiful." Almost everyone could mention certain birds they think beautiful to look at or listen to, and many more would count this a significant pleasure in their lives than would rush to see some drab vagrant, cast up in a bizarre location. Think of the huge popularity of the BBC's *Springwatch* programmes and of David Attenborough's *Life of Birds* (1998).[1] These are surely driven to a large extent by the delight people take in the *appearance* of birds as well as by a more anthropomorphic curiosity about their behaviour and family arrangements. The beauty of birds has long been celebrated in poetry and prose and has often been represented in art and even imitated in music, but exactly what it might consist in is curiously little analysed or examined. What are the criteria and how do they interrelate? Who are the art critics and connoisseurs of the wild? This is one more area where it is easier to ask the questions than provide systematic and convincing answers, but I shall hope that just asking the questions may sometimes by itself enlarge our sense of the possibilities and show how an interest in birds can connect creatively with other parts of our lives.

This is a huge area of enquiry. Part of the problem is that we use words like "beautiful" to describe such a wide range of different things—stars, mountains, clouds, rivers, landscapes, animals, birds, flowers, butterflies, women, poems, music, paintings, clothes, and cars. Do we mean the same thing in all these cases, and what in particular do we mean when talking about birds? There are various strategies for addressing such difficult questions. One way— usually that of the poet or creative writer—is to attend closely to particular instances, describe and evoke them as well as you can, and hope that connections between them may emerge in the reader's response. That has the advantage of directness and authenticity but may in the end only elicit a succession of separate, if vivid, images. Another way is more analytical and deductive, seeking to identify and define the key categories in a sort of downwards-branching logical tree that eventually isolates the specific concept you are studying; so that in this case one might look at notions of beauty and physical attraction as they apply first to natural versus nonnatural (e.g., artistic) realms, then subdivide natural into organic versus inorganic, then further subdivide organic into human versus nonhuman, the latter into vertebrate versus invertebrate, birds versus other animals, and further as necessary. This feels more systematic but can lead to disappointingly abstract conclusions. Remember

[1] The 2007 BBC *Springwatch* programmes regularly attracted an audience of more than four million viewers, sometimes outdoing even those for *Big Brother*. Of course, both these examples of "reality television" are in fact equally contrived—and there are other parallels (think dunnocks and see N. Davies, *Dunnock Behaviour and Social Evolution* on their surprising sex life).

the cautionary tale of the schoolteacher Mr. Gradgrind in Dickens's *Hard Times*, who was wholly preoccupied with inculcating Facts into his pupils. Gradgrind criticises the ignorance of the shy young girl, Sissy Jupe ("girl number twenty"), who actually knows all about horses because her father works with them but who cannot define one on demand. He turns instead to his star pupil Bitzer:

> "Bitzer," said Mr. Gradgrind. "Your definition of a horse."
>
> "Quadruped, gramnivorous. Forty teeth, namely twenty-four grinders, four eye-teeth, and twelve incisive. Sheds coat in the spring; in marshy countries, sheds hoofs, too. Hoofs hard, but requiring to be shod with iron. Age known by marks in mouth." Thus (and much more) Bitzer.
>
> "Now girl number twenty," said Mr. Gradgrind, "You know what a horse is."

There is also a middle strategy, messier and more informal, that relies on example and analogy to explore some central ideas, without knowing or deciding in advance which of them will turn out to be connected or where they might lead. It shuttles between the general and the particular, trying to weave a web between them. And there are diversions, bypasses, and blind alleys, not all of which are shown on existing maps. I take this more exploratory and uncertain route.

Signs of Life

It's hard to know where to start, but I suggest the Windmill Theatre. The Windmill was celebrated in the mid-twentieth century for its risqué shows and especially for its revues involving nude or scantily dressed women. As such it regularly attracted the attention of the Lord Chamberlain's Office, which had the responsibility for maintaining "a decent level of propriety" in the British theatre. In 1940, when Britain was threatened by German invasion, this came to seem to the authorities a vital patriotic objective and on 16 April of that year a conference was summoned at St. James's Palace involving representatives of the Home Office and police, London County councillors, and administrators from all branches of the entertainment industry. They gravely debated this threat to national security and duly issued an agreed communiqué that dealt in particular with the problem of female nudity on stage. They determined that "actresses may pose completely nude provided the pose is *motionless and expressionless*" (my italics). In the case of the Windmill's revues, photographs of poses were to be submitted for the Lord Chamberlain's

24. Nude revues from the Windmill Theatre. These were photographs submitted for
approval by the Lord Chamberlain's Office: the top two were probably approved; the
bottom left is marked "approved," but the bottom right is marked "No" (in J. Johnston,
The Lord Chamberlain's Blue Pencil, 1990)

advance approval (and pleasure, presumably) and there are records of the various cases authorised and declined.[1]

The key thing was the effect of *animation* on the observer. This is surely
fundamental to our reactions to birds as well. We are fascinated by their movement, literally their liveliness. This encompasses all their habits of locomotion
and behaviour—how they hop, run, or jump on the ground; how they move
through bushes and trees; how they fly in the air; how they swim, dabble, or

---

[1] The proud motto of the Windmill in the war years was "We never closed"; but it finally did
close in 1964, for the ironic reason that its shows were by then far too tame for progressive appe-
tites and had been completely outflanked, as one might say, by the burgeoning strip-club industry.

a

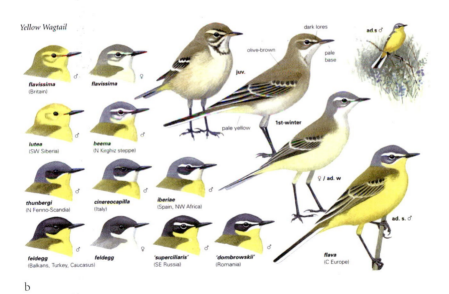

b

1. (a) Detail of swallows from the "spring fresco," from Room Delta 2, Akrotiri, Thera (about 1650 BC)—see p. 3; (b) yellow (flava) wagtails (Dan Zetterström)—see p. 63

WARBLERS OF NORTH AMERICA
THE ARBOREAL SPECIES

2. American spring warblers (Ramiel Papish) with inset prothonotary (David Quinn)—see p. 81

a

b

c

3. (a) Hoopoe (photo: Shootov Igor/Shutterstock)—see p. 110; (b) roller (photo: Bill Baston)—see p. 116; (c) barn owl in flight (photo: Bill Baston)—see p. 44

a

b

c

4. John James Audubon, *The Birds of America* (1827–38): (a) wild turkey;
(b) golden eagle; (c) Leach's fork-tailed petrel—see p. 120

a

b

5. (a) Bruno Liljefors, *Golden Eagle and Hare* (1904)—see p. 121; (b) sea eagle in flight (photo: N. Stepkin)—see p. 227; (c) Edward Lear, *Eagle Owl* (1837)—see p. 220

c

a

b

c

6. (a) Peacock (photo: L. Kelly / Shutterstock)—see p. 129; (b) the four blue macaws (in Tony Juniper and Mike Parr, *Parrots*, 2003)—see p. 135. Top row from left to right: hyacinth, Lear's, glaucous. Bottom left: two perching Spix's macaws (a young bird on the right). Bottom right: "the four blues" in flight. (c) Australian fairy-wrens—see p. 229. Clockwise from top left: red-backed (photo: Bill Jolly), variegated (photo: Bill Jolly), splendid (photo: Graeme Chapman), superb (photo: Graeme Chapman)

a

b

c

7. (a) World "robins"—see p. 245. From left to right: white-throated robin, European robin, Siberian blue robin, American robin, rufous bush-robin (RSPB, Birds magazine). (b) Christmas card robin (by Sarah Adams)—see p. 34; (c) Christmas biscuit tin (Crabtree & Evelyn, 2007)—see p. 189

a

b

8. (a) North American sports logos—see pp. 280–81. Top line: Toronto Blue Jays, 1977 version and 2004 version; Pittsburgh Penguins, 1967 version and 2000 version. Bottom line: Atlanta Thrashers, Atlanta Falcons, Arizona Cardinals, Philadelphia Eagles.
(b) British stamps (Kate Stephens / Royal Mail)—see p. 225

dive in water; how they display, court, and threaten; how they feed, drink, and preen. It is their animation, even more than their shape, size, and colour, that is often what gives them both their attraction and their special identity. Unfortunately, we do not know what physical tests the valiant Windmill censors submitted themselves to in judging the precise degree of excitement different nude poses might (literally) give rise to, but you can test the claim about birds quite easily. Go to a museum with a collection of stuffed birds and see the difference between these dead specimens posing "motionless and expressionless" in glass cases and the live ones you can observe in the wild. One thinks again of Ted Hughes's brilliant characterisations of birds through their distinctive movements: the "bounce and stab" of the song thrush, the "steep / controlled scream of skid" of the swifts, "the plummeting dead drop" of the skylark at the end of its song flight, or the starlings "limber and saurian on your hind legs, / tumbling the sparrows with a drop kick" at the bird feeder.

It can actually be quite difficult to recognise familiar species in a museum display, even though you are closer than you will ever be in the wild. For example, in the wader cabinet: that redshank should be starting nervously, ducking a little before raising its wings to fly; the sanderling, twinkling to and fro in a small party following the edge of the surf and lightly dotting the sand with quick pecks; the common sandpiper, bobbing up and down before quickly launching itself on a stiff-winged, flicking flight low over the water; the jack snipe doing its deep knee bends as if on springs; the knot in dense formation flights rather than standing rooted and alone. Here they are all just stiff, static, and solitary. Similarly, warblers no longer reveal their characteristic movements through the vegetation: chiffchaffs flicking their tails downwards while moving lightly through the upper foliage, reed warblers shinning up reed stems, whitethroats launching themselves in a short display flight and then diving down into a hedge, blackcaps on a more furtive flit between bushes. Birds of prey all look smaller close-up than you expect and are reduced to a common lifelessness instead of variously gliding, soaring, hovering, darting, dashing, plunging, and diving. My point is emphasised, not contradicted, I think, by those species whose *immobility* over a long period can be a striking feature—like a long-eared owl roosting motionless a few yards away in a tree, a stone curlew statuesque in a bare field, or a heron rigid with concentration and menace when fishing. The immobility here is palpable, a deliberate, purposeful pose. Curators do their best. They try to position the specimens in naturalistic poses and may construct appropriate backdrops and settings for them, but the life has literally gone out of the birds. The Audubon Society has as its motto, "A bird in the bush is worth two in the hand," and this turns out to be a point not just about conservation but also about appreciation.

The study of birds has changed in this respect, and so perhaps have our perceptions. Up to at least the early twentieth century the standard way of looking closely at birds and identifying them was by inspecting dead specimens. There were a few exceptional observers like White, Thoreau, and Clare who had the patience, fieldcraft, and interest to come to know birds in a fuller sense and the facility to communicate their experiences; but in general the collector's adage obtained that "What's hit is history, what's missed is mystery." It is only recently that technical advances in optical equipment have enabled all of us to enjoy close-up views from a distance, without disturbance to the bird's natural behaviour, indeed sometimes without its even knowing it is being observed. Television has taken the process even further and now brings extraordinarily good and intimate pictures of birds right into our living rooms. As a result, we can now see almost all the plumage details of the bird as it would be in the hand as well as all the characteristic movements of the bird as it is in the bush. Perhaps we give the latter a higher priority as a consequence, now that it has become a part of what we routinely see and respond to. Certainly many earlier descriptions of birds are more restricted to questions of markings and coloration. Here is Sir Thomas Browne describing "a very rare bird ... which seemed to be some kind of jay," which had been killed locally in Norfolk and brought to him for identification. He says (original spelling, my punctuation):

> The bill was black, strong and bigger than a Jaye; somewhat yellow clawes tipped black, three before and one clawe behind; the whole bird not so bigge as a Jaye. The head, neck, and throat of a violet colour, the back upper parts of the wing of a russet yellowe, the fore and part of the wing azure, succeeded downward by a greenish blewe, then on the flying feathers bright blewe; the lower parts of the wing outwardly of a brown, inwardly of a merry blewe, the belly a light faynt blewe; the back toward the tayle of a purple blewe; the tayle eleven fethers of a greenish coulour, the extremities of the outward feathers thereof white, with an eye of greene. ("Notes on Certain Birds Found in Norfolk," 1668)

This is a good and recognisable description of a roller, one of my Volga Delta garden birds. But it is a dead roller. I watched the roller outside my front door there quite closely for several days and became very familiar with its movements and behaviour (I was even able to watch it "rolling" in flight sometimes). I could probably have identified it in profile or flight at a great distance, but I couldn't have recalled the exact patterning of all these different blues and greens as Browne described them (and I never noticed the claws at all).

This is a tiny illustration of an important change in what we now look at and see. This is driven in part by the technological advances I referred to, which have transformed the possibilities of seeing the live bird in its natural context. But it is driven in part too by our changing cultural attitudes towards the natural world in general, which is a large and fascinating story in itself and one I return to at the end of this chapter. The origins of this change seem to lie in the eighteenth century, in a reaction against the exploitation and destruction of nature that was literally fuelling material progress. There was also a growing secularisation and a decline in the anthropocentric view of the world that religion had seemed to encourage, and this was given a massive further boost, and apparent justification, by Darwin's revolutionary theories. He demonstrated that man was just one species among many, subject to precisely the same forces of creation and change as the rest, and had indeed evolved *from* other species. Among the many consequences of this dramatic shift in our view of ourselves and the world at large was the emergence of new life sciences such as ecology (the study of organisms in relation to their environment) and the huge growth of a popular (and therefore political) interest in the environment itself and in conservation issues more generally. We have moved a long way from a time when Henry More could in 1653 write that God had given life to cattle and sheep so as to keep their meat fresh "until we shall have need to eat them" to a time now when academic journals in law and philosophy carry earnest articles on the moral rights of individual trees.

Image and Imagination

The history of the depiction of birds has reflected some of these changes and the major bird artists have made their own contribution to our perceptions of the world. But this is not a simple or straightforward story with the movement all in one, increasingly naturalistic, direction. It is complicated by the different purposes this art was intended to serve, which might include Art with a capital A but also more practical and indeed commercial purposes of ornamentation and illustration, including the specialised requirements of identification guides. There has undoubtedly been a general move towards representing the living bird in its natural context, but even now leading field guide artists make great use of skins or specimens to give their work the accuracy of detail that has come to be demanded and that is difficult to observe directly or to derive even from high-quality photographs. Formerly, of course, artists were almost wholly reliant on this source and it showed. Birds used to be depicted in fixed poses that conveyed little or nothing of their active behaviour. Compare, for example, the portrait of a male great spotted woodpecker by the Dutch painter Pieter Holsteyn the Elder (ca. 1580–1662) with illustrations of the same species by Lars Jonsson in his field guide *The Birds of Europe* (1992).

(a)

(b)

25. Great spotted woodpecker comparisons: (a) Pieter Holsteyn the elder (ca. 1580–1662) and (b) Lars Jonsson (1992)

The Holsteyn is quite accurate in its feather maps but has the bird perching like a pigeon or crow. The Jonsson, by comparison, catches perfectly its apparently magnetic adhesion to the trunk, the way it addresses the cone—poised and ready to give it a short sharp stab, and also the way it is braced by its tail; even the young bird whose head is just poking out of the nest-hole has some real character, looking expectant and demanding.

There are several signal stages on the road from Holsteyn to Jonsson, though they do not all point forward in quite the same direction. The two great beacons early on in this process were Thomas Bewick and John James Audubon (who were contemporaries and became friends).[1] Bewick (1753–1828) is best known for his charming and beautifully finished woodcuts. He was a good naturalist and observer, but his originality lay not in any specific contributions to ornithological knowledge but in his skill at imparting a distinct personality to the birds he depicted. After publication of his *Land Birds* in 1797, a Captain Stuart wrote him a letter of appreciation from the Ipswich barracks, saying, "I never before saw the *character* and *attitude* of the birds so admirably drawn," and Audubon remarked, "Look at his tail-pieces, reader, and say if you ever saw so much life represented before." Bewick himself made an interesting distinction between working from stuffed specimens and working from dead birds. He found a "very great difference between preserved Specimens and & those from nature, no regard having been paid at that time to place the former in their proper attitudes nor to place the different series of the feathers, so as to fall properly upon each other." Despite working as much as he could "from nature," however, by which he mainly meant from newly shot birds, Bewick too sometimes had problems in suggesting the correct mode of movement or "attitude" of a species, as can be seen from his blue tit (fig. 26), which is actually sitting stiffly in a horizontal posture like a chaffinch, not like the agile and bouncy little bird you see clinging upside down to twigs and bags of nuts. The "natural" still hadn't quite come alive.

Audubon (1785–1851), by contrast, went almost too far in the other direction. His famous portraits in *The Birds of America* are sensational in every way, dramatic and exaggerated action shots, which give the impression of enormous vitality and movement even at the cost of improbable contortions in the subject. Audubon, like Bewick, painted not from life but mainly from freshly killed birds, in his case usually birds he had just killed himself. He was an enthusiastic hunter, who boasted, "I call birds few when I shoot less than one

[1] It was Audubon who caused Bewick's wren to be so called, in gratitude for his support for Audubon's *The Birds of America,* for which Bewick found eight new subscribers. Meanwhile Bewick's name is in danger of disappearing from the other species that once bore it, now that the Bewick's swan is regarded as merely the Eurasian race of the tundra swan *(Cygnus columbianus).*

26. Thomas Bewick's blue titmouse (1797)

hundred a day," and his biographer, Edwin Way Teale, added dryly that "probably the most terrifying sight a bird could see was the approach of John James
Audubon."[1] He would pin the specimens he had thus despatched to a drawing
board marked out with small squares, which he replicated on his drawing
paper in order to depict the size and proportions accurately. This also enabled
him to force the bird into unnatural postures to illustrate key plumage features
and render the portrait in that way more informative. The result, unsurpris-
ingly, was often more artistically exciting than it was authentic. Some of the
classic Audubon images are wonderfully evocative but others are quite misleading. Compare, for example, the paintings in plate 4 with Audubon's depiction of the black guillemot in figure 27, where the flying bird looks as though
it has just been projected from a torpedo tube rather than whirring along, as it
should be, with rapid and stiff wingbeats that seem barely to keep it airborne.

Audubon was a massive influence on all succeeding wildlife artists. Britain
was a special case since it was here that the nineteenth-century interest in natural history flourished most fully. It is striking, for example, that Audubon's
great work, *The Birds of America* (1826–38), was first published not in the
United States but in Edinburgh and London, and that of the 180 subscribers he
listed in 1831 all but eighteen were British, with twenty-nine coming from the
Manchester area alone. Nonetheless, the artist I would pick out next for particular mention was a Swede. Bruno Liljefors (1860–1939), like Audubon, was a

[1] It may now seem an irony of course that this dedicated hunter should have given his name to
one of the premier conservation societies in the United States, but in fact he did often express
views about topics like habitat loss and overhunting that were probably advanced for his day (see
Welker, *Birds and Man*, pp. 104–5). Hunting and conservation interests continue to have a complex relationship, not a simple antagonism.

27. Audubon's black guillemot (*The Birds of America,* 1927–38)

devoted hunter. He specialised in portraits of avian predators—golden and white-tailed eagles, goshawks, and eagle owls—and clearly identified with them in portraying the moment of the kill with great vitality and enthusiasm. His credo was that "Organic life, especially the animal, is the apex of creation and movement is the highest expression of natural life," and he set new standards in the convincing portrayal of birds in flight and in their natural environment. One has the strong sense of an artist at home in the scenes and with the creatures he depicted. He too, though, was sometimes tempted to dramatise his paintings for artistic rather than strictly naturalistic effects and the trade-off poses a nice problem in aesthetic judgement. His famous painting of a golden eagle pursuing a hare has been subject to detailed technical criticism by ornithologists and the following quotations demonstrate the standards of sensibility and expertise that now obtain in this area, for example in the detail about the overpainted primary tips (see plate 5a). To reverse my earlier dictum, there are connoisseurs in green anoraks as well as in velvet smoking jackets.

Nicholas Hammond, in his very thoughtful survey in *Modern Wildlife Painting,* explains the background to the aerodynamics of the painting like this:

> The hare has been flushed by the eagle, an immature bird with a white tail band, flying low enough for its wings to skim the ground vegetation. The

outcome of the encounter is not certain. The hare almost certainly knows the terrain better than the eagle and is jinking. To have a chance of catching its prey the bird must turn and is beginning to do so, its first and second primaries have turned, the third and fourth are quivering, blurred shadows, while the secondaries on the right wing are slanted to spill air.

He then quotes Jonsson, a sympathetic admirer and a supreme technician himself, who tries to weigh the advantages of an artistic impression against the disadvantage of a deviation from naturalism:

A golden eagle has seven primary feathers, the six outer ones are deeply fingered and are more flexible under the effects of air pressure. Liljefors has deliberately portrayed this in the lefthand wing. He has painted the back fifth, sixth and seventh feathers curving upwards and then painted over them to correct what he himself found visually incorrect. But the overpainted feathers show through and reinforce the impression of movement. The righthand wing shows four almost identically shaped feathers, indicating a strong wing beat. However, it is doubtful whether the eagle is turning; rather, it is gliding towards the hare in a straight line. The position is thus impossible and as now represented the eagle would hit the ground. But despite this and other objections—the way the wing feathers allow the air to slip through has no basis in reality and the positioning of the feet is incorrect—the picture gives balance and beauty to a circling golden eagle and at the same time describes the harmony between the ground and the bird's plumage.

Liljefors might be regarded as a genuine artist who happened to have a passion for wildlife; other paintings of his show strong influences from French impressionism and therefore remind us again that the fundamental questions raised here are not limited to bird art as such. Does a Monet haze or a Turner sunset give a more "real" sense of the phenomenon than a photographic representation? Nor are the questions limited to art, for that matter. Does the speech Shakespeare put into Henry the Fifth's mouth before Agincourt give a truer account of the event than would a transcript of the words actually uttered? (Or a better or deeper account—and are these different questions or the same?)

One could pursue this theme by studying the way other artists after Audubon responded to the challenge he had set. Figures like Louis Agassiz Fuertes in North America and Archibald Thorburn, Joseph Wolf, Edward Lear, and John Gould in Europe all found their own ways of negotiating this tension between the demands of art and of nature and responding to the ever-growing requirement for lifelike accuracy, whatever that was taken to mean, and each of them had their own special strengths.[1] In Britain the tradition continued through the twentieth century in gifted artists such as Richard Talbot Kelly[2] (1890–1971), Peter Scott (1909–89), Keith Shackleton (1923–), Eric Ennion (1900–1981), Charles Tunnicliffe (1901–79), Robert Gillmor (1936–), and John Busby (1928–) along with several other present-day practitioners of real distinction. To pursue my particular theme of animation, though, I turn instead to a figure more important than any of these in terms of popular influence and success, and that is Roger Tory Peterson (1908–96).

Peterson belongs firmly in the tradition of illustrators rather than artists. He began by scratching a living from painting furniture, especially floral designs for bedroom furniture probably destined for New York's uptown bordellos, but he soon attracted wider attention as a dedicated bird artist and obsessive identification expert. In 1934 he published his first *Field Guide to the Birds,* an illustrated introduction to the birds of eastern North America. This revolutionised the presentation of such reference material and helped popularise an interest in birds among a massive lay audience in North America, with sales of more than two million copies. He went on to produce a European equivalent, in collaboration with Guy Mountfort and P.A.D. Hollom, which was eventually published in 1954 and itself achieved more than a million sales, with translations into thirteen languages. The Peterson *Field Guide* format was extended to other regions (Mexico, western birds) and to other subjects (fish, wildflowers, animals, and so on). Peterson became a brand. His special genius was in what Mountfort described as "diagnostic portraiture." He arranged related species on the same page, all in identical settings for easy comparison, and literally pointed to their special distinguishing features with little markers (see fig. 23, p. 110). The accompanying text was similarly simplified and limited to the essential differentia. Like other apparently obvious ideas, this turned out to be completely novel, instantly intelligible, and phenomenally successful. Of course, in the usual human way, after achieving unprecedented success in one genre Peterson always regretted that he was not better known in another, and longed to be appreciated as a "real" artist. His other paintings are in fact very fine, though less well known, and so Peterson himself in his work, and more especially in his aspirations, illustrated just the same tension between different objectives that his predecessors had.

[1] Gould had the unattractive habit of claiming credit for the work of other artists he commissioned for his magnum opus, *The Birds of Europe* (1832–37), and Lear in particular may have suffered as a consequence. Edwin Landseer said of Wolf's uncanny ability to catch the essence of a living bird, "he must have been a bird before he became a man."

[2] Probably the least known of these artists, but his murals of birds in the Museum of Zoology in Cambridge are at least as good as animations as the famous dioramas in the American Museum of Natural History in New York.

28. Common tern jizz (John Busby, 1990)

Peterson, however, represented a move in a quite different direction from them since it was his actual *intention* to simplify and to exclude extraneous and distracting features of animation and context. Later developments in field-guide design were in part a reaction against that, leading to another extreme, which is well represented by *Birds by Character: The Fieldguide to Jizz* (ed. Rob Hume) and *Birds by Behaviour* (Dominic Couzens); in these, various leading field ornithologists such as Ian Wallace and John Busby offer short, impressionistic sketches that are almost all jizz and no detail, just a line or two catching the feel of some characteristic movement or posture, more like a quick cartoon than a portrait.

Meanwhile, the search went on to achieve the holy grail of combining all these different virtues in one treatment. There are two outstanding candidates

29. Long-tailed ducks in flight: (a) Lars Jonsson (1992) and (b) Collins (1999)

for that award. The first is Lars Jonsson's *Birds of Europe* (1992). Jonsson (1952–) has an astonishing virtuosity and a feel for lifelike movement and character that have rarely been equalled; he also has a relentless passion for accuracy in depicting the whole bird in all its variations. Most pages are enlivened with a little vignette showing a head from a different angle or the bird in some active pose. The gannet twists in flight to dive; the night heron hunches, turned away, roosting on a branch; a honey buzzard on straight wings glides over a common buzzard on slightly bowed ones; a black guillemot whirrs away with its wings a blur; a tawny owl lands on a chimney clutching a mouse. He reminds us why we respond so strongly to movement, activity, and flight.

The second candidate is more of a team effort, the *Collins Bird Guide*, which finally appeared in 1999 and is now regarded as the European birders' field guide of choice, unsurpassed for its all-round excellence as a guide to identification. The two principal artists are Killian Mullarney (1958–) and Dan

Zetterström (1954–), who manage to combine the reference functions of Peterson with the other qualities of accuracy, animation, and sense of context. If
they perhaps lack quite the nerve and confidence and sheer panache of Jonsson, they compensate with their access to the very latest advances in identification knowledge, the range of different plumages exemplified, and a thor-
oughgoing integration of illustrations, text, and maps. Figure 29 shows extracts
from each of these outstanding guides for a comparison of the styles.

I have pursued the history of illustration to this very satisfactory point to
emphasise just how important the ideas of animation and movement are to
our appreciation of birds. But on the principle that you shall know things by
their opposites, I will end this section, as I began it, with a piece of vaudeville.
Even the most gorgeous birds—even, for example, a Norwegian Blue parrot—
can lose all their charms when comatose or dead:

> *Customer (Cleese):* I wish to complain about this parrot what I pur-
>   chased not half an hour ago from this very boutique.
> *Shopkeeper (Palin):* Oh yes, the, uh, the Norwegian Blue . . . What's,
>   uh . . . What's wrong with it?
> *C:* I'll tell you what's wrong with it, my lad. 'E's dead, that's what's wrong
>   with it!
> *S:* No, no, 'e's uh . . . he's resting.
> *C:* Look, matey, I know a dead parrot when I see one, and I'm looking
>   at one right now.
> *S:* No no he's not dead, he's, he's restin'! Remarkable bird, the Norwe-
>   gian Blue, idn'it, ay? Beautiful plumage!
> *C:* The plumage don't enter into it. It's stone dead.

This metaphysical dispute ends with a clear verdict:

> *C:* 'E's not pinin'! 'E's passed on! This parrot is no more! He has ceased
>   to be! 'E's expired and gone to meet 'is maker!
> 'E's a stiff! Bereft of life, 'e rests in peace! If you hadn't nailed 'im to the
>   perch 'e'd be pushing up the daisies!
> 'Is metabolic processes are now 'istory! 'E's off the twig!
> 'E's kicked the bucket, 'e's shuffled off 'is mortal coil, run down the cur-
>   tain and joined the bleedin' choir invisible!!
> THIS IS AN EX-PARROT!!![1]

[1] The famous Monty Python "Dead Parrot" sketch, first broadcast in 1969. There is no such
bird, alas, and no endemic parrots of any kind in Norway, though paleontologists have recently
found fossil remains in Denmark of a very early parrot species, *Mopsitta tanta* (but dated fifty-five
million years ago, before the formation of the Norwegian fjords!): see David Waterhouse et al.,
"Two New Fossil Parrots," *Paleontology* 51, no. 3 (May 2008).

Colour and Form

Animation is not, of course, the only feature of a bird's physical appearance that draws us to it. There is a group of other qualities such as size, form, shape, colour, and patterning that play an important part too, sometimes in interaction with one another or with a bird's characteristic movements. These are the factors we are usually referring to when we talk of a bird being "beautiful." There's a strong temptation to produce another list at this point—which birds do you, or people in general, find most beautiful and why? There's no shortage of candidates or of answers in popular culture and in our poetry and prose literature. To start with, let's look at some of the claims made for ten possible international choices—swan, crane, peacock, hummingbird, bird of paradise, bee-eater, kingfisher, quetzal, hyacinth macaw, and satyr tragopan—all of which have had their devotees. We plunge deep into subjective judgements here, but I shall want to argue that they are indeed "judgements" and can therefore be discussed, criticised, refined, and often agreed on. At any rate there are enough shared preferences to make it possible to generalise about the sources and stimuli for our reactions, even if the reactions themselves turn out in the end to be personal and anthropomorphising in some limiting way. That after all is a large part of what we are investigating. The more serious difficulty, in fact, is that all the relevant physical elements—such as size, shape, pattern, and colour—that one wants to analyse are fully integrated in the design of the living bird and have their strongest effects in combination. I do treat them separately in order to make some points about the special contribution each quality can make, but this is in the end an artificial procedure. We shall also find that we want to broaden the notion of "catwalk" beauty to include kinds of physical attractiveness better described by terms like "magnificent," "subtle," or "delicate." With these important qualifications, then, let us look more closely at the beauty parade and assess both the candidates and the judges.

Size seems to matter in the case of the first three species, possibly the first four. The swan, crane, and peacock are all conspicuously large birds, commonly regarded as "statuesque" or "stately." The combination of size with an appropriate bearing and movement contributes powerfully to this impression, of course. Consider the swan (in this context usually the mute swan, in its natural medium on water) gliding smoothly but strongly, with arched neck and wings slightly raised like sails, massive enough to evoke respect, even apprehension, but gracefully proportioned. The size remains impressive in flight, and is further expressed in the rhythmic wingbeats, but on land it makes the bird come across more as threatening than beautiful as it stumps about rather awkwardly. Here then is an early pointer—the medium affects the message.[1] There is colour only in the beak, the eye, and the legs (usually invisible), and the bird's overall whiteness seems to emphasise the lineaments of size and form as well as feeding into associations of purity that we register only at some deeper level.

> With that I saw two swans of goodly hew
> Come swimming softly down along the lee;
> Two fairer birds I yet did never see . . .
> So purely white they were,
> That even the gentle stream, the which them bare,
> Seemed foul to them, and bade his billows spare
> To wet their silken feathers, lest they might
> Soil their fair plumes with water not so fair,
> And mar their beauties bright,
> That shone as heaven's light,
> Against their bridal day, which was not long:
> Sweet Thames! Run softly, till I end my song.
> (Edmund Spenser, *Prothalamion*)

The crane has something of the same stately bearing, in this case usually on land, where its long legs and neck and the elegant "bustle" behind give it a special grace of movement, whether rocking gently forward as it probes the ground or displaying excitedly with others in the famous "crane dance." Its size can startle and impress, especially if it is standing near a lapwing, which we think of as a medium-sized bird, or a heron, which we think of as a large one. In fact almost everything about the crane impresses, as I suggested before in my section on charismatic birds (pp. 28–31, 50), and contributes to its symbolic role in many different cultures and genres. Here is a tiny selection from the many available quotations:

> These elegant birds, in their stature, grace and beauty, their wild fierce temperament, are striking metaphors for the vanishing wilderness of our once bountiful earth. (Peter Matthiessen, U.S. naturalist, *The Birds of Heaven*)

> Cool seascape with cranes
> Wading long-legged in the tideway pools

---

[1] Interestingly, wild swans (Bewick's and whoopers) seem more beautiful in flight, perhaps because of their sonorous bugling calls and one's knowledge of their long migrations from Arctic lands.

Between Shigoshi's dunes
(Basho, seventeenth-century Japanese poet, haiku)

The cranes were dancing a cotillion as surely as it was danced at Volusia.
Two stood apart, erect and white, making a strange music that was part
cry and part singing. The rhythm was irregular, like the dance. The other
birds were in a circle. In the heart of the circle, several moved counter-
clockwise. The musicians made their music. The dancers raised their
wings and lifted their feet, first one and then the other. They sunk their
heads deep in their snowy breasts, lifted them and sunk again. They
moved soundlessly, part awkwardness, part grace. The dance was sol-
emn. Wings fluttered, rising and falling like outstretched arms. The
outer circle shuffled around and around. The group in the centre attained a slow frenzy. . . . Suddenly all motion ceased. (Marjorie Kinnan
Rawlings, twentieth-century U.S. novelist, *The Yearling*)

> Now they are standing close together
> Others are flying
> Closely approaching
> Others are following from Karangarri
> They are remembering
> Now they are telling
> Others are flying from Karangarri
> (Didjeridu song, traditional Australian Aborigine)

In the case of the male peacock, it is the size of its organ of sexual display
that counts, that extraordinarily overdeveloped tail, shimmering with coloured
eyes and rattling with excitement (see plate 6a). The peacock's tail[1] posed a serious problem for Darwin. He wanted to say that its evolution was powered
and controlled by female sexual selection—the males with the biggest and
brightest tails standing the best chance of attracting desirable mates. But a tail
of these proportions was surely an impediment to mobility and therefore a
threat to survival. How could it possibly be worth the peacock's while to carry
that disadvantage? Darwin thought that female choice in this respect was
purely aesthetic and nonutilitarian, on the model of human aesthetic sense.

---

[1] We always call this the "tail," but as Gilbert White characteristically noted (letter 35, to Thomas
Pennant, 1771), he "could not help observing" that the train in fact consists of hugely elongated
upper-tail coverts, which are propped up by the short stiff brown feathers that form the true tail
and act as a fulcrum.

He suggested that "the most refined beauty may serve as a charm for the female, and for no other purpose" *(The Descent of Man),* and a hostile (male) reviewer of the book in 1871 noted that this seemed to make male physical characteristics alarmingly dependent on what he called "the instability of a vicious feminine caprice." In any case, this just seems to defer the problem—why should females make such perverse choices? The difficulty is of course not necessarily an objection to Darwinism as such, since the same problem would seem to present itself to the opposing supporters of "intelligent design": why *is* this an intelligent design? The question is not as yet fully resolved, but the difficulty does serve to underline just how beautiful that tail must be, to us and to peahens.

Size may also be a factor in our attraction to hummingbirds, in this case their lack of it. People are often mesmerised by these tiny jewels, fizzing in all directions like supercharged bumblebees. The wonderful coloration and unpredictable movement are surely enhanced by the tiny proportions of a creature small enough to penetrate a flower, as much insect or moth as bird (the French name is in fact *oiseau-mouche*). W. H. Hudson makes all these connections:

> After all that has been written, the first sight of a living hummingbird, so unlike in its beauty all other beautiful things, comes like a revelation to the mind. The minute, exquisite form, when the bird hovers on misty wings, probing the flowers with its coral spear, the fan-like tail expanded, and poising motionless, exhibits the feathers shot with many hues; and the next moment vanishes, or all but vanishes, then reappears at another flower only to vanish again, and so on successively, showing its splendours not continuously, but like intermitted flashes of the firefly—this forms a picture of airy grace and loveliness that baffles description. *(The Naturalist in La Plata)*

And, again, it is the connections that are important. Extremes of size are not by themselves usually sufficient to excite an aesthetic reaction rather than just one of crude astonishment: I wouldn't say that ostriches, emus, cassowaries, and rheas were made especially beautiful by their mighty dimensions, striking though they may be. Hummingbirds, on the other hand, incorporate such a combination of attractions that they can overcome the disadvantages even of immobility and death. John Gould's exhibit of 320 different species of the tiniest and most colourful birds in the world was undoubtedly one of the highlights of the Great Exhibition of 1851.

The Victorian public flocked to see these "tresses of the day star," as Charles Dickens called them in his rave review in *Household Words,* and the Queen herself noted in her journal for 10 June of that year, after leading a full state

INTERIOR OF THE HUMMING-BIRD HOUSE, IN THE GARDENS OF THE ZOOLOGICAL SOCIETY

30. John Gould's hummingbird display in the Great Exhibition of 1851
(*Illustrated London Magazine*)

visit with Prince Albert and her entourage, "It is the most beautiful and complete collection ever seen, and it is impossible to imagine anything so lovely as
these little hummingbirds, their variety, and the extraordinary brilliancy of
their colours." The word "complete" here is interesting, of course. Linnaeus had
known just eighteen species of hummers, while Gould had organised the collection of more than three hundred, many only recently discovered and named
at the time. This was yet another impressive demonstration of the reach and
power of British influence, the taking of a new species being, as *Household
Words* explained, one of the most prestigious forms of plunder to be had from
a foreign country. Not everyone was admiring, however. The great field naturalist W. H. Hudson, whom I quoted above, found Gould's personal collection
of stuffed specimens deeply artificial and depressing:

> I had just left tropical nature behind me across the Atlantic, and the un-
> expected meeting with a transcript of it in a dusty room in Bedford
> Square gave me a distinct shock. Those pellets of dead feathers, which
> had long ceased to sparkle and shine, stuck with wires—not invisible—
> over blossoming cloth and tinsel bushes, how melancholy they made me
> feel. (Hudson, *Idle Days in Patagonia*)

He goes on to accuse Gould of being an addicted collector rather than a real
lover of nature, someone who "regarded natural history principally as a 'science

of dead animals—a necrology.' " Hudson was right about Gould's lack of field experience. Gould himself based his great monograph on hummingbirds (1849–61) on the inspection of skins and he commissioned others to collect all the birds for him for that study and for the Great Exhibition. He did not actually see a live hummer until 1857, when the monograph was well advanced and well after the Great Exhibition that had celebrated the birds' attractions so successfully.

Form, shape, and *proportion* are closely related to function, of course, but "fitness for function" is not by itself usually held to be sufficient to define beauty. You could say that any bird that has evolved thus far and has survived is by definition "fit for purpose," but not all adaptations of form strike us as especially beautiful. By "form" here I mean just the two-dimensional silhouettes or the three-dimensional architecture, abstracted from other properties. For example, puffins and penguins are thought very lovable, mainly I suspect because of their upright humanoid posture and cuddly shape,[1] and they are wonderful swimming machines, but they would not usually be described as "beautiful" for these reasons. Pigeons surely have heads too small and hawfinches heads too large? The legs of the turnstone make it look squat, those of the stilt can appear spindly. The crane and the swan (on water) again score well on design structure, but I would suggest that the most attractively proportioned birds in general are the smaller wading birds, especially those of the sandpiper family, and among those perhaps in particular the wood sandpiper, which has always seemed to me to have a physical structure in perfect balance between its different elements. Some flight silhouettes also have a grace of form approaching beauty, though it is hard to see these in isolation from the functions they serve: the lissom elegance of the swallow and the hurtling bolt the peregrine becomes; the swift, "with wings and tail as sharp and narrow / As if the bow had flown off with the arrow" (Edward Thomas); the outlines of the red kite, the frigate bird, long-tailed skua, and the arctic tern, all cases where the tail streamers combine with the angled wings to give a beautiful effect of lightness and buoyancy (see fig. 31).

Birds en masse can have their own attractions through the form and shape of the flock, behaving like some larger organism.[2] Think of the swirling clouds of starlings before a roost, shaping and reshaping themselves like a shoal of

[1] See pp. 43–44 above. The scientific name for the large penguin family is *Spheniscidae,* meaning "wedge-shaped."

[2] The mechanisms of communication that make this possible are still not fully understood but it is unlikely to be the kind of telepathy suggested in a seriously dotty book by Edmund Selous that appeared in 1931 under the wonderful title *Thought Transference (or What?) in Birds.* He was, however, a very good field naturalist and the book contains some excellent, if rather repetitive, descriptions of these communal displays in a wide range of species.

31. Flight silhouettes: (a) swallow; (b) swift; (c) arctic tern; (d) long-tailed skua;
(e) peregrine; (f) red kite; (g) frigate bird

fish or a swarm of bees (fig. 32). Or a densely packed group of many thousand knot pouring over a mudflat like a fast-moving raincloud. Or a looser skein of geese or cranes, first stretched out in the sky, then whiffling to the ground and forming a new and different unity there. These effects too are a function of size, scale, and form.

Pattern is a sort of link between form and colour, the shapes within shapes, formed by different shades and hues. The bee-eater is a conspicuous example of a bold patterning effect produced by bright and strongly contrasting colours. But we should remember that there are subtle pleasures to be had as well as *sensations fortes*. In my view some of the loveliest patterning effects come from much more delicate and irregular shading in a range of subdued colours like brown and grey. I think, for example, of the nightjar, woodcock, and wry-neck, all beautifully marked for camouflage purposes; or even the humble dunnock, which came to mind in the Volga Delta. And the drake smew and the black-throated diver in summer plumage show what can be done with a very limited palette of black, grey, and white. This sort of perception really does vary by person and place, though it can be learned over time. An eye accustomed to the watery light and flat landscapes of East Anglia in England may initially find a tropical landscape just too dramatic and glaring to see

32. Starling flock with peregrine in Rome (photo: "Sky Chase," Manuel Presti)

properly, while the virtues of the former may be so understated as to be invisible to an inhabitant of the latter. In winter in the Cambridge Fens, for example, light and colour drain away very fast in the afternoon, and to adapt another dictum from Yogi Berra, "It gets late early out there."[1]

Colour is clearly a major attractant and must figure centrally in the qualifications of almost all the birds on my initial list. Of those not so far discussed, the birds of paradise must be among the most gorgeously coloured. This is David Attenborough's bird of choice, though the reason he revealingly gives is not so much that he wanted to see it as that he wanted to film it. His particular favourite is the blue bird of paradise, which "hangs upside down and makes a noise like a malfunctioning electronic device and throbs in sync with it, with a cloud of azure ultramarine gossamer." An earlier explorer reacted with similar enthusiasm:

> The bird itself [the great bird of paradise] is nearly as large as a crow, and is of a rich coffee brown colour. The head and neck is of a pure

[1] He was actually referring to left field in baseball, and specifically to Yankee Stadium in New York, where the shadows from the edifice greatly reduce the midafternoon light in that part of the pitch.

straw yellow above, and rich metallic green beneath. The long plumy tufts of golden orange feathers spring from the sides beneath each wing, and when the bird is in repose are partly concealed by them. At the time of its excitement, however, the wings are raised vertically over the back, the head is bent down and stretched out, and the long plumes are raised up and expanded till they form two magnificent golden fans striped with deep red at the base, and fading off into the pale brown tint of the finely divided and softly waving points. The whole bird is then overshadowed by them, the crouching body, yellow head, and emerald green throat forming but the foundation and setting to the golden glory which waves above. When seen in this attitude the Bird of Paradise really deserves its name, and must be ranked as one of the most beautiful and most wonderful of living things. (Alfred Russel Wallace, *The Malay Archipelago*, 1869)

Similar encomia could be culled for the bee-eater and kingfisher, of course. The hyacinth macaw is an interesting case—the collectors' choice. This is the largest and most spectacular of the blue macaws, all of which have excited the interest and greed of professional collectors, to the point where they are either endangered or already extinct. The big four (plate 6b) are the glaucous (extinct), Lear's (down to about 750), Spix's (declared extinct in the wild in 2001), and hyacinth (rare and under pressure, with a retail value of some fifteen thousand U.S. dollars). Is blue a special trigger? Certainly the blue flash of a departing kingfisher is electric both in appearance and effect, and the metallic blue of the swallow's back is a powerful attractant too. The natural and cultural history of blue as a colour is interesting in itself, as Tony Juniper remarks in wondering why the blue parrots are so desirable:

Blue land animals are rare. There aren't any blue mammals and very few blue birds. Since earliest times people have placed a great value on blue and gone to great lengths to manufacture the colour. Plants from the genus *Isatis* (woad) yielded a blue dye called indigo that once held great ceremonial importance. Later on, this plant attained considerable commercial value. Until the advent of synthetic dyes, woad was cultivated in great plantations that were for some time a mainstay in some colonial economies. Indigo was, for example, the main export of El Salvador until coffee took over in the 1870s. (*Spix's Macaw*, p. 63)

One might quibble about blue mammals (there are blue whales, blue bulls, and blue sheep?), but what is certainly true is that blue parrots have always been greatly prized, and priced accordingly. The same is of course true of

33. A one quetzal coin from Guatemala

many other brightly coloured and rare parrots. It is an agreeable fancy, as Juniper says, that Long John Silver spent so long in search of buried treasure when something of far greater value may actually have been sitting on his shoulder. In fact the internal evidence in Robert Louis Stevenson's *Treasure Island* (1883) is inconclusive, but Captain Flint was probably one of the Amazon "green" parrots.

The quetzal is the Aztecs' choice, a bird so beautiful that they worshipped it (as had the Mayas before them) as the "god of the air" and a symbol of goodness and light. The full name is the "resplendent quetzal," and the male bird is resplendent indeed with a red breast and a green body that can iridesce anywhere in the range from green-gold to blue-violet. Today it is Guatemala's national bird and perhaps the only bird to have given its name to a whole currency (the quetzal, or GTQ, which was adopted in 1925); much earlier, in Mayan times, the long tail-covert feathers effectively *were* the currency since they were widely used for trading purposes.

The last bird on my list, the satyr tragopan of the Himalayan foothills, is on the other hand very much a birders' choice, best described by Mark Cocker in his introduction to *Birders: Tales of a Tribe* and offered there as an explanation of how the experience of a bird like this can have such an effect on a life, how, as he puts it, "the human heart can be shaped by the image of a bird." He saw it for just a few seconds:

> Satyr tragopan is amongst the most beautiful names for any of the world's 10,000 species of bird and a loose translation might be "horned god of the forest." But this is a creature even more lovely than its title. It's a type of pheasant [but] comparing a tragopan to the hand-reared

pheasants we know in Britain is like trying to evoke an Apache warrior by describing a balding overweight London businessman.

Imagine, perhaps, a bird the size of a really large cockerel with an electric blue face, erectile black feather horns that it can raise at will and a body plumage of the deepest blood red. Overlay that magical colour with hundreds of white ocelli so bright they look luminous. Then surround each of the glowing eyes with an intense black margin and you have a sense of this extraordinary creature. And that's only the appearance.

It is time to move on from such appearances to other factors, as Cocker does himself, but first let us enjoy with him the moment of epiphany:

After a long and complicated stalk we all finally got to see the bird itself. For about two or three seconds it was in view as it rushed down a tree stump, from which it had been calling, and ran off over a steep brow—a blur of crimson studded with a hundred silvery eyes. We never saw it again. The horned god was gone. Yet it is still, undoubtedly, the most beautiful, wondrous and thrilling wild bird I've seen in my life.

Art and Nature

The purely physical features I've just surveyed would be relevant to the attractions of most other forms of animate life. Colour and pattern play a large role in our attitudes to flowers, butterflies, and fish; size and form in the case of trees and animals; activity in all cases, I would think (including the nonlocomotive movement of trees and flowers).[1] I leave to a later chapter the discussion of sound, which is mainly (though not exclusively) relevant to birds, and I have little to say here about the senses of smell, touch, and taste, which are least relevant to our perceptions of birds compared to other animate creatures. But what about the rest of the natural world: the inanimate world of the stars, clouds, winds, rivers, mountains, and seas, and the landscape generally? Is that the same or different? Certainly most of the same categories still seem to apply and we use much the same language: we talk of the grandeur of a mountain, the awesome scale of the stars, the expanse of an ocean, the purity of an Arctic or desert scene, the colour, texture, and pattern of woods and fields, the mobile beauty of cloud forms, rivers, and seas; indeed the borderline between the animate and inanimate soon becomes blurred when thinking about landscape.

[1] It's interesting that the other wildlife interests birders seem most naturally to migrate to are dragonflies, butterflies, and moths, all taxa where jizz, colour, and flight are important in identification; and dedicated sea-watchers transfer naturally to cetaceans (whales, dolphins, and porpoises), where size, shape, and movement, usually perceived at a distance, are the key determinants.

We are very drawn by the movement of water, or of the wind across waving grasslands, or of fire, although we know these are not deliberate animated movements like the stoop of the peregrine and the butterfly settling on a flower. But is a flower reaching for the sun, to take an intermediate case, more purposeful and directed than a tree bending in the wind or a waterfall tumbling over rocks? Maybe there's a continuum here? In any case a "landscape" seems to comprise all these elements, both animate and inanimate (as well as human artefacts), so the distinction breaks down that way too.

Perhaps the more important distinction is between the whole of what we think of as the natural world and something more intangible: the world of ideas, imagination, and associations. This sounds promising. Maybe we ourselves supply the context that converts these sensations into something more deeply felt. William Hazlitt, at any rate, was in no doubt that our attachment to natural objects and the beauty we find in them has another source altogether from the immediate objects of our attention. He concedes the sort of descriptions I gave above:

> No doubt, the sky is beautiful; the clouds sail majestically along its bosom; the sun is cheering; there is something exquisitely graceful in the manner in which a plant or a tree puts forth its branches; the motion with which they bend and tremble in the evening breeze is soft and lovely; there is music in the babbling of a brook; the view from the top of a mountain is full of grandeur; nor can we behold the ocean with indifference . . .

but concludes that the true source of all these notions is from "the recollections habitually associated with them," that is from "the association of ideas." It turns out, though, that the recollections he means are of earlier experiences of the same kind and the associations are therefore just generic ones:

> Thus Nature is a kind of universal home, and every object it presents to us an old acquaintance with unaltered looks. . . . For him, then, who has well acquainted himself with Nature's works, she wears always one face, and speaks the same well-known language, striking on the heart, amidst unquiet thoughts and the tumult of the world, like the music of one's native tongue heard in some far-off country. (Hazlitt, "On the Love of the Country")

He puts all this very nicely but it only seems to defer the problem to an earlier stage. Why did we feel like that in the first place? The question about the source of the attraction therefore stands. Nor does this explain the pleasures of novelty, surprise, and *discovery* we may feel when we find what is for us an unusual bird "in some far-off country," as I was in the Volga Delta. Here it is the *contrast* with the familiar that matters, surely, even if the distinction between the exotic and the familiar later becomes more blurred or complicated, as again it did for me in the case of the Central Park warblers, with which I became sated.

Wordsworth makes a more radical association of ideas. He sees the ultimate source of our reactions to nature, in this case his feelings at the sight of the River Wye above Tintern Abbey on 17 July 1798, in something Other, which is Out There (or perhaps In There?):

> . . . And I have felt
> A presence that disturbs me with the joy
> Of elevated thoughts; a sense sublime
> Of something far more interfused
> Whose dwelling is the light of setting suns,
> And the round ocean and the living air
> And the blue sky, and in the mind of man:
> A motion and a spirit, that impels
> All living things, all objects of all thought,
> And rolls through all things.

We are thus led out of ourselves, but then in the immediately following passage (which is less often quoted), back again to nature:

> . . . all things. Therefore am I still
> A lover of the meadows and the woods,
> And mountains; and of all that we behold
> From this green earth; of all the mighty world
> Of eye and ear,—both what they half create,
> And what perceive; well pleased to recognise
> In nature and the language of the sense
> The anchor of my purest thoughts, the nurse,
> The guide, the guardian of my heart, and soul
> Of all my moral being.

This sort of approach will appeal to those who want some ultimate, *external* reason and justification for our most passionate feelings about nature, whether they think of that as God, Gaia, Cosmos, a Platonic Form, or some other transcendent agent beyond human imagining. This is a more spiritual response, for some a religious response—whether the god in question is outside the world or, as here, somehow infused with it in a kind of pantheism. Such an explanation certainly does more justice to the strength of our aesthetic reactions to nature and the sense of connection or communion we may feel with something that is both larger than ourselves and includes ourselves. But do we really need metaphysics as well as physics to explain this? And are we now in danger of forgetting the relevance of context and our own powers of imagination and association?

Oscar Wilde had a more outrageous thought, as you might expect. He didn't much like nature anyway. In his essay mischievously called "The Decay of Lying" (1889), his spokesman complains that "nature is so uncomfortable. Grass is hard and lumpy and damp, and full of dreadful black insects." He argues that, far from art imitating nature, it is the other way round. Nature is just an unsatisfactory imitation of art. Once art has created something unique and wonderful it then moves on, but nature bores us with repetition:

> Nobody of any real culture, for instance, ever talks nowadays about the beauty of a sunset. Sunsets are quite old-fashioned. They belong to the time when Turner was the last note in art. To admire them is a distinct sign of provincialism of temperament. Upon the other hand they go on. Yesterday evening Mrs. Arundel insisted on my going to the window, and looking at the glorious sky, as she called it. . . . And what was it? It was simply a very second-rate Turner, a Turner of a bad period, with all the painter's worst faults exaggerated and overemphasised.

In the same vein he asks:

> Where, if not from the Impressionists, do we get these wonderful brown fogs that come creeping down our streets, blurring the gas-lamps and changing the houses into monstrous shadows? To whom, if not to them and their master, do we owe the lovely silver mists that brood over the river, and turn to faint forms of fading grace curved bridge and swaying barge? The extraordinary change that has taken place in the climate of London during the last ten years is entirely due to a particular school of art.

Well, there's a novel explanation of climate change that might appeal in some quarters. Banish the artists, close down the galleries, forget about carbon footprints—and we might yet save the planet! Of course, Wilde only says it to tease, but there's a serious point here too. We do have to *learn* to see things, and as I suggested in chapter 4, we look at a lot of things we don't at first really see. Art is one factor in shaping our perceptions, and is probably more pervasive than those who think they aren't interested in art realise. In the case of birds the illustrations in our guides and reference books certainly affect how we see them, as I tried to show in my very brief survey: they shape our expectations and can limit or extend them. But there must also be more to it than this. It can't just be that we derive our sense of beauty wholly from our own artistic creations and project that back on nature. Flowers don't only become beautiful because we make beautiful representations of them. They have objective qualities we are responding to subjectively.

We need to see things both ways simultaneously if we can and acknowledge the force of both objective and subjective aspects of our appreciation of nature.[1] The difficulty is holding them in the mind together. On the one hand, we do inevitably bring to our perceptions a large and rich range of associations, which draws on our emotional lives and needs, and our personal memories and imaginings. Some of this is frankly anthropomorphic, or at least anthropocentric. When we think of a mountain as "bleak," or a crane as "elegant," or a black poplar as "rugged," we know we are referring to a human reaction as well as to what prompted it, not just to a brute physical fact like weight, height, or material composition. But that's where we start from, unavoidably; we're referring to a relationship between a subject and an object, so any description needs to involve both of them; it may or may not be appropriate in context but can at least be recognised and discussed; it won't be true for all times and all people but that doesn't make it less authentic and significant for us now. On the other hand, that doesn't mean that all reactions are equally valid. It isn't just a free-for-all of mushy sentiment. There may be trivialisation, distortion, ignorance, sentimentality, and all manner of misunderstandings in our attitudes to nature as there are in the case of art, and these can then be subjected to the same corrective disciplines of discussion, criticism, and reflection. Just to say, "I know what I like," usually reveals a distinct *lack* of knowledge both of oneself and of the possibilities available in the world.

We should also remember that our ideas of beauty themselves have a history—not only a personal history as we develop and refine our sensibilities through experience, but also a larger cultural history, which has varied by time and place. Robert Macfarlane makes this point in plotting the history of the human fascination with mountains:

> What we call a mountain is thus in fact a collaboration of the physical
> forms of the world with the imagination of humans—a mountain of the

---

[1] I use these chill philosophical terms "objective" and "subjective," which Ruskin called "two of the most objectionable words that were ever coined by the troublesomeness of metaphysicians," because they have nevertheless continued to have currency. See my further references in the note section.

mind. And the way people behave towards mountains has little or nothing to do with the actual objects of rock and ice themselves. Mountains
are only contingencies of geology. They do not kill deliberately, nor do
they deliberately please: any emotional properties which they possess
are vested in them by human imaginations. Mountains—like deserts,
polar tundra, deep oceans, jungles and all other wild landscapes that we
have romanticised into being—are simply there, and there they remain,
their physical structures rearranged gradually over time by the forces of
geology and weather, but continuing to exist over and beyond human
perceptions of them. But they are also the products of human perception; they have been *imagined* into existence down the centuries. (*Mountains of the Mind*, p. 19)

He reminds us, for example, that the current Western ideas of landscape have
their origins very much in the Romantic movement of the nineteenth century.
Dr. Johnson toured some of the finest scenery in Scotland and grumpily dis-
missed as "considerable protuberances" the mountains a later generation was
to find sublime and awe-inspiring. Our general attitudes to nature and wilderness have surely been shaped by our increasing urbanisation and exploitation
of the physical world for human purposes. There is an irony in the thought
that our capacity to enjoy some aesthetic pleasures may be dependent on our
capacity to destroy their source. As Wallace was admiring the extreme beauty
of the birds of paradise, he also reflected on the poignant circumstances in
which he supposed this would be appreciated:

I thought of the long ages past, during which the successive generations
of this little creature [the king bird of paradise] had run their course—
year by year being born, and living and dying amid these dark and
gloomy woods, with no intelligent eye to gaze upon their loveliness;
to all appearances such a waste of beauty. Such ideas excite a feeling
of melancholy. It seems sad, that on the one hand such exquisite creatures should live out their lives and exhibit their charms only in these
wild inhospitable regions, doomed for ages yet to come to hopeless
barbarism; while on the other hand, should civilised man ever reach
these distant lands, and bring moral, intellectual and physical light into
the recesses of these virgin forests, we may be sure he will so disturb the
nicely-balanced relations of organic and inorganic nature as to cause the
disappearance, and finally the extinction, of these very beings whose
wonderful structure and beauty he alone is fitted to appreciate and
enjoy.

NATIVES OF ARU SHOOTING THE GREAT BIRD OF PARADISE.

34. Aru hunters in New Guinea (from Alfred Russel Wallace,
The Malay Archipelago, 1869)

This may well be doubly mistaken: first, the "barbaric" Aru could evidently make similar discriminations, since they hunted the most attractive birds and prized their plumage for ornamentation as well as exchange; second, and more important, birds of paradise are themselves presumably "fitted to appreciate and enjoy" (one might quibble over "enjoy") other birds of paradise and are almost certainly sensitive to more visual distinctions between them than we are, hence the evolution of these natural extravagances. Wallace goes on, however, to reach the right, nonanthropocentric conclusion:

This consideration must surely tell us that all living things were *not* made for man. Many of them have no relation to him. Their cycle of existence has gone on independently of his, and ... their happiness and enjoyments, their loves and hates, their struggles for existence, their vigorous life and death, would seem to be immediately related to their own well-being and perpetuation alone, limited only by the equal well-being and perpetuation of the numberless other organisms with which each is more or less intimately connected.

Our sense of ourselves as a species—the ways we are both like and unlike other species—has changed with the progressive acceptance and understanding of Darwinian ideas about evolution. That process will go further and may eventually give us a better understanding at a biological level of the origins of some of our specifically human values. That won't make them less real though, or less deeply felt. "Birds are beautiful" remains more than just a good slogan. It is a fact of life, a fact about some of *our* lives.

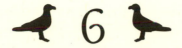

6

The Sense of Sound

A bird does not sing because it has an answer—
it sings because it has a song.
Old Chinese proverb

If I keep a green bough in my heart, a singing
bird will come.
Another old Chinese proverb

Little Thurlow, Suffolk, 18 May 1997

It is 3.30 AM and I've walked down the lane to a little wood to wait for the dawn chorus. This is the dark before the dawn, the silence before the crescendo of early morning sound that is one of the most exciting (and available) experiences in the natural world. You can hear it in a muffled kind of way from bed but you really need to be out there to get the full effect—it's the difference between attending a live concert and listening to a cheap tape through earphones. And there's the same sense of hushed expectation before the concert begins. It's never absolutely quiet, of course. The murmur of conversation here takes the form of the soughing poplars, the running stream, and a host of invisible and unidentifiable rustlings in the undergrowth. There is the occasional hoot from a tawny owl and one loud klaxon note from a pheasant. I thought I heard the soft call of a moorhen down by the river too. I am concentrating hard, waiting for the first real song, and feeling a delicious sense of anticipation. I know in a general way what is coming but I don't know quite how the performance will go this morning. The official time of sunrise today is 0502 BST but the birds usually start about an hour earlier at this time of year. I count down the minutes. Then at last at 0405 a robin sings softly close by and breaks the tension, quickly followed by several other robins, then the song thrush and dunnock at 0406, blackbird at 0407, wood pigeon at 0410, and wren at 0411. I am writing these times down in the dark with the aid of a little pocket torch, but by the time the blackcap comes in at 0421, the great tit at

0425, and the chiffchaff at 0426, there are streaks of light in the east. The volume of noise is now simply tremendous but I still haven't actually *seen* a single bird. The cuckoo joins the chorus at 0436, the chaffinch at 0441, and the turtle dove at 0459; and by the time of the official dawn at 0502 I have pretty much the full orchestra playing. By 0600 I have heard some twenty-five different species in song but the peak of noise is past and the great excitement has subsided; the birds are now having to combine singing with other necessary activities such as feeding, copulation, and housework, all of which are easier in the light. I brush the dew from my beard and head home. The final performer is *Homo sapiens,* delivering the papers at 0615 and whistling a feeble little jingle, rather like blackbird subsong, I fancy.

This performance is repeated every day, reaching peak intensity and volume in April and May in the northern hemisphere. The regularities are very striking. I started doing dawn choruses as a young boy in the Colchester area of Essex and still have all the records my brother and I kept then. The order of entrants is largely invariable and the time of day they start up on any particular date is almost exactly the same to the minute every year, just varying a bit by the prevailing light conditions and weather. (And interestingly, at the other end of the day, in the "dusk chorus," they bow out pretty much in reverse order.) There are other variations that depend on one's exact location and some chance factors. For example, I would have expected to hear the local mistle thrush at about 0430 this morning (wonder why it's usually so much later than the song thrush, despite singing from a high perch?), but that didn't figure at all this particular day (a fatal accident?). And if I'd been nearer the open fields I would have heard the skylark first, catching the early light in the open fields. Then there are the larger variations by latitude and longitude, of course. But otherwise for each location it is very predictable: in mine the robin, song thrush, and blackbird all come in first (perhaps because they all have large eyes and better night vision?); a little later on the warblers, the tits, the dunnock, and wren; and so on to relatively late risers like the finches and buntings.

You can check it out. But to do that you need to be able to identify the songs, which is in any case a skill well worth learning and not so difficult. Most species have very distinctive songs and calls and if you take the trouble to get to know them this is by far the easiest way to find and identify birds at this time of year since you always hear so much more than you see, particularly in woodlands and hedgerows. With practice you can even begin to identify individual birds, which isn't so remarkable when you think how easy we find it to recognise a friend's voice on the phone. We must assume that birds can identify one other just as effectively, if not more so. Moreover, some birds seem to have their own regional dialects, which like humans they learn from their families and neighbours, so you can learn to tell a Yorkshire chaffinch from a Suffolk one by its phrasing and rhythms.[1] Birds don't just sing for pleasure, of course—either theirs or ours. In spring and summer the dawn chorus is very much a male choir, and they are using their voices to express their virility and so defend their territories, attract their mates, and defeat their rivals. That's not such a bad system, when you think of the human alternatives, but it does make you wonder if "singing" is necessarily the best description of what they are doing.

There are many unsolved problems to do with bird songs and calls that are basically scientific questions about bird biology and behaviour. For example, we don't really know why they do all sing so early; or whether the songs are in fact more elaborated than they need be for strictly functional purposes (the peacock's tail problem again). But the questions that most interest me here are those that relate more directly to the themes of this book. How important is the dimension of sound to our response to birds? How does identification by ear compare with identification by eye and what cues does it rely on? How can we best represent and remember these? How does our appreciation of birdsong compare with our appreciation of the other forms of beauty I considered in the last chapter and what are the criteria? Is it affected in the same ways by association and context? And are the obvious and tempting analogies with human language and music actually helpful or do they lead to yet new forms of misunderstanding, sentimentality, and anthropomorphism?

Sound and Silence

Birders who are much concerned with their personal lists and records and have a strongly competitive approach to their activities are, as I described in chapter 4, liable to curious neuroses and anxieties. One of the more absurd of these is the earnest worry as to whether they can "count" a bird identified by sound alone. What a relief to have an easy question at last. Of course you can! That is precisely how, usually, you do identify a corncrake or a quail in the grass, a nightingale in a thicket, a grasshopper warbler or a bittern in a marsh, whimbrel or redwing migrating high overhead through misty cloud, a nightjar on a heath at dusk, and a tawny owl at midnight. It's nice to catch sight of these birds as well, but you don't need to do so in order to be sure what they

---

[1] It's hard to say whether some of these dialects are in fact more than just geographical variations, but certainly the chaffinches of Eastern Europe, for example, have a very distinctive *tic* at the end of the song sequence, which has no counterpart in the standard British chaffinch song. Is "dialect" a description or an analogy?

are, and they can all be very elusive. In fact, the only interesting thing about this question is why it should arise at all. I shall have a lot more to say later about the importance of sound-recognition in identification but I want first just to stand back and muse more generally about the role of sound in our world.

Ever since Aristotle it has been assumed in Western culture that sight is the primary sense, followed by hearing and the others in some sort of descending sequence.[1] Our whole language is infused with this assumption. "I see," we say, meaning "I understand." Similarly, even when the contexts are not primarily visual ones we use expressions like: "see for yourself," "I see where you are coming from" (ugh), "watch what you're saying," "look after him," "mark my words," "point to a solution," and "show me." (Indeed, Missouri calls itself the "Show Me" State, to indicate its sturdy scepticism and even displays this slogan on its licence plates.) The same assumptions get incorporated into idiom and proverbial wisdom: "second sight," "only have eyes for," "seeing is believing," "the writing is on the wall," "love is blind," "show your hand," and so on. Even God is implicated. "Let there be Light" is his first instruction in Genesis and after each day's labour he is only satisfied when "He saw that it was good." There are good practical and biological reasons for this, of course. We rely hugely on sight to interpret the world, navigate in it, and engage with it. But ours is a world of sounds as well as sights and the sense of hearing is sometimes the more important means of experiencing it or interacting with it. Think of human speech itself, and our extraordinary (and universal) ability to decode meaning from different tones of voice. It is the voice, not the content, that often most moves us in politics as in poetry and love, which is why when the Conservative government under Mrs. Thatcher wished to neutralise the impact of the Sinn Fein leader Gerry Adams at a critical stage in Anglo-Irish relations, it banned not his words or face on television but his actual *voice*. Think also of the crucial role of sound in communications media like telephones and TV, in music, entertainment, play, and city life, and the natural sounds of river, sea, wind, and fire, which are as much a part of the significance of these phenomena for us as is their visual appearance.

Even in our own tradition there have been myths that recognise this. In Alain de Lille's epic *Anticlaudianus* (1183), the senses are represented by five horses that pull a carriage conveying Prudence and Wisdom to the higher regions of the planetary system. But the coach cannot penetrate the heavenly

[1] Aristotle, *On Sense and Sensibilia*, 437a, though as usual he goes on to make some interesting distinctions. He says sight is the most important sense for dealing with "life's necessities" but hearing is the most important for the mind because of its connection with speech.

35. Bartolemeo Delbene's *Gate of Hearing*, from *Civitas Veri*, 1609

mysteries and Theology persuades Prudence to abandon the coach. She un-harnesses one of the horses, Hearing, and rides on with him alone. In another very striking allegory, in the didactic poem *Civitas Veri* (City of Truth, 1609) by the Florentine author Bartolemeo Delbene, the soul is pictured as a city with five gates representing the senses; and it is through the Gate of Hearing that the poet is led to the innermost temples because it is through speech and hearing that the most important truths are transmitted.

Moreover, not all cultures privilege sight over the other senses as we tend to do. For the last twenty-five hundred years or more we have been heirs to an al-phabet, to the ability to read, write, record, document, and later to print, film, televise, and digitise. Our culture has been dominated by vision as the most important means of acquiring and transmitting knowledge. This is what, liter-ally, gives us our "picture" of the world. But as you might expect, oral or non-literate cultures may sense the world quite differently and they thereby remind us that there are other dimensions or, if you like, other worlds to be perceived as well. Constance Classen describes cultures that appear to order the world principally by sound (the Andean Incas), temperature (the Tzotzil of Mexico), smell (the Ongee of the Andaman Islands), and colour (the Desana of Colom-bia). Colour, in this last case, is described as "colour energies"—very different, it seems, from the visuality of the West with our emphasis on detached obser-vation and surface appearance. It can be hard for us to imagine, or even quite believe in, these alternative ways of responding to the natural world and conceptualising it, but it is liberating at least to try. And liberation may be the thing more literally at stake for some, as Classen explains:

> Andean culture was exclusively oral until its encounter with European civilisation in the sixteenth century. The Inca empire itself, with a population of approximately ten million, was organised without the aid of writing. The abrupt introduction of writing which occurred with the Spanish Conquest disrupted the continuity of the oral traditions of the Andes and presented an alien system of ordering the world.
>
> The deeply traumatic experience of the Conquest for the Andeans infected the local conception of writing. Thus, while in the West writing has tended to be viewed as the *sine qua non* of civilisation, the inhabitants of the Andes perceive it as a sorcerous tool of conquest, employed by the Spanish to silence the collaborative oral dynamics of the Andean world and impose an exploitative sight-based culture onto it. (*The Five Senses,* p. 10)

Similar examples could easily be culled from other parts of the world. We think of the spread of literacy as so obviously a benefit and a political priority that we forget there may be losses in how we hear the world as well as gains in how we manage it.

Silence has its own huge significance too, by way of contrast with our ever-present experience of noise, or certain kinds of noise. We have one-minute silences in crowds, silent prayers, silent rooms, and silent carriages on trains. In speech itself we convey a great deal in the pauses between words or sentences, whether in ordinary conversation or in a more studied way in telling jokes, in theatrical performances, or in political addresses. This is taken to some sort of logical extreme in the famous "composition" by the postmodern composer John Cage entitled 4′33″, which calls for exactly four minutes and thirty-three seconds of complete silence (to be performed by any instrument or combination of instruments). This is invariably followed by admiring applause for the orchestra, I gather.

There is never complete silence, of course, only different kinds and degrees of internal and ambient noise. In the natural world too silence is only ever relative, but the silence of remoteness or night can greatly enhance the quality of one's listening:

> I went down towards the wood. A tawny owl called *kee-wick,* the first true sound of night. Slowly I walked down the long slope of the field and up into the hushed unanimity of oaks that rose on the far side. As I came nearer, they seemed to move apart. Their stillness was dark and

immense, a weight upon the eyes, a pressing-in of the ear-drums. The afterglow in the west reddened the trees' rough bark. I touched it to be sure that it was not some strange luminosity that would come off on to my fingers. My hand cast a faint shadow. The sun had set half an hour before. It was the stillness of the trees that made them so vividly alive. They seemed to be holding themselves upright in a tall silence, like hunters that do not wish to be seen. They were drawing together across the last remaining light, closing in, massing. The soft greyness of the wood was hardening to a unity of black; inimical if you believed the dumb are your enemies. . . . A smoke of sounds drifted from the distant village: the fraying bark of a dog, a dusk of voices.

The tawny owl's dark release of song quavered from the pinewood. The sleek dusk bristled with it, like the fur of a cat. I moved under the gloomy trees. The owl surfed out across the rising night. He could hear the turn of a dry leaf, the relaxing of a twig, the loud scamper of a soft-skinned mouse. To him the silence was a flare of sound, a brilliant day of noises dazzling through the veins of dusk.

J. A. Baker again, who else? One reason why Baker's prose is so striking is his daring in crossing sensory boundaries in phrases like "a smoke of sounds" and "a dusk of voices." We do this, quite unconsciously, in ordinary speech too when we apply visual adjectives to auditory contexts (bright tones, clear voice, dim or blurred sound, the blues, white noise) or the reverse (loud colours, screaming pink); but some other metaphors are more deeply buried and long dead: "absurd" comes from the Latin *surdus* (deaf or mute) and "logical" from the Greek *logos* (word, speech, explanation), both pointing again to the significance of hearing in thought and understanding.

We can perhaps appreciate even more fully the importance of sound in our experience of the world if we consider the extreme consequences of the disabilities of blindness and deafness: in the one case sound becomes all-important and in the other it is largely absent. There are many very moving memoirs of how people have responded to these desperate conditions and I am struck by how often birdsong is mentioned as one of the deprivations in the second case and one of the compensations in the first. In her memoir *The Open Cage,* Phoebe Raddings explains how she herself didn't realise that she had the disability of deafness, so well had she compensated by lip-reading and other means, until she was told about it by her parents at the age of eleven. She then developed an extraordinary repertoire of techniques to enter as far as possible into the world of sound, including placing her fingers on a musical instrument being played or on the throat of a singer to "hear" the vibrations.

She also had the most acute powers of observation of human behaviour and "body language" and could join confidently in conversations and make shrewd judgements about the character and veracity of any speakers she observed. She would even go to concerts with enjoyment and "hear" the music, which she constructed in her mind from the movements of the orchestra and conductor. But the two things she said she really missed were hearing the actual notes of instruments to see if they corresponded to her imaginings and hearing the song of birds, which she had no conception of apart from what she had read.

In another extraordinary memoir, the poet and translator David Wright, who became totally deaf at the age of seven, gives an even more remarkable account of how he converted seen movement into sound. This has a particular relevance here because of the emphasis I gave to animation in the last chapter. Wright talks of movement as "eye-music":

> In my case, silence is not absence of sound but of movement. Suppose it is a calm day, absolutely still, not a twig or a leaf stirring. To me it will seem quiet as a tomb though hedgerows are full of noisy but invisible birds. Then comes a breath of air, enough to unsettle a leaf. I will see and hear that movement like an exclamation. The illusory soundlessness has been interrupted. I see, as if I heard, a visionary noise of wind in a disturbance of foliage. Wordsworth in a late poem exactly caught the phenomenon in a remarkable line: "a soft eye-music of slow-waving boughs."

Wright goes on to explain that some "sounds" he hears, like the sound of gales and rough seas, are probably distant memories of sounds he did once actually hear before deafness struck. Not all, however:

> On the other hand I also live in a world of sounds which are, as I know quite well, imaginary because non-existent. Yet for me they are part of reality. I have sometimes to make a deliberate effort to remember I am not "hearing" anything, because there is nothing to hear. Such non-sounds include the flight and movement of birds, even fish swimming in clear water or the tank of an aquarium. I take it that the flight of most birds, at least at a distance, must be silent—bar the creaking noise made by the wings of swans and some kinds of wild geese. Yet it *appears* audible, each species creating a different "eye-music" from the nonchalant melancholy of seagulls to the staccato flitting of tits.

Probably the best-known account of all these afflictions and how they can be transcended, or at least accommodated, is that of Helen Keller, who suffered both blindness and deafness simultaneously but had this to say about the comparison:

> I am just as deaf as I am blind. The problems of deafness are deeper and more complex, if not more important, than those of blindness. Deafness is a much worse misfortune. For it means the loss of the most vital stimulus—the sound of the voice that brings language, sets thoughts astir and keeps us in the intellectual company of man.

It is no accident that when in 1962 Rachel Carson published her pioneering work warning of the growing dangers to the environment from pesticides and pollution—the book that first inspired conservation movements and Green politics in the West—the title she chose to dramatise the poverty of a world without birds and birdsong was *Silent Spring.*

But despite all this we always talk about bird*watching.* Are we missing something important?

Sounds Different

My opening anecdote of a dawn chorus showed how crucial the dimension of sound was in that context. Obviously so. I couldn't see the birds at all most of the time, I could only hear them; and not only could I identify them all quite easily that way but that was the only way I *could* identify them. To put that more crisply, sound was both the necessary and the sufficient means of identification. A dawn chorus is a very particular kind of occasion, of course, but I think the point has much more general application. There are many environments and occasions when you hear a bird before you see it: nearly always in woodland and reedbeds; often in gardens, countryside, farmland, grasslands, and marshes; commonly with birds in flight. In strictly urban environments, and increasingly near motorways,[1] it is true, the ambient noise restricts one's hearing and both we and the birds rely less on aural cues. And when birding at reservoirs, lakes, estuaries, or in open country we probably find more by eye than ear initially, at least when birds are on the water or the ground. But it is only in the rather specialised activities of sea-watching and raptor-watching that we rely almost wholly on the recognition of flight-silhouettes and visible features. Most of the time and in most places sound trumps sight.

There are good reasons for this, of course. Sound travels round or through visual obstacles like bushes, hedges, crops and trees; it issues from concealing

---

[1] There is some evidence that birds with softer and less far-carrying songs are unable to use the suitable nesting sites in planted motorway verges because they can no longer be heard by others of their species, including prospective mates. And some others are learning to raise the pitch or turn up the volume (the so-called Lombard effect) to counter urban noise.

seawalls, ditches, ledges, moorland, heath, hillocks, and dunes; it approaches us from all sides and at all angles; it reaches us at all times of day and in all light conditions; and it carries just as finely discriminated signals as do visual messages. Most birds prefer to conceal themselves as much as possible, for equally obvious reasons, and rely on sound to a large extent to communicate with one another about life's essentials (sex, territory, food, mutual protection, social solidarity, information-sharing, and so on). Even in the rather extreme environment of a seabird colony on open cliff ledges, which is as visually accessible as anything could be, the chicks and parents can recognise one another's individual voices and use these to home in on the right nests in a very crowded and noisy environment.

There's a sort of analogy here, I suppose, in the extent to which we rely on speech rather than reading for many kinds of verbal communication with one another—wholly so in the case of the nonliterate societies we mentioned. Exclusion from this, as the memoirs of the deaf testify, is potentially a very limiting experience. So why should we exclude ourselves voluntarily from such access as we have to the communications of birds? The range of sounds in which birds operate overlaps substantially with ours so we can overhear many of these exchanges even if we cannot fully understand them.[1]

Moreover, for those who have a special interest in identification this is an essential skill. There are many well-known problem pairs that can most easily, and in some conditions can only, be told apart by sound rather than sight: in Europe, marsh and willow tits, willow warbler and chiffchaff, reed and marsh warbler; in North America, long- and short-billed dowitchers, the empidonax flycatchers, and so on. In many other cases it's just quicker, easier, and more reliable to use your ears when you only get a glimpse of a disappearing wader, pipit, or bunting that nonetheless helpfully calls.

Most field guides pay lip-service to these undeniable facts, but curiously not much more than that. I've just looked through a half dozen on my shelves. They all have a section in the introduction called "Identification," with subheadings on things such as size, moult, behaviour, flight, habitat, and plumage (with those elaborate feather-maps showing things such as median coverts, alula, primary emargination, and so on, any of which you would do well to see with the bird pinned down at two-foot range under arc-lights, let alone in field conditions); and then as a sort of afterthought they include a section on song or voice. These last are almost always quite brief and perfunctory: in

---

[1] Birds communicate at higher frequencies on average than do humans, between 1 and 5 kHz, though reaching up as high as 6 (grasshopper warbler) or even 7 (goldcrest) and as low as 200 Hz (bittern); our hearing is most sensitive between 400 Hz and 3 kHz, but we can hear these extremes too if the volume is sufficient (though the upper limit comes down with age).

North American guides—a half page in the *National Geographic,* one column in Sibley, not at all in Peterson (though a two-paragraph note before the introduction explains the omission and refers readers to some sound recordings), and two pages in the *Golden Guide* (mainly about the sonagrams it unusually includes in the passerine entries as its USP). In European guides—Peterson, one paragraph; the *RSPB Guide,* ed. Hume, not at all—hard to believe; Collins, one paragraph with an earlier note on transcription conventions in the text; Jonsson, one page out of a thirty-page introduction, but a good one. That isn't a very impressive record. It's even more baffling because they usually seem to agree with me: "Song and calls are among birds' most obvious attributes" (Jonsson), "Expert ornithologists often rely on their ears as much as their eyes, to identify birds" (Peterson, *European Guide*), "It is sometimes said that expert birders make 90 percent of their identifications by ear" (Sibley), "A bird's songs and calls not only reveal its presence but also, in many cases, its identity" *(National Geographic).*

Birders will vary in this skill as in others of course, but I have witnessed one or two amazing feats of identification by voice alone. I think the most remarkable was when a buff-bellied (American) pipit, which is an extreme vagrant to the United Kingdom and very similar indeed to the commoner pipits here, both in voice and appearance, was successfully identified in flight on the basis of a single call by Paul Holt on the Isles of Scilly in the autumn of 1996. The rest of us subsequently saw it on the ground, watched it through high-powered telescopes, had a chance to compare its calls with those of the meadow pipits in the same flock, and just about made out all the key features in the course of the day. He just heard one flight note and confidently put a name to it, the second record ever for Scilly at the time and only the fifth ever for Britain. On the other side of the world, the American Ted Parker established an unrivalled reputation for his knowledge of neotropical birds and was said to be able to identify more than four thousand species of bird by sound alone. In the rain forest this is an even more essential skill than elsewhere, but Parker took it to quite a new level by his ability to extrapolate from the known to the unknown; he more than once successfully identified a species new to science on the grounds that its calls where unfamiliar to him, as Kevin Zimmer recalls in his affectionate obituary:

Not long ago Ted was listening to a tape of the dawn chorus made by a colleague in a remote site in Bolivia. In the midst of other sounds on the tape, he picked up one that was different, and announced that it had to be an undescribed species of *Herpsilochmus* antwren (one member of which is already named in Ted's honour). Within a year, a European worker visiting the site found Ted's antwren, and sure enough, it was a *Herpsilochmus* species that was previously unknown to science. Ted could listen to a one-minute cut of tape and not only tell you what you had recorded, but *where* you had recorded it (e.g., south bank of the Amazon between the Rios Madeira and Tapajos), simply by listening to other birds in the background.

But you don't need these grandmaster skills to extend your own capacities and interest in birds in the dimension of sound. You don't even need to be in the field. There's a game some birders of a sedentary disposition play of listening to the bird sounds TV sound engineers dub into their films. Move to the coast and there's that Desert Island Discs herring gull; back to the country and there are the rooks cawing in the churchyard; a wistful romantic parting in the garden and the robin sings its sad autumn song; expect a happy ending if the skylark sings and a bad one if the raven croaks. You can have fun spotting the anomalies too. From my armchair I have heard tawny owls hooting in Ireland (there aren't any there), swifts screaming in February (June is more like it), and canaries singing in a Jane Austen country garden (come off it). BBC producer Stephen Moss tells me that the BBC used to have a tape of bee-eater calls that was routinely applied to "farmland" situations until the purists noticed it and objected. And in America, CBS Sports had to apologise for dubbing white-throated sparrow and hermit thrush song into the "wrong" live broadcasts of golf tournaments in states where these species do not occur.[1] Roger Tory Peterson had an even better story from Hollywood:

> When I was a young man, one of my lists was from soundtracks of movies. I had a very special list for the wrentit, a common bird around the studios of Hollywood—a bird with an unmistakable voice. The range of this species is almost entirely within the state of California, but my researchers in movie theaters over the years extended its range to Wyoming (in the Wallace Beery movie Wyoming), Kentucky (National Velvet), Lake Champlain (Northwest Passage), and even Austria (The Waltz King).

Popular songs aren't any better. How about "and a nightingale sang in Berkeley Square" (must have been a robin disturbed by the new streetlights)[2] or "there'll be bluebirds over / the white cliffs of Dover" (swallows, I suppose—

---

[1] See *New York Times*, 17 September 2000 (reprinted 27 November 2007). They then had to apologise again for printing a picture of house sparrows to go with the apology about the white-throated sparrows.

[2] To be fair to the lyricist, Eric Maschwitz, however, he does in context make it clear that this was just another impossible event: "There was magic abroad in the air. / There were angels dining at the Ritz. / And a nightingale sang . . ." The year was 1940.

bluebirds are strictly North American and would cause a twitchers' stampede over the white cliffs if they appeared here).

There are literary games too. John Clare has this very fine evocation in the *Shepherd's Calendar* (March):

> Down the edge of the distant sky
> The hail storm sweeps . . .
> While far above the solitary crane
> Swings lonely to unfrozen dykes again
> Cranking a jarring melancholy cry
> Thro the wild journey of the cheerless sky

But that couldn't have been a crane, which bugles sonorously. It's the heron that utters a "cranking cry." And then you discover that Clare refers to herons indifferently as herons, heronshaws, storks, and cranes.[1]

A more teasing case comes in the classic Sherlock Holmes mystery *The Hound of the Baskervilles*. Watson is being conducted over the moor near the great Grimpen Mire by the creepy entomologist, Stapleton (who turns out to be the villain in the end):

"Halloa," I cried, "What is that?"

A long low moan, indescribably sad, swept over the moor. It filled the whole air, and yet it was impossible to say whence it came. From a dull murmur it swelled into a deep roar and then sank back into a melancholy, throbbing murmur once again. Stapleton looked at me with a curious expression on his face.

"Queer place, the moor!" said he.

"But what is it?"

"The peasants say it is the Hound of the Baskervilles calling for its prey. I've heard it once or twice before but never so loud."

I looked round, with a chill of fear in my heart, at the huge swelling plain, mottled with the green patches of rushes. Nothing stirred over the vast expanse save a pair of ravens, which croaked loudly from a tor behind us.

"You are an educated man. You don't believe such nonsense as that?" said I. "What do you think is the cause of so strange a sound?"

"Bogs make queer noises sometimes. It's the mud settling, or the water rising, or something."

"No, no, that was a living voice."

---

[1] Clare's verse is actually (mis)quoted as the epigraph to the chapter on the East Anglian cranes in Peter Matthiessen's *Birds of Heaven* (2002).

"Well, perhaps it was. Did you ever hear a bittern booming?"

"No, I never did."

"It's a very rare bird—practically extinct—in England now, but all things are possible on the moor. Yes, I should not be surprised to learn that what we have heard is the cry of the last of the bitterns."

Now, Watson would not have been fobbed off with this had he consulted the magisterial work by W.S.M. D'Urban and the Rev. M. A. Mathew, *The Birds of Devon,* published in 1892 (that is, ten years before *The Hound of the Basker-villes*). That makes it clear that a bittern on Dartmoor would have been un-precedented and specifically warns against the mistake of *omne ignotum pro magnifico est* ("supposing everything unknown must be something wonderful," Tacitus, but not translated in D'Urban and Mathew!), which the authors apply to supposed sightings of bustards, cranes, and other exotica on the moor. But Watson would in any case have seen through the deceit had he ever listened to a bittern, whose deep foghorn *uh-BOOH* is nothing like the sound described.

My suggestion, then, is that we can both enlarge and enrich our perceptions of birds, and in particular aid our recognition of them, by attending more to what we can hear than what we can see. You can test this easily enough for yourself by alternately using a blindfold and earplugs to discover what you find and what you miss. I will do a little test right now by taking a walk out from the village for a half hour and noting which species I can identify and whether I do so by sound or sight or both. It is 3 PM on 18 October 2007 and I am at home in my small Suffolk village. It's sunny and windless, with just a touch of autumn chill in the air—good conditions for both watching and lis-tening. I'm going to walk up a quiet minor road that runs out of the village and has an avenue of trees on one side and a well-established hedge on the other; after about four hundred yards it reaches a small grass paddock where there may be horses, and it then goes on into the open countryside between arable fields bordered by hedges, with some copses in the middle distance. A typical piece of East Anglian countryside. This is quite a demanding test for my thesis, as it happens, first because very few birds are singing this time of year (I've heard only robin, wren, and starling at all regularly this week, with occasional bursts from dunnock and collared dove), and second because midafternoon is in any case generally the quietest time of day; moreover, we're going into fairly open country, not dense woodland, so you might expect more birds to be readily visible. Anyway, I'll transcribe the notes just as I make them and then see what they amount to:

Robin singing somewhere in the bushes under the trees, in fact more than one; also a couple of wrens (all out of sight). Fieldfare calls in the distance (probably in flight but I can't pick it up)—good, first one of the autumn. Also redwings in flight somewhere, that penetrating wheezing call, must be several; yes, I can see four small thrushes disappearing over the trees in that rapid dodging flight they have. Stand still for a moment. A clattering in the branches as wood pigeons take off (does that count as hearing or feeling?); a pheasant calls loudly (could be half a mile away, though); dunnock calls weakly from hedgerow and I think I glimpse it flitting away as I approach. Walk on. Corvids flying high over fields—must be jackdaws from the size; yes, one calls—a clipped *kak* or *tchak*. Ah, a *conversazione* of soft, high-pitched calls from the other side of the hedge and the lower branches of a conifer—almost certain to be a mixed party of tits and goldcrests; I can hear long-tailed tits and blue tits at least, and now at least one goldcrest; there they are, inspect the flock with binoculars (thinks, unbalanced experiment this, I don't have an ear-trumpet with me to improve my hearing); I can see one great tit and two blue tits and perhaps half-a-dozen long-tailed; a coal tit is also calling, and now the full hand—a marsh tit just gave its explosive, almost sneezing *pitch-eeou* call; still can't see the goldcrest(s), though.

Have got to the paddock now. Scan the grass. Something flies up calling, a weak *zeep, zeep*—meadow pipit; and a skylark goes up with it, also calling, a strong dry *chirrup*. I hear a yellowhammer call, a hoarse *zheez*—it's on the telephone wires ahead. I'm now in open country. A soft in-drawn *hwee* from the blackthorn thicket—bullfinch, maybe two of them. Scan around with binoculars. Sometimes there are little owls here. Nothing at all, except more pigeons in flight over the fields, and some smaller ones—must be stock doves. I look directly up (easy to forget to do this) and there are four lapwing flying by high overhead. Now stop to listen again. A buzzard cries, the so-called "mewing" note, very distant but unmistakeable—they've just moved into our area in their very welcome eastward advance (actually a return). Very quiet otherwise. A great spotted woodpecker calls *tchick*, not sure whether it is in the copse or maybe on a telegraph pole round the corner. A rattling call as a mistle thrush flies fast overhead and loops on to the crown of our veteran black poplar; it came from behind me and I might easily have missed seeing it. A finch-like bird flies over silently and disappears into the hedge; not sure what that was, maybe greenfinch or chaffinch. I do hear, then see, a chaffinch on the way back; and a pied wagtail skittering over a roof, making the familiar *chissick* call. There are starlings on some of the roofs too, and as I approach I hear the *sotto voce* clicking, whistling and gurgling that passes for a song. Funny, no black-bird yet, but now one starts *chinking* in the hedge, a sign that the light has started to go and they are going to roost. Back home, with some house sparrows chirping somewhere and a collared dove bleating on the aerial.

This all sounds rather breathless, but in fact it was very quiet indeed, with very little to see *or* hear, relatively speaking. If this had been early morning or a spring or summer month then I would certainly have heard a great deal more. But for what it's worth the upshot is:

> *Heard but not seen:* robin, wren, fieldfare, pheasant, coal tit, goldcrest, marsh tit, bullfinch, buzzard, great spotted woodpecker, house sparrow.
> *Heard first and then seen:* redwing, dunnock, blue tit, long-tailed tit, meadow pipit, yellowhammer, skylark, mistle thrush, chaffinch, blackbird, pied wagtail, collared dove.
> *Seen but not heard:* lapwing, stock dove.
> *Seen first then heard:* jackdaw, woodpigeon, great tit, starling.

It is a very unscientific test, of course, but I think the Ears have it over the Eyes.

Signs of Sound

If the argument of the previous section is broadly right, then why is this so little recognised? And even when it is recognised, as it is in the quotations I gave from those excellent field guides, why is it so little acted on? I think part of the answer must lie in the weight of cultural inheritance I described in the first section, which has shaped our habits and expectations more perhaps than we consciously realise. Reading and writing are the ways we record the accumulated knowledge of the species, the ways we transmit what we know and validate it. It hasn't always been so, and it isn't so even now in some parts of the world, but it is something we take so for granted in the "developed world" that it seems surprising even to query it. And the consequence of this, I think, is that even when we are talking about sounds, we prefer to represent them in some visual medium we can refer back to and remember them by. That may not be a bad thing in itself, and it may even be unavoidable for us to some degree given what we are and have become. But it is on the face of it likely to be difficult to represent one medium by another—think of doing the reverse (sight into sound), or translating sight into touch or smell, or the reverse of that—the mind reels. So it is not surprising if our conversion of sounds into some visual code leads to our forgetting or downplaying the original medium.

We can look at some of the ways this conversion has been attempted. One of the commonest is to use *transcriptions* into what seem the nearest equivalent human sounds in our own spoken language. We all learn this at a very early age: rooks say *caw,* ducks say *quack,* owls say *tu-whit tu-whoo,* and cuckoos say, well, *cuckoo.* Let's start with this last one. Lots of birds have onomatopoeic names: some very obviously so, such as the cuckoo, chickadee, towhee, curlew, jackdaw, and chiffchaff; in many others an imitation of a characteristic sound may be present but has been obscured by the evolution of the word forms, as in kite (this comes from the shrill cry, not the name of the toy, which was probably based on the bird rather than vice versa), dove (our Middle English ancestors thought they said *douve* not *coo*), rook (from the Anglo-Saxon form *hroc,* though doesn't its cawing actually sound more like *kraa,* which is the original form of "crow"?), and knot (probably from the older forms *gnat* or *knat,* with the *g* or *k* pronounced).

You may already be getting suspicious about the cuckoo and you may get more so when you look at the other European names for it. The French is *cou-cou,* the German *kuckuck,* the Dutch *koekoek,* the Italian *cuculo,* the Spanish *cuco,* Faroese *geykur,* Hungarian *kakukk,* Icelandic *gaukur,* and the Russian *ku-kushka.* How on earth does it manage to learn so many languages? The fact is, of course, that it's the other way round. We all listen to the same bird making the same noise and represent the call in whatever way seems most natural in the phonology of our own language. We then actually hear it that way. This isn't just a fact about bird sounds but a much more general fact about human language. The newborn infant is in principle capable of speaking and pronouncing any language on earth but it rapidly learns, usually from its mother in particular, to select for the range of sounds and sound combinations it needs for its own. Later in life it may be very difficult even to recognise sounds one has never needed. That is why different foreigners, for example, speak English with such different and distinctive accents—we can all do hammy imitations of the stereotyped German, French, or Italian "English" accent. And of course it's true of English speakers in reverse—most of us can't even pronounce the Scottish *loch* correctly, let alone something from "tone" languages such as Japanese or Chinese (where you can change the meaning of a word simply by changing the pitch at which it is spoken) or the African "click" languages such as !Xu (which has forty-eight different click sounds produced by moving the tongue round the mouth in various ways, as in the scolding sound we represent in English as *tut tut*). So *cuckoo* is at best a very approximate imitation, a sort of phonetic reminder, in the sounds that best suit the English ear. It also has its own history as a word. The earliest citation in English is in the well-known song of about 1240:

Sumer is icumen in
Loude sing cuccu.[1]

Later spellings included variants such as *cokkow* (in Chaucer's *Parliament of Fowles*), *cucko, cuckow, kukkowe, cucco, cocow, cocow, cuckoe,* and even *guckoe, gugko,* and *gukkow* (this last one quite a good rendering, actually).

This is not in itself too unsettling. We know that languages, spellings, and their pronunciation evolve over time and that elements within them may carry all sorts of echoes and associations from the past. The words like "cuckoo" or "rook" are just our current written symbols that happen to have this aural origin. But surely we can do better than this now? And so we can. Field guides all without exception, I think, offer careful transcriptions of the commonest calls and, where relevant, songs; and these can be very useful, especially if the transcription gives an indication of relative stress, as in *huitt* for the willow warbler's disyllabic call and *huitt* for the chiffchaff's (Collins) or *uh-BOOH* for the bittern (Jonsson—very different from a canine howl!). But in the end these too turn out to be of limited value, for various reasons.

First, there is an irreducibly subjective element, even here. Jonsson hears *uh-BOOH,* Svensson (also a Swede, in the Collins) hears *uh-whump*. That doesn't matter much in the case of the bittern, so remarkable a noise as to be once heard and never forgotten, especially if you are standing in a huge reedbed at dawn or dusk. But it may matter more to the casual "garden birdwatcher" listening to an unseen bird calling from a low bush—is it *check* (Jonsson), *zeck* (Collins), or *tit-tit-tit* (Peterson)? This is in each case a transcription of the ticking call of the wren. It gets worse for the serious birder. A pipit flies up calling from a seawall on a late winter afternoon as it's getting dusk; no chance of a decent view; you think it's probably a meadow pipit but you wonder about rock pipit or even a rare red-throated pipit. You check the books afterwards and find this:

	Meadow pipit	Rock pipit	Red-throated pipit
Peterson	*weesk, tseep*	*seest, weesp*	*peese*
Collins	*ist-ist*	*visst*	*pssiih*
Jonsson	*pseet*	*peest*	*speeeeeh*

---

[1] Less often quoted is the next verse introducing other familiar sounds of the countryside: "Ewe bleateth after lamb / Low'th after calfe cow, / Bullock starteth, bucke farteth, / Merry sing cuccu."

And you would lose heart altogether if you dared wonder about the even rarer olive-backed pipit (*spiz* in Collins), or the vagrant buff-bellied pipit Paul Holt latched on to *(psipp)*. None of these transcriptions is "wrong," of course, just not very helpful.

The next problem is that the variation in transcriptions tends to get conflated with the natural variations between individual birds and between the different calls or "vocabulary" each species has for different purposes. The grid of possibilities then threatens to expand uncontrollably. When I was in the Volga Delta, for example, I was very interested in hearing and trying to distinguish the large range of skulking reedbed and steppe warblers that can occur in this region but which are notoriously hard ever to see clearly. I did a lot of work beforehand on books, tapes, and recordings to prepare myself, but if I'd relied on transcriptions alone I would have been confronted with this:

	Peterson	Collins	Jonsson
Reed (warbler)	*churr, skarr, tchar*	*che, chk, chreech, chrrre, trr-rr*	*kresh, kek-kshe, kche*
Sedge	*tuc, churr*	*tsek, errrr*	*check, trrr*
Moustached	*tac-tac-tac, trrrt*	*treek, trk, trrt*	*trr-trr, tcht, tr-trrrrr*
Paddyfield	*tschik, chek-chek*	*check, chre, zack*	*dzak*
Blyth's reed	*tack, tchik*	*zeck*	*chek, chek-tchr trrr*
Marsh	*tchuc, tuc, stit, churr*	"similar to reed"	*check, tret, terrrr*
Great reed	*chack*	*kshack*	*krek*
Olivaceous	*tec, click*	*tsack, chack*	*tch che-ch-ch, chr, trrr*
Booted	*click, zett*	*zett, zerrr*	*tsek*

And I haven't even mentioned Savi's, river, and grasshopper warblers, which were all there too. The Collins cop-out on the marsh warbler is my QED.

And third, there is the problem of longer vocalisations like songs. Most of the guides accept defeat on these and find another way to describe them. But there are some heroic attempts and failures too. The Collins that capitulated so feebly in the foothills of the marsh warbler calls nonetheless feels brave enough to attempt the North Face of the sedge warbler song and comes up with this:

zruzru-trett zruzruzru-trett zruzruzru psit trutrutru-purrrrrrrrrrrurrrrrr **vi-vi-vi** lululu *zetre zetre.*

Got it? This reminds me, by a natural train of thought, of the Russian phrase book I took on the same trip, which advised me to prepare for unexpected opportunities by memorising the following:

Mi azheeda-yem vza-eemavemavigadnava dyelavova saatroodneechyestva

It means "We look forward to a mutually beneficial business relationship." In the event, I only learnt *da* (yes), *nyet* (no), *spaseeba* (thank you), and *bormo-tushka* (booted warbler—well, just in case).

If transcriptions won't do, then, what other imitative devices or representations are available to us? There is literal *imitation,* of course, though that need not detain us long. There have been gifted mimics like Percy Edwards, who used to entertain BBC Radio audiences years ago with his uncanny ability to reproduce a whole range of nonhuman sounds with extraordinary fidelity. Dr. Johnson's comment on dogs walking on their hind-legs applies here—surprising that they can do it at all. And at the other end of the artistic scale, many great composers have included musical representations of birdsong in their works—most famously, I suppose, Beethoven in his Sixth Symphony, *The Pastoral* (where there are recognisable imitations of quail, nightingale, and cuckoo) and Vaughan Williams's *Lark Ascending* (where the solo violin traces in sound the upward, spiralling flight song of the skylark).

36. Beethoven score from the *Pastoral* Symphony (in the Readers' Digest *Book of Birds,* 1969)

Other composers such as Clément Janequin, Ottorino Respighi, and, most systematically, Olivier Messiaen mimic features of birdsong, adapted and accommodated to musical conventions, or even include "quotations" from actual birdsongs as integrated extracts in their work.[1] None of this helps us much with identification, though, except perhaps in the indirect sense of arousing our curiosity about the originals.

There is, however, a more interesting intermediate case in the sort of very approximate imitations that any experienced birder can produce to indicate rhythm, stress, and phrasing to a beginner. This is the aural equivalent of jizz

---

[1] For example, in works such as Respighi's *Pini di Roma* (nightingales—but see appendix 3 for a warning of what can go wrong) and Rautavaara's *Cantus Arcticus* (curlew, crane, shore lark—brought down by two octaves, and migrating whooper swans). There is even a work by the American composer James Fassett called *Symphony of Birds,* which consists *wholly* of the songs and calls of real birds.

and it may be very useful to produce one's own sound-sketches as an aid to identification and memory. Some of these aide-mémoire get stylised and incorporated into proverbial lore, like *a little bit of bread and no cheese* for the yellowhammer's song in Britain. That isn't terribly helpful in fact, since there is rarely any *and no* in it—it just goes *little bit of bread CHEESE*. Another memorable version is the male fantasy of "the reluctant milkmaid"—*no, no, no, no, no, PLEASE*. There are less silly North American equivalents in *please, please, pleased to meetcha* for the chestnut-sided warbler and *old Sam Peabody Peabody Peabody* for the white-throated sparrow.

The only systematic attempt I have seen to exploit mimicry for identification purposes was years ago in a locally produced tape featuring the mimic Jake Ward (pictured on the label in regulation woolly hat on Cley marshes), under the arresting title *Big Jake Calls the Waders*. The blurb says that these are "sounds specially recreated by the human voice for the human ear" and there was an expert commentary from Bryan Bland on each of the twenty-eight wader calls included. This was a clever strap-line. One reason why bird sounds can never be fully represented by transcriptions of human sounds is that the mechanics of the two sound production systems are quite different.[1] Perhaps if the translation were to occur at an earlier stage, so to speak, the difficulty could be at least partly avoided? A more radical and remarkable development of the same thought is the project by the artist Marcus Coates in which he first slows down selected bird songs to "their" speed, then gets human vocalists to sing along and imitate them at that slower speed, and finally speeds the result back up to the original speed. This produces some quite extraordinary and realistic "imitations," which threaten to bring into question several conventional assumptions about the differences between human and bird vocalisations.

A natural question at this point is whether there can't be some more scientific way of doing all this, some way not dependent on the vagaries of subjective interpretation and misleading forms of representation. And there is. The first attempts date back to at least 1650, when Athanasius Kircher tried to transcribe birdsong into *musical notation* in his *Misurgia universalis*. That failed for much the same reason as transcriptions into written languages fail: birds produce their sounds as differently from the musical instruments for which these notations are designed as from human voice boxes.

But in the mid-twentieth century there was a quite different and much more promising technological development. In the course of the Second World War

---

[1] Birds do not use lips, tongues, and teeth, as we do, to articulate a sound produced in a larynx high up in the throat; they have a syrinx, much lower down and subdivided into two parts that can operate independently and may in the case of songbirds be controlled by several pairs of muscles so that it can produce very complex combinations of sounds and even duet with itself.

37. Athanasias Kircher's notation of bird voices. The six lines at the top represent the song of the nightingale (*Misurgia universalis*, 1650)

scientists at the Bell Laboratories in New Jersey developed a technology that could be used to detect and recognise the underwater "sound signatures" of enemy submarines; and after the war ethologists and other behavioural scientists saw that these sound spectrograms or *sonagrams,* as they came to be called, might be usefully applied to the systematic study of animal communication, in particular the relative importance of instinct and learning, which was the hot topic of the day. William Thorpe, working in Cambridge, England, inspected the Kay Sonograph at the National Physics Laboratory (the only one in England at the time) and saw its potential. He persuaded the university to buy one for him and set him up with a special laboratory to pioneer the application of this to birdsong. Here at last was a device that could produce detailed and objective visual images of sound. He produced a series of studies of chaffinch song, which was ideal for his purpose since it was already known that the chaffinch displayed different regional "dialects" whose variations could now be reliably recorded this way; he could then study to what extent they learned from their neighbours and to what extent the song patterns were innate. The technology and its applications have now become enormously more sophisticated, of course, and sonagrams of bird songs of all species are readily available. As far as I know, however, the first and still the only field guide to have made any real use of them is the U.S. *Golden Guide* (1983), which includes sonagrams for all the songbirds and promotes their advantages enthusiastically in the preface. This never really caught on, it would be true to say, largely, I suspect, because readers shied away from these unfamiliar and very technical-looking graphs in much the same way as those who can't read music flinch from musical scores. The cause has now been taken up again, however, with almost evangelistic fervour in a new publication, *The Sound Approach to Birding* (2006) by Mark Constantine, which offers some very rich and well-produced materials for study in its text, illustrations, and accompanying CDs. I suspect the psychological resistance will remain for most people, but it is worth setting out what can now be achieved by those willing to make the effort. Who knows? In 1977, Ken Olsen, the president of Digital Equipment Corporation, said "There is no reason for any individual to have a computer in his home."

What a sonagram does, basically, is plot frequency against time. The vertical axis indicates changes in frequency, the horizontal one measures time. So you can quickly tell from this whether sounds are going up or down (pitch) and how long each of them lasts (duration). You can also see the repetitions and pauses (phrasing), any changes in acceleration or slowing (tempo), and, if a depth of shading is used, changes in volume (loudness). What is more difficult to pick up is voice quality or timbre (the sort of thing we usually describe with words like *dry, buzzy, clear, harsh, flutey,* or *screeching,* or more anthropomorphic terms like *sad, cheerful,* and *angry*), but with sufficient experience and cross-reference to sonagrams of other known noises apparently the real experts can manage this too.

Figure 38 sets out a few sonagrams of some songs and calls already mentioned, to show how they work. Note the sharply rising inflection in the willow warbler call, the rhythm of the white-throated sparrow song, and the familiar double note of the cuckoo. This doesn't have to be high-tech to be useful. You can make little field sketches indicating the essentials in a sound-cartoon (as in fig. 39).

I think this has real utility. It may continue to have both the practical and psychological disadvantages I've mentioned, but it can certainly supplement

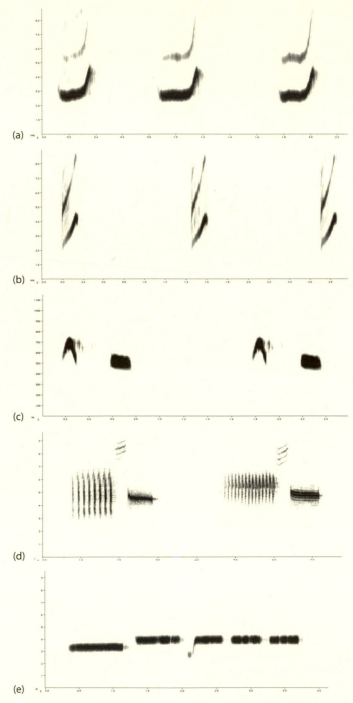

38. Sonagrams (Geoff Sample): (a) willow warbler; (b) chiffchaff; (c) cuckoo; (d) yellowhammer; (e) white-throated sparrow

39. Sound cartoon of white-throated sparrow (in David Sibley, *Birding Basics*)

other approaches. It does at least underline the need to give much more emphasis to sound in identification guides and, equally importantly, it provides a language in which to do it. We should surely give as much attention to the structure of a bird's sounds as we do to the visible structure of its physical parts and the technology of sonagrams makes that structure explicit and accessible in a way it never was before. But technology has in the meantime also delivered a way of doing this more directly than through any of the forms of "representations" we have been considering. There are now excellent recordings of actual bird vocalisations for almost all species in the world and all regions and these are readily available on CD and tape. These are a natural first point of reference both before and after one needs help in identifying particular bird sounds, and there are further technological developments coming through that will soon make it as easy to take a large and relevant selection of bird vocalisations into the field for instant comparison as it already is to carry a large field guide with you in electronic form. Some of us may never want to do this, for quite other reasons, but the possibilities are there.

But prose descriptions will always be needed too, if only as verbal reminders, especially to convey character and tone, and there is no reason why these should not be metaphorical or even poetic, provided that we do not confuse memorable description with sentimental attributions of mood. We can call the golden plover's call "plaintive" (Collins) or "melancholy" (Jonsson) as long as we don't think the birds must be sad, and these sorts of descriptions will probably remain more meaningful to most people than the sonagram in figure 40.

So to end this section I list some of the descriptions and similes of this kind that I have found most striking (and therefore memorable) in my favourite field guides.

Coot: "an explosive, at times incredibly high *pitts* as if a light bulb had been dropped onto a stone"

Jack snipe: "a very peculiar muffled [call] like a distant galloping horse"

Sandwich tern: "a loud grating *kerrick* like pressing amalgam into a tooth"

Roller: "a harsh and sonorous *rak* or *rak rak,* like rolling two dried walnuts between the palms of the hands"

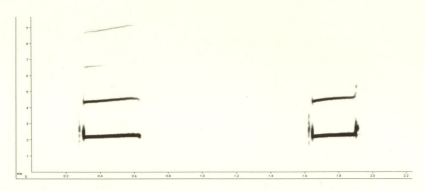

40. Golden plover's "plaintive call" (sonagram: Geoff Sample)

Robin: "a sharp ticking *tic* like winding up a clockwork toy"
Bluethroat: "*chak* like a halyard striking against a flagstaff"
Sardinian warbler: "sudden, startlingly loud burst like a stuttering engine"
Wood warbler: "an accelerating series of sharp, metallic, call-like notes
     ending in an almost pulsating trill . . . often likened to a spinning
     coin on a marble slab"
Tristram's grackle: "very vocal, has characteristic meandering whistles
     recalling tuning in a short-wave radio, e.g., *wioowiooweet.*"

I've never encountered a Tristram's grackle, but if I'm ever in the Syrian desert
I shall now know one when I hear it.

"And the winner is . . ."

Does the capacity to identify birds by ear enable us to refine our responses to
bird sounds, and in particular bird songs, as well as our descriptions of them?
Does it help to make us sensitive to more distinctions and so appreciate the
songs the more? On the face of it you might expect so. Surely we are likely to
get more pleasure from, say, a sedge warbler's song if we know it *as* a sedge
warbler and can tell it from the similar reed warbler song rather than just
hearing it as a generic warbler song of some kind. After all, the birds themselves, at whom these songs are directed, make much finer discriminations
than we do: they will respond selectively to the voice of their own species and
they form their own preferences among individuals on the basis of factors like
the size of repertoire, complexity, variation, volume, tone, and all the variables
we have been trying to identify. Most human lovers of birdsong have found it
easiest to explain their preferences too by reference to comparative distinctions of this kind. I have already quoted Lord Grey distinguishing blackcaps

and garden warblers (pp. 39–40). He prefers the blackcap in the end. In fact
the blackcap turns out to be on his short list of winners and he starts making
the awards:

> For perfection or moving quality of voice I should place the blackcap
> with the blackbird and the nightingale in the first class of British song-
> birds. His song is loud, exceedingly sweet, but also spirited: it is not very
> long, but is frequently repeated: there is not great variety but the thing
> done is absolutely perfect. There is not a note that fails to please or to
> be a success. The tone does not stir us so inwardly as that of the black-
> bird, but it is a sheer delight to listen to it. Of the blackcap, indeed, it has
> been said that, like the gipsy before the castle gate, "he sang so very
> completely."

With a very gentle let-down in the end for the popular favourite:

> The nightingale's song has compass, variety and astonishing power; it
> arrests attention and compels admiration; but it is fitful, broken and
> restless; it is a song to listen to, but not to live with.

Others want to take this game further and use these sorts of distinctions as
a basis on which we could grade the songs in a systematic ranking of some
kind. A rather touching and innocent attempt of this kind is given in an appendix to Stanley Morris's book *Bird-Song* of 1924. A score of 20 in any dimension, he says, is "absolute perfection."

Species	Mellowness of tone	Sprightly notes	Plaintive notes	Compass	Execution	Total points
Nightingale	19	14	19	19	19	90
Linnet	12	16	12	16	18	74
Blackcap	14	12	12	14	14	66
Skylark	4	19	4	18	18	63
Titlark	12	12	12	12	12	60
Woodlark	18	4	17	12	8	59
Robin	6	16	12	12	12	58
Goldfinch	4	19	4	12	12	51
Chaffinch	4	12	4	8	8	36
Greenfinch	4	4	4	4	6	22
Hedge-sparrow	6	0	6	4	4	20
Thrush	4	4	4	4	4	20
Wren	0	12	0	4	4	20

Species	Mellowness of tone	Sprightly notes	Plaintive notes	Compass	Execution	Total points
Siskin	2	4	0	4	4	14
Blackbird	4	4	0	2	2	12
Redpoll	0	4	0	4	4	12
Reed-sparrow	0	4	0	2	2	8

Who knows how the redpoll equalled the blackbird? But that's show business for you.[1]

Charles Hartshorne takes this much further still in his far more ambitious study of the structure of birdsong, *Born to Sing* (1973), which draws on a great deal of science and scholarship but shows an alarming determination to quantify exactly his chosen parameters of Loudness, Scope, Continuity, Tone, Organisation, and Imitation. He ploughs on remorselessly through these spurious calculations and emerges with a World List of Superior Singers, 194 species in all, each with its precise score; within this he distinguishes 22 triple-starred "superlative songsters" and a further 61 double-starred "superb songsters." Top of the pops, you'll be eager to know, is (let's hear it for Oz) the superb lyrebird; the only U.S. candidates to make the top nominations are hermit and wood thrushes, mockingbird, brown thrasher, and (surprisingly?) Carolina wren; while the leading U.K. entrants are woodlark, skylark, nightingale, and blackbird (Grey's blackcap is only in division two, and one of my own favourites, the curlew, is excluded in advance for reasons of taxonomic prejudice—not a songbird!). Hartshorne's supposedly rigorous scoring system clearly favours the loud and lengthy over the delicate and wistful (the British robin bombs badly). It reminds one of nothing so much as those equally spurious cost-benefit analyses that determine all the outcomes in advance in the way they quantify the key subjective variables. Once it has been decided that "economic development" scores 9.62 and "conservation of the environment" scores 6.13, it is rather easy to demonstrate the case for building that new factory on reclaimed marshland.

The more interesting question that the analysis of distinctions between songs does perhaps raise is what I think of as Kant's question. The great philosopher was not a bird man, as far as I know, but he did raise a tricky question about the natural world in the course of examining aesthetics as a kind of knowledge. He asks whether our pleasure in listening to a birdsong like that of

[1] Some of these vernacular names have, of course, changed: hedge sparrow to dunnock, reed sparrow to reed bunting, and titlark to pipit (more likely to be tree pipit than meadow pipit here since it scores so highly, but the line of straight 12s still looks suspicious to me).

a nightingale would be affected by the subsequent discovery that the source of the sound was just a mechanical imitation. He thinks the answer is probably yes, on the grounds of our resulting sense of deception and disillusion; but of course it could also be argued that one is just responding to a sound, which has whatever qualities it has, and that it shouldn't matter to one's aesthetic response what kind of bird it is or indeed whether it is a bird at all. Typical philosopher's question, which you either find intensely irritating or troublingly difficult. Anyway, for our own more modest purposes I feel Kant must be right, that fuller knowledge, and in particular fuller knowledge of context, must affect what is perceived and how it is evaluated. I don't think this is "unweaving the rainbow," as Keats famously complained philosophers were wont to do. You surely do appreciate a sedge warbler's song the more when you hear it fully enough to know that it *is* a sedge warbler's song; and you also respond to it as part of your larger response to the circumstances in which you hear it.

I don't propose, however, to analyse the constituents of song that most appeal to us in quite the way as I did for features of visible beauty such as animation, size, colour, form, and so on. There are things one could say on these lines, noting, for example, the importance of rhythm in the chaffinch's song; tone in the blackbird and wood thrush; variety in the marsh warbler, mockingbird, thrasher (and incidentally the sedge warbler and starling, both altogether absent in Hartshorne's rankings); purity in the blackcap and song thrush; richness in the garden warbler and nightingale; the way the songs of the skylark, curlew, and tree pipit are linked expressively to their display flights; and the powerful effects of birds calling in a flock, like geese rising from a field, rooks coming in to roost, and migrating cranes. But I think that in the case of song, even more than in the case of visible beauty, it becomes very difficult to consider such factors in isolation, either from each other or from the crucial factors of context I discuss in chapter 7.

I will just indulge one personal choice. The woodlark is probably my favourite British songster, surpassing even the better-known skylark, the nightingale, and the curlew (my second choice). The woodlark's Latin generic name, *Lululla,* gives a musical clue,[1] as does its French name, *alouette lulu.* The song is composed of a series of pure trills interspersed with deeper, yodelling *luu-luu-luu* notes, which are structured very simply but with sufficient changes of pace, pitch, and volume to allow for almost infinite variations. The result is complex, subtle, and piercingly beautiful. The male may sing from a perch on a bush or tree (hence the specific Latin name, *arborea*) or may choreograph a

---

[1] In fact, in 1758 Linnaeus christened it an *Alauda,* like the skylark, but from 1829 it has been assigned the genus *Lululla* all to itself.

beguiling song-flight that will sweep the bird upwards in slow ascending spirals until the song ends abruptly and he plunges silently to the ground. Gerard
Manley Hopkins tried hard to capture the elusive music of the phrasing in his
poem "The Woodlark," which starts,

> Teevo cheevo cheevio chee
> O where, what can that be?

and ends,

> With a sweet joy of a sweet joy,
> Sweet, of a sweet, of a sweet joy
> Of a sweet—a sweet—sweet—joy.

This is a bird of woodland glades and margins—and the song is often a fugitive
sound, just around the corner. Today it is flourishing in the clearings created
by forestry activities, and there are now some three thousand pairs breeding
in Britain, mainly in the south and east. But when I first heard it as a boy in
the 1950s in dawn chorus excursions to the woods round Colchester it was a
rare bird, with only one hundred pairs in Britain, and it still conjures up for
me that early sense of discovery, excitement, and innocence.

The Sound of Music

Whatever your personal favourite, almost everyone responds positively to
birdsong in a general way. It's official. Governments cite listening to birdsong
among the key indicators of our "quality of life"; doctors offer doses of birdsong in a "sonic stream" designed to repair bodies and minds in hospital;
managers of British Airways airport lounges include it in their Muzak to
soothe stressed travellers; and when as a species we try to contact other worlds
and life forms to tell them what is most important about our own, the top scientific selection committee includes a snatch of birdsong among all the technical data.[1] But we didn't need the suited professions to tell us this. Poets and
ordinary people have been quite clear about it for centuries. We mention birdsong as naturally as we do the weather to strangers in chance encounters on a
walk. We mark the seasons by it. We go into the countryside to hear it, eyes
closed and listening deeply, just as we go down to the sea or up hills to stare
out into those far distances. There are whole anthologies of poetry and prose
celebrating birdsong as a sort of natural miracle, and there are tapes and CDs

---

[1] NASA incorporated a snatch of birdsong in the Golden Disk on *Voyager 1* and *2*, giving our
"Greetings to the Universe." The bird calls selected are a bit disappointing, to be honest, being
mainly background to elephant and hyena cries, but the thought was good.

to share the best of the best from all round the world. And we always talk of it as bird*song* and think of it as a kind of music.

But is this right? Do these words really convey what is going on? Most of the time this way of talking is just an implicit assumption on our part, so natural that we no longer consider if "birdsong" is really a description rather than a sort of metaphor; but sometimes the assumption surfaces more consciously, as in these extracts from Thoreau, whose favourite songster was the wood thrush:

> The wood thrush has sung for me sometime. He touches a depth in me which no other bird song does. He has learned to sing and no thrumming of the strings or tuning disturbs you. Other birds may whistle pretty well but he is the master of a finer toned instrument. His song is musical not from association merely—not from variety but the character of its tone. It is all divine—a Shakespeare among birds and a Homer too.

Then, a month later:

> As I come over the hill I hear the wood thrush singing his evening lay. This is the only bird whose note affects me like music—affects the flow and tenor of my thought—my fancy and imagination. It lifts and exhilarates me. It is inspiring. It is a medicative draught to my soul. It is an elixir to my eyes [sic] and a fountain of youth to all my senses.

The claims get stronger and stronger:

> It changes all hours to an eternal morning. It banishes all trivialness. It reinstates me in my dominion—makes me the lord of creation—is chief musician of my court. . . . All that was ripest and fairest in the wilderness and the wild man is preserved and transmitted to us in the strain of the wood thrush. It is the mediator between barbarism and civilisation. It is as unrepentant as Greece.

But then the natural observer takes over again, rather suddenly:

> I find my clothes covered with young caterpillars these days.

That's rather a relief, isn't it, after all the high-octane prose? One sometimes feels the need for the same sort of shuddering anticlimax after reading Keats on the nightingale, Browning on the thrush, and Shelley on the skylark, splendid though these poems are, if only to remind oneself that the birds are not actually singing for *us*. But in fact it is not only these glamorous, charismatic songsters that attract this kind of language. Here is a celebration of the song of

Bachman's sparrow, a drab and now uncommon bird of the southeastern United States and parts of the Midwest:

> The song of the Bachman sparrow is a thing of surprising beauty. In delivering it the bird chooses a prominent station at the top of a weedstalk, fencepost, or sapling, or stands well out on a bare limb of a tree. Here he throws his head back and draws, as it appears, a full breath in a note of ravishing sweetness; then sends it forth again in a tinkling rill of uniform or varied notes. Nothing can excel the fine poetic rapture of the inspirited note. It sets the veins a-tingle and makes one wish to put his shoes from off his feet. The characteristic opening note is given with constantly varying pitch and intensity. Sometimes it sounds like a dream voice floating gently from the summer land of youth and again it vibrates with startling distinctiveness like a present call to duty. Occasionally a dainty trill is substituted for this inspired and inspiring opening, while the remainder of the song may consist of a half-dozen notes precisely alike, or of a succession of groups three or four in number. There is a soulful quality, an ethereal purity, and a caressing sweetness about the whole performance which makes one sure the door is opened into the third heaven of bird music. (W. Leon Dawson, *Birds of Ohio*)

If Bachman's *sparrow* can be thought to be producing music, just as much as Keats's nightingale, we had better take the question seriously. Is birdsong actually "song," then? Is it really a kind of music or is it just *like* music, and if so how? As with most interesting questions of this kind, the journey is more important than the destination. Like Humpty Dumpty we can use the words any way we want, of course, and the answers we are looking for are not just "yes" or "no"; what we really want to know is how bird vocalisations are like and how unlike other kinds of music, and whether the similarities seem more important than the differences. There certainly *are* some similarities.

First, birdsong clearly has an internal structure of the same general kind as human music. There are recognisable melodies, rhythms, symmetries, repetitions, variations, refrains, and reprises and some species can have a repertoire of many thousand separate phrases; there is even duetting between two birds in some tropical species. And as with human language and music, the individual acoustic elements in birdsong achieve their effects only in combination—they don't actually refer to anything or mean anything in isolation. On the other hand, these formal structures tend to be less complex in the case of birds and the repeatable patterns are not usually sustained over more than a few seconds. Nor is there large-scale coordination: the dawn "chorus" does indeed make a huge impact on us and probably stimulates the birds too, but it is the impact of a swelling combination of individual sounds, not an organised cho-rus where the voices are interacting in deliberate harmony.

Second, birdsong sounds much more similar to human music than do the vocalisations of the other primates, though these are of course closer to us on the evolutionary tree. Most apes don't sing in any recognisable way (though you could argue about howler monkeys and gibbons). Whales and dolphins (and possibly seals) seem to be the only other mammals to produce anything comparable. And it is a shared feature of human musical productions and these, and only these, bird and animal songs that they are to a high degree learned, not innate. Apes will sound like apes, however they are reared, but chaffinches need other chaffinches to develop their distinctive songs. That sounds significant, but it could of course all be explained by an accidental and unrelated convergence of two quite different communication systems rather than a shared one; rather like the "panda's thumb," which turns out not to be, anatomically, a thumb or a finger at all and therefore not an example of the dextrous, opposable thumb we are told was so important to human evolution-ary success.

Third, the elaboration of birdsong seems to go well beyond anything that might have a selective advantage in evolutionary terms. The principal biologi-cal functions of birdsong are agreed to be the defence of territory (repelling rivals) and sexual selection (attracting mates), but many songs seem so elabo-rate, so sustained and so exquisitely expressive that it's hard to see how they could have evolved in that way just for those limited functional purposes. This is the peacock's tail problem again (see chapter 5, pp. 129–30), which has puz-zled and divided scientists from Darwin onwards, and those who want to press the analogy with human music make much of this feature.

Fourth, relevant to that point but distinct from it is the question of whether the birds themselves take any aesthetic pleasure in their own performances. That would not be inconsistent with an evolutionary explanation of music, in their case or in ours, since "taking pleasure" could be a very natural motiva-tor and reinforcer if there were other benefits to be had. No one would suggest birds had any *self-conscious* aesthetic sensibilities, of course, but that need not mean they are not *somewhere* on the continuum from pleasure to appreci-ation. Some musicians, at least, feel they merit the use of this vocabulary. François-Bernard Mâche makes the interesting point that the idea of gratu-itous aesthetic pleasure is in any case only a small part of musical behaviour in humans and has only become seriously important in the last two centuries or so of European civilisation. In many musical traditions people would have no idea what a "concert" is, and many cultures make their music mainly in ritual and social contexts. Mâche wonders if music might develop from a certain "lavishness of nature" in extending its limited utilitarian purposes; diversity or superiority in song may at first have enabled an individual bird to prevail over a competitor, before gradually overshooting the mark and turning the excess not into a disadvantage but into an unexpected pleasure, something to be valued beyond mere survival. After describing the musical virtuosity of various species he ends with this affirmation:

> I leave my conclusion to the tape-recorder. I can only say, as a composer, that *Craticus nigrogularis,* the pied butcher bird, is a kind of colleague.

And Messiaen would have agreed:

> It is probable that in the artistic hierarchy birds are the greatest musicians existing on our planet.

But there are some evident differences between birdsong and human music to be noted as well. First, in most species and for most of the year, singing is a function of male birds only. There are exceptions, but singing is evidently tied very much to the need to attract mates and protect territory. Second, singing of the kind we are talking about is a capacity enjoyed only by the order of *Passerines* and within that the suborder of *Oscines,* which is a little less than half the known bird species. The majority of species have no song as such, though some have mechanical equivalents to song (the drumming of woodpeckers and the vibrating tail feathers of a snipe), and some calls can have analogous pair-bonding functions. Third, birds take no detectable interest or pleasure in the singing of any other species of bird than their own, except for the purposes of mimicry (which in most cases is probably just an alternative way of generating variety in song). Nor do they generally have a reciprocal interest in human music, though here at least one apparent exception is famous enough and fun enough to be worth recalling.

In the 1920s, the British cellist Beatrice Harrison moved to the Surrey countryside and got into the habit of practising outdoors in her large garden in the spring. To her great delight, one evening a nightingale began to sing along, matching her notes "in thirds, and always perfectly in tune with the cello." Entranced, she persuaded the BBC, in the person of the very sceptical Lord Reith, to mount its first ever live "outside broadcast" to share this phenomenon with the world. On the appointed night of 19 May 1924 there was a tremendous sense of expectation, since the BBC had advertised the event very widely. The idea was to break into its regular Saturday night dance programme as soon as the birds were in good voice. Conditions were perfect—a clear, warm night with a full moon. Harrison put on her best concert frock, went out into her garden and played, for what might be the biggest audience of her

41. Beatrice Harrison playing the cello in the woods at Foyle Riding for the "Nightingale Music Festival" of 1933 (Hulton / Getty)

life or anyone else's. An estimated million listeners were tuned in and the suspense must have been almost unbearable (especially in Lord Reith's office). She tried "Danny Boy." No response. She launched into the Elgar Cello Concerto. Nothing. Then just after 10.45 PM, not long before the BBC was due to close down and go off the air, she started Dvorak's "Songs My Mother Taught Me" and the bird began, and continued, and sang as only a nightingale can in what was clearly a series of responses, if not technically a duet. The reaction among listeners was ecstatic; news spread round the world and the BBC had made a sensational international coup. Beatrice received more than fifty thousand letters of appreciation, including one from an old gentleman in New

Zealand, who said he had left the old country when he was a boy and that to hear this song once again out on his New Zealand farm "was a prayer answered." Public demand required that the event be repeated, and so it was every year until 1942.

Now, what actually happened that night? Any hard-nosed experimenter in a white coat would probably have been lynched for suggesting that this was just an effusion of anthropomorphic sentiment on a national scale. The reactions were clearly deeply felt and genuine, but what exactly were they reactions to? It is recorded that one year in the repeat performances a chorus of frogs was also stimulated to join in with Harrison, but presumably no one hailed that as "music." And in 1942, the programme was not actually broadcast, though it is preserved in a historic recording, because that night the nightingales were responding to the very different noise of approaching aircraft, which an alert BBC engineer rightly judged it imprudent to broadcast in wartime. Perhaps the nightingales and we were not quite as "attuned" as we supposed, in either direction? The more one studies this whole story the more mysterious it becomes, and I begin to have suspicious thoughts (see appendix 3).

For one final problem with the assumption that we are hearing birds "sing" is that we and the birds are actually hearing different things. We both operate within broadly the same frequencies, with birds generally occupying the higher parts of the range, but we have very different powers of discrimination among individual sounds. Birds have far greater "temporal resolution": they can distinguish time differences of between one and two milliseconds, while we can only do so between three and four milliseconds; and if you slow down birdsong to nearer our speed, you hear all kinds of details and elaborations that we would normally miss altogether but which birds are sensitive to and can hear clearly. But it then no longer sounds like song to our ears or like any conventional kind of attractive music. Are we now closer to hearing what the birds hear, or did the original recalibration to suit our physiology give a more realistic impression? You can make your head spin thinking through these sorts of relativities. We are told that mice and humans have the same life span in terms of the number of heartbeats each is allotted. It's just that mice use theirs up in a year or two, whereas ours may be spread over seventy years or more. We live at different speeds, but does that mean we all "really" live the same length of time or not?

I think I would conclude from all this that the analogy between music and birdsong is a rather weak one in most respects. It is at its strongest in the undoubted emotional effects each can produce in us and these need not be weakened by the knowledge that they may each have a quite different source. In fact the subjective human reaction may be all the stronger for recognising that birdsong is quite "other." We should not in any case assume that human beings all react the same way to the same sounds of music, whether human or avian. Here I refer you back to the last section of the last chapter, for the beauty of birdsong is indeed another form of physical beauty to which many of the same considerations apply. In this case too there is no one "correct" response, invariant across history, background, and culture. We each hear with our own ears and bring to our listening our own associations and experience. And so I dispute Keats's famous lines on the nightingale:

> Thou wast not born for death, immortal Bird
> No hungry generations tread thee down:
> The voice I hear this passing night was heard
> In ancient days by emperor and clown:
> Perhaps the self-same song that found a path
> Through the sad heart of Ruth, when, sick for home,
> She stood in tears amid the alien corn;
> The same that oft-times hath
> Charm'd magic casements, opening on the foam
> Of perilous seas, in faery lands forlorn.

These "self-same songs" may mean very different things at different times, even within the history of a single life, and the differences may be precisely what makes them emotionally significant. In particular, that meaning will be sensitive to the contexts of time and place, and it is to the crucial importance of these factors in determining our reactions to birds that I now turn.

7

A Time and a Place

If a given combination of trees, mountains, water,
and houses, say a landscape, is beautiful, it is not so
by itself, but because of me, of my favour, of the
idea or feeling I attach to it.
Charles Baudelaire

The Flannan Isles, 2 June 2004

Leach's petrel is on my list of "charismatic" birds. It is in truth a rather drab
little thing in general appearance, a sort of sooty brown in colour with a pale
band on the upper wing and a narrow white rump. It's about the size of a swallow and has longish narrow wings and a shallowly forked tail. Some are seen
in Britain every year passing down the coasts, usually in conditions of bad vis-
ibility and most often after severe gales from the northwest. Its attraction and
mystique, however, have another source. There are only four sites in the British Isles where Leach's petrels regularly breed, all of them isolated, remote, and
uninhabited islands in the North Atlantic, beyond even the Outer Hebrides:
St. Kilda, the Flannan Isles, North Rona, and Sula Sgeir. The species is actually
quite numerous, with many thousand birds in the St. Kilda colony and a few
hundred supposedly on the Flannans, but it remains very hard to encounter
(and so is "rare" in a practical sense), partly because of the inaccessibility of
these small, rocky islands and partly because of its elusive nocturnal habits.
The Leach's is a truly pelagic species and uses the islands only in summer for
breeding purposes. Even then it feeds way out in the open ocean all day, up to
one hundred miles from its nesting site, returning to its burrows only late at
night—at about 2 AM, in fact; and just to make things more difficult, the nesting burrows are usually on the side of precipitous rocky slopes. So even if you
brave the long (and certain to be uncomfortable) journey by small boat to one
of these distant locations you still won't see a Leach's unless you venture out in
the wee hours onto the right cliff ledge and cling there in the dark in whatever

weather conditions happen to obtain (the odds being heavily in favour of strong winds and rain). But then your reward may be great. If you are lucky the returning birds will mill around you on all sides, exchanging an extraordinary range of weird cries with their mates in the nest burrows. These calls are supposed to act as a kind of air-traffic control to bring them home in the dark to just the right hole in the ground, but the effect is of hysterical banshee wailing. I had only ever heard these island spirits on tape but they sounded quite "other," even in the reassuring surroundings of my own living room. I wanted to hear the real thing, and at the right time and place.

I had already tried the year before in St. Kilda, but although we had reached these fabled islands, battling through very heavy seas, the waves and the swell were just too great to let us stay for more than a few hours; so back we sailed again, leaving somewhere in our wake about fifteen thousand Leach's petrels, unseen and unheard. The next year I determined to try the Flannan Isles instead, where I could hope to put off for the night in my tent and be right on hand for the performance if there was one. The Flannans are just as remote as St. Kilda but much less well known and less visited. I should have the islands to myself. Moreover, there was an intriguing unsolved mystery there. The Flannans have never been properly inhabited in human memory but there was a manned light there once. In December 1900, after a violent storm, it was noticed by a passing vessel that the Flannan light was dark. A relief boat was duly dispatched to investigate but on arrival the crew could find no sign of the three keepers. A meal was still on the table, the last logbook entry had been neatly completed, and everything seemed to be in working order; but no trace of the men was found, then or ever. This Marie Celeste–type story provoked a great deal of speculation at the time and at least one long narrative poem, which ended with the portentous lines:

> We seemed to stand for an endless while,
> Though still no word was said,
> Three men alive on Flannan Isle
> Who thought on three men dead.
> (Wilfrid Wilson Gibson, "Flannan Isle," 1910)

So even if I dip on the Leach's again, there are perhaps other spirits to look for. I am duly landed (and abandoned, since the skipper of our small boat has decided to retreat to the relative safety of the Isle of Harris). It's raining and I set up my small tent to wait. It stays light until nearly midnight this far north and west and there is quite a lot to listen to: the resident raven croaks, a deep thudding bass, and I hear two whimbrel wittering in flight (could they be nesting here?—unlikely, I suppose); then in the dusk a cuckoo calls close by—goodness, Wordsworth was right when he spoke of "the cuckoo-bird / Breaking the silence of the seas / Among the farthest Hebrides" (but it must be a migrant here on the bare Flannans, surely, though on other, better-vegetated Hebridean islands they do breed, parasitising the pipits). Even after dark the noise from birds goes on: the oystercatchers break into a nervy piping every so often; there are occasional grunts from puffins and harsh cries from the herring and lesser black-backed gulls; and once I hear the clear calls of some golden plovers, migrants forced down by the misting rain, no doubt. Presumably the birds are all disturbing one another since there is no one else to disturb them (is there?). In the background is the continuous roar of surf and in the foreground squalls of rain rattle against my tent. All very atmospheric.

At 1.45 AM I put on my boots and rainwear and unzip the tent-flap to have a recce. Immediately I hear a strange, muffled call nearby, something between a chuckle and a gurgle. Can it possibly be . . . ? As soon as I get outside the tent I hear it again, more clearly, and then several more, and then a longer sequence of calls in a wild, chattering rhythm, and then the whole devil's chorus. I walk in what seems to be the direction of these screaming spirits, just the other side of the lighthouse; and suddenly here they all are, whirling round me in their bat-veering, butterfly-floating flight, even brushing me with their wings, several hundred birds, shrieking like Gaelic goblins on acid, as someone put it—the full Leach's experience. Each time the beam from the great light comes round I see them briefly illuminated in the air, as if blown in like leaves; they are pitching down right by my feet to enter their nesting-holes; I can pick out individual birds with my torch at ranges of down to a yard as they crash-land and then flop into a burrow.

Magic. I stay with them for an hour or so and decide that it isn't worth going to look for the related species, storm petrels, which are nocturnal too and are likely to be nesting in the dry-stone walls of the old cleits I noticed at the other end of the island. Storm petrels have class but not charisma, and I don't want an anticlimax. By about 3.30 AM the Leach's have stopped flighting in and the colony is falling silent. I return to my tent, with light already appearing in the northeast, and it is only now that I realise how wet I've got in the rain. I sleep. In the morning light they are all gone, leaving me wondering if it was all just a marvellous dream. As another and better poet put it (Shakespeare in *The Tempest*):

> Be not afeard: the isle is full of noises,
> Sounds and sweet airs, that give delight, and hurt not.
> Sometimes a thousand twangling instruments
> Will hum about mine ears, and sometimes voices

> That if I then had waked after a long sleep
> Will make me sleep again

I had seen Leach's a few times before, storm-tossed birds flicking and gliding low over the waves when driven close inshore by rough weather off the
East Anglian coast. That was always exciting—it's a test to pick them out and
identify them in these conditions and they are unusual sightings. Such encounters also convey something of the birds' wild pelagic existence, though
they are in truth displaced on these occasions, as are other and much rarer vagrants who may be victims of extreme weather conditions. To have seen a
long-billed murrelet at Dawlish Warren in November 2006 or a golden-winged
warbler in a supermarket car park in Kent in February 1989 is to have had a
remarkable experience of a kind, though no one would suggest that the massed
twitchers were experiencing the "whole bird" in anything like its natural setting.[1] But to encounter the Leach's on the Flannans at two in the morning was
to feel as though I was seeing and hearing them very much in *their* place and
at *their* time.

I want in this chapter to explore this thought further. To what extent does
our experience and appreciation of birds depend on when and where we see
them? Do they acquire part of their significance and "meaning" for us from
these dimensions of place and time? And is the reverse true—can the cycles
of the year and day or the landscapes we inhabit be at least partly defined by
the birds we associate with them? Can a bird be a genius loci?

The Sense of a Season

There was a government crisis on 14 March 2007 in Japan. The official meteorological agency forecast the start of the cherry blossom season incorrectly.
This really matters in Japan. There is a brief period when the delicate pink
flowers bloom at their best and everyone plans celebrations to mark this great
event, a brief honeymoon period between the contrasting rigours of winter
and summer. Travel agents put on tours to the best localities, towns plan festi-
vals, and Japanese companies have parties where salary-men and office-ladies
can celebrate under the trees each night until the blossoms fall. Nor is this
some new "invented tradition." In Kyoto, the former Japanese capital, the
cherry blossom records go right back to AD 705. But despite this wealth of
historical data the forecasters got it wrong by three crucial days in 2007 and

---

[1] The number of those present to see the warbler was impressive, however. An estimated three
thousand people saw it on the Saturday after its discovery and another twelve hundred on the
Sunday; but few returned and the numbers dropped off quickly. The bird remained in the area
until April, though it was sometimes unreported for days at a time towards the end of its stay.

the embarrassment was profound. Whether acts of defenestration actually occurred is not recorded, but the bows of apology could not have been deeper. "We have ruined the spring for those who relied on us," the meteorologists abjectly confessed, before very sensibly going on to blame a computer bug. Meanwhile in Britain, we knew it must be spring because someone wrote to *The Times* about the first cuckoo, swallows appeared on the south coast, daffodils appeared at Gowbarrow Park,[1] and Bill Oddie appeared on television.

People have always had seasonal markers of this kind, and very often the markers have included birds. Literature and art are full of these references, as are the conversations and diaries of quite ordinary men and women. Spring is generally the season most eagerly awaited and the one that attracts most attention, but all the seasons are regularly characterised by the comings and goings of familiar birds. Here are just a few examples, some well-known, some maybe less so:

> For, lo, the winter is past, the rain is over and gone. The flowers appear on the earth; the time of the singing of birds is come, and the voice of the turtle is heard in our land. (*Song of Solomon*, about third century BC)

> I have news for you; the stag bells, winter snows, summer has gone.
> Wind high and cold, the sun low, short its course, the sea running high.
> Deep red the bracken, its shape is lost; the wild goose has raised its
>   accustomed cry.
> Cold has seized the birds' wings; season of ice, this is my news. (Irish anon., ninth century)

> It is remarkable how the American mind runs to statistics.... Every shopkeeper makes a record of the arrival of the first martin or bluebird to his box. Dodd, the broker, told me last spring that he knew when the first bluebird came to his boxes; he made a memorandum of it. John Brown, merchant, tells me this morning that the martins first came to his box on the 13th he "made a minute of it." Beside so many entries in their day-books and ledgers, they record these things. (Thoreau, *Journal*, 17 April 1854)

> Then, quite suddenly, one morning, the change came. The wind went to the south, came off the sea warm and soothing. In the afternoon there were little gleams of sunshine, and the doves began, without interval, slowly and awkwardly, to coo. The doves were cooing, though with a

[1] The location near Ullswater in the Lake District where Wordsworth had his "daffodils" epiphany on 15 April 1802 ("ten thousand saw I at a glance ... ").

laboured sound, as if they were still winter-stunned. Nevertheless, all the afternoon they continued their noise, in the mild air, before the frost had thawed off the road. At evening the wind blew gently, still gathering a bruising quality of frost from the hard earth. Then, in the yellow-gleamy sunset, wild birds began to whistle faintly in the blackthorn thickets of the stream-bottom. (D. H. Lawrence, "Whistling of Birds," 17 February 1917)

Touching my arm, the shepherd pointed downstream at something in the dark-shadowed east high above the river and just discernible in the failing sky. Ragged and flocculent, fading to grey, scattered with specks of pink from the declining sun, varying in width as random fragments were dropping away and recohering and agitated with motion as though its whole length were turning on a single thread, a thick line of crowd-ing storks stretched from one side of the heavens to the other. Mounting Africa along the Nile, they had followed the coast of Palestine and Asia Minor and entered Europe over the Bosphorus. Then, persevering along the Black Sea shore to the delta of the Danube, they had steered their flight along that shining highway until they had come to the great bend a few miles downstream. Defecting from the river, their journey was now following a westerly as well as a northerly bias; they were bound for Poland, perhaps, and shedding contingents as they went at hundreds of remembered haunts. We gazed at them in wonder. It was a long time before the rearguard of that great sky-procession had vanished north. Before nightfall the whole armada would subside in a wood or settle all over some Slovakian hamlet—astonishing the villagers and delighting them, for storks are bird of good omen. (Patrick Leigh Fermor, *Between the Woods and the Water*, 1986)

The same general point can be made, even more strikingly perhaps, by a *failure* to pay proper attention to these seasonal indications:

If the Emperor Napoleon, when on the road to Moscow with his army in 1811, had condescended to observe the flights of storks and cranes passing over his fated battalions, subsequent events in the politics of Europe might have been very different. These storks and cranes knew of the coming-on of a great and terrible winter; the birds hastened towards the South, Napoleon and his army towards the North. (Frank Buckland in George C. Bompas, *The Life of Frank Buckland*, 1885)

In Britain, it is the swallow, the cuckoo, and the swift that carry the main symbolic weight of spring and summer for most people. In other parts of

42. Cranes of the world on stamps. Top: Siberian white (Russia), black-necked
(China), sarus (Burma). Middle: white-naped (North Korea), common (Romania),
red-crowned (Japan). Bottom: black-crowned (Niger), demoiselle (Turkey). In
P. J. Lanspeary, *The World of Birds on Stamps* (1975)

Europe also the white stork, the crane, and the turtle dove, depending on location and latitude. In North America this necessarily varies across such a very
large continent and there are a number of regional differences: in some eastern states the bluebird, the purple martin, and the American robin perform
this role, in parts of Canada and the Midwest people may rush outside to greet
the returning geese or (for some lucky few) whooping cranes; in Southern
California the swallows (cliff) return every year from Argentina to San Juan
Capistrano and are celebrated in the festival of St. Joseph on 19 March each
year (memorialised in the song "When the Swallows Come Back to Capistrano"). This symbolism has great potency, as governments well understand,

and most of these species (especially cranes and storks) have featured on national stamps, coins, and flags.

Manufacturers understand its commercial value too and you see similar images emblazoned on articles as various as clothes, crockery, carpets, and wallpaper. Things get more complicated, however, when religious symbols are also involved. Have you ever thought, for example, about the curious appearances of different species in the familiar carol "On the First Day of Christmas"? It starts off harmlessly enough with twelve drummers drumming and eleven lords a-leaping, and one can't really have an ornithological problem with seven swans a-swimming or six geese a-laying. You begin to get suspicious, though, when you come to four calling birds (which birds are calling?) and three French hens (why French?). And you may be positively mystified when you reach two turtle doves and a partridge in a pear tree. As we all know, you don't get turtle doves in Britain at Christmas—they are summer visitors, usually arriving in Northern Europe in May. As for the partridge, this is presumably a common (or "grey") partridge since this is a traditional carol and the red-legged (or "French") partridge was an introduced species that didn't breed in Britain until 1790; on the other hand, the French for "partridge" is *perdix* and if you pronounce that in French it does sound rather like "pear tree." Anyway, I've never seen a partridge on top of a tree of any kind, let alone a pear tree. Poetic licence? No, it's more interesting than that. One theory is that all the twelve "presents" are really religious symbols and the whole carol is in a kind of code because it was composed at a time when it was dangerous to express a public commitment to Catholicism. Then it all makes sense: the twelve drummers are beating out the twelve doctrines in the Apostles' Creed, the eleven pipers are the eleven faithful apostles spreading the word, and so on, down to seven beautiful swans as the seven gifts of the Holy Spirit, six laying geese as the six days of creation, five gold rings (maybe ring-necked pheasants?) as the first five books of the Bible (the Pentateuch), four colly birds (the old country name for blackbirds) as the four evangelists, three French hens as the three virtues, and two turtle doves as the two Testaments. Finally, the partridge is lifted aloft as the resurrected Christ, and that draws on an even older Greek myth in which Athena (who was the goddess of pear trees among many other things) raised from the dead her lover Perdix (the Greek name for a partridge) and carried him to heaven in the branches of a pear. That's already a heady mixture of the pagan and the Christian.

But the manufacturers won't leave it at that. I saw a fancy gift tin of biscuits one recent Christmas with the cover illustrated in plate 7c. There's the partridge on the pear tree—a grey partridge, quite correctly. But what birds are those winging in at the top, left and right—two swallows, very Christmassy!

And it gets worse. There are two even more remarkable strangers sneaking in below the swallows, common terns (or could they be arctics, if the artist was being careful in depicting such a sharply delineated leading underside edge to the wings?). Terns are also summer visitors, and are more often seen in estuaries than in orchards. Presumably they are there on the tin because their angled wings and forked tails were thought to reemphasise the swallow theme by the designers responsible. Who says we no longer believe in archetypes?

Birders can always spoil a bit of harmless fun or a favourite carol with these deconstructions, but they have their own special marker species too, as you might expect. In Britain they will be looking for the first wheatear or sand martin and listening for the first chiffchaff from early March (the habit persists, though chiffchaffs are now increasingly overwintering because of climate change). Many birders keep such annual lists of arrival and departure dates for their local patch. Arrival dates are easy since the birds are active, usually singing, and just have to be noted when first seen or heard. Departure dates can be harder work and require more systematic record-keeping: the cuckoo itself, so eagerly awaited and instantly recognisable in spring, is rarely noticed again by most people once it stops calling in early July and you need to maintain a daily diary to be sure of remembering which was the last swift scything past high overhead in August. But these are precisely the sorts of records bird enthusiasts have always liked to keep. As with the recording of rare birds, the main interest and value in them come not from the occasional freakish outrider—a swallow in December or a waxwing in May—but from the regularities and trends they demonstrate, a particular issue now, of course, with the concerns about global warming and climate change. And to establish patterns, the records need to be kept very systematically over a long period of time and for a very specific locality.

In Britain, records of this kind have been kept by naturalists at least since the eighteenth century. There is a particularly famous sequence of records maintained by the Masham family in Stratton Strawless in Norfolk. In 1736, Robert Masham began to record twenty-seven "indications of spring," mostly flowering, leafing, and migration dates, and successive generations maintained these observations until 1958, so they constitute an extraordinarily detailed and continuous list of records for one small place. Others were meanwhile putting their experiences into prose. In 1790, Robert wrote an enthusiastic letter of congratulation to the clergyman author of a new book that contained a wealth of similar observations, all expressed in an inquisitive and unsentimental style. This work has endeared itself to readers worldwide ever since. It is the particular and indeed parochial character of Gilbert White's *The Natural History and Antiquities of Selborne, in the County of Southampton* that has been its universal appeal, thus demonstrating an important point about the human imagination more generally. In his study *The Naturalist in Britain,* David Elliston Allen identifies White's key virtue as a writer as

> his gift for empathy, his ability to infuse deep feeling into what he described so carefully and soberly. He was perhaps the first writer on natural history in Britain to display this much more modern gift, and for that reason alone *Selborne* is of special historical interest. White's preference for patient observation, in an age when most people stopped merely to collect, is, similarly, far in advance of its time. But over and above even these there still remains that one ingredient without which no work attains the status of an irresistible classic: somehow, it enshrines a portion of our necessary collective mythology. Lowell came very close to the truth in calling *Selborne* "the journal of Adam in Paradise." For it is, surely, the testament of Static Man: at peace with the world and with himself, content with deepening his knowledge of his one small corner of the earth, a being suspended in a perfect mental balance. Selborne is the secret, private parish inside each one of us. We must be thankful it was revealed so very early—and with such seemingly unstudied simplicity and grace.

Masham and White got into a lively correspondence about the mystery of bird migration and their shared love of swallows and martins in particular.[1] It was indeed the swallow that White especially looked for each spring and it was his simple diary note of 13 April 1768 that betrays the significance its arrival had for him each year: *"Hirundo domestica!!!"*

There is a long history of such welcomings going back far before White's time and in many other countries and cultures. And sometimes the emotional significance can be so great as to be traumatic, especially in the absence of expert information:

Madame Butterfly: When do the robins build their nests in America?
American consul: What was that?
Butterfly: Before or after they do here?
Consul: Why do you ask?
Butterfly: My husband promised me he'd return in the season when the robin rebuilds his nest. He's already done it three times here.

---

[1] White summarises his own list of migrant dates in his first letter to Daines Barrington (30 June 1769), including, one notices, in his list of regular summer migrants the wryneck "about the middle of March," the stone curlew "end of March," and the landrail (no date). He notes that some wheatears "are to be seen with us the winter through."

Consul: Maybe there it happens less often. . . . I'm sorry. I never studied
   ornithology.

Pinkerton was lying, but in any case they weren't the same kind of robins! You
could argue that *Madame Butterfly* is a good illustration of the dangers in making facile comparisons between different cultures, which may mean very different things by apparently similar words and practices. Anthropologists hope
to have the antidote to this by immersing themselves in the society they are
studying and reporting on it from the inside. And they make it clear that the
seasonal significance of birds is by no means limited to the Western, developed
world or to temperate regions. It may be even more marked in some nonliterate
societies in the tropics for which birds seem to act as both clocks and calendars
to some degree. Steven Feld describes the world of the Kaluli people who live in
the tropical rain forest in the Southern Highlands of Papua New Guinea:

> Kaluli are quick to remark on the relationship between this [seasonal]
> cycle and that of the avifauna. The appearance of the rainbow bee-eater,
> *bili,* is a prominent feature of *ten,* roughly April to September. At the
> beginning of *ten* in 1977, I heard several youths running across the
> courtyard yelling, "*Ten's* really here; we heard the *bili.*" During *ten, bili*
> stays in the gardens and forest openings. The season from October or
> November to mid-March corresponds to *dona,* and Kaluli know it to be
> the time that *yoma* "Mountain Pigeons" come in large groups to feed on
> *dona* and other tree fruit. Kaluli say *dona* is the season when pigeons
> and fruit-doves are highly present and vocally conspicuous.
>
> Perhaps more significantly, the daily cycle of events is marked by the
> presence of birds. Kaluli say "Only bats work at night: people are like
> birds; we get up with their calls in the morning and sleep when they do."
> Women note that the early morning calls of *bolo,* the Brown Oriole and
> New Guinea Friarbird, and *sagelon,* the Hooded Butcherbird, tell chil-
> dren to gather with their families. Others told me that the late afternoon
> appearance in the courtyard of *bas,* the Black-breasted Woodswallow,
> and *defalen,* the Uniform Swiftlet, with the former calling *bas bas bas*
> "brother-in-law" to the swiftlet, means that people should come and sit
> together and have food. In these instances the presence of birds stands
> for the passage of time and the cycle of sociality.

The human fascination with migration has as long a pedigree as our everyday observations of the arrivals of regular visitors, whether swallows or wood-
swallows. In the ancient Western world the two great encyclopedists of natural
history, Aristotle (384–322 BC) and Pliny (AD 23–79), both puzzled over it,

reporting a large number of relevant observations as well as toying with some wild theories, including the notion that the birds hibernated (which was still thought possible as late as Gilbert White's time) or that they even metamorphosed into other species (for example, the robin into the redstart). The first actual experiment appears in a story told of the Cistercian prior Caesarius von Heisterbach in the thirteenth century. He is supposed to have taken a swallow from its nest and attached to its foot a piece of parchment with the message, "Swallow, where do you live in winter?" The next spring the bird returned, bearing the answer "In Asia, in the home of Petrus." Well, the story deserves to be true, at any rate. Eventually, of course, the scientists took over and studied the question properly. Recording arrival and departure dates became "phenology" and enquiries into migration became "bird navigation studies," though amateurs and enthusiasts continued to provide much of the data for the scientists to work on and are probably still the people who care most about the findings.

If it turns out, as now seems very likely, that the climate is changing in a progressive way then the effects will indeed be far-reaching. We are already noticing the changes in behaviour of several migratory species. Blackcaps have been commonly wintering in the United Kingdom for years (though usually not the same ones that summer here); now chiffchaffs are starting to do the same and perhaps other species will follow suit. If they can obtain sufficient food and shelter the gains are obvious: they save themselves the need to make these massive, exhausting, and hazardous migrations that take such a huge annual toll in mortality. This isn't a straightforward issue, of course, because climate changes of this kind can affect different natural phenomena at different speeds and the complex synchronisation that has evolved between food supply, nesting site, and arrival dates may be seriously disturbed. Changes in temperature are, after all, only one of the relevant factors and have no effect, for example, on the length of daylight hours. Birds interact with their total environment, including prey, predators, parasites, competitors, and resources. Change one factor and the whole system may be destabilised. And this destabilisation may include not just practical consequences but symbolic ones. One swallow may not make a summer, but would swallows still be swallows if they were with us all the year round? Would summer still be summer, come to that? What would happen to the seasonal cycle of expectation and recognition? Would we lose a whole repertoire of metaphor and reference, and if so at what cost?

Keats again, but this time I quote him with approval as he reflects in his *Ode to Autumn* on the transience of the individual human life and the futility of regret; the departure of the swallows is indeed a premonition of the coming winter but it is also an intimation that they will return; each season has its own delights and pleasures; and he even seems to notice that the British robin sings a different song in the autumn:

> Where are the songs of spring? Ay, where are they?
> Think not of them, thou hast thy music too,—
> While barred clouds bloom the soft-dying day,
> And touch the stubble-plains with rosy hue;
> Then in a wailful choir the small gnats mourn
> Among the willow sallows, borne aloft
> Or sinking as the light wind lives or dies;
> And full-grown lambs loud bleat from hilly bourn;
> Hedge crickets sing; and now with treble soft
> The red-breast whistles from a garden croft;
> And gathering swallows twitter in the skies.

This should strike a chord with most birders. Anyone who watches a particular patch regularly becomes very sensitive to all the gradual and small changes going on throughout the year. This goes way beyond noticing the first cuckoo and the last swift. Every bird has both its daily and seasonal rhythms and so therefore do the places they inhabit. There are regular appearances and disappearances to observe; occasional visitors to note; habits, trends, and patterns to detect. Absences and silences can be as striking as presences and arrivals if you are finely attuned in this way. Small variations on a theme can be as exciting as large surprises. Birders love to keep records of these regularities and irregularities and you will find them in every local ornithological magazine. Here is just one representative example, taken from Wiltshire in southwestern England, where a dedicated observer has been visiting Liddington Hill for many years to track the autumn migration, of ring ouzels in particular. This is an extract from his 2001 records. I quote it at length to show the kind of detail that is characteristic of such observations (numbers, age, sex, behaviour, location—even down to individual trees):

> The visits started well with a juvenile hobby circling the Castle on 22 August and five wheatears around the ramparts and got better when an immature marsh harrier "played with" a buzzard, eventually drifting off south-west (25th). Supporting cast included redstart, yellowhammer in partial song—a very late date for song—and another carrying food. 23 yellow wagtails was a notable count (28th) plus six wheatears, four whinchats and four whitethroats.
>
> On the first September visit (3rd) there was some evidence of buzzard migration with four south west at 10 AM followed by another five drifting south west at 10:30 AM. Wheatears were present on six dates during

the month with five on 4th. Over 40 meadow pipits arrived on 5th when there was a lone corn bunting close to the trig point, three yellow wagtails and seven kestrels. Redstarts were in the hawthorn hedge to the west of the Castle on 12th and 26th with the last whitethroat there on 18th. Ploughing of fields adjacent to the Castle attracted good numbers of gulls from 12th when 430 lesser black-backed gulls and a common gull were feeding; this increased to 820 lessers on 18th and included a herring gull on 26th. The field edges also attracted coveys of grey and red-legged partridges. Signs of winter were the first siskins (22nd) followed by a male merlin hunting a linnet (24th). Migrants on 26th included 200 linnets, 80 meadow pipits and 45 greenfinches.

October started with two wheatears (3rd) and two chaffinches (5th). Visible migration included passage swallows and house martins with 55 of the latter (12th). A male peregrine circled the Castle (15th) and the first three stonechats arrived (17th) increasing to seven (20th). The warm weather of October . . . was no doubt responsible for the large number of "late" butterflies. This included 55+ red admirals and a "fresh" painted lady (both 17th) with a small tortoiseshell (24th). An interesting sight on 19th was a siskin accompanying a party of eight redwings.

Just when I was giving up hope of ring ouzel there was one flying from the hawthorn hedge "with" a mistle thrush (20th). It flew across to the next hedgerow and perched in an elderberry bush facing me—a female or immature. Interestingly, I found ring ouzels here on 20th October 1998 and 18th October 1999. Birds occurring after 8 October are likely to be Scandinavian in origin.

The sequence of visits goes on, to end in early November:

Two November visits on 3rd and 5th proved worthwhile. Another ring ouzel appeared on 3rd when a woodcock was put up on wet pasture. On the final visit . . . the highlight was a count of 8 stonechats, indicative of an excellent autumn for this species; also noted were two sparrowhawks, two corn buntings, a small movement of starlings southwest and a "late" red admiral. (Stephen Edwards)

Every birder has records like this, if not usually quite as thorough and good as this, and the whole country is a mosaic of local patches that are watched intently, not for the great rarities that may occasionally turn up or for general scientific hypothesising but for the daily variations in the ordinary and the particular. On every walk you take in a familiar landscape, you are moving through a dense web of signs and signals, and therefore through a whole terrain of meaning that can be sensed and explored. And when you are on unfamiliar ground, as I was in the Flannan Isles, a good part of the pleasure comes from trying to ask the right questions of the place and starting to piece together the answers. Some of those answers, as we have seen, are to be found in an awareness of season and time, but we should now turn to the other and complementary dimension of place.

Birds in a Landscape

In 1955, W. G. Hoskins published his classic work *The Making of the English Landscape,* which practically invented the subject of "landscape history," a very attractive blend of geology, history, and natural history that has since become a hugely popular topic for whole series of books, evening classes, and of course TV programmes. In the latter a jovial presenter will be striding about the countryside (usually wearing clothes, it must be said, that don't seem to have seen much action) and talking to local savants who are able to "read" the landscape. The analogy with reading a text is very compelling. You need skill, attention, practice, and experience to do it well; you can learn from other people but the experience is all your own; the more reading you do the more you are likely to get out of it; but everyone can do it to some degree and you can do it anywhere you happen to be. I want to make the further suggestion that seeing birds in and as part of the landscape is essential to a full and satisfying reading.

Some writers are very good readers as well. The heroes of this book so far have been the much-quoted team of Gilbert White, John Clare, Henry Thoreau, Richard Jefferies, and J. A. Baker, each of whom is very different from the others in what they bring to their writing but all of whom have an exceptional rapport with the landscapes they are describing. Their descriptions are almost too good for present purposes, though, since we (and occasionally they) can get carried away by the writing itself. I want first to approach this question from the standpoint of the more ordinary birder in his or her patch. What most birders do most of the time is visit familiar places and have unsurprising experiences there. If their primary interest is in finding and identifying rare birds, they will of course make specific excursions for extraordinary purposes—the supermarket in Kent for the 1989 golden-winged warbler, or St. Mary's airport in the Isles of Scilly for the 2004 cream-coloured courser;[1] they may also go on organised bird tours to parts of the world where everything is, to them, new and exotic. But these are only apparent exceptions to my point. Even the most highly motivated twitchers will usually devote their

---

[1] Some people got off the helicopter, inspected the bird on the airfield from the airport buildings, and went back home on the next flight—not a large exposure to the local landscape.

unusual energies to a local patch as well and will transfer the same obsessions to that, with sometimes curious results. If your local patch actually *is* Scilly it then becomes as important to see a magpie there as a courser (or even better a green woodpecker or little owl), while if your patch is Hyde Park in London a report of a house sparrow, a yellowhammer, or a snipe would bring people running. Green woodpecker was last recorded in Scilly in 1901 (the only record) and little owl has yet to appear. In Hyde Park, jackdaw, house sparrow, and snipe are relative rarities. Interestingly, a rook or a yellowhammer is a good bird in both places.

This just confirms what we already know about the relativity of the rare. There are no exotic birds any more than there are exotic languages, people, or places; there are just exotic experiences. In any event, the interest in the exotic is itself just the flip-side of our interest in the familiar: in both cases we are aware of how certain things, in this case birds, either do or don't fit in with our usual expectations and in both cases that awareness depends on a prior sensitivity to place.

Local patches can be almost anywhere, as these examples already indicate. They may be as large as a whole county, a state, or a separate island (which has the additional satisfaction of being physically "bounded"); they may be as small as a parish, a wood, a marsh, a gravel pit, a garden, or even a prison window ledge;[1] they may be rural or urban, wild or tame, beautiful or despoiled. What they have in common is that the regular visitor becomes unusually close to them, intimate in quite a strong sense of that word, often with a feeling of personal attachment, which like all such emotions may then develop into or fuse with other feelings, some of them positive (belonging and understanding) and some less so (possessiveness and resistance to change). The intimacy comes from an accumulation of very particular observations over time, each of which helps gradually to build up a set of informed expectations that it then becomes a pleasure to test, modify, extend, and enrich. There is a wealth of publications that speak to this interest: country diaries, nature notes, memoirs, blogs, and chronicles of "a year in the life of (some favoured spot)." Every naturalist or birder of whatever stripe has kept such records. Here is just one example, which shows how the ordinary becomes special when you give it this kind of devoted attention:

> Can it really be only two years since I first visited my local patch? Some
> mornings, as I walk or cycle along the narrow path around the reservoir

[1] The case of Robert Franklin Stroud, the "Birdman of Alcatraz," at least as portrayed by Burt Lancaster in the film. Stroud was actually the birdman of Leavenworth—he was only transferred to Alcatraz later—and he gave most of his attention to tame canaries he kept in his cell.

and watch the bird activity, it seems as if I've been coming here forever. This is partly down to the comforting familiarity of everyday landmarks. There's the little reedbed at the north end, summer home for a couple of pairs of reed warblers. The patch of sallows at the southern end, where I always hope to come across some scarce migrant, but never do. And the row of old black poplar trees, so late to come into leaf this spring. Every birdwatcher enjoys coming across the unexpected. But one of the best things about making regular visits to your local patch is the usual birds: the resident pair of mute swans, the arrival of the first swifts in spring or the flocks of wintering shovelers in autumn. Even the customary flock of carrion crows, squabbling noisily in the trees by the gate, are a welcome sight.

I suppose it's not really surprising that I find the sights and sounds of this place familiar. I have, after all, made almost 200 visits there since July 1994. Why? What's the point in going to one place so many times, especially when it is just one of thousands of ordinary sites up and down the country? Well, apart from the fact I enjoy being out in the fresh air (always the standard birder's excuse), it's because even a small, landlocked location like this can turn up a surprising number of different kinds of birds. . . .

Some of these are commonplace birds elsewhere—but locally rare in this particular part of the London suburbs. They include sightings of jackdaws and wigeon—hardly likely to cause a mass twitch. Nevertheless, to me they were as exciting as any storm-driven rarity. For these were my birds.

He goes on to record one or two special sightings, including a hobby one May, and concludes:

In the end, the real joy in patch-watching is the knowledge that I am helping to create a permanent record of the birdlife of one tiny corner of the British Isles. It may not be a famous place for birds, like Minsmere or Cley, nor a remote or majestic one, like Fair Isle or the Cairngorms. But it is still a place where birds come and go, act out the dramas of their daily lives, and continually enthral at least one person passionate about birdwatching. (Stephen Moss, on Lonsdale Road SW13)

The important point here, I think, as in the quotation from the patch-watcher in Wiltshire, is the relish in the ordinary and the particular. I said before that birders spend most of their time having unsurprising experiences. Unsurprising, but not therefore unrewarding. In fact, often rewarding because unsurprising; the pleasure comes in the confirmation of what we have learned to expect and the confirmation therefore of our own increased awareness. We come to know that at this time of day and year there should be a reed warbler singing in that patch of reeds, that there could be a wigeon on the water, and that there just might be a hobby hawking overhead. In that sense we have *made* the experiences unsurprising by refining our expectations and enlarging our sense of what is likely and what is possible; and there is always just enough variation and uncertainty to keep us interested. We can also then respond more fully to what is genuinely surprising because we understand the context that makes it so and have a sharper sense of the probabilities. You can either say we are making the ordinary special or put it the other way round and say we are learning to expect the unusual. Either way, we are in effect making ourselves more at home in the natural world, and "home" is of course the root meaning of "ecology," the study of things in their home surroundings.

There can be a special satisfaction in testing such expectations in less familiar locations. A good birder should be able to eye up a piece of terrain and make some pretty good predictions about what might be there at any given time. The predictions are not exactly self-fulfilling but they certainly improve your chances, since attention is necessarily limited and selective. If you don't actually *look* for birds like a nightjar, a jack snipe, a long-eared owl, and a dotterel in the right places at the right times you're most unlikely ever to see them; if you're not *listening* for the kingfisher speeding along a stream, some twite rising in a flock of linnets from a coastal marsh in winter, and a hawfinch hiding deep in the crown of a tree, you will probably never pick them up at all.

Most birders with a local patch have in their heads a sort of hit-list of birds they think they ought to encounter there in due course and a shrewd idea of just when and where they will find them. There can be great satisfaction in seeing a barn owl over the ideal patch of rough pasture, a ring ouzel on the ridge on autumn passage, or a spring wheatear one early morning in the dunes. I waited for years before finally hearing a Cetti's warbler on my coastal patch, singing from just the area of flooded willows I knew it would one day appear in if their expansion through East Anglia continued; likewise the grasshopper warbler on passage that sang for just an hour one dawn from the dense vegetation between the reedbed and the drier grassland I had marked out as the likely spot. The water pipit on the boggy grass by the marsh was a longer shot (which felt like a coup); and I still await the winter shore lark on the spit that runs out from the shingle bank and the red-breasted flycatcher flitting in that copse set back from the beach one October morning when the wind has been in the east. Believe it and they will come . . . one day.

You can use the same sort of informed expectations to do detective work of this kind in reverse, that is identifying a location from an account of the birds there. You can try yourself out by using one of those "Where to Watch Birds in *X*" books backwards, as it were: look at a list of birds and try to work out the likely time and place. For example, *marsh harrier, bittern, avocet, nightingale, woodlark, Cetti's warbler, tree pipit, and little tern* gives you a large reedbed location (marsh harrier and bittern), with overgrown surrounding scrub (Cetti's) and woodland (nightingale), including lagoons (avocet) and a shingly beach (little tern) and some heathland (tree pipit, woodlark). This will be in the south or east of England, almost certainly Minsmere or Walberswick. If you also have *swift and whimbrel* it is probably not before late April (the swift) and not after mid-May (end of whimbrel passage, on their way north). That one's easy, but here is a master detective at work. James Fisher was not only a leading scientific ornithologist of his day but was also enough of an Anglo-Saxon scholar to translate this passage from the Old English poem "The Seafarer":

> There heard I naught but seething sea,
> Ice-cold wave, awhile a song of swan.
> There came to charm me gannets' pother
> And whimbrels' trills for the laughter of men,
> Kittiwake singing instead of mead.
> Storms there the stacks thrashed, there answered them the tern
> With icy feathers; full oft the erne wailed round
> Spray-feathered . . .

Fisher then applies his powers of deduction to it:

> My guess is that this scene, so tenderly described, was observed by a young Anglo-Saxon ornithologist in some year before AD 685, at the Bass Rock in what his present heirs call East Lothian, most probably between what we would call 20 and 27 April by our calendar. Birds change their distribution, but not so much their season; just at this stormy time the winds can blow cold in the Firth of Forth, and the great whooper swans pass north to their breeding-grounds on the moorland wetlands, and the whimbrels utter their trilling titter, usually of seven beats, on their flight to the moorland drylands; and the common terns' main arrival is due; and the gannets and the kittiwakes and the white-tailed sea eagles hold their nest-sites on the ocean-facing cliffs. At least the ernes did: they have gone now, from the Bass, though a statement from the late, great Professor Alfred Newton of a century ago . . . indicates that the white-tailed eagle still has an eyrie on the Bass in our bird-historical times (that is, since 1600) a thousand years after the Seafarer saw them there.

This dating, and placing, of perhaps the first bit of true-sounding, wild-inspired field ornithological record since the Romans gave up their colony is of course no more than an (I hope) educated guess. The Bass is the only place I can think of within the Anglo-Saxon realm where all these birds could have been seen together under the circumstances which the unknown author of *The Seafarer* describes. There is today, it is true, a small gannet colony on the chalk ledges of Bempton Cliffs in Yorkshire, with kittiwakes, where terns and whimbrels pass. But it is quite new. Nowhere else in England save on Lundy in the Bristol Channel have gannets nested since "Domesday Book" times; and the description of the Seafarer is no description of Lundy. The gannet colony of the Bass is one of the old, ancient ones.

Watson would have blinked at him in amazement at this point.

Sometimes just the name of a bird or two, or an illustration, can trigger a whole series of less scholarly associations, as in this example from *Jane Eyre* by Charlotte Brontë. Jane is absorbed in her copy of Bewick, the field guide of the day, and imagines scenes not unlike those the Seafarer must have encountered:

> I returned to my book—Bewick's *History of British Birds:* the letterpress thereof I cared little for, generally speaking; and yet there were certain introductory pages that, child as I was, I could not pass quite as a blank. They were those that treat the haunts of seafowl; of "solitary rocks and promontories" by them only inhabited; of the coast of Norway, studded with isles from its southern extremity, the Lindeness, or Naze, to the North Cape. . . . The words in these introductory pages connected themselves with the succeeding vignettes, and gave significance to the rock standing up alone in a sea of billow and spray; to the broken boat stranded on a desolate coast; to the cold and ghastly moon glancing through bars of cloud at a wreck just sinking. . . . With Bewick on my knee I was then happy: happy at heart in my way. I feared nothing but interruption.

Jane's mood is consciously escapist. But Stanley Baldwin seems to be trying to deceive himself as well as other people in this extraordinary idyll from the 1920s:

> To me, England is the country, and the country is England. And when I ask myself what I mean by England, when I think of England when I am abroad, England comes to me through my various senses—through the ear, through the eye and through certain imperishable scents. . . . The sounds of England, the tinkle of the hammer on the anvil in the country smithy, the corncrake on a dewy morning, the sound of the scythe

43. Jane Eyre's Bewick vignette (*The Ship* from Bewick,
A History of British Birds, volume 2, *Water Birds*, 1804)

against the whetstone, and the sight of a plough team coming over
the brow of a hill, the sight that has been England since England was a
land . . . the one eternal sight of England. (Stanley Baldwin, "Speech to
the Annual Dinner of the Royal Society of St. George," 6 May 1924)

Local authorities are encouraged by developers to exploit similar fantasies
in their naming of streets. The line of thought is that certain birds have very
positive associations with attractive environments and landscapes, so that by a
process of sympathetic magic using the name in itself makes the locality more
attractive. Hence the large number of Kingfisher Drives, Swan Lanes, and
Nightingale Avenues in places where the relevant species have yet to be recorded. But one sometimes suspects a frustrated patch-lister may be loose in
the naming department. I have a local example of this in the unlovely town of
Haverhill, Suffolk. There is a little estate there that has a "bird theme," including the predictable Kingfisher and Robin Closes, the delightful-sounding if
surprising Sandpiper, Osprey, Gannet, and Tern Closes, and the astonishing
Rosefinch Close.[1] (Have you ever seen a drab, washed-out October rosefinch—the usual kind in the United Kingdom? Personally, I wouldn't cross
Robin Close for one.) The limiting case of this sort of bureaucratic thinking
must however be in the outback town of Longreach in Queensland, where *all*
the streets are named after birds; and you can orient yourself handily if you
have an Australian equivalent of Bewick's original two volumes organised by
habitat, since streets named after water birds run east-west and streets named
after land birds run north-south. So if you go south down the main Eagle

---

[1] Funnily enough, though, I did see a pair of waxwings on cotoneaster bushes in the adjacent
Gannet Close in the winter of 2003. Now, Waxwing Way would be a street name really worth
having.

Street, turn left at Pelican Street, then take the 6th left up Cassowary Street and first left at Swan Street, you get back again to Eagle Street (wedge-tailed, presumably).

This nostalgia for landscape and the identification of landscape with certain species of birds can take a more serious form in times of war. The famous naturalist Peter Scott (son of the doomed Antarctic explorer) served in the navy in the Second World War. He found himself in a destroyer on patrol in the Western Approaches and thought about what he was defending:

> For most of us [England means] a picture of a certain kind of country-side, the English countryside. If you spend much time at sea, that particular combination of fields and hedges and woods that is so essentially England seems to have a new meaning.... I remember as dawn broke looking at the black outlines of Star Point to the northward and thinking suddenly of England in quite a new way—a threatened England that was in some way more real and more friendly because she was in trouble. I thought of the Devon countryside lying behind that black outline of the cliffs; the wild moors and ragged tors inland and, near the sea, the narrow winding valleys with their steep green sides; and I thought of the mallards and teal which were rearing their ducklings in the reed beds of Slapton-Leigh. That was the countryside we were so passionately determined to protect from the invader.

Scott was of course protecting the people and the culture as well as the place (and the ducklings), but it is striking that the references are all to the physical geography and the wildlife. James Fisher struck the same note in the preface to his classic introduction to ornithology, *Watching Birds*, which was first published in 1941:

> Some people might consider an apology necessary for the appearance of a book about birds at a time when Britain is fighting for its own and many other lives. I make no such apology. Birds are part of the heritage we are fighting for.

In the same spirit, but a very different idiom, was the 1944 film *Tawny Pipit*, directed by Bernard Miles. This Ealing-style comedy has a pair of tawny pipits, great rarities from the steppe, nesting near Burford in Oxfordshire. An unlikely patriotic alliance of eccentric villagers and the army combines to protect the birds against dastardly egg-collectors and against unfeeling farmers who want to plough up the field where *Anthus campestris* has favoured them with its presence. "The eggs belong to England," declares the bird-loving corporal; and a lady of the village expresses their local pride in a song of tribute in the

Church, "It's a very great honour we're all agreed / That they came to Lipsbury
Lea to breed." There is some discussion in the film as to whether it was acceptable to use the word "breed" in church.

And finally, a quotation from Julian Huxley, another eminent scientist and
"public intellectual," as we might now call him, also writing in the 1940s when
feelings of national attachment inevitably fused with those other feelings about
"birds in their place" that have been the subject of this section:

> One of the birdwatcher's most obvious rewards is that the countryside
> soon becomes alive to him in a new way. Every kind of bird has its own
> particular quality and character, so to speak, which derives partly from
> its size and colouring and voice, partly from its temperament and habits,
> partly from the surroundings where one is accustomed to see it.
>
> To go out on a country walk and see and hear different kinds of birds
> is thus to the birdwatcher rather like running across a number of famil-
> iar neighbours, local characters, or old acquaintances. The walk becomes
> a series of personal encounters instead of a mere walk. . . .
>
> An appreciable part of the feelings which you have for a countryside
> will, if you are a birdwatcher, be derived from its birds. An American
> landscape may now and again look surprisingly like an English one; but
> its birds will speedily remind you of its alien character. The blue jays and
> American robins, thrushes and cat-birds, chipping sparrows and vireos—
> what a different quality they give from our English blackbirds and rooks,
> thrushes, redbreasts and wagtails, chaffinches and whitethroats.

Birds, Huxley concludes, give us a unique sense of time and place:

> In the same sort of way the yellowhammer's song seems the best possi-
> ble expression of hot country roads in July, the turtle dove's crooning of
> midsummer afternoons, the redshank's call of sea-breeze over saltings
> and tidal mudflats, the robin's song of peaceful autumnal melancholy as
> the leaves fall in a sun which has lost its warming power.

These extracts are themselves very much of their times and places. But they
do help make the point, which has been the argument of this chapter, that neither birds nor places can be described or imagined in isolation. Anything that
purports to give a full account of our experience and understanding of any
given bird—its identity in a cultural as well as a taxonomic sense—needs to
address this dimension of context. And conversely, any evocation of a place
may miss a crucial aspect if it does not include in the account of its natural
setting some reference to its characteristic bird life. Everyone can immediately
see this in the case of natural wonders like the Great Barrier Reef, St. Kilda,

the Serengeti, the Galapagos, or the Everglades; but it's true much more generally, if not quite so conspicuously, of other much-visited places too, though
you can search in vain through popular travel literature and topographical
guides for any recognition of this. Can you visit the shrines of Delphi in Central Greece without being aware of the rock nuthatches trilling in the temple
ruins or the eagles above? Can you climb Ayers Rock without seeing galahs,
crested pigeon, the gorgeous painted firetail, and perhaps a wedge-tailed eagle?
Or the Taj Mahal without black kite and vultures,[1] Stonehenge without
skylarks? Or, to take less numinous destinations—Waikiki beach in Hawaii
without the fairy terns, Brighton Pier on a late winter's afternoon without the
starlings, Barbados without the frigate birds and the bananaquit, Stanford
University campus without the acorn woodpeckers and Steller's jays, London
and Venice without the pigeons? It's true that only a birder would go to the
Pyramids at Giza *mainly* to see a pharaoh eagle owl and hoopoe lark or to
Petra in Jordan for the Dead Sea sparrows and the Hume's tawny owl, but in
these places too the birds become part of the extended sense of the place if
you are aware of them.

This lacuna doesn't occur only in popular travelogues. Even major works of
scholarship can be blind to this aspect, or at least partially sighted. There is a
small French village called Montaillou, in the mountains some one hundred
kilometres southeast of Toulouse, which was made famous by the massive
study published by the historian Emmanuel Le Roy Ladurie in 1978. His book
was an immediate, if surprising, best-seller of the day, and a trail of literary
tourists now find their way to Montaillou in spring and summer months to
picture the life of the medieval society he so vividly describes. Ladurie's book
is nothing if not comprehensive, more than six hundred pages in the French
edition, covering every aspect of life, work, love, marriage, society, religion,
culture, and death in this remote community in the fourteenth century. Or almost every aspect. As far as I can see, birds are mentioned only once, as being
either omens of death (the magpie and the owl) or as symbols of Christ (the
pelican).[2] But what immediately strikes a visitor now is that on the roof of
almost every building in Montaillou there is a black redstart singing, the bird

---

[1] The vultures are only just hanging on, I gather, the numbers of the native Indian species in
particular having been massively reduced by diclofenac poisoning. But that just makes my point.
Will it be the same place without them?

[2] In fact Ladurie deliberately *excludes* birds and the rest of the natural world from his history on
the grounds that life was too hard then for the people to have time to admire natural beauty, "Ils
ne vibrent pas, devant leur montagne ni devant la nature." He does, however, concede that as a
farming community "the village and the region had the feeling—a feeling tinged with anthropomorphism—that they shared in surrounding nature."

that is the common "house redstart" of continental Europe. When I visited Montaillou in late April 2003 there was even one singing from the memorial plaque in the eponymous Espace Le Roy Ladurie. I don't doubt they were there in the fourteenth century too, noticed and welcomed as the harbingers of spring, along with the tree pipits, cuckoos, and blackcaps I heard singing in the fields roundabout and the swifts passing through high overhead.

In all these ways a bird may be the one thing we most associate with a place, the genius loci, and we can no longer think of either the bird or the place without the other.

◄ 8 ►

Wild Nature: The Politics of Preference

So I eagerly wandered on and rambled along the
furze the whole day until I got out of my knowledge
when the very wild flowers and birds seemed to
forget me and I imagined they were the inhabitants
of new countries.
John Clare, *Autobiography*

Old Hall Marshes, Tollesbury, 15 February 2002

I'm returning to one of my favourite places, after a gap of very many years. This is where I used to go birdwatching as a boy. How many times have I worked my way round this familiar eight-mile circuit of seawalls, in foul weather and in fine, rarely ever meeting a single person en route? Outside the protecting banks are the creeks, saltings, and oozing mudflats of the Essex marshes and beyond them the deep channels of the River Blackwater as it issues into the sea. I can see Mersea Island to the northeast, open sea to the east, Bradwell Power Station to the south, and a distant ridge of arable fields with their irregular grid of hedgerows to the west. Within the seawalls is a huge area of grazing-marsh with a few areas of open water, some patches of reed, and one or two larger lagoons, "fleets," as they are known locally. This is where I saw my first short-eared owls, found my first marsh harriers (rare birds in those days), and on one glorious May day discovered my first spoonbill (at Pennyhole Bottom, satisfyingly at the farthest point on the walk round). Old Hall was the nearest thing we had to a wilderness locally: the land too poor to sustain any farming beyond rough-grazing for sheep and a few cows, the fields too vulnerable to flooding to support any kind of development, the access too difficult for car owners, and the going too overgrown, wet, and muddy for most weekend walkers.

For birds, however, Old Hall was a real haven. In winter you could expect to see divers, grebes, and goldeneye in the channels; huge flocks of brent geese and wigeon on the saltings; owls and raptors of various kinds hunting over the grasslands; waders in the creeks and mudflats; and finches, buntings, larks, and pipits on the weedy seawalls and grasslands. I roamed over the whole of the area, never quite sure whether I was trespassing or not, and I got to know all its secret pools, hollows, hedges, and ditches. For the initiated there was one isolated reedbed in the middle that supported bearded tits, one thick hawthorn hedge that sometimes had a winter roost of long-eared owls, a favourite perch for a merlin in a line of shattered fence-posts, and one wet meadow where Lapland buntings were fairly regular. All these birds were great prizes for me at the time, and over the years I saw well over one hundred different species there. I revelled in the sense of freedom and discovery the place gave me, and even in the discomforts of the weather and the terrain, which seemed like a kind of membership charge to a club I wanted to remain exclusive.

It's always a risk to go back. I wasn't the only one who had found the place and seen its importance. Old Hall became an official RSPB reserve in 1984 and I'm wondering how it might have changed. To be sure, they would be protecting the star birds and would probably have attracted others by skilful land management; and they would have saved the site as a whole from gross forms of despoliation like caravan parks, chalet shanty-towns, and leisure complexes (dire examples of each are now very close nearby). But would I still know it? Would it still be wild?

I am at first reassured. There is, it's true, a small car park now, so that you can drive to the edge of the reserve instead of cycling or walking the mile or two from the nearest access point; and there's a notice board in the car park with a map and a list of recent sightings (Slavonian grebe, merlin, and short-eared owl yesterday, I see). But the "Visitor Centre" is just a beaten-up old caravan in the farmyard and there is no evidence of any staff there today; nor do I see any other visitors. I start out on the familiar walk and soon I am mentally ticking off species in the places I expect them: a mixed flock of goldfinches, greenfinches, and linnets twittering in the bushes at the start; redshank and curlew fly up calling from the creek on the right, and further out I hear the plaintive call of grey plover on the mud; as I round the big bend to head out over the seawalls I catch sight of the first fleet and I can already hear the wigeon and teal (large numbers) and can see gadwall, shoveler, and tufted duck on the water. Then I get two new ticks, species I had never seen here as a boy—a little egret flies up from a ditch with a hoarse strangulated cry, and on the fleet itself I can see a little party of ruddy duck cruising round the edge of the reeds. Both these species were great rarities back in the 1950s and '60s but are commonplace now, the latter even officially classified as a pest in need of culling.[1] As I go on I am rewarded with other happy reunions: a huge flock of brents rise from the marshes in the distance, with a loud murmur of conversational rumblings that become a hubbub as they fly almost overhead; two short-eared owls quarter a reedbed; there are turnstones on just the same tiny shingle-spit where I always used to see them in winter; and there are goldeneye and dabchick in the same deep channel. I automatically scan a narrow creek that runs diagonally away from me and spot a kingfisher sitting on exactly the same plank-bridge that one used to fish from all those years ago. There are other sightings I wouldn't have had as a boy: a flock of avocet wintering on Pennyhole Fleet, more than one hundred black-tailed godwit out in the estuary, and, as I complete the circuit and return to the car park, a wintering chiffchaff in the tamarisks and a pair of collared doves in the farmyard.

So, has it been spoiled or improved? Certainly, there are "improvements" to the site for a new kind of visitor. Proper stiles have been erected and fences repaired. You don't have to stagger through waist-high vegetation or leap over unbridged dykes, and you do now know when you are trespassing. There is even a constructed hide overlooking Pennyhole Fleet positioned just where I used to crawl through the long grass and peer over a bank. The land is being sensitively managed with quite a light touch—some drainage here, a little controlled flooding there, the enclosure of one or two fields, the reinforcement of certain banks. The RSPB is both protecting it and promoting diversity within it, and with the fuller observer coverage it now gets they had recorded a remarkable total of 232 species on the reserve by 1995, including a number of real rarities such as Forster's tern, sociable plover, and Wilson's phalarope. These are not disruptive or unwelcome changes, surely? Yet, I must confess to an emotional twinge. I do feel a change and I can't wholly welcome it. But is that just nostalgia for past innocence? Is it really a change in the place or in me? John Clare spoke of going "out of his knowledge" when he ventured out of the parish he knew so well, and the critic Jonathan Bate says of this experience:

> Clare spent many of his happiest days wandering alone on Emmonsales Heath. He grew intimate with the flora and fauna of his village and its

---

[1] It is in fact a little more complicated. The ruddy duck was introduced into Britain from North America as a captive species in wildfowl collections. It escaped, inevitably, in the 1950s and a wild population developed rapidly. The cull, however, was a response to a request from Spain, where the ruddy duck was interbreeding with and threatening the indigenous white-headed duck, a much rarer species, and Britain's ruddies were seen as a staging population for the invasion of Iberia. The RSPB controversially backed the government in this, on the interesting grounds that Spain's endangered native species was more important than our successful immigrant.

surrounding parishes. His sense of his own identity was bounded by the horizon of his locality. To leave his home parish was to go out of his knowledge. To return was unsettling: the known and loved place seemed different. In reality, the village was the same. It was Clare who was different. Once a native has gone away, he can never fully return.

This chapter is about responses to change, in particular changes in the landscape and the environment as they affect birds and our perceptions of birds. I look at examples of different kinds of change—some extreme, some mild, some natural, some imposed—and see how these might complicate our experience of what is "natural" or "wild." I also look at various attempts deliberately to intervene in the natural world in the name of conservation and biodiversity and ask whether these attempts might involve us, if only unconsciously, in imposing our preferences on what it is we are conserving, thus making it even less "natural." Is nature in the end a matter of political choices?

Disturbance and Disorientation

The changes at Old Hall Marshes have been relatively minor and gradual. But what happens when there is a dramatic and disruptive change to a landscape we have come to know and have painstakingly learned to read in the way I described in the last chapter? Some such changes are natural—that is, if extreme weather events still count as natural. The Great Storm of 1987 in Britain was such an extreme event. On 15–16 October of that year hurricane-force winds overnight changed many familiar landscapes in southern England in what was literally the most radical way, uprooting or flattening some fifteen million trees. It produced not just physical chaos but also emotional trauma, and it changed some long-held beliefs about how to manage the environment. The head forester of the National Trust described it as follows:

> The initial response to the storm was urgent. It was an instinct. Something awful had happened to places people loved. They were devastated and it had to be put right immediately. After a while, we stopped to ask why it matters, why are trees and woodlands so important? It became about human need. . . . Nature shows us what we need, and we explored ways of working with nature.

There were significant effects on birdlife, of course, but not all negative. Fallen trees were left to regenerate, new plantings were undertaken, glades and open spaces emerged, some heathland reappeared, insects thrived on the fallen timber, birds thrived on the insects, and woodlarks, tree pipits, and nightjars recolonised areas from which they had long departed. In short, the

44. After the Great Storm (16 October 1987): the National Trust's Emmet House, near Sevenoaks (photo: Mike Howarth)

wildlife changed and adapted. This was the largest storm of its kind in Britain since 1703, though we are told they may now become more frequent. In other parts of the world they are already common, indeed so regular as to be part of the seasonal experience. What was especially upsetting in England was the speed and scale of the change.

Wartime can also produce radical changes to a familiar landscape, in this case through gross acts of human interference, though in these circumstances too the birds may adapt surprisingly well. There is a classic description by "Saki" (H. H. Munro) of the effects of trench warfare on the birdlife of the western front in the First World War, which is well worth reading in its entirety and from which I quote just two short extracts here. The owls did very well, he tells us, especially the barn owls, which had a more than ample supply of the rats and mice that infested the fighting line to feed on and a wealth of ruined buildings to nest in. Similarly, kestrels and sparrowhawks thrived (though for some reason not buzzards). Partridges and skylarks continued to rear their broods in land "seamed and bisected with trenches and honeycombed with shell-holes." Even the shy members of the crow family held their ground:

> The rook is normally so gun-shy and nervous where noise is concerned that the sharp banging of a barn-door or the report of a toy pistol will sometimes set an entire rookery in commotion; out here I have seen

him sedately busy among the refuse heaps of a battered village, with shells bursting at no great distance, and the impatient-sounding snapping rattle of machine-guns going on all round him; for all the notice that he took he might have been in some peaceful English meadow on a sleepy Sunday afternoon. Whatever else German frightfulness may have done it has not frightened the rook of northern France; it has made his nerves steadier than they have ever been before, and future generations of small boys, employed in scaring rooks away from the sown crops in this region, will have to invent something in the way of super-frightfulness to achieve their purpose.

In the case of magpies, the tables were completely turned. They had been driven from their usual nesting sites in the rows of now-shattered poplar trees, but they had become bolder than their human persecutors:

> Affection for a particular tree has in one case induced a pair of magpies to build their bulky domed nest in the battered remains of a poplar of which so little remained standing that the nest looked almost bigger than the tree; the effect rather suggested an arch-episcopal enthronement taking place in the ruined remains of Melrose Abbey. The magpie, wary and suspicious in his wild state, must be rather intrigued at the change that has come over his erstwhile fearsome human, stalking everywhere over the earth as its possessor, who now creeps about in screened and sheltered ways, as chary of showing himself in the open as the shyest of wild creatures.

The war zone would soon recover anyway. Other kinds of landscape change can be engineered more deliberately and have longer-lasting effects. The Enclosure Movement of the eighteenth and nineteenth centuries, whereby common land was by Act of Parliament "enclosed" and parcelled out into private lots, is the classic example here, and John Clare was the classic voice of protest. He found the reconfiguration of the countryside he knew so intimately to be profoundly alienating, and in poems such as "The Lamentation of Round-Oak Waters" and "The Lament of Swordy Well" he imagines the land itself speaking out against its abuse:

> Of all the fields I am the last
> That my own face can tell.
> Yet, what with stone pits' delving holes
> And strife to buy and sell,
> My name will quickly be the whole
> That's left of Swordy Well.

Indeed, in "The Moors" he counts the birds themselves as much the victims of the new laws of trespass as were the poor:

> Each little tyrant with his little sign
> Shows where man claims, earth glows no more divine.
> On paths to freedom and to childhood dear
> A board sticks up to notice "no road here"
> And on the tree with ivy overhung
> The hated sign by vulgar taste is hung
> As though the very birds should learn to know
> When they go there they must no further go.
> Thus, with the poor, scared freedom bade goodbye
> And much they feel it in the smothered sigh,
> And birds and trees and flowers without a name
> All sighed when lawless law's enclosure came . . .

Clare was responding to changes less violent and sudden than those arising from hurricane and war but in some ways more insidious, far-reaching, and permanent. These were changes we had willed, as part of a deliberate political process. His familiar reference points had gone. There is an historical irony in this, of course, since one effect of the changes he deplored was the landscape of small fields and hedgerows that we in turn have found familiar and attractive and that we have sought to defend against subsequent changes to agricultural practice and land use.[1] Birds form part of the rhetoric of defence, for us as well as Clare. But there is one real difference. In both cases the birds react and adapt, with consequent changes in distribution and populations, but in our day the adaptation has taken the form not just of change, as some species replace others, but of disappearance and retreat, with a clear overall impoverishment and loss of diversity.

Clare's social sympathies were with the displaced poor, but his reaction also sounds like an extreme case of conservatism, arising from an extreme sense of affinity with the land and from his attachment to it. Jonathan Bate makes the link with the attitude Australian aborigines have to their "Songlines," the invisible trackways across their ancestral lands, and suggests that, far from sentimentalising the land through the poetic device of a personification onto which he projects his own feelings, Clare may be thinking of himself as doing exactly the reverse, echoing the sorrows of the land in which we share. If that were so he might be seen as anticipating the sort of ecological ideas associated with

---

[1] And there was another, more poignant, irony in the fact that Clare himself had to take work as a labourer, making fences and planting the hawthorn hedges he deplored.

the Gaia hypothesis of James Lovelock, the idea that the whole earth is a single, living ecosystem with its own interests and reactions.

Clare was a poet, however, not a theorist. What I intend these and the earlier quotations to illustrate is just the thought that the idea of "nature" is by no means a simple one and that there are no easy contrasts between natural and human landscapes or between wild and artificial ones. Did the Great Storm replace one natural landscape with another one, or were both equally manmade? Was the Storm itself natural? Were not Clare's wild moors themselves an unnatural effect of an earlier deforestation? Is a hedge more natural than an open field? There are of course real differences between the human and the nonhuman world, but as the critic Raymond Williams once famously observed, "The idea of nature contains, though often unnoticed, an extraordinary amount of human history." Even the idea of landscape is an artificial one: a "land-scape" is literally land as painted or seen by a human viewer, and the word itself was invented only in the seventeenth century, first to denote a kind of painting and then later the scenery represented in it. One can at best think of "the natural" as a kind of continuum, though one with many discontinuities and dimensions. At one end might be totally artificial constructions like Wild Blue Yokohama in Japan, which is a massive indoor beach with simulated waves, palm trees, sand, rivers, and rain forest—a manufactured paradise interspersed with convenient sunlamps and Jacuzzis and without the discomforts of scorpions, jellyfish, or bad weather. In this confection of concrete and rubber, refugees from the city can safely explore "the great indoors."[1] At the other end might be the Antarctic continent, still populated by only about one thousand people in winter months in its 5.4 million square miles, but of course wholly dependent for its wildness on human decisions to keep it so and in that sense also an artificial construct; and vulnerable in any case to climate change, which itself has human origins to some degree. In between these extremes are the majority of the world's habitats and environments, none of them untouched by change or by human history.

Moreover, birds and other wildlife keep confounding our expectations about their own natural preferences. The last red-backed shrike known to have nested in England chose to do so within twenty yards of an ice-cream van on a public picnic site at Santon Downham when it had the whole of Breckland and

---

[1] See Web site and the *New York Times* article on 15 June 1993, "To Surf and Ski, the Japanese Are Heading Indoors." California is now following suit in Anaheim with a planned 450,000-square-foot "surf and ski" complex; and Dubai is going the whole way and creating a complete fantasy world in a five-million-square-foot "dedicated theme park" constructed by DreamWorks Animation and described as "an exciting destination where families and tourists will enjoy the unique opportunity to interact with DreamWorks branded content within Dubailand."

Thetford Forest to choose from. The black redstarts that were so much in evidence at Montaillou expanded into Britain after the war by colonising the bomb-sites in London, before moving on later to industrial sites such as nuclear power stations, factory complexes, and warehouses. The best places to find rare gulls and refine your skills in splitting the herring gull complex are rubbish tips and sewage outfalls. Peregrines move into central London and house sparrows move out. Meanwhile "the most polluted square mile in the United States" at the Rocky Mountain Arsenal in Denver, Colorado, where the most toxic substances imaginable were manufactured and deposited in huge quantities, has been colonised by the national symbol, the bald eagle, where, ironically, it enjoys protected status. Ferruginous hawks are apparently considering moving in to enjoy the same benefits.

So it starts to get confusing. And it gets worse. . . .

Intervention and Conservation

The Rocky Mountain Arsenal is an unusual and ironic case because it has now travelled full circle and become a nature reserve—the intention being to make a Beauty Spot of the former Black Spot. Most nature reserves have had a less paradoxical history, often starting like places such as Old Hall Marshes, visited and cherished by a few enthusiasts, and then, as their importance to wildlife becomes recognised, getting increased degrees of protection until they are finally bought by a conservation body of some kind. In Britain the Royal Society for the Protection of Birds, Natural England, and the various Wildlife and National Trusts have "saved" an enormous number of prime sites this way, as have the Audubon Societies in the United States; while organisations such as BirdLife International Partnership, the World Wildlife Fund, the International Union for the Conservation of Nature, and Friends of the Earth operate worldwide to target individual species that have become endangered and act to protect the often very specific habitats they require to survive. Everyone with an interest in wildlife in general and birds in particular must applaud the work these organisations do to preserve the biodiversity of the planet, protect wild places against hostile forms of development, and make it possible for ordinary people to visit them in a controlled way. This all seems rather obvious and uncontroversial, doesn't it?

Well yes, but only until you have to make some actual decisions. These bodies have members; they have directors, staff, and organisational structures; they raise funds and have to allocate these funds; they have budgets and targets; they have to select among different desirable objectives; they have to deal with governments, companies, and other bodies that have different kinds of

20 bald eagles dare to roost at Arsenal

By Lou Chapman
Denver Post Environmental Writer

The Rocky Mountain Arsenal contains what's called the "most polluted square mile in America," but now it's also a home to America's endangered national symbol, the bald eagle.

Twenty eagles have taken up residence at the Arsenal, once used to make chemical weapons and pesticides and now a federal Superfund cleanup site.

The eagles, an endangered species in Colorado, began building a communal roost in a grove of trees along First Creek in the Arsenal's southeastern corner last November, Army officials said Friday.

Researchers don't know whether the eagles will stay at the Arsenal permanently or will move to higher elevations as the weather warms.

If the birds are just wintering at the Arsenal, they probably will return for subsequent winters, experts said.

Whatever the birds' travel plans are, the decision is completely theirs. As members of an endangered species, the eagles are protected from any activities that would disturb them or disrupt their roost.

The eagles' protected status could have an impact on how the Army goes about cleaning up the contaminated soil and groundwater at the Arsenal. The presence of the roost may even be a good enough reason for the Federal Aviation Administration to reconsider the environmental impact of expanding Stapleton International Airport, which lies immediately to the south.

Certainly, the eagles will be considered in any plans for a new airport east of the Arsenal, officials said.

"But right now I can't see there's any conflict with air navigation," said Walt Barbo, manager of the regional office of the FAA.

Right now officials don't know enough about the eagles and the new home to predict if it will affect either ongoing Stapleton expansion or construction of the new airport.

The four adult and 16 immature eagles are being watched carefully by the consulting firm that is helping the Army investigate the extent of contamination at the Arsenal.

The U.S. Fish and Wildlife Service also is very interested in the birds, in part because the agency's regional office is studying the effect of contamination on eagles in Colorado and Utah.

"All of a sudden, we have a large concentration of bald eagles at the Arsenal that we can study," said Jeff Opdycke of the agency's field office in Grand Junction.

Opdycke and his staff also noticed an unusually large population of ferruginous hawks at the Arsenal recently. That species is being considered for inclusion on the endangered species list.

"I guess we didn't fully appreciate the value of the Arsenal as a wildlife habitat until this year."

Some might say that is putting it mildly.

Beginning in 1942, the Arsenal produced tons upon tons of military supplies that included nerve gas, mustard gas, hydrazine rocket fuel and white phosphorous grenades. Shell Oil Co. and smaller companies made pesticides and herbicides at the Arsenal until 1982.

Seepage from the Arsenal has polluted nearby groundwater sources, and one 93-acre pond of liquid hazardous waste and its surrounding land have been dubbed "the most polluted square mile in the United States" by the U.S. Environmental Protection Agency.

45. The Rocky Mountain Arsenal, article by Lou Chapman in *The Denver Post* (14 February 1987)

objectives; they have to negotiate, compromise, and reconsider; and then they have to make decisions. Nature becomes a matter of choices, preferences, and possibilities. In short, it becomes political.

On 23 March 2006, the House of Lords had two major items on the agenda for the morning, both of them involving the history of Britain's relations with North America. The first was the Iraq War and the question of whether to withdraw British troops. This the noble lords debated for nine minutes, as

Hansard records. The second debate took longer. For two hours and thirty-one minutes they discussed the fate and the future of the British red squirrel and the threat to it from the larger and more aggressive North American grey squirrel. The latter is an immigrant and a very successful one. Since its arrival here in the late nineteenth century, when some were released in the park at Woburn Abbey and a few other places, the grey squirrel has spread throughout most of the country, displacing its smaller native rival wherever they meet, and the much-loved red squirrel now survives only in a few embattled enclaves. The red, though, is the one we all learned to love: "an iconic creature," Earl Peel explained, introducing the debate, "immortalised by Beatrix Potter, through the charismatic character of Squirrel Nutkin." The grey by contrast, the Lord Plumb declared, was nothing more than a "tree rat"; one "with good PR," as Lord Livsey of Talgarth added. They were actually animal hooligans, thugs, and killers; they would kill off trees, damage property, eat songbirds, spread disease; they were pests; indeed they were *vermin*. Once that was established, it was easy to see the answer to the problem. They should be culled, perhaps exterminated. Lord Inglewood even wondered if one means of achieving this would be to eat them:

> I invite each and every one of the front bench Environment, Food and Rural Affairs Department team to a hotel in the Lake District where I am a director—and which, I hasten to add, has one AA rosette for fine food—to dine on grey squirrels to launch an "Eat a Grey and Save a Red" campaign![1]

Lord Chorley thought a European Squirrel Initiative might be the answer. He said he had actually had tea with Beatrix Potter in 1941 (goodness, how old *is* he?) and was sure she would have supported robust action. Everyone agreed the government had to *do* something.

It is indeed governments that have to decide in the end when something is a "pest," usually on grounds of likely threats to health and safety or to legitimate commercial and leisure interests. So they have to listen to farmers concerned to protect their crops against wood pigeons, fishermen wanting to cull cormorants, residents of south coast towns worrying about the gulls fouling their roof tops, poultry farmers frightened about bird flu, and air traffic controllers guarding against bird-strikes. In all these cases you have to weigh the

---

[1] He went on to cite the *L. L. Bean Game and Fish Cookbook,* which pronounces that "squirrel meat is the most delicious of all small game. Young squirrel is better than rabbit or chicken." Squirrel stew and squirrel stroganoff are especially recommended, and we are told that mustard goes well with any squirrel recipe. And Lord Inglewood's Big Idea has now been revived by various entrepreneurial restaurateurs, I see (*The Observer,* 11 May 2008).

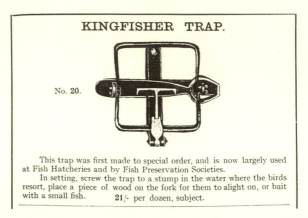

46. Kingfisher trap (in S. Haddon-Riddoch, *Rural Reflections: A Brief History of Traps, Trapmakers and Gamekeepers in Britain*, 2007)

human interest against the wildlife interest, and though the decisions may be controversial or difficult we can usually see what the issues are. It gets more complicated, however, when the human interest involves weighing one wildlife interest against another. Should we let a gamekeeper prefer pheasants to magpies, salmon to otters, or grouse to hen harriers? Is the slope getting slippery? How about lambs against eagles or perch against kingfishers? Every predator of game, actual and potential, has been persecuted at some point in the past—and there even used to be traps designed specifically to catch kingfishers to protect fishing interests (fig. 46).

In the case of highly prized birds like kingfishers, hen harriers, and golden eagles, we have now decided in favour of the wildlife interest by making it illegal to kill them, even if some measure of harm to human interests can be proved. But is that rational? What are they being prized *for?* This takes us right back to the theme of chapter 2, which is a thread through the whole book. Why do we find certain birds so attractive, or even charismatic? What part do rarity, beauty, context, and association play in our experience? These political issues of conservation and control may help us focus on some of the answers, or at least some the reasons we give ourselves as answers. The justifications may become even more revealing if we go on to look at cases where human interests don't seem to enter into it at all, at least not in the direct ways we have so far been considering. I mean cases where it seems to be a matter of just *preferring* one species over another. What reasons do we give then?

In the example of the red squirrel debate the main reasons given seemed to be a combination of the aesthetic and the autochthonic. The reds are prettier, brighter, bushier, cuter, and undoubtedly more cuddly; but they also *belong* here—they are the original squirrels, the natives, British residents threatened by an invading immigrant population; what's more, the alien is larger and more aggressive, and is winning; the reds are endangered. These sorts of emotive descriptions crop up in most such debates. And this contrast of what is alien with what is native (or, by a small sophistic step, "natural") is deployed over other domains and battlefields too, involving trees, fish, ladybirds, bees, flowers, and even crustaceans. American imperialism is a convenient culprit not only in the squirrel world but also the underwater world of the crayfish, where the American signal crayfish is displacing the British white-clawed variety in the rivers. The usual stereotypes are recycled in popular reports of this incursion—oversized, oversexed, and over here—despite the fact that the "invaders" were introduced by British fish farmers for commercial purposes (in ignorance, apparently, of the fact that crayfish can crawl as well as swim and so could escape from the ponds into which they were deposited).

The traffic is not all one-way, of course. It was the British who inflicted rabbits on Australia, and rats and cats on various Pacific islands where they wiped out all the ground-nesting birds. They also tried to introduce several species of birds into the United States to make it seem more homelike. Songbirds such as skylarks, nightingales, blackbirds, and European robins were imported into North America in large numbers in the mid-nineteenth century, but none of them lasted long (although curiously the skylark still survives in the very British redoubt of Vancouver Island). Two other less welcome species did make it, though. In 1853, house sparrows were released in Brooklyn, and then a few other places on the East Coast; by 1898, they had reached the Mississippi, and of course they are now common coast to coast. And in the 1890s a wealthy drug manufacturer and philanthropist, Eugene Schiefflin, is supposed to have had the bright idea of introducing into New York all the species of birds mentioned in Shakespeare to raise the tone of the place. The starling only just makes it into Shakespeare (as a mimic and *agent provocateur*),[1] but it flourished in America: eighty pairs were released in Central Park, New York, in 1890–91; within fifty years it had replicated the migrations of European immigrants, crossing the mountains and plains to reach the Pacific coast, and there are now an estimated two hundred million of them in the United States. The other forty or so species Schiefflin introduced all met with some terminal demise (though it is not recorded whether he included the phoenix in his original list).

And now the collared dove is making the same journey. It's hard to remember that the collared doves reached the United Kingdom only in 1952, exotic

---

[1] *Henry IV, Part 1*, 1.3.230, "Nay, I'll have a starling shall be taught to speak / nothing but 'Mortimer,' and give it him / to keep his anger still in motion."

immigrants from Turkey and the Near East. They have progressed from pioneer to pest in about fifty years. They were later released in the Bahamas in the 1970s, and a friend told me recently that they have now just reached Northern California. They may well fit into the landscape there, but it doesn't follow automatically. Pheasants were first introduced into Britain by the Normans in the eleventh century, but they still don't seem to me to suit the landscape here (or indeed the landscape in California, where they were introduced in 1857).

The arguments in favour of what is native have some force, if only because of the disastrous consequences of some of these ill-informed introductions of aliens. And the idea of "belonging" is an important one, to which I want to return. But first I want to show how this line of argument also throws up some hard cases, which may be deliciously ironic. There is a small number of eagle owls nesting in the United Kingdom at present—a charismatic bird if ever there was one (see plate 5c)—and there is a lively debate as to whether any of these are recolonists that have found their own way here or whether they are all feral birds released or escaped from captivity. This matters a lot to some birders (who want to "count" them) and to some conservationists (who want to protect them and reintroduce more) as well as to some sheep farmers (who want to kill them). One pair of these massive birds nested in a conspicuous site near a public footpath in the Forest of Bowland in 2007 and so became national celebrities. They successfully fledged three young, under police protection, and later the nest site was examined to determine what their prey species had been. Rabbits were the main item of diet (no surprises there) but it also turned out, to the embarrassment of their supporters and the delight of the gamekeeping fraternity, that they had killed and eaten three hen harriers (a male, a female, and one juvenile), thus wiping out one of Britain's few remaining breeding pairs of this heavily protected species. If eagle owls continue to prosper, other raptor species may well be under threat, since the eagle owls are quite capable of taking goshawk, merlin, and all the other native owls too.

These wildlife dilemmas are quite common, and are in fact unavoidable when one moves on from considering pest control to more interventionist acts of positive discrimination and reintroduction. It's one thing to control and perhaps cull the numbers of rampant immigrants like ruddy ducks or Canada geese (and maybe one day ring-necked parakeets?) and to curb exploding populations of urban gulls, wood pigeons, or magpies; but it's quite another to decide that what we need are more bitterns, red kites, or sea eagles. Who decides these questions and on what grounds? They certainly do involve decisions because there may well be incompatibilities and conflicts here. The reedbeds that ideally suit the bitterns may be less good for bearded tits or marsh harriers, or may involve the flooding and transformation into reedbed of land once occupied by lapwing, yellow wagtail, and redshank. Sea eagles may compete for nest sites, and possibly prey, with golden eagles. Avocets, red kites, ospreys, and corncrakes—all "badges of success" for the RSPB and other conservation bodies—each have their special requirements, which may exclude other possibilities. And even if there were no conflicts there would still be choices to make, since costs are involved and budgets are limited. Is it more important to the nation to have cirl buntings in Cornwall, bustards on Salisbury Plain, or sea eagles in Suffolk?

Belonging?

How can one pick one's way through these uncertainties, and how do they relate to our main theme here of the way birds form part of our landscapes (or, more precisely, our experience of landscapes) and change with them? We need some distinctions between different kinds of immigrant and the different circumstances of their arrival, in order to take us beyond emotive appeals against "invaders," "aliens," and "vermin."

The *time of arrival* makes little difference by itself, I would suggest, though time and habituation may dissolve some of the prejudices, in the natural world as in the human. Many of the familiar birds in Britain were at one time immigrants, whether artificially introduced (like the red-legged partridge and little owl in the eighteenth and nineteenth centuries) or self-propelled (like the little egret, collared dove, and Cetti's warbler in the twentieth). But there's no neat scale that plots residency qualifications against time. If you go back far enough, to the time when Britain was connected to the Continent by a land-bridge, eagle owls were no doubt resident, along with wolves, beavers, lynx, boar, bear, and a host of other animal and bird species, any of which might be hailed as a candidate for reintroduction on grounds of ancestral rights, if that were the criterion.

You get similar discussions about trees, which brings in the different criterion of *continuity*. There was an earnest debate in the eighteenth century at the Royal Society as to whether the sweet chestnut, *Castanea sativa,* was a native or an alien. The Hon. Daines Barrington, better known as one of Gilbert White's correspondents in *The Natural History of Selborne,* argued against its acceptance as an indigenous tree on the grounds that it did not occur "in any considerable masses" in Britain and that "with us the nuts by no means ripen kindly." The argument went back and forth, with appeals to supposed references in medieval documents and place-names, particular veteran specimens, large and flourishing chestnut woods, timbers in old buildings, and so on. Its status was eventually resolved in the twentieth century, but in a way that just confirmed the ambiguity: pollen analysis revealed that it was a very ancient introduction, ancient enough to have acquired sufficient characteristics of a native to satisfy the sceptics. The unrelated horse-chestnut, by the way, was a far later arrival and is undoubtedly an alien, though very much a "traditional favourite" and a part of the culture (think conkers).

I don't think the *numbers* make much difference either, at least in the case of birds. The ring-necked pheasant is an ancient introduction and is certainly here "in considerable masses," while two other exotic pheasants were introduced from China in the nineteenth century, the golden pheasant (which is rare and localised) and Lady Amherst's (which is probably dying out). But all are equally nonnative and will always remain so. If species like the little egret and collared dove achieve a different kind of acceptance it won't be because they are common but because they arrived in a different way.

Physical impact is perhaps more relevant: collared doves are relatively discreet and their songs and calls no more than tedious; ring-necked parakeets, by contrast, have a noisy, rackety presence and both sound and look flagrantly out of place.

But I think the *circumstances of arrival and dispersal* are the really significant thing. There are very important distinctions, it seems to me, between species that find their own way to a place and those that have to be imported or assisted. I have allowed myself to use the word "natural" as a shorthand label for the former class of arrivals, though that begs other questions I try to confront later. *History* is also important, including the history of any earlier residency and the reasons for the last departure. One can broadly distinguish the following categories in the U.K. context:

1. Natural transnational movements. Birds are expanding and contracting their ranges and population numbers across the world all the time. Whether because of climate change or other changes to food supply and habitat, Britain has more or less lost as breeding birds species like the red-backed shrike and wryneck that were common in Clare's day, while we have gained others like the little egret and collared dove, perhaps to be followed soon by other Mediterranean species like the cattle egret, black kite, glossy ibis, and spoonbill.

2. Natural local movements. Similarly, some existing but scarce residents have been expanding within the country (Dartford warbler, wood lark) while others have been contracting (corncrake, willow tit, tree sparrow).

3. Natural returns after persecution. There are species returning of their own accord after they had earlier been ousted by direct human persecution (for example, ospreys returning to Scotland in the 1950s after disappearing in the nineteenth century).

4. Natural returns of species that find their way back on their own after departing more as a consequence of habitat loss (cranes returning in the 1980s after a four-hundred-year absence, and avocets returning in the 1940s after more than one hundred years). An important subclass here would be raptors such as peregrines reestablishing themselves after a decline from inadvertent poisoning. Collecting usually becomes a further and sometimes terminal factor in both (3) and (4) as the birds become rarer and therefore more prized, but initially the human agency in (4) is indirect and unintentional in its effects.

5. Reintroductions to the country from abroad. Wildlife conservation bodies have been reintroducing species that had ceased altogether to be breeding species in the United Kingdom a long time ago, like sea eagles (reintroduced into Scotland in the 1980s) and the great bustard (into Wiltshire in 2004).

6. Local reintroductions of birds still present in the United Kingdom. These are species that have not become extinct as breeding species but have greatly contracted their ranges in this country and are becoming endangered here (corncrakes, cirl bunting, red kite). As with (3) and (4) the reasons for their decline may include either human persecution (especially the raptors) or habitat shrinkage.

7. Accidental immigrants with no history of residence, usually escaping from captivity, like the ring-necked parakeet, Egyptian goose, and mandarin in the twentieth century, or going back further probably the gadwall (mid-nineteenth century) and certainly the Canada goose (mid-seventeenth).

8. Deliberate introductions of birds with no history of residence, usually for game and domestic purposes, like the pheasant (probably eleventh century, possibly earlier), the red-legged partridge (from the 1770s), and the mute swan (twelfth century, though there may also have been wild birds much earlier).

These categories can be somewhat blurred in the case of individual species, of course. Cranes probably qualify in both (3) and (4) since they were hunted for the table as well as suffering from the drainage of wetlands. And birds that start in (3) or (5) can get themselves included later in (6) when people try to build on the original success of establishing a new colony in the country. Sea eagles and ospreys both come into this mixed category. You could cut the categories other ways too, and recast them into more or fewer. But my purpose is not a definitive analysis or indeed a systematic policy paper. I just want to illustrate that there are many different kinds of immigrants and that it might make a difference to our feelings about them if we consider both the means of immigration and the history (theirs and ours). My form of classification does at any rate suggest a few further general points about the politics of preference.

First, I have taken these examples from the United Kingdom because there are active and successful conservation bodies here and so the questions arising are politically real ones with practical outcomes. Moreover, because of the United Kingdom's island situation and relatively small size, issues of immigration and reintroduction here tend to be more dramatised. But the same issues of principle arise elsewhere and in equally challenging ways. The United States, for example, is the country that lost the passenger pigeon and the heath hen, and may have lost the charismatic ivory-billed woodpecker. There was a powerful Endangered Species Act of 1973 and since then extraordinary measures have been taken to protect species such as the bald eagle (now delisted), California condor, whooping crane, Kirtland's warbler, piping plover, and northern spotted owl. Meanwhile, the Audubon Society is producing a series of scientific reports on the sharp decline of "meadow species" like the northern bobwhite, Eastern meadowlark, loggerhead shrike, and field sparrow, and these include comments that sound very familiar: "The song of Eastern meadowlarks used to be the soundtrack of summer," said Scott Weidensaul, a naturalist and author born in eastern Pennsylvania who has reviewed the report. "Now it's a rare thing. The landscape is changing." All the same questions and problems arise, *mutatis mutandis,* in Hawaii, New Zealand, Australia, Brazil, South Africa, India, and Japan.

Indeed, it is noticeable what a national, indeed sometimes nationalistic, form these questions sometimes take. We demonise the Japanese knotweed and the North American mink or grey squirrel. We may think of the yellowhammer (or the meadowlark) as the sound of an English (or American) summer. We feel a certain pride in our own endemic species if we have any and make symbolic use of them on flags, coins, and stamps. The cruder and more ludicrous aspects of this may be thought just an exaggerated form of the sympathetic identification of birds with certain landscapes; but national pride can also have parochial effects in terms of strategic conservation efforts. For example, there is a current project to reintroduce corncrakes into suitable wetland and grassland habitats in East Anglia, on the grounds that they are now endangered and rare breeders in the United Kingdom, just hanging on in the Hebrides and the extreme Northwest. That is, they are in categories (2) and (6) in my listing. But they are not seriously endangered internationally—up to two million pairs breed in Europe, including up to 1.5 million in European Russia alone. Perhaps they should be allowed to stay in (2), if this is a secular decline in the United Kingdom related to climate change, while giving them a little local assistance in the Hebrides as necessary. Corncrakes do after all migrate through Britain to reach their current nesting areas in the Hebrides, sometimes stopping off at traditional sites, and they could no doubt settle in the Nene Washes if they found the conditions suitable there.

Another practical consequence of national pride in such matters is the way taxonomy can affect politics. I mentioned endemic species, which tend to be a special badge of national honour and appear regularly on the coinage and postage of the countries concerned. This is complicated in the United Kingdom by the fact that our only candidate, the red grouse, was downgraded into a subspecies of the willow grouse in 1956 and is in any case conserved mainly so that it can be shot in large numbers from the "glorious" twelfth of August each year. We can leave it to these sporting interests to ensure that population levels are maintained at reasonable levels, at least up to every 11 August. But consider the case of the crossbill complex, *Loxia curvirostra*. There is a Scottish population largely dependent on the remnants of the Old Caledonian Forest in the north of the country, and they seem to have characteristics intermediate between the common crossbill *curvirostra* and the parrot crossbill *ptyopsittacus* (a native of the boreal forests of Russia and Scandinavia but an occasional visitor and breeder in the United Kingdom). These Scottish crossbills used to be thought of as just a race of *curvirostra*, but in 1980 were accorded full specific status as *Loxia scotica*. It may be important to them and to their pine forests to hang on to that status, because with the downgrading of the red grouse they are now Britain's only endemic species, with the further advantage of being purely "Scottish" (which the red grouse isn't). The Famous Grouse whisky brand, which has long promoted itself as being named after "Scotland's national game bird" shows no sign yet of seeking an icon that has more scientific support, but you can see how such a question might arise. And in the conservation business, fund-raising to support a proper species is going to be much easier than it would be for a subspecies or a mere geographical race. St. Kilda wrens should follow this debate with interest.

But they should not hold their tiny breaths. Charisma affects politics at least as much as taxonomy does. The species that tend to get favoured in conservation and reintroduction programmes are generally large and spectacular ones— raptors, cranes, bitterns, avocets, and the like. The cirl bunting is an exception, but one doesn't hear much discussion about bringing back unobtrusive waders like the Kentish plover (which left in the mid-twentieth century, along with the wrynecks and red-backed shrikes); or establishing new colonies of small passerines like willow tits, spotted flycatchers, or tree sparrows, all of which are declining fast; or introducing crested larks, serins, and fan-tailed warblers from the Continent, or crested tits from Scotland. There may well be all sorts of good, scientific reasons why such attempts would not work, of course, but these are not even on the agenda for major interventions, though in terms of biodiversity a "little brown job" should count as much as a big

raptor does, surely? The political fact, however, is that the lbj's would not attract enough public support and interest to justify the operation. The interesting question, and the one I have been exploring throughout this book is why,
exactly? How do we rank criteria such as relative rarity, beauty, association
with time and place, symbolic importance, and the other factors we have been
looking at? Conservation issues sharpen the questions and may depend on the
answers to them, but they do not themselves solve them.

There would be a general feeling, I expect, that a sense of "belonging" matters in deciding what deserves conservation and support. There is a real and
important difference, that is, between birds artificially introduced into a landscape and environment of which they had never formed any part and those
that once lived in it or subsequently found their own way to it (a difference
between my categories 7–8 and 1–6, that is). Bluntly, we care more about ospreys and cranes than about ring-necked parakeets and ruddy ducks. We may
argue about which former residents to reintroduce, but no one would suggest
reintroducing an introduction that was failing (like Lady Amherst's pheasant)
or bringing back the bobwhite quail (there were colonies once on Tresco and
elsewhere). There may also be an aesthetic aspect of this, in a feeling that some
of the exotic introductions don't "look right" in this landscape, or in the case
of the parakeets don't "sound right" either. There might be surprises and argu-
able cases when one sees what falls the wrong side of the line (the little owl
and gadwall?), but the distinction is fairly clear on the whole and probably not
controversial. Indeed, it has been part of the purpose of chapters 7 and 8 to
show how and why this should be so.

But there is also a difference between natural movements (as in 1–4) and
reintroductions (as in 5–6), and another of a more subtle kind between introductions of a bird that has altogether left the country (5) and those that still
survive here, albeit in reduced numbers (6). I may well be in a minority in
feeling this quite strongly, and I am in a way quite surprised that I do make
these distinctions since I generally support all conservation projects against
the opposing forces; but my hesitations relate to the anxieties I felt on returning to Old Hall. I see every reason to offer a high degree of protection to a species establishing a new niche or returning to a niche it once occupied. The
hope, of course, is that the bird will flourish, will spread further, and will eventually become self-sustaining. The stories of the return of the avocet, first to
East Anglia and now to the whole south coast, and the spread of the osprey
throughout Scotland, are great success stories, rightly celebrated by those involved. The return of the Cornish chough is exciting in just the same way—
and in this case the choughs narrowly anticipated the plans to reintroduce
them by arriving at the Lizard peninsula in 2001 and breeding successfully in

2002. I also see good reason, by direct implication, to protect these niche environments and to conserve or even perhaps create others into which such species can expand.

That "even perhaps create" is the first intimation of my unease, however. We should surely conserve threatened habitats like wetlands, heathland, grassland, hedgerow, moorland, meadow, and forest and we would hope that their existing inhabitants will be thereby protected and new species enabled to move into them (whether brand new arrivals as in (1) or birds like Dartford warblers in (2) expanding into new areas). I can also see the case for enlarging and connecting discrete patches of such habitat (as in the ambitious Great Fen Project in East Anglia) to create more substantial and viable tracts of such environment. But when such a conservation area becomes a flagship "Reserve" of an official kind there is then a temptation to develop it further. The sponsors may reasonably want to maximize its species count, attract new star birds, and of course to encourage as many visitors as possible to enjoy and support these achievements. The new visitors need an infrastructure of staff, services and buildings, the infrastructure needs maintenance, investment and management and you may soon be on a slippery slope that leads in the end to the birds promoting the interests of the Reserve or the Organisation rather than vice versa. The rhetoric may be all about biodiversity and conservation but the commercial reality is rather different. Whole sites can be reengineered to provide an entirely artificial habitat. And then you are on the way to theme parks, leisure complexes, and zoos, where the sights and sounds and experiences can be guaranteed. I don't say that this is the intended outcome or that it is inevitable, but you see the risk. These are points about places and *their* meaning as well as about birds and theirs. Old Hall fortunately hasn't yet become a flagship reserve.

My other concern was about another slippery slope, the one from (5) to (6), from helping to reestablish a bird in its original home to a whole series of organized dispersals. It seems to me one thing to reintroduce the sea eagle to remote parts of the Hebrides, still a natural habitat for the bird, and one from which it was driven only by hunting and persecution. The human effort was considerable, but one accepts that the occasional visiting migrants from Scandinavia would probably not have managed to recolonise it on their own. It is another thing, however, to go on from this to reintroduce it to other parts of the United Kingdom in which it might once have occurred centuries ago. I have seen sea eagles in Suffolk and Norfolk and it was a great thrill; the birds make a stupendous physical impression anyway but I also knew they were very rare visitors to these parts, probably prospecting immigrants from the Hebridean stock or from Scandinavia that might or might not linger and return.

47. "Great Bustard Ale" from
Wiltshire (Bryn Parry and the
Great Bustard Group)

However, I wouldn't feel at all the same if they were forcibly implanted there (as is now proposed). They won't *belong* again unless they make the move themselves and readapt to what is now a different place.

In the case of the great bustard, I'm not sure it's even worth getting it into category (5) and I certainly wouldn't inspect the birds, either inside or outside their pens on Salisbury Plain, with any sense of having seen a wild bird in its natural home, much less any sense of having *discovered* one. They are more like a local tourist curiosity or an animated historical exhibit, with no real chance of expanding to other earlier haunts like Breckland, let alone Newmarket Heath. They are embattled, in the literal sense of being dependent on the protection of the surrounding military ranges, and unlikely to establish a viable, self-supporting population even there except under the most artificial conditions. The project has taken on the character of a local marketing exercise, attracting significant funding and even leading to spin-off commercial exploitations, as in the newly branded Great Bustard Ale (fig. 47). If I'm wrong and they do by any chance survive a bustard generation or two, I suppose their young may in any case meet an ironic fate at the feet of the then-burgeoning populations of eagle owls and sea eagles that have jumped off the same bandwagon.

Birds too can go "out of their knowledge," like humans.

9
Naming Matters

I know'd my name to be Magwitch, christened Abel.
How did I know it? Much as I know'd the birds'
names in the hedges to be chaffinch, sparrer, thrush.
I might have thought it was all lies together, only as
the birds' names come out true, I supposed mine did.
Charles Dickens, *Great Expectations*

Kakadu, Northern Territory, Australia, 14 January 1999 ·

I talked in the last chapter about John Clare being "out of his knowledge" when he left his own parish and I'm certainly out of mine here. Everything seems unfamiliar and exotic and I can't employ my usual reference points to get a bearing. I'm sitting on a rock in the middle of this vast wilderness area at the Top End of Australia, some two hundred kilometres east of Darwin. Kakadu is about the size of Wales or New Jersey, but decidedly unlike either. It's hot and very humid; the light is eyeball-dentingly fierce; the landscape is a phantasmagoria of rock formations, waterfalls, creeks, and lush rainforests in colour combinations I have never seen before; and all around me I can hear and see birds I can't identify. Not only can't I identify them, I don't know where to start in many cases. It's positively embarrassing when they are sitting right in front of me like this. The categories I am used to don't seem to fit at all, so I can't eliminate the impossible and home in on the probable in the usual way. What's more, the variety is bewildering. There are some 280 bird species recorded here, about a third of the Australian total, and many of them are endemics not found elsewhere in the world.

I thumb rather desperately through my already damp and steaming field guide. Surely the names will help, at least? Yes, they do, up to a point. I know what wrens are, after all, and I've seen superb fairy-wrens (the gorgeous blue ones—see plate 6c) on other, less adventurous trips out of urban centres like Sydney and Melbourne. "Superb" by name and by nature—but there are also "splendid" ones, just as good, so these adjectives are not very helpful as identifiers. Up here I have to look out for the red-backed fairy-wren (should be easy if I see one, which I do later) and also the rarer purple-crowned one (ditto, though I notice there's also something called a "variegated" in the book with the alternative name of "purple-backed," which could be confusing). In addition there is a genus of emu-wrens, though not up here (why *emu* I can't imagine; they're tiny), and another of grass-wrens (which is an easier move to follow). In fact I'm in just the right place for the rare white-throated grass-wren, I discover, but they seem to be very elusive and in any case I'm not really interested on this trip in seeing birds "rare in Australia" since they are all equally rare to me.[1]

I can also recognise other general groups such as cuckoos, pigeons, and parrots, of course, and without too much difficulty I manage to identify a clutch of cuckoos (is that the right collective noun?—it might suit the parrots better): little bronze cuckoo (a bit like a wryneck to look at), brush cuckoo (another small one, with a grey head and olive underparts), common koel (also a cuckoo, and must be named after the call, a slow but penetrating *koeeel*), and the amazing channel-billed cuckoo (just what it says on the tin). The pigeons eventually resolve themselves into the Torresian pigeon (a.k.a. pied imperial or nutmeg pigeon) and three different doves (peaceful, bar-shouldered, and diamond). The gaudy parrots aren't as easy as you might think, since they always seem to be just flying away, but in the end I make out the red-winged parrot, the very numerous sulphur-crested cockatoos, and the rainbow and varied lorikeets, though I'm still not sure when a parrot becomes a cockatoo, lorikeet, or rosella.

I have to work harder with the flycatchers. My guidebook says there are ten thousand insect species in this area and most of them seem to be very close by. They are at any rate attracting lemon-bellied and brown flycatchers (the latter also called "Jacky Winter," I see, which is nice, and "stump bird," which is clearly accurate). These look like our Old World flycatchers but are related to the Australasian robins (which in turn are nothing to do with the European robins, or indeed the American ones). However, there are also leaden, restless, and shining flycatchers around, which belong to a quite different family of "monarch" flycatchers, more like fantails. The restless flycatcher soon reveals to me why it has another vernacular name of "scissors grinder" when it vocalises,

---

[1] Sean Dooley visits Kakadu to mop up the local rarities in his record-breaking twitch of more than seven hundred birds in a year in Australia and gets his white-throated grass-wren right here at Gunlom Falls (*The Big Twitch,* chapter 32). He also makes an interesting point about the name of the place: apparently it used to be called UDP Falls, but that stands for Uranium Development Project, which was a bit of a turn-off for the eco-tourist trade, so they found an Aboriginal name instead (and they also got the falls into the first *Crocodile Dundee* movie).

and the shining flycatcher makes me think of the American phainopepla, which is also a glossy black fly-catching bird (whose name translates charmingly as "shining gown"), though it is quite unrelated to the Australian bird.

This feels like progress. But then there are all the species that don't seem to have any kind of counterpart at all in North America and Europe. A lot of them sound like hybrids or chimeras, which is no doubt how they got their names from early settlers who were struggling in the same way as I am: cuckoo-shrikes, shrike-thrushes, owlet-nightjar, quail-thrush, magpie-lark, and parrot-finches. They are not hybrids at all of course, just different genera that don't fit our preconceived patterns. Other birds are so different that they may have defeated any attempt to assimilate them to something known. In the northern hemisphere we just don't have anything like pardalotes, manucodes, or friarbirds, so quite new names had to be found for those. In other cases the European immigrants must have decided that they could adapt the existing Aboriginal names and they ended up with evocative words like galah (another cockatoo, also very common), currawong (some bell-magpies), budgerigar (yes, there are wild ones up here), brolga (a crane), and of course kookaburra (which is a gigantic "tree" kingfisher, whose maniac laughter I can hear nearby). The native languages did not exist in any written form at this time so presumably the terms that were easiest to borrow were the onomatopoeic ones like kookaburra and currawong.

Occasionally you get some help from a prominent physical feature. That burly roller-type bird on a distant dead tree makes a little foray after some large flying insect and reveals the distinctive white spots on the wings—ah, yes, the dollar bird; I've read about that. It is so named because the spots were thought to look like Spanish silver dollars. By a similar if less whimsical process of inference I work out the spangled drongo, blue-faced honeyeater, pied butcherbird, and silver-crowned friarbird, though in no cases do I initially recognise them as such. But gradually I get my eye and ear in and start to understand how things fit together and relate to one another, and by the end of the day I find that I have identified about seventy species securely, with a few more "probables" and several "what on earth was that!"s.

In the next few days I visit some different local habitats, including the creeks and rivers (all swollen with water at this time of year). Herons, ibises, storks, wildfowl, kingfishers, kites, and eagles now start to fall into place with a bit of effort, as do egrets, though here there are great, little, and intermediate kinds to distinguish (the last one not a very inspired choice of name, surely[1]—was

---

[1] But still better than its alternative name of plumed egret, which doesn't distinguish it at all from other kinds.

the taxonomist just getting tired?). My best bird of the week is probably the rainbow pitta, which I glimpse only for a second or two in thick leaf litter on the ground in an area of dense monsoon forest, briefly illuminated by a shaft of sunlight that brings out more than enough colours for a very decent rainbow. When I look this up later I find that it's a kind of ground-thrush and that "pitta" comes from an Indian language Telugu and means "young bird" (suggested perhaps by its stumpy appearance and tameness?). So there are foreign imports here too. Indeed, the name Kakadu may itself be an import. With a show of political correctness this is carefully explained in my guidebook as a mispronunciation of the Aboriginal name Gadudju; but this area was first opened up in the nineteenth century to European settlement (not to say exploitation) by the German explorer Ludwig Leichenhardt and the German word for cockatoo is in fact "Kakadu." So who knows?

Anyone interested in words as well as birds can get quite absorbed in tracing some of these derivations for their own sake, of course. There are quite a few surprises. You might think that such quintessentially Australian birds as cockatoo, jabiru, drongo, emu, and cassowary must have names derived from local Aboriginal languages, when in fact the words are all imports from abroad. And who could have guessed the origin of the names for apostlebird, hardhead, burdekin, and rosella? I set out what I discovered about all this (including the answer to the emu-wren question) in appendix 4. At any rate, the names I've so far mentioned do illustrate more generally something of the variety of sources bird names can have and the way the names can affect how we see, hear, or think of the birds so described. I want in this chapter to explore this aspect further. Are names ever more than just labels? Does it matter what name a bird has and can we say some names are "better" or more "real" than others? What criteria do we use to invent them? And readers who have persevered this far won't be surprised to hear me wondering not only what the names tell us about the birds but also what they may tell us about ourselves.

What's in a Name?

Everyone now knows that names are just the artificial labels we put on things, and that they can't affect the things themselves. Names are invented: they can be modified, changed, replaced, or abolished at our discretion. To think otherwise would be to go back to some primitive, superstitious belief in the magical power of words, to a prescientific world where you think you can harm your enemies by chanting their names in a spell, where to use secret names is to have special powers; that is, to a world where the names are very much part of the things they are attached to. Shakespeare, as usual, puts our more enlightened attitude into its classic formulation when he has Juliet say:

> What's in a name? That which we call a rose
> By any other word would smell as sweet,
> So Romeo would, were he not Romeo called,
> Retain that dear perfection which he owes
> Without that title. Romeo, doff thy name,
> And for thy name, which is no part of thee,
> Take all myself.
> (*Romeo and Juliet,* 2.2)

Philosophers have been discussing this issue since the start of Western philosophy:

> For my part, Socrates, I have often discussed this question with Cratylus and many others and I cannot be persuaded that there is any correctness of names other than by convention and agreement. For it seems to me that whatever name is given to a thing is its right name. And if another name is exchanged for that later the new name is no less correct than the earlier one, just as we can change the names of our servants, since no name belongs to any particular thing by nature but only by the custom and practice of those who use the name and call it that. (Hermogenes in Plato's *Cratylus*)

And J. S. Mill is making essentially the same hard-headed point when he says that proper names attach to their objects, not their attributes:

> A proper name . . . is merely an unmeaning mark . . . which we endeavour to connect with the idea of the object in our minds in order that whenever the mark meets our eye or occurs to our thoughts, we may think of that individual object. Not being attached to the thing itself, it does not enable us . . . to distinguish the object when we see it; but it enables us to distinguish it when it is spoken of. . . . Objects thus ticketed with proper names resemble, until we know something more about them, men and women in masks. We can distinguish them from one another, but can conjecture nothing with respect to their real features. (*System of Logic*)

We all know this. It's just rational, twenty-first-century common sense, isn't it? But why then do we still *care* so much about names? Consider the following, for example:

- In 2007 the U.K. Deed Poll Service helped some forty thousand people change their names by deed poll, as has been a legal right in the

United Kingdom since 1760. Some of these were people wanting to put an end to some tiresome combination wished on them by their parents, like Neil Down or Marshall Law; some were hopefully choosing names like Darth Vader or David Beckham to improve their chances in life; while others were dealing with arguably more serious problems arising from immigration (anglicising "foreign" names, for example).

- Women in most Western countries routinely face a decision about whether to change their names on marriage (not straightforward, as is evident if you ask men whether they would cheerfully do the same), and then whether to change them again in the event of a separation or divorce (ditto); civil partnerships pose similar problems.
- *Taboo* is a Tongan word meaning "untouchable," but all societies, modern as well as traditional, have their taboo words that are not used in polite society, even though other words describing the same objects or functions may be.
- Celebrities in show business have often felt they needed more marketable names, quite rightly in the following cases: Reginald Dwight (Elton John), Frances Ethel Gumm (Judy Garland), Marion Morrison (John Wayne), Archibald Alexander Leach (Cary Grant), Issur Danielovitch Demsky (Kirk Douglas), Robert Allen Zimmerman (Bob Dylan), Norma Jean Baker (Marilyn Monroe), Allen Stewart Konigsberg (Woody Allen); and this extends to stage "couples" like Frederick Austerlitz and Virginia Katherine McMath (Fred Astaire and Ginger Rogers), who wanted something that tripped as lightly off the tongue as they did on the dance floor. This sort of nominal reinvention is now a standard part of the overall cosmetic surgery required in these professions.
- Authors also often invent "better" names for themselves: for example, George Orwell (who thereby also generated a new adjective, "Orwellian"), and George Eliot and Currer Bell (who wanted to be taken for men). Sir Walter Scott made a point of *not* having a name (and his mysterious anonymity as "the Great Unknown" did wonders for his sales, as it did later for the author of *Primary Colors*).[1]

---

[1] *Primary Colors* was the novel published in 1996 that told the story of an American politician whose career and habits corresponded suspiciously closely to those of Bill Clinton. There was a media frenzy to discover the author's identity, which helped Random House sell a half million hardback copies and sell paperback rights for $1.5 million and film rights for $1.5 million. Handwriting analysis eventually revealed the author to be a journalist with the modest-sounding name Joe Klein. Ironically, Charles Dodgson was another author who craved, but failed to find, anonymity.

- Parents agonise over finding the "right" name for their children, and there is research to suggest that their names can indeed affect their lives: the U.S. educationalist David Figlio has produced a study relating popular girls' names to their perceived "femininity rating" (with Isabella, Anna, and Elizabeth near the top and Ashley, Abigail, and Alex near the bottom); the report suggests that girls at the top end are less likely to study mathematics and physics (subjects considered "masculine"), at least partly as a consequence of the expectations engendered by their names.
- Family history and onomastics (name research) are booming leisure activities; watch someone pick up a dictionary of place names or first names in a bookshop and they all automatically turn to the names of their own families or home towns to see what they "mean." More sinisterly, name theft and identity theft are now serious and growing criminal activities.
- Countries and people change names for political reasons to do with the history and associations of particular words: Muhammad Ali (Cassius Clay), St. Petersburg (Petrograd, then Leningrad), Zaire (Congo), Sellafield (Windscale), Zimbabwe (Southern Rhodesia) and Harare (Salisbury), Mumbai (Bombay), and Myanmar (Burma).

These examples all seem to suggest that names *matter*. And there is plenty of traditional support for the view that names somehow *belong* to things. Adam's first job, after all, was to give names to the creatures of the earth:

> And out of the ground the Lord God formed every beast of the field, and every fowl of the air; and brought them unto Adam to see what he would call them: and whatsoever Adam called every living creature, that was the name thereof. (Genesis 2:19)

But the examples cited also suggest, in the case of people at least, the more alarming thought that there might be a sort of nominal determinism at work, whereby the name you carry can affect the way you are perceived, and therefore to some extent the way you behave, and so eventually the way you *are*. There is popular and literary support for this notion too:

> People always grow up like their names. It took me thirty years to work off the effects of being called Eric. If I wanted a daughter to grow up beautiful I'd call her Elizabeth, and if I wanted her to be honest and a good cook I'd choose something like Mary or Jane. (George Orwell [Eric Blair], Letter to Rayner Heppenstall, 16 April 1940)

Birds and places don't know what names they have, of course, but as
Humpty Dumpty reminds us, we may still have to be careful what we call
them lest the words run away with us:

> "When I use a word," Humpty Dumpty said in rather a scornful tone, "it
> means just what I choose it to mean—neither more nor less."
>
> "The question is," said Alice, "whether you *can* make words mean dif-
> ferent things."
>
> "The question is," said Humpty Dumpty, "which is to be master—
> that's all."
>
> Alice was too much puzzled to say anything, so after a minute Humpty
> Dumpty began again. "They've a temper, some of them—particularly
> verbs, they're the proudest—adjectives you can do anything with, but
> not verbs—however, I can manage the whole lot! (Lewis Carroll, *Alice
> through the Looking-Glass*)

Nearly one hundred years later it was another comic writer, the journalist
Paul Jennings, who helped make popular the game of intuiting hidden mean-
ings in familiar proper names. In a classic article for his weekly column in *The
Observer* newspaper he revealed the deeper senses of the names of various
English towns:

> There is surely about most English words an ultimate rightness which
> ought to strike everyone, including foreigners, as the final perfection
> reached in man's art of naming. . . . If anyone doubts this let him con-
> sider the very names of our towns. For they not only describe places.
> They carry wonderful overtones, they seem to have been drawn from
> some huge, carelessly profuse stock of primal meaning, to have come
> out of the very bag from which Adam got his names.

Jennings then gives us some examples "from this vast English treasury of sub-
conscious meaning":

Babbacombe n. An idle or nonsensical rumour. "It's just a lot of b."
Beccles n. An ailment of sheep, cf. the Staggers, the Twitches, Quarter-ill, the
    Jumps.
Bovey Tracey adj. Headstrong, wilful. "None of your b.t. ways here, Miss!"
Brasted adj. (colloq.) Term of humorous abuse. "The b. thing's come unstuck."
Dunstable adj. (arch.) Possible. "If 'tis dunstable he'll do it, my lord." (Shak.)
Erith v. (obsol.). Only in third pers., in old proverb "Man erith, woman
    morpeth."
Morpeth See Erith.
Stevenage n. (legal). Ancient nominal rent paid to lord of manor for stones.

And so on to his final example, which still feels appropriate for the spiritual home of English football:

Wembley adj. Suffering from a vague *malaise.* "I feel a bit w. this morning."

One could play similar games with the names of birds and there does seem, to use Jennings's notion, an obvious "rightness" about names like wren, eagle, finch, twite, and sparrow, even if we can't guess their etymological origins. How could that be? I'll come back to this, but first it may be helpful to analyse some of the categories of bird names whose meanings are more obvious and transparent.

Facts and Fancies: Naming the Birds

Let's start with some of the categories obviously descriptive of the physical appearance (1–4) and then go on to behaviour (5–7) and other factors (8–10). I shall allow myself to include as examples some of the more exuberant names that it is a pleasure just to roll off the tongue. It adds zest to one's birding in unfamiliar regions to know that out there somewhere may be a Coxen's double-eyed fig-parrot, a sapphire-vented puffleg, or an oleaginous hemispingus (see fig. 48).

1. Colour. Many, perhaps most, birds are named after the colour that is the most striking aspect of their overall appearance. Sometimes it is just the colour *tout court,* as in blackbird (a thrush in Western Europe, but in North America a group of "icterids" related to grackles and orioles); bluebird (North America); and yellowbird (popular Caribbean name for the North American yellow warbler). More usually, however, there is at least some family or generic qualifier: blue jay, greenfinch, sooty tern. Then there are myriad colour-names relating to specific parts of the bird: black-headed gull (actually brown), blue-winged teal, wheatear ("white arse"), red-rumped swallow, yellow-vented bulbul, and so on, and there are occasionally combinations like black-throated blue warbler, white-winged black tern, and black redstart. Quite unusual colours are sometimes distinguished: azure-winged warbler, flammulated antpitta, cinnamon teal, ochre-rumped bunting, flavescent and ultramarine flycatchers, fulvous-breasted flatbill, sepia-brown wren, ferruginous duck, icterine (that is, "jaundiced") warbler, plumbeous warbler, and hyacinth macaw, though these must be the inventions of taxonomists in laboratories rather than the instinctive appellations of ordinary birders in the field. It would take a keen-eyed observer to discern the exact shades of the yellow-tinted honeyeater, the violaceous trogon, and the rufous and rufescent flycatchers. A nice note of ruminative hesitation is struck with the greenish warbler.

48. Birds with exotic names:
(a) Coxen's double-eyed fig parrot;
(b) oleaginous hemispingus;
(c) sapphire-vented puffleg

2. Patterns and shapes. Similarly, there are many species called the pied, speckled, spotted, barred, striped, striated, banded, masked, vermiculated, or chequered something. There is also the harlequin duck, and there are pied, collared, and semi-collared flycatchers. Some others need a bit of working out: the pectoral sandpiper has a very clear breast band (Latin *pectus,* meaning "breast"); while "shag," in case you wondered, refers to the jutting crest. Occasionally there are etymological traps, however: "ruff" looks as though it must be derived from the elaborate collar that was a fashionable item of clothing in the sixteenth century, very like the remarkable frill of feathers sported by the male ruff in breeding plumage. But in fact the word probably predates the

Elizabethan ruff and the female name "reeve" is more of a clue.[1] That still carries the sense of bailiff or sheriff (as in "shire-reeve") and "ruff" may have related origins in the Old English *gerofa* meaning registrar or commander; and that fits well with the aggressive display the male puts on when he parades before his rivals. As Potter and Sargent put it, "Certainly 'field marshal' seems a better title than 'collared dandy' for *Philomachus pugnax*" (and the French agree, with their *Chevalier combatant*).

3. The so-called bare parts of the bill and legs are sometimes the features singled out. Most of these are easy to understand, as in redshank (that is, "red legs"—similarly greenshank and yellowlegs), stilt, shoveler, spoonbill, long-billed curlew, thick-knee (stone curlews), wrybill (a New Zealand wader with a unique sideways curve to the bill), crossbill, grosbeak ("fat beak"), bullfinch ("bull-necked"), and gull-billed tern. Less obvious are "pomarine" skua (a contraction of "pomatorhine," literally, "nose-lid," referring to the protective rim over the nostrils) and "phalarope," which also comes from the Greek and literally means "coot-foot." In some other cases the meaning is clear, but you may need to perform feats of hyperperception in the field if you are relying only on the name: short-toed lark (and eagle and treecreeper), sharp-shinned hawk, red-eyed vireo, semi-palmated sandpiper, Lapland longspur, thick-billed warbler, slender-billed gull, long-toed stint, and hook-billed kite are all easier to identify by other means.

4. The size is often a part of the name, either on its own, to separate closely related species in a group, or in combination with other features: great snipe, giant coot (a terrifying thought), great/intermediate/little egrets (and there's also a "lesser" one in Southeast Asia), dwarf bittern, Goliath heron, pygmy owl. Comparatives are also quite common, though they obviously imply a knowledge of at least two species to make sense. They can also be faintly ridiculous; at least, terms like "lesser-spotted" seem to lend themselves easily to parody when bluff humorists are ridiculing birders for nerdish tendencies: "Are you looking for a lesser-spotted whatsit, then?"

5. Activity: swift (unusual to have an adjective on its own stand for a name), swallow (not what it seems),[2] diver, kingfisher, shoveler, sapsucker, dipper, treecreeper, foliage-gleaner, trembler, leaf-tosser, roadrunner, woodpecker, wryneck, roller (the flight), spiderhunter, and goatsucker (in Latin *caprimulgus,*

---

[1] Readers of James Thurber may recall at this point that "reeve" has several other meanings too: "They are here with the reeves," in "What do you mean it was brillig?" from *My World and Welcome to It* (1942).

[2] Not from the verb "swallow"; more likely from the proto-Germanic *swalwo* meaning "cleft-stick" in reference to the tail or from the Old English *swealve* meaning "move rapidly."

but false either way). And presumably the fearful owl of the Solomon Islands and the shy albatross of the southern oceans betray these qualities somehow?

6. Voice. Another very large category. I have already discussed the general phenomenon of onomatopoeia and the history of some bird names like that of the cuckoo (see chapter 6, pp. 161–62). There are many names where an imitative reference to a characteristic call or song is very evident (cuckoo, kittiwake, curlew, chickadee, towhee, veery, chiffchaff, koel, and boobook) and others where it is present but obscured by the evolution of the word-forms (owl, kite, crane, dove, jay, and probably goose). There are also many names, both of species and families, that incorporate descriptions rather than imitations: nightjar (from the "jarring" = churring song), nightingale ("night singer"), whistler, barking owl, whooping crane, cirl bunting (another buried meaning—it probably comes from a word meaning "to chirp"), song thrush, warbler (transferred from the European warblers, which do warble, to the quite different group of American ones, which on the whole don't), melodious babbler, clinking currawong (a Tasmanian speciality), and another nightmare candidate, the horned screamer.[1]

7. Food. The main or preferred food items are often part of a name: figbird, fish eagle, mistle thrush (mistletoe berries), crab plover, bee-eater, snail kite, hawfinch, acorn woodpecker, corn bunting. But inevitably some of these are not quite accurate: honey buzzards are after the larvae, not the honey; oyster-catchers will eat "most any kind of mollusc" (Peterson, see p. 101 above); and antbirds are also quite omnivorous. The activity and the food source get combined in the case of the flycatchers, gnatcatchers, and berrypeckers.

8. Place. Some birds are named after what is, or once was, a favoured habitat: wood pigeon, reed bunting (now common in farmland and other "dry" habitats), olive-tree warbler, mangrove heron, meadowlark, skylark, house martin, desert wheatear, junglefowl (the wild ancestor of the domestic chicken, of course), reef egret, and thicketbird (Vanuatu). Some of these too now sound rather inappropriate: tree sparrow (in many parts of the world an urban bird), marsh tit (mainly a bird of woodland in Europe), garden warbler (ditto), and seagull (no such bird anyway). Then there are birds named after early associations with particular locations: for example, Dartford warbler, Sandwich tern, Kentish plover (strange that one county of England should account for all three), and Manx shearwater; in North America, Connecticut, Kentucky, Tennessee, Nashville, and Canada warblers (none of them really appropriate), Carolina wren, and Ipswich sparrow (the Ipswich in Massachusetts); and in Australia, Burdekin duck, Torres Strait pigeon, and Port Lincoln parrot.

[1] From the same cast list as the satanic eared-nightjar (Sulawesi).

9. People. Various ornithologists, explorers, and collectors bestowed their own names (or, in a few cases, those of their wives) on birds. The number of personal names applied in this way totals well over one thousand and more than two thousand species are involved (some names being applied to many different species). Familiar examples for Europeans are Montagu's harrier, Bewick's swan, Leach's petrel, Radde's and Pallas's warblers, White's thrush (the only tribute of this kind to the great man), and for Americans, Wilson's petrel, Swainson's thrush, Bonaparte's gull, and Blackburnian and Grace's warblers (two of the women). The nationalities contributing most of these are: first the United Kingdom (with 331), then the United States (201), France (161), and Germany (137), reflecting the distribution of imperial power from the eighteenth to the early twentieth centuries, when most of these possessive eponyms were established. In this spirit there is even one Carruthers involved, a certain Alexander Douglas Mitchell Carruthers (educated Trinity College, Cambridge), who managed to "discover" Carruthers's cisticola as well as publishing books with "Boys' Own" titles like *Unknown Mongolia* (1913) and *Arabian Adventure* (1935). The individuals scoring highest in the naming stakes include the expected figures of Gould (24), Blyth (16), Hume (13), Pallas (13) and Wilson (7), as well as some less well known ones such as Sclater (21 species between father and son, mainly South American), Swainson (17), Temminck (17), and Salvin (15). The last of these, Osbert Salvin, was an Englishman who was the first European to record a resplendent quetzal, which he described as "unequalled for splendour among the birds of the New World" and then shot.

Women fare badly in this, I'm afraid, and not just numerically. "Isabelline," describing the sandy colour of the Isabelline wheatear and shrike has been explained by a bizarre reference to Isabella, the archduchess of Austria and daughter of Philip II of Spain. He laid siege to Ostend in 1601 and in a moment of filial loyalty she vowed not to change her underwear until the city was taken. Unfortunately the siege lasted until 1604, by which time the garments were the colour in question.[1]

These personal names never describe any characteristics of the birds themselves, of course, though one could perhaps argue that they sometimes lend a certain romance to an exotic species. I think I prefer "Pallas's gull," for example,

[1] The *Oxford English Dictionary* reports this anecdote only to refute it by pointing out that the word was first used to describe this colour in 1600. But as Michael Quinion suggests in his "World Wide Words" note on the Internet, the reference may well be to another Isabella and another siege, the siege of Granada by Ferdinand and Isabella that ended in 1492 (this one lasted eight months—quite long enough for the purpose). A more prosaic derivation would be that the word comes from the Arabic *izah* meaning "lion-coloured," but the Isabella story deserves to be true.

to the more accurate but rather boring "great black-headed gull" as a name for this charismatic species; and there is a certain charm to Murphy's petrel, Mrs. Moreau's warbler, Muriel's chat, and Spix's macaw. In just a few cases the name does actually have a meaning that transfers to the bird (Orphean warbler, a wonderful songster), and in one or two more you feel there might be some deeper connection if only you knew more about the personage involved (was Lady Amherst as grand as her pheasant, and would Aurelia have been glad to have the greenish puffleg named after her?). Otherwise, names of this kind are surely just arbitrary labels in exactly the sense J. S. Mill was suggesting.

10. Other. The great majority of bird names fall into one of the nine categories so far considered, but there are a few other miscellaneous ones. Some are little more than vague expressions of admiration: the Australian superb fairy-wrens, for example (there are also superb starlings and pittas), and similarly splendid ones (along with splendid sunbirds, white-eyes, and woodpeckers). Magnificent frigate birds come into the same category (as do magnificent hummingbirds and birds of paradise). There is also a beautiful tanager and a mysterious starling (now extinct), which won't help you much in the field, and invisibility can scarcely be the key distinguishing feature of the invisible rail, surely? There is at least one example of *dis*approbation too with the fulmar ("foul bird"), and a sort of cop-out with the variable screech-owl, seed-eater, and wheatear. Some other birds are just "common" of course (though none seem to be "rare"). One or two names defeat the imagination entirely (does the cloud-scraping cisticola have an Icarus complex?), and the etymologists themselves are baffled about the origins of "woodchat" in woodchat shrike.[1]

In most of the cases in these ten categories we can fairly quickly see how the name came about, even if it doesn't always incorporate the most obvious or helpful feature by which to remember the bird. Apart from those called after people, the names are like little shorthand descriptions, though when you use them regularly you tend to forget the etymology and just think of the name *as* the bird. That is, although we can immediately see why a bluebird, a curlew, or a swift came to be so called if we think about it for a moment, we don't usually have that thought uppermost in our minds when we casually refer to them. A swift is a swift is a swift. In general the names incorporating the fullest literal descriptions are likely to be those of birds regarded as exotic—"collected" and discovered as part of some zoological expedition into little-studied areas and

---

[1] The word first appears in 1713 (Ray's *Synopsis methodica avium et piscium*) and may just be a printing error. The "chat" part could conceivably be onomatopoeic ("chatterer," as in stonechat), but the bird is very rare in Britain and can't have acquired this sort of popular name. All the European languages in countries where the bird does occur regularly have names that refer to the brilliant chestnut colour on the head and nape and Ray himself says that he was very struck by that.

later named by museum taxonomists or scientists, often on the basis of skins. That would account for some of the names that seem to emphasise features not very evident in the field (bristlebird, lesser short-toed lark) or that lack, shall we say, flair (intermediate egret, dull-coloured grassquit, variable seed-eater). Is it fanciful to imagine a dispirited taxonomist on a wet Friday afternoon at the London Natural History Museum in the Cromwell Road opening yet another crate of skins from the mountains of central Asia and saying wearily, "Oh, let's call this one a plain leaf-warbler *Phylloscopus neglectus,* shall we?" or possibly even, "Do you think old Allan [Hume][1] would like to have one of these leaf warblers named after him as *Phylloscopus humei?*" If you look, for example, at the page of tyrant flycatchers in *The Birds of Venezuela* or the honeyeaters in an Australian field guide, it isn't surprising if invention sometimes flags (see fig. 49).

Native species, on the other hand, are likely to have names with a longer history and to have evolved from popular names whose original meanings may now be hard to recognise or even recover. They are like stones, shaped and polished by centuries of geological activity, with only a distant relationship to the physical landscapes from which they came. This brings us back to the wrens, gulls, finches, and eagles, and I want in due course to look at how names like these can act as carriers of meanings and what that tells us about our attempts to invent and change names.

Invention and Discovery

But we should first recognise that birds do not just have one name: they always have at least two, often three, and sometimes more. I refer of course to the differences between the standard common names we have so far been looking at, their Latinised "scientific" names, and their various other possible national, local, dialect, and slang names. This is a quite different set of categories, which cuts across those so far considered. I took most of my examples to illustrate the ten categories of *sources* for names from the standard common names like greenfinch, koel, and cuckoo, but you could just as well use examples from all these other *kinds* of names. And if we now look at each of these we find that they in turn suggest other ways in which names can have meanings for us.

Every bird has a *Latin scientific name* that uniquely identifies it and places it in the family to which it belongs, whatever the misleading similarities and differences of the common names. So the European robin is *Erithacus rubecula,*

[1] Allan Octavian Hume (1829–1912), a civil servant in India for most of his professional career, actually had thirteen species named after him, including the leaf warbler.

49. "Tyrant flycatchers" page (Steven L. Hilty, *The Birds of Venezuela*, second edition, 2003)

the North American robin is *Turdus migratorius* (placing it clearly in the same genus as European thrushes), the Australian scarlet robin is *Petroica multicolor,* the African bearded scrub-robin is *Cercotrichas quadrivirgata,* and so on, most of the world's many "robins" being named originally out of nostalgia for the British robin redbreast and the word then being attached to other small birds with prominent red plumages (see plate 7a).

The scientific name always comes in two parts (the "binomial system") with the first part (always capitalised) denoting the genus and the second (always lowercase) the species; there is then sometimes a third name denoting a race or subspecies, as in *Erithacus rubecula rubecula,* denoting the continental race of the robin, and *E.r. melophilus,* denoting the British race. The main point of these Latin names is to enable scientists to communicate internationally without any possibility of confusion. It can have its practical uses for the rest of us too, as I discovered in the Volga Delta where my Volga boatman spoke as much English as I did Russian, but he was able to locate various rare warblers for me because we both knew the Latin names. The system also enables you to place each bird in a larger hierarchy of family relationships, like a huge filing system that starts with the class of birds *(Aves)* and works its way down through the order of passerines *(Passeriformes)* to the family of Old World flycatchers *(Muscicapidae),* the tribe of chats *(Saxicolini),* and finally to the genus of *Erithacus* and the species *rubecula* ("little red one"). It was Linnaeus's[1] remarkable achievement to invent this whole system, which he applied first to plants (in the *Species plantarum* of 1753) and then to animals and birds (in the *Systema naturae,* tenth edition, 1758). Scientists have since of course refined, evolved, and changed his original categories in many ways but the basic system still stands. Latin was chosen as the language in which to express all this, since that was then as much the international language as English is now.

Quite often the scientific name just translates a popular name, so the white-fronted goose is *Anser albifrons,* but sometimes it picks out a quite different feature. For example, the little owl becomes *Athene noctua,* which adds a historical dimension: Athena was the Greek goddess of wisdom, war, and the night, and the owl was her symbol; the image of the little owl was stamped on ancient Greek coins, which became known as "owls." A rather different little history lesson comes from the Latin names of the Manx shearwater and puffin. The former is *Puffinus puffinus* and was a reference to the "puffiness" of the nestling shearwaters, which were once harvested in places like Scilly and

---

[1] It is a fitting professional tribute that we know the great Swedish naturalist by the name Carolus Linnaeus, Latinised from his real name, Carl von Linné.

the Isle of Man and sold as cured delicacies; the trade name then transferred both to the adult birds and (by confusion) to the puffins that nested in burrows in these places and were also fat and "puffy," though they were usually known by local names like sea parrot or coulter neb ("plough bill"). The puffin, meanwhile, has the quite different Latin name *Fratercula arctica,* which means "hoodie from the Arctic" or, more literally, "little brother," a reference to the "friar's cowl" black-and-white pattern.

Some people shy away from these technical-looking Latin names, which may remind them of painful educational experiences, and which often look cumbrous and hard to pronounce, but they can sometimes have a wonderful aptness just from the way they sound. I particularly like *Crex crex* for the corncrake, for example, *Upupa epops epops* for the Eurasian hoopoe and *Bubo bubo* for the eagle owl (all three onomatopoeic, of course); and doesn't the specific name in *Lanius excubitor* summon up something of the fierce, dominating posture of the great grey shrike even if you don't know that *excubitor* means "sentinel"?

Not all the taxonomists are dry sticks, anyway. They sometimes cheer themselves up by playing games, as when they called the kookaburras by the generic name *Dacelo* which is an anagram of *Alcedo,* the generic name of the European kingfisher, as is *Lacedo* for the Asian banded kingfisher. Richard Fortey tells some nice stories of this kind in his charming book about the London Natural History Museum, *Dry Store Room No. 1.* In chapter 2 he discusses the naming of various molluscs: there is apparently one with the generic name *Abra,* and two scientists had the wit to christen a species in that genus *cadabra* in 1957, only for some spoilsport to decide that it really belonged to a different genus altogether and meanly rename it *Theora cadabra.* In the same spirit, there is a beetle called *Agra phobia,* along with crustaceans whose Latin names are suggestive of enormous sexual organs and must have amused someone no end for a short time.

Then there are the common names that are standard in forms of English other than British English, the most important being *North American English.* Many of the differences are quite trivial, as in the following:

American	British
Greater shearwater	Great shearwater
Great cormorant	Cormorant
Common eider	Eider
Great egret	Great white egret

And no one in Britain is going to be in any real doubt about what is intended by ruddy turnstone, black-legged kittiwake, red crossbill, or greater scaup, even if they prefer to use the shorter and simpler version while on home territory. There can, however, be confusion between some other pairs, where the names have diverged further and there may even be quite different designations for the genera involved:

American	British
Common loon	Great northern diver
Arctic loon	Black-throated diver
Horned grebe	Slavonian grebe
Eared grebe	Black-necked grebe
Brant	Brent goose
Northern harrier	Hen harrier
Common merganser	Goosander
Black-bellied plover	Grey plover
Red phalarope	Grey phalarope
Parasitic jaeger	Arctic skua
Mew gull	Common gull
Common murre	Guillemot
Horned lark	Shore lark
Barn swallow	Swallow
Winter wren	Wren
Lapland longspur	Lapland bunting

Inevitably, there is an urge in some quarters to standardise these, one way or the other, though in practice that seems usually to mean standardising in favour of the American usage. But such official agreements are not always observed by the troops on the ground, so to speak, and since there is in any case already an agreed common language for serious scientific purposes, it seems unnecessary to strive too hard for complete uniformity in this area any more than in others where these two major dialects of English differ. In any case the paired species are not always precisely the same, even if they only represent different geographical races, as the full scientific names of the larks and harriers indicate (the Northern European shore lark, for example, is *Eremophila alpestris flava* and the North American *E. a. alpestris*).

On the contrary, it's quite interesting to compare some of the differences and note the different impressions they give rise to in the two different contexts. The history is sometimes complicated and tends to undermine possessive claims about who has the original or "real" name. "Great northern diver," for example, has a fine romantic ring to it, especially for British readers brought up on the Arthur Ransome children's classic *Great Northern;* it suggests a rare and impressive visitor from the North on the edge of its breeding range, which is exactly right in Britain. And "diver" is clearly a good descriptor. But "loon" is quite evocative too and was in fact a local name in parts of England in the seventeenth century for both divers and grebes.[1] The name is onomatopoeic— from the weird wailing cry that is indeed a common sound in northern lakes in the New World (but almost never heard in Britain)—so the name "common loon" is entirely appropriate there. Let's keep both, and use the local language when abroad.

In the same way, "winter wren" is quite inappropriate in Britain (where wrens are common residents all the year round), though it is migratory in America, where there are also several different wrens to distinguish. But in some cases one or other of the names does seem to fit better. The American "brant" is closer to the original sense of "burnt" (that is, blackish), and that was also once the common name in Britain, as was "horned grebe," which is surely more helpful than "Slavonian," and "murre" ("growler"), which is more satisfyingly onomatopoeic than "guillemot."[2] Some other American names are less appealing. Political correctness played a part in causing Americans to drop the vernacular "oldsquaw" in favour of the European "long-tailed duck," since the former managed in one short word to be simultaneously racist, ageist, and sexist! Then there are examples of apparent misnomers. All skuas/jaegers are parasitic to some degree so why attach that name to just one of them? Don't the names of the ring-necked duck and the red-bellied woodpecker pick out the wrong key features? And aren't "long spurs" difficult to spot on a bunting crouched close to the ground in grassland or tundra? In the case of the confusing "red" and "grey" phalaropes, the two names describe the summer and winter plumages respectively of the same bird, the former of which is almost never seen in Britain and is seen only in the far Arctic regions of North America. One could argue endlessly about other borderline cases and we may just have to agree to continue to be "divided by a common language," as George Bernard Shaw famously put it. The Australians are in any case sensibly

---

[1] Though the splendid insult in *Macbeth,* 5.3.11, "thou cream-faced loon," refers to another meaning of loon as *lown* or "stupid."

[2] "Guillemot" comes from the French, or more exactly from the Breton *Gwelan,* and like the old Norfolk name *Willock* is supposed to recall the high-pitched cries of the young birds of this species. But Yarrell wrote in his *British Birds* of 1843, "In England the commonest [name] is the onomatopoeic 'Murre,' from the murmuring noise of the assembled multitudes at their breeding haunts," and that seems a much happier association.

eclectic. In the cases of the few species in the last table that have occurred there: they follow U.S. usage for barn swallow, U.K. usage for grey plover and grey phalarope, and a hybrid for arctic jaeger.

English may be the world's dominant language for many purposes, but of course from a linguistic point of view it is only one among about six thousand. All of these will have their own names for their native birds and it is worth looking briefly at some of these in the commoner *European languages* that are naming the same birds as we are in British English. For example, I do like the French *Le grand duc* for eagle owl and *Jean le blanc* for short-toed eagle; and doesn't *Alouette lulu* beautifully convey the lilting song of the woodlark, as does *zilp zalp* in German the refrain of the chiffchaff and *kluut* in Dutch the call of the avocet? *Grote Burgermeester* (also Dutch) captures something about the dominant bearing of the glaucous gull, and *ballerina bianca* in Italian gets the dancing steps of the white wagtail perfectly. And who could resist the Italian for the black redstart, *codirosso spazzacamino* ("red-tailed chimney-sweeper")? But it's also interesting to compare a set of common names where the foreign equivalents may be less striking than these, just to see what features are particularly emphasised and what different generic connections are made. We stayed a few days in late April one year at the house of some friends in a small village south of Toulouse in the Ariège, and they asked me to make up a "garden list" of birds for them. That gave me a chance to learn some French bird names and become more aware both of the similarities and the sometimes subtle differences in the perceptions implied by them. The house is an isolated old farmhouse, set among rather unkempt pastures and with woodland round about, and the list went as follows:

Canard colvert (mallard)

Milan royal (red kite)

Milan noir (black kite)

Buse variable (buzzard)

Falcon crécerelle (kestrel)

Fasan de Colchide (pheasant)

Caille des blés (quail)

Perdrix grise (grey partridge)

Gallinule poule d'eau (moorhen)

Tourterelle turque (collared dove)

Tourterelle des bois (turtle dove)

Coucou gris (cuckoo)

Effraie des clochers (barn owl)

Chouette hulotte (tawny owl)

Engoulevent d'Europe (nightjar)

Martinert noir (swift)

Huppe fasciée (hoopoe)

Pic vert (green woodpecker)

Pic épeiche (great spotted woodpecker)

Pic épeichette (lesser spotted woodpecker)

Alouette des champs (skylark)

Alouette lulu (woodlark)

Hirondelle de rivage (sand martin)

Hirondelle de fenêtre (house martin)

Hirondelle rustique (swallow)

Pipit des arbres (tree pipit)

Bergeronnette grise (white wagtail)

Traquet motteux (wheatear)

Traquet pâtre (stonechat)

Troglodyte mignon (wren)

Accenteur mouchet (dunnock)

Rouge-gorge familier (robin)

Rossignol philomèle (nightingale)

Rouge-queue noir (black redstart)

Grive musicienne (song thrush)

Grive draine (mistle thrush)

Merle noir (blackbird)

Fauvette á tête noire (blackcap)

Fauvette grisette (whitethroat)

Fauvette babillard (lesser whitethroat)

Fauvette des jardins (garden warbler)

Pouillot fitis (willow warbler)

Pouillot véloce (chiffchaff)

Pouillot siffleur (wood warbler)

Gobe-mouche noir (pied flycatcher)

Mésange à longue queue (long-tailed tit)

Mésange nonnette (marsh tit)

Mésange bleu (blue tit)

Mésange carbonnière (great tit)

Sitelle torchepot (nuthatch)

Grimpereau des arbres (treecreeper)

Loriot d'Europe (golden oriole)

Geai des chênes (jay)

Pie bavarde (magpie)

Choucas des tours (jackdaw)

Corneille noire (carrion crow)

Grand corbeau (raven)

Étourneau sansonnet (starling)

Moineau domestique (house sparrow)

Moineau friquet (tree sparrow)

Pinson des arbres (chaffinch)

Serin cini (serin)

Verdier d'Europe (greenfinch)

Chardonneret élégant (goldfinch)

Bouvreuil pivoine (bullfinch)

Linotte mélodieuse (linnet)

Bruant jaune (yellowhammer)

Bruant zizi (cirl bunting)

Bruant proyer (corn bunting)

Not a dramatic list by any means, though I wouldn't mind being able to hear from *my* back garden golden orioles, quail, nightjars, woodlarks, nightingales, and cirl buntings (isn't *zizi* nice for that?); and the list is also a nostalgic reminder of how many of these birds we have *lost* in the English countryside. I won't try to translate or explain all the French terms here, since you'll see what I mean about the different emphases immediately and you might prefer to work out the meanings you don't know yourself. The point of the exercise is not so much to learn another language but to become more self-aware about one's own.

Cultures and countries more distant than the French may use more radically different principles of classification and description, of course. *Native languages* of hunter-gatherer societies are likely to distinguish those species and characteristics that are of most practical interest for hunting, food, ornamentation, and ritual. I have already referred to the use of birds as markers of times and seasons in preliterate societies (pp. 192–93) and the discriminations New Guinea hunters might make between different birds of paradise (pp. 142–43), and there is a lot of anthropological source material on all this.

Jared Diamond, for example, presents a detailed comparison between the taxonomies of the Foré people of New Guinea and those of Western ornithologists. In a volume of studies on E. O. Wilson's biophilia hypothesis, he writes that the Foré have 110 names for the 120 species we would distinguish: in 93 of the cases there is a one-to-one correspondence with Western taxonomy; they then have 8 names for 4 sexually dimorphic birds of paradise species (where the males and females have quite different plumages and so have a different utility for the Foré); and in 9 cases they lump species we would split. (I assume there are more than 2 species for some of those 9 names, to make the arithmetic work.) They distinguish the visually very similar *sericornis* family of scrubwrens (one of which has the English name of "perplexing scrubwren," I notice) by behaviour and call, since those are the key field criteria. In fact they generally rely far more on hearing than sight in identifying birds in these densely vegetated habitats and have an expert knowledge of songs and calls. They use this knowledge to distinguish the edible from the inedible, separate out confusion species, and track species that are indicators of special habitats and food sources. Birds are valued as food, clothing, and especially decoration. Indeed, the feathers of a Pesquet's parrot cost a good deal more than a wife does locally. Interestingly, Diamond tells us that the Foré did not on the whole distinguish butterflies, which had no such utility for them, at least not until the European collectors arrived and presented them with a commercial opportunity. Other authors in the same volume record the poignant loss of such experience and terminology when a culture of this kind is destroyed, as in the case of those North American Indians who have moved into the cities.

More radical differences in taxonomy emerge when dealing with groups like the cassowaries, kiwis, or penguins, which are exceptional in various ways. The very notion of a "bird" starts to seem a "fuzzy definition" in itself, just as the notion of a hedge or a bush is. There is a celebrated article by Ralph Bulmer under the title "Why Is the Cassowary Not a Bird?" which shows how the whole animal kingdom might be divided up in quite different ways for different purposes. The Karam people of New Guinea apparently have one general term for the 180 or so kinds of flying birds and bats they distinguish and another for the cassowary, which is of course flightless, almost wingless, huge, and very powerful. This thought could be deeply disturbing for twitchers and listers, who have to maintain a strong belief in "natural kinds" if they are to tick a cassowary for their Australian lists. But nothing like as unsettling as the taxonomy attributed to Tai Ping Kuang Chi in an ancient Chinese encyclopedia entitled the *Celestial Emporium of Benevolent Knowledge:*

> It is written that animals are divided into (a) those that belong to the Emperor, (b) embalmed ones, (c) those that are trained, (d) suckling pigs, (e) mermaids, (f) fabulous ones, (g) stray dogs, (h) those that are included in this classification, (i) those that tremble as if they were mad, (j) innumerable ones, (k) those drawn with a very fine camel's hair brush, (l) others, (m) those that have just broken a flower vase, (n) those that resemble flies from a distance.[1]

What would it be like to see the world that way? The classification may not be as completely fanciful as it seems. In some Australian Aboriginal languages, for example, one finds quite different ways of categorising nouns. The linguist Robert Dixon tells us that Dyirbal has four grammatical genders, represented by the following: (1) men, kangaroos, most snakes, possum, moon, storms, boomerang; (2) women, bandicoots, most birds, sun and stars, hairy mary grubs; (3) honey, edible fruit, and vegetables; and (4) parts of the body, yam-sticks, noises, grass, mud, and stones. Birds are believed to be the spirits of dead women and are therefore grammatically "female." And there are other examples closer to home, which show how circumstances alter cases. In 1869 *Punch* magazine published a cartoon illustrating a lady proposing to travel by rail with a menagerie of pets, including a tortoise (fig. 50). The railway porter is explaining the fares in the caption:

> Station Master say, mum, as cats is "dogs," and rabbits is "dogs," and so's parrots; but this 'ere "tortis" is an insect, so there ain't no charge for it.

I must now return to the more familiar world of our *national names* in English. Here too there are more distinctions to make. All our present standard names for local species have a history, even if the history is just to have been unchanging over centuries. Where the species is a common or familiar one, however, there will usually have been popular names or a range of different *dialect names* in the past, one of which may become the standard name, while others may still survive even when the official name becomes the dominant and agreed one. The Shetlanders (and birders) still talk of bonxies (great skuas) and tysties (black guillemots), and we are all likely to know what a redbreast,

---

[1] Tai Ping Kuang Chi (AD 981), cited approvingly, of course, by Borges in *Other Inquisitions, 1937–1952*, and by Michel Foucault in *Les mots et les choses*.

50. "This 'ere 'tortis' is an insect" (*Punch* cartoon, 1869)

peewit, tomtit, and spadger are. Some of these old folk names sound very apt. Here are some British examples:

Mollymawk (fulmar)
Scart (cormorant or shag)
Butter-bump (bittern)
Windhover or windfucker (kestrel)
Sea-pie (oystercatcher)
Stone runner (ringed plover)
Bog-bleater (snipe)
Whaup (curlew)
Cushie doo (wood pigeon)

Cock-up (pheasant—the call, not the design)
Devil screamer (swift)
Snake-bird (wryneck)
Yaffle (green woodpecker)
Dishwasher (wagtail)
Shufflewing (dunnock)
Bum-barrel (long-tailed tit)
Butcherbird (shrike)
Chatternag (magpie)

In one or two cases an ancient name may give a clue to modern place-names, as with the erne (sea eagle), which is unwittingly celebrated in Earnley, Earnwood, Arncliffe, Arnold, Arnwood, and Yarnfield. And the Suffolk name of awl-bird for the avocet might just explain the unusual name of the splendid pub, the Eel's Foot at Eastbridge, on the edge of the flagship Minsmere reserve; if "eel" there is a corruption of "awl," it would be a happy historical celebration of one of the first places in Britain to which avocets returned to breed in the 1940s.[1]

---

[1] See Greenoak, *British Birds,* p. 82, for this rather brave speculation. The avocet is of course the official logo of the RSPB, and its lovely name comes from the Italian *avocetta,* and perhaps ultimately from the Latin *avis* meaning "bird."

The Americans have their own equivalents in stiffy (plus sixty other less suggestive names for ruddy duck, from the tail), harrywicket (plus more than a hundred others for northern flicker, from the call), bogsucker (American woodcock, not really accurate), quank (white-breasted nuthatch, the nasal call), preacher (red-eyed vireo, with its endlessly repeated song), redbird (Northern cardinal), ricebird (bobolink, raiders of rice and other crops on migration south), shitepoke (herons, conspicuous defecation of), teeter-bob (spotted sandpiper, from the bobbing gait), and water-witch (pied-billed grebe, mysterious disappearance on diving). As you might expect, the Australians are not short of colourful vernacular terms either. I have mentioned some of those in appendix 4, and one could produce similar examples for other forms of regional English in South Africa, India, and New Zealand.

A rather different kind of dialect, which cuts across local boundaries, is *birders' slang*. In Britain at least this consists of special names, often in the form of pidginlike simplifications, for particular birds or genera. And here the birds are not necessarily the common ones (which would have attracted other kinds of folk names), but some rarities (which wouldn't). Like other kinds of slang, this is the private language of a special group or guild, whose members are "insiders," partly defined and recognised by their use of a common language. It is a curious mixture of abbreviations (sometimes of Latin genera), contractions, acronyms, references to confusion pairs and ID problems, insider jokes, and occasional flights of fancy. Here are some examples:

Acro (*Acrocephalus* warbler)
Barwit (bar-tailed godwit)
Blackwit (black-tailed godwit)
Commic tern (common or arctic tern)
Crest (goldcrest or firecrest)
Dick's pipit (Richard's pipit)
Goldie (golden plover or golden eagle)
Gropper (grasshopper warbler)
Grotfinch (common rosefinch)
Guillie (guillemot)
Hippo (*Hippolais* warbler)
Icky (icterine warbler)
Lancey (lanceolated warbler)
Lap bunt (Lapland bunting)

Lesserlegs (lesser yellowlegs)
Lesser spot (lesser spotted woodpecker)
Lesserthroat (lesser whitethroat)
LRP (little ringed plover)
Med (Mediterranean gull)
Melody (melodious warbler)
Mipit (meadow pipit)
Monty (Montagu's harrier)
Oyk (oystercatcher)
Paper bag (little egret)
Pec (pectoral sandpiper)
PG tips (Pallas's grasshopper warbler)
Phyllosc (*Phylloscopus* warbler)
Pom (pomarine skua)

RB fly/flicker (red-breasted
 flycatcher)
Sabs (Sabine's gull)
Semi-p (semi-palmated sandpiper)
Sibe (Siberian species)

Spot-red or spotshank (spotted
 redshank)
Sprosser (thrush nightingale, from
 the German)
Tuftie (tufted duck)

This is like a real language in the sense that you can learn to apply it creatively to new situations. One technical feature is the appropriation of certain qualifiers as nouns. For example, an aquatic warbler discovered in Britain will be referred to colloquially as "the aquatic," a black-and-white warbler as "the black-and-white," and a Blyth's reed warbler as "the Blyth's." So when Britain is finally favoured with its first black-throated blue warbler from America (very likely arriving one October at the small garden known as The Parsonage on St. Agnes in the Isles of Scilly) it will inevitably be referred to as "the black-throated blue,"[1] while the American redstart just down the lane by the Fruit Cages will immediately become "the Yankstart."

There is one final set of names, which is a sort of subclass of the vernacular British and American species names, and this is the category of *Collectives*. These too can affect the way we think about the creatures so assembled, and the words themselves—often archaic and much beloved in quizzes and word games—are an odd mixture of the vernacular and the technical, the apt and the artificial. Many of them are everyday words we use unthinkingly, of course—a herd of cows, a flock of pigeons or sheep, a pack of hounds, a brood of chickens, a swarm of flies, and so on; but there are many others less familiar and some quite bizarre ones. I include a few other creatures as well as birds to give a fuller flavour:

Badgers, a cete	Geese (on the ground), a gaggle	Mallard, a sord or suit
Bears, a sloth		Monkeys, a troop
Bittern, a siege	Goldfinches, a charm	Nightingales, a watch
Boars, a sounder	Hares, a down, mute, or husk	Owls, a parliament or stare
Choughs, a chattering		Parrots, a pandemonium
Coot, a covert or raft	Hawks, a cast	Partridges, a covey
Crows, a murder	Herons, a siege	Peacocks, a muster
Dotterel, a trip	Kangaroos, a mob or troop	Pheasants, a nid or nide
Dunlin, a fling	Larks, an exaltation	Porpoises, a school
Geese (in the air), a skein	Lions, a pride	Quail, a bevy or covey
	Magpies, a tiding	Ravens, an unkindness

[1] Though this won't work for the first yellow warbler or black woodpecker, since the shorter common colour names are not used on their own this way.

Rooks, a parliament or	Snipe, a wisp	Toads, a knot
clamour	Starlings, a murmuration	Whales, a pod
Ruffs, a hill	Swans, a herd	Woodcock, a fall
Shelduck, a dopping	Teal, a spring	Wrens, a herd

A lot of these appear to have their origins in hunting terms and come to us through the Normans, whose sportsmen no doubt felt themselves as distinct a class in their devotion to the chase as do present-day birders. "Siege" means a sitting, "nide" is a nesting, and "covey" a covering or hatch. The "herd" of swans is a historical reminder that the swan was a protected, even royal, bird and was kept in herds like sheep, goats, and swine (with a swanherd alongside the shepherd and swineherd), though the further application of "herd" to wrens in the fifteenth-century manual on hawking the *Book of St. Albans* must surely be some sort of joke? It's easy to make fun of these names and play games inventing others, and I can't quite believe in the authenticity of the very literary-sounding exaltation of larks, murmuration of starlings, and unkindness of ravens. Some others make sense, however, when you realise that the chattering "choughs" were actually jackdaws and that the watch of nightingales was a "wakefulness." And some of the names are very apt and revealing indeed: a wisp of snipe and a spring of teal are exactly right; a trip of dotterel is nicely ambiguous as between their short visits to traditional stop-over points on spring migration and their quick little runs; and a fall of woodcock perfectly conveys their sudden, silent arrival in the season still known in North America by its older English name of "fall."

Birds are not the only creatures to enjoy this rich variety of different names and naming systems, of course. Just the same issues arise with butterflies, for example, which also have common names, scientific names, and folk names that may refer to aspects of their physical appearance, behaviour, or history. Does a painted lady look any different if you think of it by this current English name, for example, by its more polite French name, *la belle dame*, or by the fuller Italian *bella dama o cardero* (lovely lady of the thistles)? Would you rather see a Camberwell beauty (British) or a mourning cloak (U.S.)? Don't you just love the idea of a clouded yellow, a silver-washed fritillary, and a grizzled skipper, even if you never get to encounter one? Who was the Monarch and who the Duke of Burgundy? What are the mythological links suggested by the *Inachis io* (peacock), the *Papilio machaon* (swallowtail), and the *Vanessa atalanta* (red admiral)? And if you move from the seventy-odd British butterflies to the two thousand or so British moths, you'll soon be lost in a welter of waves, wainscots, pugs, footmen, snouts, sprawlers, and chimney sweepers.

Is this profusion of names and systems a messy disorder we should clean up and regularise in the interests of good order and unambiguous communication? Or is it a rich heritage of meanings and significance we should relish and preserve? Do we take our lead from Linnaeus or from Paul Jennings?

Regulation and Resistance: The Esperanto Illusion

There have always been those who would like to take control of the language, arrest change, and impose good order. As early as 1672 John Dryden was complaining about "those who corrupt our English Idiom by mixing it too much with the French"; and in 1697 Daniel Defoe suggested that the establishment of an Academy might stem the inundation of swear words into the language, "the Frenzy of the Tongue, a vomit of the Brain." Jonathan Swift actually put up "A Proposal for Correcting, Improving and Ascertaining the English Tongue" in 1712. His hope was that "if it [English] were once refined to a certain Standard, perhaps there might be Ways found out to fix it for ever," and he submitted his plan for a National Academy for English to the Earl of Oxford:

> My Lord; I do here, in the Name of all the Learned and Polite Persons of the Nation, complain to your LORDSHIP, as *First Minister,* that our Language is extremely imperfect; that its daily Improvements are by no means in proportion to its daily Corruptions; that the Pretenders to polish and refine it, have chiefly multiplied Abuses and Absurdities; and, that in many instances, it offends against every part of Grammar.

The idea never got off the ground in Britain, though it already had done so in France (in 1635) and the French still have their Académie Française, whose function is to maintain the purity of the language, resist the inflow of foreign (especially English) words, and publish an approved dictionary. It was another dictionary maker, Dr. Johnson, who saw the difficulty with this, though, remarking in his preface:

> When we see men grow old and die at a certain time one after another, we laugh at the elixir that promises to prolong life to a thousand years; and with equal justice may the lexicographer be derided, who being able to produce no example of a nation that has preserved their words and phrases from mutability, shall imagine that his dictionary can embalm his language, and secure it from corruption and decay.

Johnson saw the principal purpose of his great *Dictionary* of 1755 as an attempt to describe the language, not arrest it or reshape it; but he did also see the need to introduce order where there had been chaos:

I found our speech copious without order and energetik without rules: wherever I turned my view, there was perplexity to be disentangled and confusion to be regulated.

That is of course a more prescriptive idea, and this ambivalence between prescription and description has pervaded the efforts and intentions of dictionary-makers ever since. And the bodies that produce "official" lists of bird names are no different. They too have to decide what is the "correct" term to use and whether divergences from this are mistakes, acceptable regional variations, or evolutions of actual usage that in their turn will become "correct." They certainly confront almost as much potential confusion as Dr. Johnson did. Think of the anomalies among the names of gulls for a start. In Britain we have a black-headed gull (with a brown head), a common gull (which isn't really),[1] and a herring gull (when did one of them last see a herring?). The Latin versions only make it worse. The black-headed gull is *Larus ridibundus,* meaning "laughing gull"; the American laughing gull is *atricilla* (black-tailed, though only the immature has that feature); and the Mediterranean gull is *melanocephalus* ("black-headed"). The herring gull is *argentatus* (silvery) and the Australian silver gull is *novaehollandiae* (New Holland). Meanwhile the Iceland gull is *glaucoides* ("like the glaucous") and the glaucous is "Arctic" *(hyperboreus),* just as the ivory is "frost-loving" (in a different genus, *Pagophila*). In the United States, the British common gull becomes the mew gull (*Larus canus,* meaning "grey," though "mew" is already an old word meaning "gull," so this is in effect "gull gull"), the ring-billed gull is *delawarensis* (from the Delaware River), Bonaparte's gull is *philadelphia* (from the city), and Franklin's gull is *pipixcan* (an Aztec word, meaning unknown, though Franklin was a British Arctic explorer). Little gull *(Larus minutus)* is spot-on all round, though—well done, somebody.

So it isn't surprising that bodies like the British Ornithologists' Union, the International Ornithological Congress, and the American Ornithologists' Union, together with their various taxonomic subcommittees, are constantly considering ways of making the nomenclature more consistent and intelligible. They periodically produce lists of "recommended names" for international use, which are dutifully followed by most key journals and learned societies, though not so readily by ordinary birders or the general public. Everyone should accept, of course, that some changes are required by advances in scientific knowledge: booted warbler, for example, was split into two species because there were detectable physical and regional differences between what is now the booted warbler *(Hippolais caligata)* and Sykes's warbler *(Hippolais rama);* in

[1] Unless common meant "plain" (Greenoak) or was really "commons" (a bird of open fields).

the same way we now have both eastern and western olivaceous warblers, houbara and Macqueen's bustards, red-breasted and taiga flycatchers, and lesser and common redpolls (though this last one remains confusing since the "lesser" is the common one and the "common" is the rarer "mealy"). In the same way, some of the scientific names change in the light of the most recent hypotheses about generic relationships (great white egret joins the herons as *Ardea alba,* having formerly been *Egretta alba,* and alpine swift rejoins the common swift as an *Apus*). Even the sequence in which the names are presented in lists and reference works changes to reflect the latest thinking about evolutionary development (working from the oldest through to the most recently evolved species) and birders of three-score years or more have had to learn successively the Wetmore (1930), Vous (1977), Sibley (1988), and now Dickinson (2003) sequences to find their way around field guides. All this is understandable and quite interesting, even for the nonscientist, since it can give a new insight into family relationships and resemblances.

It gets more controversial, however, when the common names are changed for the sake of international consistency. The national journals and societies may then have to allow for consumer resistance on the part of their members and produce their own modifications for local use. The leading U.K. journal *British Birds* went through an exercise of this kind recently and made some very sensible pragmatic decisions. Names like rufous nightingale, tundra swan, great ringed plover, horned lark, Eurasian jackdaw, and hedge accentor had been impolitely ignored by British birders and were therefore dropped in favour of the familiar and traditional names. As a gesture to international solidarity, though, they loyally persisted with a further list of "suggested names for use in an international context." But one wonders why that is so important when we already have a "second language" of Latin scientific names for precisely these international purposes? Isn't this the Esperanto illusion—the belief that if you devise a new language purged of the inconsistencies, irregularities, and oddities of real languages everyone will want to adopt it as a new international standard? What you get instead is a bland and bloodless laboratory language, born dead, with none of the associations and historical echoes of a living one. Philosophers have sometimes emphasised just how finely evolved and adapted our vernacular languages are, for all their messiness and inconsistency:

> Our common stock of words embodies all the distinctions men have found worth drawing, and the connections they have found worth marking, in the lifetime of many generations: these surely are likely to be more numerous, more sound, since they have stood up to the long

test of survival of the fittest, and more subtle, at least in all ordinary and reasonable practical matters, than any that you or I are likely to think up in our armchair of an afternoon—the most favourite alternative method. (J. L. Austin, "A Plea for Excuses")

For the reasons already rehearsed in this chapter, I therefore suspect that few British birders are going to find it natural in field situations to refer instinctively to northern pintail, mew gull, pied avocet, Eurasian oystercatcher, Atlantic puffin, wood nuthatch, or winter wren. Why talk of a northern sparrowhawk in Sussex or a western marsh harrier in Essex, where other kinds have never been recorded? Nor should we expect familiar songs, proverbs, and Christmas cards to be adjusted to allow for the European turtle dove, black-billed magpie, common blackbird, or European robin. Come on—would Americans rejoice in a white-headed fish eagle for their national symbol, *Haliaeetus leucocephalus*? Would Australians swap the kookaburra and the emu for the New Guinea arboreal kingfisher *(Dacelo novaeguineae)* and the New Holland runner *(Dromaius novaehollandiae)*? Would the New Zealand Kiwis take the field as flightless southerners *(Apteryx australis)*, let alone as Australians?

Names do matter. And our most familiar bird names are often themselves the product of a long period of slow evolution. In the course of that history they become embedded in the language, part of a web of interconnections that run off in all directions. Think of the many similes and metaphors adopted from bird names. We have expressions like "craning one's neck," "goose-stepping," "eyes like a hawk," "swanning around," "larking about," "crowing over." We also form new words based on the connotations of bird names: nouns like cuckold, kite, and crane, adjectives like ravenous, verbs like quail and gull. We know what it is to call someone a magpie, grouse, gannet, dodo, or booby. In these and innumerable other cases you can't just artificially exchange one name for another without upsetting the whole system. Could Jenny Lind as well have been called the Swedish corncrake as the Swedish nightingale?

We saw in looking at the sources of bird names how common it was for the names to be based on onomatopoeic factors of sound, and sensory connotations of this kind run very deep in language and naming more generally. Some of this is obvious: words like "thud," "slurp," and "bang" imitate sounds, while "mushy" and "slippery" convey tactile sensations. But what is sometimes called "sound symbolism" goes a good deal further than this. Some linguists think they detect links between certain vowel or consonant sounds and the meanings they intuitively imply. Is it a coincidence that venomous, vitriolic, vile, vicious, vindictive, and vulture all start with a snarling *v*, or that slide, slither, slouch, sluice, slope, and slump all indicate downward movement? Don't words

like swagger, swivel, swat, and swerve somehow *describe* a characteristic movement, just as swift and swallow do? Isn't shingle just perfect for loose stones
on the beach?

Poets certainly trade on this belief. The famous Lewis Carroll "Jabberwocky"
poem wouldn't work at all (and certainly couldn't be so easily memorised) unless we could conjure up meanings for the nonsense words for ourselves:

> 'Twas brillig, and the slithy toves
> Did gyre and gimble in the wabe:
> All mimsy were the borogoves,
> And the mome raths outgrabe.

You can check your intuitions against Lewis Carroll's own "explanations" and
the Tenniel drawings in *Alice through the Looking-Glass.*

And more conventionally there is Tennyson, imitating the sounds of summer:

> The moan of doves in immemorial elms
> And murmur of innumerable bees.

Or W. H. Auden demonstrating the effects of rhythm:

> This is the Night Mail crossing the border,
> Bringing the cheque and the postal order . . .

Some anthropologists such as Brent Berlin have suggested that the names
chosen by some native peoples for fish and birds might suggest a similar sense
of what sounds intuitively "right"—for example, that the bird names have a
relatively large number of segments of acoustic high frequency, which denote
quick and rapid motion, while the fish names have more low-frequency segments with connotations of smooth, continuous flow.

This sort of thing is hard to test and probably impossible to prove, but it
may help explain why some bird names seem so deeply rooted. Words have
roots, just as trees do, and though they may now be invisible to us and deeply
buried they can still nourish the meanings we use and understand.

10

Birds Are Good to Think With

Natural species are chosen [as totems] not
because they are "good to eat" but because they
are "good to think."
Claude Lévi-Strauss, *Totemism*

Delphi, Greece, 6 April 1990

I have a dramatic view, in every sense. I am sitting in the top tier of seats in the ancient theatre cut into the mountainside at Delphi. Behind and to the northeast of me is the massive bulk of Mount Parnassos, rising to nearly twenty-five hundred metres (more than eight thousand feet), its peaks still snow-covered in the early spring. The crags of the Phaidriades Rocks ("the shining ones") are immediately above me and the Kastalian Spring emerges from a chasm in the rock at their foot. Directly in front of me is the River Plaistos gorge, which runs away south in a deep valley, eventually broadening out into a silvery-grey sea of olive groves that extend to the Gulf of Corinth in the distance. We are in the heart of central Greece. Indeed, the ancient Greeks thought this place was the centre of the universe itself. The legend was that Zeus, father of the gods, wanted to know what was the middle point of his kingdom and sent two eagles out to explore, one starting from the furthest west and one from the furthest east. They met over Parnassos and identified the exact middle at the *omphalos,* the navel stone at Delphi. The *omphalos* is still here, and so are the eagles, I see. There are two golden eagles soaring over the valley right now, very much a part of the majestic grandeur of the whole scene. They look huge—unmistakable as eagles even to the naked eye. The leisure of their slow, sweeping circles in the sky seems to express a total assurance in their own power and an unchallenged authority over the terrain they scan.

There are other birds closer to hand in and near the archaeological site, and in fact this is just as good a place for birding as it is for cultural history. The

51. Delphi scene from ancient theatre (photo: William Shepherd)

tourists haven't yet arrived in full force, and there are rock nuthatches trilling all over the ruins, together with a blue rock thrush singing from the shattered columns of the Temple of Apollo; and several black redstarts are pouncing on small insects from the stone seats in the theatre. The nuthatches, thrushes, and redstarts don't distinguish between natural rocks and human ruins, it seems. On the scrubby hillside I can hear lots of Sardinian warblers singing their scratchy songs and also the more tuneful notes of an Orphean warbler. Up above me somewhere there may be some of the rarer Rüppell's warblers, and down in the valley a few olive-tree warblers (though it's bit early in the season for them). I don't go hunting for these, but I do scramble round the hillside nearby and find black-eared wheatears among the scree and sombre tits in the bushes. A hoopoe floats along the roadside, a good omen this—they are supposed to be messengers to and from the gods. Cuckoos are calling and I wonder about the possibility of wryneck, the "cuckoo's mate," mainly a passage migrant in Greece nowadays, but well known to the ancients and credited with magical properties. There was an old tradition that "golden wrynecks" once sang from the Temple of Apollo and the wryneck was thought to have great efficacy as an erotic charm. No such luck today, though I do find a woodpecker (middle-spotted, I think). This is also great bunting country. There are six species regularly found in the area in summer and it's a wonderful place not only

(a)

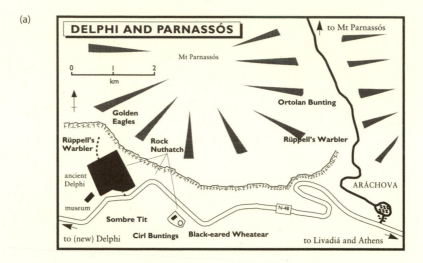

(b)

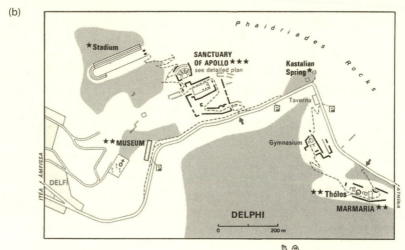

52. Two site-maps of Delphi: (a) birdwatchers' guide (in *Where to Watch Birds in Turkey, Greece and Cyprus*, 1996); (b) archaeological guide (in Michelin's *Green Guide Greece*, 1987)

to glimpse the bright colours of the male black-headed, rock, and cirl buntings but also to sort out the differences in all their songs and calls, especially those of the very similar ortolan and Cretzschmar's. The sixth bunting in the area is the more familiar corn bunting, the plainest of the lot but, paradoxically perhaps, the easiest to find and the most readily identifiable by both sight and sound.

The visitors are now arriving in their coach-loads from Athens and pouring out all over the site, maps in hand. It's rather fun to compare the two sets of maps I have: one of the ancient remains for cultural tourists, and one for birders from a guidebook to the best ornithological sites in Greece (fig. 52). Two quite different ways of seeing the same place.

I come back to the eagles, now just distant outlines, and search the skies for other raptors. There are usually peregrines around the gorge here and there's a possibility of griffon vulture and an outside chance of lammergeier too. Each of these great raptors is charismatic in its own way and each, of course, carries its own freight of legend, folklore, and association. The peregrine is the prince of falcons, reputedly the fastest bird in the world when plunging vertically downwards in its killing stoop, the bird of choice for falconers and kings. Vultures are as large as or larger even than eagles and different vulture species have been revered in many cultures: this too was a bird of augury for the Greeks and Romans, not always distinguished from the eagle; it was the bird of Mut in Egyptian mythology, associated particularly with women; it appears in Pueblo Indian lore and the Mayan calendar; and it is the principal agent in contemporary Parsee rituals of "sky burial" in India. The lammergeier is also a vulture, the bearded vulture, known in Greek as the "bone-breaker" and "tortoise-eater" from its habit of dropping bones from a great height to smash them open and expose the marrow. Hence the old story that the bird was supposedly responsible for the death of the Greek dramatist Aeschylus, when it dropped a tortoise onto his bald head, mistaking it for a bare slab of rock. There are also ravens around, another mythic bird both for us and the Greeks. The travel writer Pausanias tells us how ravens attacked the statue of Athena at Delphi at the time of the disastrous expedition the Athenians made against Sicily towards the end of their great war with Sparta in the late fifth century BC:

> When the Athenians were preparing their Sicilian expedition a huge flock of ravens descended on Delphi and pecked the image all over and tore away the gold with their beaks. (Pausanias *Guide to Greece* 10.15.5)

Alfred Hitchcock might have nodded knowingly had he read this ominous anecdote.[1] But he didn't need to read Pausanias when Edgar Allan Poe was no

---

[1] The corvids in Hitchcock's *The Birds* (1963) were mostly mechanical models or the products of special effects, though he was said to have been influenced by a real incident in Capitola in 1961 when sooty shearwaters, a maritime species that migrates down the California coast near here in huge numbers each autumn, invaded the town. The Daphne du Maurier story of 1952 on which the film is based, is set in Cornwall; and in her story it is gulls that start the attack.

doubt to hand. Ravens appear in the folklore and literature of almost every culture and have deep, and usually dark, associations in all of them. For the North American peoples of the Pacific Northwest, ravens have had a more ambiguous status as creator and hero but also as trickster and mischief-maker, causing death and natural disaster. The local urban myth in Britain is that ravens have existed in the Tower of London for centuries, and if they ever desert it that will signal Britain's downfall. In fact, the tradition is a Victorian invention; all the birds were in any case killed in the course of bombing raids in World War II and new ones secretly introduced from Wales for the official re-opening in 1946. The august post of Ravenmaster dates only from 1968.

I'm interested in how certain birds acquire these roles and reputations and how those in turn affect what we see in them. And Delphi seems like a good place to be asking difficult questions like this. That's what it was famous for, after all, and this is how it acquired its own mythic status and so invested these spectacular surroundings with such numinous significance for travellers from early antiquity onwards.

The origins of the sanctuary here go back to the second millennium BC, when it was already a place of worship devoted to Gaia, the earth goddess. But its fame really depends on its later roles as a centre for the cult of Apollo, as the site of the Pythian games at which sporting and poetry contests were held (rivalling those at Olympia), and above all as the location of the Delphic Oracle. The "oracles" were answers to questions posed by visitors and were generated by a priestess (the Pythia), who supposedly self-induced a trance by drinking from the sacred spring and inhaling the fumes from burning laurel leaves, and so made herself the inspired voice of the god Apollo himself. A secretariat of priests interpreted her convulsions and ecstatic outpourings and delivered the "answers" in the form of hexameter verses that were made available to clients for a suitable donation (with a file copy kept in the temple in case of disputes). Petitioners and pilgrims came from all over the Greek world and the consultations were taken very seriously. It would be customary to ask the advice of the oracle before undertaking any major new enterprise such as starting a war or founding a city, as well as about a host of more personal questions of the kind now dealt with in our more sophisticated society by horoscopes, fortune-tellers, agony aunts, and therapists. The answers from the oracle were famously ambiguous. For example, when King Croesus of Lydia asked if he should make war on Persia, he was told that if he attacked Persia he would destroy a great empire. So he did, and he did . . . but it was his own.

Scholars have often been sceptical, of course. One German professor solemnly ate a quantity of laurel leaves and pronounced that he didn't feel any different afterwards. But it would be easy to believe in anything here. The

writer and traveller Peter Levi tells the story of a performance in this very theatre after it had been excavated and restored in the twentieth century:

> At the first modern Delphic festival, the beginning of the revival of
> classical tragedy in ancient theatres, they played the *Prometheus* of Aes-
> chylus. The performance was interrupted by a heavy storm with loud,
> re-echoing thunder-claps for twenty minutes. Out of the storm came an
> eagle, soaring and circling over the heads of the audience. No one
> moved, and those that were there still spoke of that day with awe forty
> years later.

But nothing is quite what it seems at Delphi. This is indeed the ancient site,
but the theatre I'm in is not in fact the Greek one—that was rebuilt centuries
later by the Romans; and the original Temple of Apollo (partly financed by
Croesus, ironically) was destroyed by an earthquake and replaced with another. The Romans also replaced the agora and the stadium. The tourists photograph all these remains compulsively and get their fix, but you have to think
away the present ruins to see the original Delphi. Is there any analogy with the
birds? They were real eagles overhead, sure enough, but when a bird becomes
a symbol do you then cease to see it for itself and just look through it to what
it symbolises? Do we necessarily idealise or misrepresent the thing we symbolise? Why did I think the eagles overhead were "majestic," and why do
images of eagles appear so regularly on flags, banknotes, stamps, military standards, and other national insignia? Come to that, why in my culture are
vultures contrasted with eagles and seen as unclean scavengers, when in fact
vultures and eagles are both parasitic and both have the same glorious mastery of the air? The ancient Greeks didn't make sharp distinctions between
them, in fact, or think of either primarily as carrion-eaters, but regarded both
as important birds of omen, fit to symbolise warriors and heroes and lend
their forms to gods.

In this chapter I look at some of the ways in which birds figure in our representations of the world and ourselves. They seem to crop up all over the place
in myth, allegory, and folklore, and in practices such as augury, alchemy,
and divination. Is this primitive superstition or deep archetype? We all of us
use birds freely, if unconsciously, as symbols in everyday life and in the language of analogy and metaphor. Is the worry about anthropomorphism—the
attribution of human qualities to animals—perhaps a case of looking in dia-
metrically the wrong direction? What about all this rampant ornithomorphism—using birds to represent the human world? Why are birds so good to
think with?

A Bird Told Me

I showed in chapter 7 how birds have been used in many cultures as markers of seasons. The Greeks were no exception, and in his play *The Birds*, which I refer to several times in this chapter, Aristophanes has his chorus of birds sing their own praises as human calendars:

> All the greatest benefits mankind enjoys come from us, the birds. We reveal the times of spring, winter and autumn: the time to sow is when the crane cries out in its flight to Libya; . . . then the kite appears again to herald another season, the time for sheep-shearing; then it's the swallow—time to sell those winter woollens and buy something more summery. (*The Birds*, 708–15)

But the birds were also "signs" for the Greeks in other ways too. They were the principal agents through which the gods revealed their will to humans; hence the practice of ornithomancy, divination by the observation of birds. The exponents of this art were called *oionopoloi* (bird experts), *oionistai* (bird interpreters), or *oionoskopoi* (birdwatchers). The first "ornithologists" in this special sense appear at crucial moments in Homer's great epics to advise kings and generals: in the *Iliad* the Greek priest Calchas was the man "who knew the future, the present, and the past," while on the other side Helenus was "the best augur in Troy"; and in the *Odyssey* Halistherses "surpassed all men of his day in knowledge of birds and in uttering words of fate." The Roman word for this profession was "augur," from which of course we get "augury" and "auspicious" (literally again, "watching birds"), and the Romans characteristically put the whole thing on an organised basis with a College of Augurs to codify the rules and set professional standards. There's a further relevant piece of etymology here. The Greek word for a bird, *ornis*, was also their word for an omen, so Aristophanes' chorus of birds could go on to say:

> We are your oracles too: your Ammon, your Dodona, your Delphi, your Phoebus Apollo. Whatever you are going to do, whether it's a matter of trade, or feeding the family, or getting married, you always consult the birds. Why, you even use the word "bird" for anything that brings good luck or bad luck: whether it is a chance remark, a sneeze, an unexpected meeting, a noise, a servant or a donkey, you call it a bird! So you see, we really are the oracle you depend on most. (*The Birds*, 716–22)

In practice, divination by birds depended very much on interpreting the *flight* of birds. Here are a few examples, again from Homer. Towards the end of the *Iliad* the old king of Troy, Priam, prays to Zeus to send him a favourable omen and the god obliges:

> And straightaway he sent an eagle, most significant of winged birds, the dark hunter whom they also call the "dusky eagle." His wings were stretched as wide on either side as the well-bolted doors of a rich man's high vaulted hall. It appeared on the right as it swooped through the city, and those watching rejoiced and all their spirits were raised.[1] (*Iliad* 24.315–21)

An example of an unfavourable omen occurs earlier in the *Iliad,* when Hector is pressing the attack against the Greek ships:

> A bird had appeared to them as an omen when they were hoping to cross; a high-flying eagle skirting the army on the left. It held in its talons a monstrous blood-red snake, alive and still writhing. Nor had the snake given up the fight, but twisted back and struck its captor on the breast by the neck. The eagle in sharp pain let it fall to the ground and it dropped among the throng. Then the eagle uttered a loud cry and flew away on the currents of air. The Trojans shuddered when they saw the gleaming snake lying among them, a portent of Zeus who bears the aegis. (*Iliad* 12.200–208)

Hector is told by his augur Polydamas to hold back, on the grounds that the Trojans will eventually be repulsed like the eagle. But Hector is distinctly unhappy with this advice and impatient with all this birdwatching:

> Polydamas, I no longer like what you are saying. Surely you can come up with a better story than that. If you really mean what you say the gods must have scrambled your brains, since you are telling me to forget the advice Zeus, lord of the thunder, gave me as a promise. You tell me to follow the flight of long-winged birds, creatures that do not interest me at all. I do not care whether they fly to the right towards the morning sun or left into the western gloom. (*Iliad* 12.231–40)

Eagles are the usual omens but not the only ones, and sometimes aural identification skills are required on the part of observers. Odysseus and Diomedes are planning a raid on the Trojan camp:

> Pallas Athene sent them a lucky omen, a heron, close to their path on the right. Their eyes could not see it because it was dark, but they heard

---

[1] We still talk of eagles, especially sea eagles, as having wings "as wide as barn doors." Homer's "dusky eagle" could have been a lesser spotted eagle or maybe even a black vulture (commoner in Greece then). The eagle in the next extract is behaving more like a short-toed eagle, which specialises in catching snakes and is common in the region.

its cry. And Odysseus rejoiced at the bird of omen and prayed to Athena. (*Iliad* 10.274–77)

These examples illustrate that augury was not always a matter of predicting the future in any detail so much as seeking a reassurance that you were acting in an appropriate way. The omens were thought to be favourable when birds flew by on the right, unfavourable when on the left. I have never understood this, since the prognosis would seem to depend very much on the way the observer happened to be facing at the time. The Hector example perhaps suggests that it was the *direction* of flight that mattered, which might make rather more sense (just about). The Romans thought left was favourable and right unfavourable, which seems to be because they faced south when conducting auguries while the Greeks faced north, so that east—the auspicious quarter— was on the right for the Greeks and on the left for the Romans. But it's all rather arbitrary and you wonder if right-handedness might be a factor too. Some omens required a much more complex interpretation anyway. In Aeschylus's *Agamemnon* two eagles, one "black" and one "white-tailed" (representing Agamemnon and his brother, Menelaus) appear on the side of the spear-hand (the right, auspicious side) and are devouring a hare (Troy) that is pregnant (inauspicious, suggesting eventual retribution). And in another play (probably by Aeschylus) we are told some of the technicalities that need to be mastered by the serious ornithoscopist:

> I took pains to determine the flight of crook-taloned birds, marking which were of the right by nature, and which of the left, and what were their ways of living, each after his kind, and the enmities and affections that were between them, and how they consorted together.[1] (*Prometheus Bound*, 488–92)

What are we to make of all this? I put to one side for now the larger anthropological question of how such superstitions can survive in an otherwise rational society like theirs (or ours), and ask instead why *birds* and why *these* birds?

Signs and Symbols

The Greeks were supposed to have a word for everything, but of the various species I might have seen and heard at Delphi only a few are definitely identifiable in ancient Greek. Some that are very striking or important are specifically

---

[1] This is the translation cleverly used on the title page of Lewis Namier's famous study *The Structure of Politics at the Accession of George III* (1929), which is actually about party politics in England and renders the Greek to suggest that sense.

named, such as hoopoe *(epops)*, little owl *(glaux)*, cuckoo *(kokkyx)*, swallow *(chelidon)*, bee-eater *(merops)*, nightingale *(aedon)*, raven *(korax)*, wryneck *(iynx)*, and golden eagle *(chrysaetos)*. There are then generic names such as wheatear (*oinanthe*, "wine-flower"), redstart (*phoinikouros*, "red-tail"), crow (*korone*, alternatively a cormorant, it seems, which also has the English folk name of "sea-crow"), nuthatch *(sitte)*, lark (*korydos*, six species breed in Greece), pigeon *(peleia)*, partridge *(perdix)*, woodpecker (*dryokolaptes*, nine possible species), sparrow (*struthos*, also an ostrich, bizarrely), and several of the raptors such as kite *(iktinos)*, falcon *(kirkos)*, vulture *(gyps)*, and harrier (*phrynologos*, "toad-picker"). Raptors are especially well represented with different terms, though the different species intended are not easily distinguishable: you could have found in Greece then, often in larger numbers than today, no fewer than eight species of eagle, four vultures, four harriers, two kites, three buzzards, three hawks, eight falcons, and one osprey.

Some other names are ambiguous or are used inconsistently: the wren is sometimes *troglodytes* ("hole-diver") but is sometimes *basileus* ("king"), though that can also be the goldcrest or firecrest, which have golden crowns (American "kinglets"). Finally, there are very vague categories such as *spiza* ("chirper"), which must have been a bit like our lbj, "little brown job," and *melanokoryphos* ("black-head"), which might have referred to any one of four *Sylvia* warblers (blackcap, Orphean, Sardinian, or Rüppell's), four tits (sombre, marsh, great, or coal), or one bunting (black-headed). But no fine distinctions are made between all the small birds that don't matter for any practical or ritual purposes; and there was certainly no specific word for the corn buntings I was listening to by the roadside.[1] Before Aristotle in the mid-fourth century BC, no one took a real interest in identification and taxonomy for its own sake. Interestingly, most of Aristotle's research seems to have been done on the island of Lemnos, which is in the prefecture of Lesbos, now the most popular centre for present-day birding tours in Greece.

We can easily see why some of the species on this list would attract names. Swallows and cuckoos were the signs of spring, for the Greeks as well as for us; bee-eaters and hoopoes are too striking to ignore, as are the songs of nightingales; and the eagle, owl, falcon, and raven have perceived qualities that make them potent symbols in myth and folklore almost everywhere. Had I been

---

[1] It is a surprise, however, that there seems to be no specific ancient Greek word for magpie, which satisfies several of the usual criteria for significance. Arnott (*Birds in the Ancient World from A to Z*, p. 100) says that *kissa* (jay) was later used for magpie as well and speculates that the expansion of the magpie into Mediterranean regions is relatively recent. The modern Greek word for magpie is *karakaxa* (presumably onomatopoeic), and the birds are now common in mainland Greece (though not all islands).

further north in Greece I would have added crane *(geranos)*, swan *(kuklos)*, and stork *(pelargos)* to my list, also species that are both signs and symbols in many parts of the world.

This list of birds that mattered, in some sense, to the Greeks has its parallels in other traditions, and the overlaps and coincidences are striking, after due allowance is made for distributional variations. Consider, for example, the list of birds in the Old Testament book of Leviticus (11:13–19) that are designated "an abomination," that is, taboo and not to be eaten: the eagle, ossifrage [lammergeier], osprey, vulture, kite, raven, owl, nighthawk [nightjar], cuckoo, hawk, little owl, cormorant, great owl, swan, pelican, gier eagle [another vulture?], stork, heron, lapwing, and bat! Mary Douglas, in her classic monograph *Purity and Danger,* questions whether the listed creatures are "abominable" at all, rather than creatures it is abominable to harm. They may be more anomalous and in that sense "sacred." One further point of (somewhat digressive) interest here, apart from the inclusion of the bat (see also the New Guinea example on p. 251), is that other translations of the Bible record the species list rather differently. The list above comes from the *Authorised Version* of 1611. The *Good News Bible* of 1976 has instead, following the same order: eagle, owl, hawk, falcon, vulture, crow, ostrich, seagull, stork, heron, pelican, cormorant, hoopoe, and bat; while the *Revised English Bible* of 1990 has: griffon, black and bearded vultures, kite, falcon, crow, desert owl, short-eared owl, long-eared owl, hawk, tawny owl, fisher owl, screech owl, little owl, horned owl, osprey, "various" cormorants, hoopoe, and bat. I'm not sure whether these represent an advance in translation skills or identification skills, but there ought at least to be a warning here against literal interpretations of the Bible, as well as against a rush to the Holy Land to see the various *REB* owl species new to science.

One could easily produce similar lists of ritual species from traditional societies in other parts of the world—China, Japan, India, North America, Siberia, South America, and Africa. There are of course special local cults concerning particular species with restricted distributions such as the kookaburra (Australian Aboriginal), kiwi (Maori), sacred ibis (ancient Egyptian), quetzal (Aztec and Maya), stonechat (Celtic), diver/loon (Inuit), condor/thunderbird (Plains Indians), and hummingbird (various neotropical). But what is striking is that certain species crop up again and again in different traditions, most notably: eagle, falcon, crane, heron, crow, goose, pelican, wren, cuckoo, dove, hoopoe, nightingale, owl, peacock, raven, stork, swallow, swan, lapwing, wryneck, vulture, quail, woodpecker, and one nonbird, the phoenix. Some of the same birds provide the symbols for alchemy—the black crow, white swan, peacock, pelican, and phoenix are taken to be descriptive of the crucial stages in the alchemical process. And quite a few of the birds in these lists would be species that ordinary people, or indeed birders, might naturally include in any list of favourite species or "charismatic birds," without thinking consciously about any mythic associations. I discuss just the case of the eagle here from the very large body of material that has been collected by folklorists,[1] though it may be noticed that several of these species—the crane, the swallow, and the nightingale—have been a sort of theme running through this book.

Eagles and Emblems

As we have already seen, eagles figure very prominently in Greek folklore and mythology. Zeus nominated the eagle as king of the birds and it has always been the symbol par excellence of imperial power and authority everywhere (see fig. 53). In Rome live eagles were used in the ceremonies of "apotheosis" designed to deify a dead emperor. A waxen image of the emperor would be burnt on a pyre and as the flames leaped higher the eagle would be released to carry the emperor's soul to the gods. The eagle's mastery of the skies also made it a natural sun symbol, and there was a belief that the eagle alone could gaze directly at the sun without blinking. Female eagles were supposed to make their young look fearlessly at the sun; if they flinched their mothers considered them not to be true eagles and ejected them from the nest. Shakespeare was presumably referring to this story in *Henry VI, Part III* (2.1):

> Nay if thou be that princely eagle's bird
> Show thy descent by gazing 'gainst the sun.

The Romans sought to exploit the eagle's reputation for strength and ferocity by marching under standards surmounted by eagles, and the armies of Charlemagne, Napoleon, Bismarck, Peter the Great, and Hitler all drew on the same imagery. The double-headed eagle often features in these representations, as it does in Hittite, Sumerian, and Turkish heraldry.[2] Indeed, the eagle is conspicuous in most of the early Near Eastern and Asian mythologies. It is

---

[1] It has to be said that the folklore material is very variable in character and reliability, though it is all in a sense symptomatic of what people are prepared to believe. It ranges from the classic studies by Graves and Armstrong to more modern compilations such as Tate, Pollard (specifically on Greece), and Greenoak (on Britain)—see the list of further reading in the reference section. A very different kind of project, which ornithologists will treat with some caution, is Adele Nozedar's *The Secret Language of Birds*, which describes itself "as a tool to help readers make their own spiritual journeys."

[2] The double-headed eagle motif resurfaces in Byzantium in a very particular context, symbolising the division of the empire between the two emperors Andronikos in 1325, one based in Constantinople and one in Thrace. This symbolism would presumably not have appealed to some of the later autocrats who used the same motif.

(a)   (b)

(c)   (d)

53. Eagle motifs in national emblems: (a) Albania, based on the seal of the national hero, Gjergi Kastrioti Skanderbeg (1405–66); (b) Mexico, a golden eagle based on the Aztec eagle symbol of the Sun God, Huitzilopochtli; (c) Russia, a complicated genealogy traceable from the double-headed eagle of the late Byzantine Empire (East and West, see note on p. 273) through Ivan III (1462–1505), Peter the Great (1672–1725), and the Imperial Empire, and then restored as a symbol of the Russian Federation in 1992 after the collapse of the USSR; (d) Egypt, from 1985, supposedly based on the "Eagle of Saladin" (1137–93), and later adopted as a symbol of Arabic nationalism by Iraq, Palestine, and Yemen

difficult to trace all the patterns and paths of diffusion but, according to Armstrong, there are identifiable contributions from Persia, Egypt, India, Assyria, Babylon, and Scythia, all of which will have fed into the classical traditions. In particular, the motif of the eagle and the snake, representing a relationship (often a conflict) between the powers of the sky and the earth, is very widespread indeed, extending to Central and South America, Melanesia, and Polynesia, as well as to Europe, India, and China.

The attribute most commonly associated with the eagle in the popular imagination is probably its "eagle-eyed" sharpness of vision, the ability to see and swoop down on small items invisible to the human eye from such an enormous height in the air. The eagle is top of the food-chain and top of the tops, finding its prey in the forest canopy or on the mountainside. It is the eagle in flight that has always most excited naturalists. Here is Seton Gordon describing a gathering of five eagles one winter's day on Skye in his monograph on *The Golden Eagle* (which has the revealing subtitle *King of Birds*):

> The five eagles, poised at perhaps 1,500 feet above the hill-top, arranged themselves in flying formation and moved majestically against the wind. Higher and higher they mounted on motionless wings, until they entered a cloud layer and were a while hidden, before descending slightly and reappearing beneath the cloud. After a time one of the eagles began a series of breath-taking dives. Closing its wings, it fell headlong perhaps 500 feet. It then flattened out, and almost at once mounted until it had gained its lost height, the wings being driven fast and determinedly. As it prepared for the next dive the most spectacular part of the aerial display took place. The eagle's wings still drove it upwards, but the bird slowly tilted, as a rocket does at the end of its climb before falling to earth. The eagle at first fell slowly but when it had got its head down the velocity of the fall at once increased. But even before the flier began to fall the great wings were closed and the angle of descent was controlled by the tail. As dusk was approaching the two parties of eagles separated and made off in different directions towards their roosting places.

And Walt Whitman captured a similar aerial drama in his poem "The Dalliance of Eagles":

> Skyward in air a sudden muffled sound, the dalliance of eagles,
> The rushing amorous contact high in space together,
> The clinching interlocking claws, a living, fierce, gyrating wheel,
> Four beating wings, two beaks, a swirling mass tight grappling,
> In tumbling turning clustering loops, straight downward falling,
> Till o'er the river poised, the twin yet one, a moment's lull,
> A motionless still balance in the air, then parting, talons loosing,
> Upward again on slow-firm pinions slanting, their separate diverse flight,
> She hers, he his, pursuing.

Not surprisingly, the eagle finds a role in Christian iconography too, where it is regularly incorporated into lecterns, with the Bible resting on its outstretched wings as a symbol of divine inspiration. In representations of the four evangelists it is associated with St. John, whose gospel is said to be the most "soaring and revelatory." Richard Taylor sets all this out very helpfully in his book *How to Read a Church;* but as a warning against neat symbolic interpretations, Armstrong shows just how complicated and impure these lines of transmission can be. He quotes at length the eagle lore in Cruden's *Concordance* (for long the first point of reference for many clergy preparing their Sunday sermons), remarks on the amount of misinformation contained in it, and says of its origins:

> This passage epitomises the continuous tradition of Christian homiletic literature beginning with the Bible and the Physiologus of the first century, which contained stories from animal-books of the Egyptian priesthood and quotations from scriptural and Talmudic sources. Wedded to material from Aristotle, Aelian, Pliny and other ancient writers, it was passed on, with embroideries, by Albertus Magnus, Gesner, Aldrovandus, Bartholomew and other compilers of pandects and encyclopedias until, at last, it reached, and renewed its youth on, the Elizabethan stage. The eagles adorning church lecterns have a long, strange and splendid lineage.

This symbolic power of the eagle is still very much alive, not least in the United States. As soon as the organisers of the American Revolution had signed the Declaration of Independence in the afternoon of 4 July 1776, they turned that evening to all the pressing matters to do with managing the new nation they had founded, including the creation of an official seal to express and validate their national ambitions. The committee charged with doing this was about as high-powered as it could possibly have been—Benjamin Franklin, John Adams, and Thomas Jefferson—and quite rightly so, considering the importance of this first and fundamental act of what would now be called corporate design or branding. The committee commissioned a number of possible designs, some of them incorporating eagle motifs derived, ironically, from European models. Unfortunately, each of the distinguished committee members had his own design ideas too, never a good idea in such projects,[1] but they did in the end present a composite proposal in August 1776. That failed to find favour, but after the appointment of new committees and new artists, and a great deal of negotiation over details, including a requirement that the eagle should be the American eagle, Congress finally approved a seal on 20 June 1782.

By this act the American eagle became the official symbol of the United States, and though there have been subsequent tinkerings[2] and redesigns so it

---

[1] Jefferson's was of the Children of Israel on one side, and (bizarrely) the Saxon chiefs Hengist and Horsa on the other; Franklin's was hopelessly complicated, involving Moses, Pharaoh, a chariot, a crown, a sword, pillars of fire, clouds, and a stirring motto.

[2] For example, the European heraldic crest, which remained on the first seal of 1782, was later removed, and Truman famously adjusted the eagle's position on the presidential seal in 1946 to give greater emphasis to the olive branch of peace.

54. The first U.S. Seal, adopted 29 June 1782 (in A. Stefferud, ed., *Birds in Our Lives*, 1966)

has remained, omnipresent on coins, banknotes, stamps, flags, military insignia, toponyms, and public buildings. The president himself personifies all this and is referred to as "eagle" in all security contexts by his secret service personnel. And the laws enacting the protected status of the bald eagle now recognise its unique status:

> Whereas, by the Act of Congress and by tradition and custom during the life of this nation, the bald eagle is no longer a mere bird of biological interest but a symbol of the American ideals of freedom ... (Bald Eagle Protection Act, 8 June 1940)

Native Americans may have wondered what took the colonists so long, since the eagle had long been a totem in their own societies, especially among the Plains Indians.

There seems in the end to have been only one serious dissenting voice, and that was Benjamin Franklin's. In a letter to his daughter dated 26 January 1784 he confessed:

> I wish that the bald eagle had not been chosen as the representative of our country; he is a bird of bad moral character; he does not get his living honestly; you may have seen him perched on some dead tree, where, too lazy to fish for himself, he watches the labour of the fishing-hawk, and when that diligent bird has at length taken a fish, and is bearing it to its nest for the support of his mate and young ones, the bald eagle pursues him and takes it from him. With all this injustice he is never in good case; but like those among men who live by sharping and robbing, he is generally poor and often very lousy.

He goes on to describe the bald eagle as "a rank coward" and says that even the little kingbird "attacks him boldly and drives him out of the district." His own candidate as an emblem was the turkey, "a much more respectable bird, and withal a true and original native of America." Various indignant apologists rushed to defend the eagle, but Franklin's complaint nicely illustrates some of the complexities and confusions involved in what makes a bird a good symbol. Do the facts about it matter, do they affect how we see it, can you just *decide* that something will be a symbol, and how legitimate is it anyway to make comparisons between the human and animal worlds, in either direction? Franklin makes a fair point about the eagle's parasitic habits but he then goes on to impute to it a "moral character" a bird can't possibly have, surely. Has he moved from fact to fable here? We should also notice, by the way, that his enthusiastic commendation of the turkey provides yet another exploitation of the emotive issue we looked at in chapter 8, the importance of being a "native."

Nowadays, most countries feel obliged to have a National Bird and several have chosen a native raptor, including: Bolivia, Chile, Colombia, and Ecuador (all Andean condor), Germany (eagle), Iceland (gyrfalcon), Indonesia (Javan hawk-eagle), Mexico (golden eagle), Panama (harpy eagle), Philippines (monkey-eating eagle), United Arab Emirates (saker falcon), and Zimbabwe (fish eagle); Scotland would love to have the golden eagle too, and has now managed to rig the voting (see p. 41); while Belgium very modestly settles for the kestrel. The whole process has also extended downwards to states and provinces in some countries, though how the choices are made and validated is fairly murky and in some cases it all has the appearance of a rather unconvincing local marketing exercise. For reference, then, and for trivia enthusiasts, here are the lists from Australia, Canada, and the United States, which may in fact reveal something of sociological interest if not of great symbolic import.

Australia has the emu as its national bird (it is thought never to take a step backwards) and the state birds are:

New South Wales: laughing kookaburra
Queensland: brolga (a large crane species)
Victoria: helmeted honeyeater (an endemic subspecies of the yellow-tufted honeyeater—I wonder how many people in Melbourne could identify one?)
South Australia: Australian magpie
Western Australia: black swan
Northern Territory: wedge-tailed eagle
Australia Capital Territory: gang-gang cockatoo

Only Tasmania wouldn't play this game (why don't they settle for their subspecies, the clinking currawong?). But all these other states have a floral emblem too, and most have a mammalian one (in South Australia, it's the hairy-nosed wombat).

Canada's national bird is the common loon (great northern diver) and its provinces and territories all have their own birds as well:

Alberta: great horned owl
British Columbia: Steller's jay
Manitoba: great grey owl
New Brunswick: black-capped chickadee
Newfoundland: Atlantic puffin
Northwest Territories: gyrfalcon

Nova Scotia: osprey
Nunavut: rock ptarmigan
Ontario: common loon
Prince Edward Island: blue jay
Quebec: snowy owl
Saskatchewan: sharp-tailed grouse
Yukon: common raven

And the individual U.S. states have the following:

Alabama: yellowhammer (flicker)
Alaska: willow ptarmigan
Arizona: cactus wren
Arkansas: northern mockingbird
California: California quail
Colorado: lark bunting
Connecticut: American robin
Delaware: blue hen (chicken)
District of Columbia: wood thrush
Florida: northern mockingbird
Georgia: brown thrasher
Hawaii: nene (Hawaiian goose)
Idaho: mountain bluebird
Illinois: northern cardinal
Indiana: northern cardinal
Iowa: American goldfinch
Kansas: western meadowlark
Kentucky: northern cardinal
Louisiana: brown pelican
Maine: black-capped chickadee
Maryland: northern oriole
Massachusetts: black-capped chickadee
Michigan: American robin

Minnesota: common loon
Mississippi: northern mockingbird
Missouri: eastern bluebird
Montana: western meadowlark
Nebraska: western meadowlark
Nevada: mountain bluebird
New Hampshire: purple finch
New Jersey: American goldfinch
New Mexico: greater roadrunner
New York: eastern bluebird
North Carolina: northern cardinal
North Dakota: western meadowlark
Ohio: northern cardinal
Oklahoma: scissor-tailed flycatcher
Oregon: western meadowlark
Pennsylvania: ruffed grouse
Rhode Island: Rhode Island Red (chicken)
South Carolina: Carolina wren
South Dakota: ring-necked pheasant
Tennessee: northern mockingbird
Texas: northern mockingbird
Utah: California gull

Vermont: hermit thrush   West Virginia: northern cardinal
Virginia: northern cardinal   Wisconsin: American robin
Washington: American goldfinch   Wyoming: western meadowlark

Only three of these were adopted before the twentieth century and the reasons for the choices are very different. The brown pelican is local to Louisiana and has appeared on its seal and flag since the early days of statehood at the start of the nineteenth century. The symbol of the pelican has deep heraldic roots, drawing on the ancient belief that the bird fed its young from its own blood and so became an allegory for Christ's sacrifice of his own blood for others; it comes to stand for piety, in the old sense of filial devotion, and hence civic responsibility. The northern oriole used to be called the Baltimore oriole and has traditionally been associated with the state of Maryland from the seventeenth century, when the early colonists noted that it bore the family colours of the colony's founder, Lord Baltimore. And Utah embraced the California gull in 1848, when the harvests of the first settlers were saved by the gulls, coming from their nesting areas around Great Salt Lake to eat the horde of caterpillars that were devastating the crops.[1] Many of the later choices are evidently based on colour and physical attraction (cardinal, bluebird, goldfinch), song (mockingbird, meadowlark, thrasher), local significance (Alaska, Arizona, Colorado, Oklahoma, and New Mexico), familiarity (American robin, chickadee), sporting interests (Pennsylvania, South Dakota), and in one case an unlikely commercial alliance between poultry farmers, politicians, and supporters of the Rhode Island Red Hockey Club. There are also a few historical allusions (Alabama and Delaware). The Ladies Memorial Association of Alabama urged the choice of "yellow hammers" to commemorate the Alabama soldiers of the Confederacy, known by this name on account of their cavalry uniforms. And Delaware went even further back into history, since Delaware soldiers in the Revolution were known as "blue hens" for their fighting ability, matching that of a legendary blue hen that bore champion fighting-cocks.

In the same spirit, birds have been co-opted into the logos and names of various North American sports teams. In baseball there are the Baltimore Orioles, St. Louis Cardinals, and Toronto Blue Jays; in hockey (that is, ice hockey, of course), the Pittsburgh Penguins and Atlanta Thrashers; and in football, the Baltimore Ravens, Atlanta Falcons, Philadelphia Eagles, Arizona Cardinals, and Seattle Seahawks. It will be observed that this is not an entirely reliable guide to the distribution of the species involved and that the images in some cases have been contorted for motivational purposes into uncharacteristically aggressive

---

[1] There is even a monument in Salt Lake City called "Seagull Monument" or, more informally, "The Miracle of the Gulls."

55. County signs: (a) Cornwall (choughs); (b) Wiltshire (great bustard)

postures. Interestingly, a study of the very elaborate Web sites of these teams reveals that many current logos have evolved from more innocent designs. The Toronto Blue Jays, for example, look strikingly fiercer in their new logo of 2004 than they did in 1977, while the Pittsburgh Penguins moved from being playful endomorphs in 1967 to athletic mesomorphs in 2000 (see plate 8a).

British counties don't seem to have felt the same need to brand themselves this way, though several of them do have coats of arms featuring birds, notably the chough (Cornwall) and the great bustard (Wiltshire and Cambridgeshire). It would be easy to find convincing candidates for Suffolk (avocet) and Derbyshire (dipper), but what would be the county bird of Bedfordshire or Northamptonshire, one wonders? A nondescript corn bunting?

Why Birds?

We have seen how various species of birds can acquire special, even mythic, status, and have looked at the eagle as just one example. I now turn to the second question I raised at the end of the earlier section, not just why *these* birds, but why *birds?* As usual, the Greeks are a good place to start. The historian Plutarch, relying heavily on earlier writers such as Aristotle and his school, offers one answer in a dialogue on "The Cleverness of Animals." Some of the claims made are preposterous and easy to debunk, but others predate many much more modern treatments in suggesting that animals and birds often have more humanlike feelings and capacities than we give them credit for. One of Plutarch's characters is arguing that if animals have sensations they must also have kinds of consciousness and emotion. He protests about the need always to qualify such ascriptions:

> There are those who stupidly assert that animals do not feel pleasure or emotion or fear, or make preparations for the future or remember the past, but say that the bee "as it were" remembers, the swallow "as it were" makes preparations, the lion is "as it were" enraged, and the deer is "as it were" frightened. But I don't know what they would make of those who assert that animals can only "as it were" see and hear, that they can only "as it were" give voice, and can only "as it were" live. For the first denials are as evidently absurd as the latter. (961e–f)

One reason why birds are such good symbols in myth and fable is that they seem so *like* us in many ways. They walk upright on two legs; they have behaviour we think we can understand—feeding, hunting, fighting, washing, parading, mating, and singing; they have domestic arrangements and social gatherings we can observe; and, above all, they have roundish heads with two eyes in front, and faces into which we think we can read expressions. Field guides are full of such analogies as aids to recognition, alongside all the hard data about feather patterns, size, and structure. In the *Collins Guide,* for example, the owls are distinguished partly by the different human emotions they seem to be revealing. We are helpfully told that little owls have a "stern" expression, while the tawny has a "kind" one; the Tengmalm's looks "astonished," the short-eared "mean," the pygmy "austere," the hawk owl "grim," the Ural "deceptively gentle," and the great grey "stately" (I don't know about that last one—I found the steady gaze of the great grey terrifying when I found one staring at me close up from a tree in the Finnish taiga, but see fig. 56).

It's only a short step from this to the actual *attribution* of character, inferred from a combination of body language and behaviour. And now we move imperceptibly from helpful analogy to anthropomorphic misdescription. We want to have in our gardens the cheerful robin, the cocky little blue tit, the shy dunnock, and the bold great tit, not the greedy starling, the marauding magpie, or the merciless sparrowhawk. I gave various other examples of such blind favouritism in chapter 2, with examples there of the puffin, penguin, and eagle (see pp. 40–44). And it is in this spirit that Franklin, in the letter I quoted before, goes on to concede that even his favoured turkey has his faults:

> He is, though a little vain and silly, it is true, but not a worse symbol for that, a bird of courage, and would not hesitate to attack a grenadier of

(a)   (b)

56. Owl expressions: (a) great grey, "stately";
(b) Tengmalm's, "astonished" (Dan Zetterström)

the British Guards, who should presume to invade his farmyard with a *red* coat on.

So the first reason why birds make good symbols is because they seem in these ways to be like us. But the second reason is that in other ways they are clearly *not* like us, and it is this combination of similarity and difference, I suggest, that makes them irresistible. Birds are very *other*. They are uncanny—quick and free, in ways we can only dream of. Plutarch is also good on some of these differences. He says, later in the same work, that birds are particularly suitable for the purposes of divination:

> For their quickness and keenness of apprehension, and their powers of reaction to anything impinging on their senses, make them ideal instruments of the gods. It is the gods who direct their various movements, their calls and cries and their formations, sometimes held suspended in the air, sometimes despatched like the winds, to cut short one enterprise and bring another to its proper conclusion. That is why Euripides calls birds in general "heralds of the gods." ("The Cleverness of Animals," 975a)

Birds are above all creatures of the air, the realm intermediate between that of gods and humans in which they move with such ease. Angels have wings.

And it is the power of flight, surely, that we most envy and admire, in our conscious lives as in our dreams. What attracted the greatest imagist in the English language, Shakespeare, to draw so many of his images from birds was in particular their *movement:*

> Not primarily their song, or their shape, or their colour, or their habits; but their *flight,* and their swift, accurate, easy movements when free; their fluttering, struggling movements when imprisoned; the soaring of the eagle and of the hawk, the "fell swoop" of the kite, the wild geese flocking together or "severed," "scattered by winds and tempestuous gusts," "lagging before the northern blast," the plumed estridges (goshawks) that "wing the wind," the swift flight of the swallow, the confident flight of the falcon, "towering in her pride of place," the hungry eagle "shaking her wings" or fluttering the dovecote, the turkey-cock swelling and jetting "under his advanced plumes," the peacock sweeping his tail, stalking up and down "a stride and a stand," the fairy-light hop of bird from briar, the tiny wren fighting the owl to protect her young, the terrified dove pecking the hawk, the "new ta'en sparrow" "fetching her breath" shortly, the woodcock struggling in the gin, the imprisoned bird in a cage or on a silken thread, hopping a little from his lady's hand, the cock strutting "up and down," the Barbary hen swaggering, the lapwing running "close by the ground," the dive-dapper (dabchick) peering through a wave, the swan with bootless labour swimming against the tide. All these and many more are the quick, graceful, characteristic movements of bird life which attract Shakespeare supremely, which he knows intimately and has registered with loving exactitude. (Caroline Spurgeon, *Shakespeare's Imagery*)

And it was the flight of birds, Adam Maclean tells us, that attracted the alchemists:

> The essential thing about birds is that, having as their domain the air element, they mediate between the earthly realm and the heavenly world. The alchemist, in observing the flight of birds, recognised in them a picture of the human soul undergoing spiritual development. The soul, aspiring upwards, flying free of the restraints of the earth-bound body, is seeking the heavenly light, only to have to return to earthly consciousness again after the meditation. ("The Birds in Alchemy")

This is why birds were such a perfect subject and cast-list for Aristophanes' great comic play *The Birds* (fifth century BC). The plot, in brief, is that two Athenian citizens, disaffected by high taxation and overregulation in the city, approach the birds in the person first of their leader, the hoopoe. They propose that they found a new city in the sky in which they can live as intermediaries between gods and humans and charge duty on all communications between the two realms. The hoopoe duly summons a chorus of twenty-four birds, all introduced and identified; the two Athenians are given wings "to help them rise in the world"; and they name their new city *Nephelococcygia*, "Cloud-cuckoo-land" (that's where that expression comes from). The experiment is a great success and the Athenians all go ornithomorphic in excitement:

> But now there's been a complete change, they're all bird-mad. They're so enraptured, they model themselves on the birds and do everything the birds do. Up with the lark in the morning, and then all day long they're busy with their bills—bills of impeachment mostly. They flock together—to the courts; they brood—on their grievances; and, believe me, they're always hatching something. It's really got hold on them, this bird-mania; they've even started naming each other after birds. There's a tavern-keeper, for example, fellow with a game-leg—they call him the grouse. Then there's the Swallow—that's Menippus, of course; Opuntius is the One-Eyed Raven; Philocles is the Crested Lark; Theagenes the Ruddy Shelduck; Lycurgus the Sacred Ibis; Chaerophon the Nighthawk and Syracosius the Popinjay. As for Meidias, they call him the Quail—he winces when spoken to, just like a quail that's been flipped on the head. It's spread to their songs too: no one can write a song these days without working in a swallow or a duck or a goose or a dove, or wings, a feather or two at least. And I'll tell you another thing—they'll soon be here in their thousands clamouring for wings, hooked talons and other avian accessories. So you'd better have a supply of wings handy: there's going to be a run on them. (*The Birds,* 1284–1307)

Whether we should regard *The Birds* as a play with a message of some sort, or even an allegory, is a matter of debate. It makes perfectly good sense in its own terms as a comic fantasy, with all the usual elements of lampoon, punning, double-entendre, innuendo, and slapstick. But its relevance here is that the fantasy works so well because of this ambivalent status birds have—both of our world and outside it.

Perhaps this intermediate status is what makes birds suitable subjects also for myths of metamorphosis, the process whereby people are not just represented by birds or animals but where they *become* them, as they do in the classical tale of Tereus, Procne, and Philomela, for example. This is a violent story—involving rape, mutilation, murder, and a ghastly revenge—and at the end of it Tereus becomes a hoopoe, crying *"pou, pou"* ("where, where?"), in search of his son Itys; Procne becomes a nightingale, forever lamenting in grief and guilt *"itu, itu"*; while Philomela, who lost her tongue, becomes a swallow, ceaselessly flitting through the air and unable to do more than twitter.[1] Gods can sometimes become birds too, or at least temporarily borrow their forms (Zeus, for example, in the stories of Leda and the swan and Ganymede and the eagle). Birds are in this sense receptive as well as expressive conduits in either direction.

Another bird story, which really *is* an allegory and comes from a quite different tradition, is *The Conference of the Birds,* the long narrative poem describing the Sufi, the mystical Islamic path to enlightenment. It was written in the twelfth century by the poet Farid ud-Din Attar and has some points of similarity with Aristophanes' play. The hoopoe is again the leader of the birds and the messenger of the gods. He takes the birds on a long and dangerous journey to find the Simurgh, king of the birds. They pass through seven valleys of experience, revealing their all-too-human weaknesses and frailties as they go, and when the survivors finally reach their goal they both lose and discover themselves in the consummation of their quest.

An allegory, I take it, is a sort of symbol writ large—a narrative or dramatic structure that is itself a representation or symbol, and one with a message. The same applies to the more homely *Fables* of Aesop, with which I end this section. The *Fables* are a collection of stories, originally oral stories told and retold over generations. They usually involve animals and birds, who are personified and given human voices. Some fables are in the form of "Just So" stories (how the tortoise got its shell), but most are little moral tales ending with a punch line in the form of a proverb. Every culture has its fables and proverbs of this kind—in ours one has only to think of "the wolf in sheep's clothing," "the hare and the tortoise," and "the goose that laid the golden eggs." Aesop has his variants and versions of all these and more, dealing with the universal themes of pride and overconfidence, deceptions and misleading appearances, friendship and sacrifice, selfishness and greed, unexpected outcomes and false promises. There are beauty contests, elections, debates, trials, births, weddings, deaths, journeys, and all significant *rites de passage.* In these cases there is usually no obscure symbolism to decode; the point of the stories is made very clear. One example will suffice. In "The Eagle and the Tortoise," a tortoise looks longingly at the birds of the air and says:

> "If only I too had been given wings to fly!" An eagle turned and said to her in jest, "Well, little tortoise, what would you pay me, an eagle, if I

---

[1] Later versions of the story by Ovid and others swapped Procne and Philomela around, and this explains the later etymology whereby Philomel is the poets' nightingale and Progne *[sic]* becomes the generic scientific name for some martins.

were to help raise you lightly high in the air?" "I would give you all the riches of the East," said the tortoise. "Well then, I will show you how," said the eagle. He lifted the tortoise aloft and carried her upside down until they were hidden in the clouds, then dropped her on to a mountainside, smashing the thick shell on her back. As she breathed her last, the tortoise said, "I deserve to die. What need did I have to fly in the clouds, when I already had trouble moving about on the ground?"

The animals and birds that crop up most frequently in these stories are the standard ones: wolf, dog, sheep, fox, frog, tortoise, deer, snake, lion, eagle, crow, raven, jackdaw, partridge, crane, swallow, hawk, nightingale, owl, peacock, and rooster. None of these should by now come as a surprise. They are the familiar, archetypal species that figure prominently in myth and symbol more generally.

Aesop may have been something of a myth in himself. He is a shadowy figure, referred to as a famous author by people such as Aristophanes and Plato, but never quite emerging in his own person. An ancient biography suggests that he began life with certain disadvantages:

> He was of loathsome aspect, filthy, with a pot-belly, a misshapen head, snub-nosed, swarthy, dwarfish, bandy-legged, short-armed, squint-eyed, fat-lipped, in short a freak of nature. On top of all this he had a voice defect more serious than these physical deformities: he was a mute and could not speak.

However, he once did the goddess Isis a great favour and was rewarded with the gift of speech, which he put to very good use in becoming a master storyteller. He gained great fame as a raconteur and problem-solver and eventually went to Delphi, where he gave an exhibition of his powers. The priests there thought he was too clever by half and framed him with a charge of impiety. To try and save his life he told one final story about an eagle and a beetle, which ended with Zeus changing the time of the eagle's nesting season to prevent any further conflict with the little pest. The Delphians chose not to get the point and threw him off the cliff nonetheless. He must have fallen to his death somewhere near where I was sitting. Had he made himself into a fable? Or was he just another myth?

Seeing What You Believe

Aesop could have been a real threat to the priests and augurs even as a symbol. They were the ones who interpreted the natural signs and knew how to look at them. They didn't want them speaking directly to us in our own voices.

But this brings us back to Benjamin Franklin's problem. What happens to our normal perceptions when something becomes a symbol? Symbols are in one sense less real than the things they use as vehicles. An eagle, after all, is an actual physical object, with identifiable properties, dimensions, and characteristics we can study and observe. The eagle-as-symbol is a cultural construct, one that might be constituted from partial information and could mean different things at different times to different people. But symbols are also enormously powerful—the burning of the flag, the toppling of Saddam's statue, the iconic photographs of Che Guevara or Iwo Jima, the Cross, the Olympic flame—these can all evoke tremendous emotional responses. We see beyond the particular image or event to what we may think of as some larger and more important truth or reality. You could say that in these cases we see the symbolic objects more fully than we normally would, or at least see more *in* them. They may reveal more than they represent. But in another sense we may see less. To be effective, symbols have to select, to emphasise certain features and ignore others, to simplify and idealise. In the eagle-as-symbol we see the power of the mighty frame, the mantling of the wings, the deadly talons and beak, the soaring flight, and the mastery of the air. We may not know, or may forget about, the kleptoparasitic habits Franklin deplored or other less majestic features like its diet of rodents and carrion and its body lice. And we may never notice, since we don't need to for symbolic purposes, the subtleties of the plumage and markings that can concern birders. I have watched eagles at quite close range in the Russian steppe, frustrated at my inability to determine whether they were steppe, imperial, or spotted eagles, all of which occur in the region and have a range of different (and variable) juvenile and adult plumages. The fine distinctions that look so clear on the page of a field guide can easily be obscured and overwhelmed by the sheer *eagleness* of these dramatic birds in the field, even if you are concentrating on them hard as species. And as we saw in the last chapter, the very act of naming birds can make you aware of some features at the expense of others. There is therefore a sort of paradox, that the more familiar and significant a bird becomes as a symbol the less clearly you may see it as and in itself. Perhaps it is the humble corn buntings and their kind who alone wear no masks at Delphi?

I deferred at the outset a much larger and more difficult question, about how the Greeks, or indeed any other society including ours, could come to believe in the sorts of auguries, divinations, myths, and fables about birds that we have been considering. What did they think they were doing? This could take us deep into anthropology and philosophy and I shan't try to go very far. But it does link with the general question that we have been exploring throughout the whole book, in a meandering sort of way—the question about anthropomorphism. Is it legitimate—is it perhaps desirable, or even unavoidable—to use human concepts to describe nonhuman creatures? How *should* we talk about birds?

The Greeks were not the only ones to use oracles and divination. They have been common in many African societies too, and there is a very full account of a "poison oracle" by the anthropologist E. E. Evans-Pritchard in his classic work *Witchcraft, Oracles, and Magic among the Azande* (1937). The Azande of the Sudan kept in their households supplies of a poison that was thought to have prophetic powers. When a difficult decision was required, a small dose of the poison would be administered to a domestic chicken and the question would be posed: "Did X commit adultery?" "Is Y a witch?" "Should I make this journey, divorce this person, start this war?" or whatever; "If so, let the poison kill the fowl." There could be confirmatory and follow-up questions, and they must presumably have gone through a lot of chickens,[1] but they took the results very seriously and were guided by them in their subsequent actions. Evans-Pritchard himself cheerfully entered into the spirit of things:

> I never found great difficulty in observing oracle consultations. I found that in such matters the best way of gaining confidence was to enact the same procedure as Azande and to take oracular verdicts as seriously as they take them. I always kept a supply of poison for the use of my household and neighbours and we regulated our affairs in accordance with the oracles' decisions. I may remark that I found this as satisfactory a way of running my home and affairs as any other I know of.

He was, however, an Oxford don and recognised that others might be more sceptical:

> I have described to many people in England the facts related in the last chapter and they have been, in the main, incredulous or contemptuous. In their questions to me they have sought to explain away Zande behaviour by rationalising it, that is to say, by interpreting it in terms of our own culture. They assume that Azande must understand the qualities of poisons as we understand them; or that they attribute a personality to the oracle, a mind that judges as men judge, but with higher prescience; or that the oracle is manipulated by the operator whose cunning conserves the faith of laymen. They ask what happens if one oracle contradicts the other which it ought to confirm if the verdict be valid; what

[1] Chickens deserve a further mention here as possibly the most numerous bird in the world and the one with the most direct relationship with humankind, if only on the table. Some 850 million chickens a year are consumed in the United Kingdom alone and at any one time there are also another thirty million "layers" in the country.

happens when the findings of oracles are belied by experience; and what happens when two oracles give contrary answers to the same question.

He goes on to suggest that these are the wrong questions, that "we are trying to analyse behaviour rather than belief. Azande have little theory about their oracles and do not feel the need for doctrines." We have to understand what is going on from the inside, not the outside:

> Azande observe the action of the poison oracle as we observe it, but their observations are always subordinated to their beliefs and are incorporated into their beliefs and made to explain and justify them. . . . Their blindness is not due to stupidity: they reason excellently in the idiom of their beliefs, but they cannot reason outside, or against, their beliefs because they have no other idiom in which to express their thoughts.

This kind of thing is meat and drink to philosophers, of course, since it naturally raises the question of whether there may be forms of life and language in which *we* are similarly trapped. That is, perhaps we should see these strange, to us, practices not as primitive and mistaken forms of explanation about how the world works, but as modes of dealing with the world that may have their parallels in our own different practices. After all, we have our ceremonies and rituals too. We mark the start and end of special events: we raise and lower flags; we have ceremonies for the signings of treaties, coronations, graduations, the opening of buildings and the naming of ships; and we have religious or quasi-religious ceremonies for births, marriages, and deaths. We also commemorate things in ritual ways where it is important to observe the right details: Christmas and New Year celebrations, anniversaries—national or personal, flowers on the grave, services at the tomb of the unknown soldier. We wear special clothes for special occasions (wigs, gowns, suits) and may be required to behave in particularly formal ways such as kneeling, bowing, and saluting. Then there are all the conventions of politeness and social interaction: shaking hands, giving gifts, toasts and salutations, apologies and good wishes, greetings and farewells, waving and smiling, and so on. None of this is strictly *rational* behaviour and it would quite miss the point to demand that it should be. Should we therefore think of the ancient oracles and auguries more as rather elaborate rituals for ensuring (and so reassuring) that you are doing things the right way?[1]

---

[1] Machiavelli gives this a nice twist. In the *Discourses* (1.14) he describes the case of the general who "took the auspices" in the usual way before a battle with the Carthaginians in the first Punic War. The chickens failed to perform, so he had them thrown into the sea ("if they won't eat

But this still leaves us with a sense of tension. We may wish to achieve a sympathetic understanding of these different belief-systems, but we want also to be hard-headed about such questions as really are amenable to the advances of observational science and enquiry. We don't want to cut ourselves off from imaginative insights into other forms of life, but we don't want to harbour superstitions either. Can we have this both ways? That debate goes on. But for our more limited purposes here it may help to think of this problem of interpreting other cultures as a special case of the larger philosophical problem of "other minds"—how can we ever be sure that we really understand what other people are thinking and feeling when all we have to go on is their observable behaviour? How do we bridge the gap? And that does take us back to anthropomorphism and ornithomorphism, where some of the same tensions and uncertainties are present and where we are also trying to bridge a gap.

Like a Bird

Throughout this book I have looked at many cases where we think we are just *describing* birds, yet only seem to be able to do so through metaphors and literal *mis*descriptions that could only apply to humans. A Tengmalm's owl does indeed look "astonished," but we know that it can't always be, and that even when it is it may only be "surprised" in the narrower sense of the word. (The great American lexicographer Noah Webster held to this distinction in testing circumstances once. His wife caught him out in an amorous indiscretion and expostulated, "Mr. Webster, I am surprised!" "No madam," he is said to have responded, "I am surprised and you are astonished.") The fact is, we don't know what it is like to be a bird, and so we can't know what it would be like to produce a full and authentic description of one. We can only use our terms, not theirs. As Wittgenstein remarked, "If a lion could talk we could not understand him." This is the problem for which anthropomorphism is both the symptom and the attempted remedy.

Scientific discourse tries to expunge anthropomorphic and other metaphors as category mistakes, but it is very difficult to eradicate them altogether. Even in careful technical language we use terms like electrical *current,* radio *waves,* genetic *code,* or *clouds* of electrons, forgetting that these words were first applied to these contexts from others because they helped us picture and understand the processes involved, and at that point therefore were themselves

---

let them drink!") and went into battle anyway, but lost. He was subsequently tried and condemned at Rome, not for losing, nor for disbelieving in augury, but for demoralising his troops by destroying *their* confidence in it.

metaphors. The question is whether this picturing is always an understanding or whether it can in more controversial cases be a *mis*understanding. We may be more aware of the underlying metaphors in expressions like *natural selection, worm holes* (in space), or the *selfish gene,* and when we say the sun is *trying* to break through the mist or a cold front is *pushing in* from the east. We may even make these metaphors into other metaphors, as when we talk of a *black hole* in the economy. But such harmless usages can become a problem if they seem to beg the very questions they are addressing. In cognitive psychology, for example, it is now a commonplace to describe the workings of the human mind through terminology derived from the fields of information theory and computer science. The brain itself is described as a *computer,* thought as *information processing;* certain capacities are said to be *preprogrammed* or *hard-wired* into the brain; knowledge is *encoded* and *indexed* in the *memory-store;* memory becomes *information retrieval,* while consciousness itself becomes a *feedback* phenomenon. These may all be good heuristic analogies but they clearly prejudice any investigation into the relation between the brain and the mind by forcing it in a particular direction.

Applying this to the case of birds, we should remember that terms like *migration, courtship,* and *song* are, or once were, metaphors too. In chapter 6, I was trying to consider in what ways bird "song" is like and unlike what we would call "music," and one can now see more clearly how the language of such an enquiry might affect its conclusions. In the same way we naturally speak of animals and birds as *searching, choosing, deciding, wanting,* and, more controversially, *intending, thinking, feeling,* and therefore *suffering,* by which point we have entered difficult ethical as well as scientific territory. In deciding what language to use in such cases we are also deciding whether to think of birds principally as mechanisms or as living creatures that share some but not all of our own characteristics. People who have pets or live and work with animals might be amazed to hear that this was even a serious question, so used are they to interacting with animals and communicating with them. And indeed, most of us do choose the latter option in the end, as do most scientists, if only as a provisional assumption and a means of enquiry. Certainly, the early ethologists such as Konrad Lorenz and Niko Tinbergen committed themselves wholeheartedly to that assumption. They brought to the study of animals the anthropologists' solution to the problem of other minds—participant observation—and they immersed themselves (sometimes literally) in the lives of the animals they were studying.[1]

---

[1] Tinbergen and Lorenz had large theoretical disagreements, of course, and came to diverge in other ways too, to the point where Tinbergen could write of the older pioneer, in a letter to

57. Konrad Lorenz with his geese (Getty)

Hunters make the same assumptions:

> Bushmen acquire an extensive knowledge of animal behaviour through constant observation, careful attention to detail and continual discussion among themselves of what they have seen. Their understanding enables them to identify completely with the animal they are hunting, so that they can answer such questions as: "What should I do now if I were this animal?" And their replies are amazingly accurate. (Quoted in M. A. Fox, *The Whistling Hunters*, 1984)

Some expert birders and naturalists have similar skills. J. A. Baker, as usual, takes it to an extreme:

> To be recognised and accepted by a peregrine you must wear the same clothes, travel by the same way, perform actions in the same order. Like all birds, it fears the unpredictable. Enter and leave the same fields at the same time each day, soothe the hawk from its wildness by a ritual of behaviour as invariable as its own. Hood the glare of the eyes, hide the white tremor of the hands, shade the stark reflecting face, assume the stillness of a tree. A peregrine fears nothing he can see clearly and far

Desmond Morris, "He and his wife live with a pack of dogs—I find it rather sickening, but then I'm not an animal lover." Quoted in Hans Kruuk's biography of Tinbergen.

off. Approach him across open ground with a steady unfaltering movement. Let your shape grow in size but do not alter its outline. Never hide
yourself unless concealment is complete. Be alone. Shun the furtive odd-
ity of man, cringe from the hostile eyes of farms. Learn to fear. To share
fear is the greatest bond of all. The hunter must become the thing he
hunts. What is, is now, must have the quivering intensity of an arrow
thudding into a tree. Yesterday is dim and monochrome. A week ago
you were not born. Persist, endure, follow, watch.

C'est magnifique, mais ce n'est pas la science. Maybe not, but it led Baker to
kinds of understanding, and indeed skills of description and prediction, that
would not be available through more disengaged and objective research.

The impulse to identify with the creature hunted, pursued, loved, or studied
takes one naturally from anthropomorphism to ornithomorphism. That is the
reverse process, that leads from birds back to ourselves. And we may think of
this also either as an opportunity or an inevitable failure. I have suggested various ways in which birds have proved "good to think with," in augury, myth,
and fable. In these cases we are *using* birds, consciously or unconsciously and
successfully or unsuccessfully, for our own human purposes. And as we have
seen, that may involve us in various acts of perception and misperception of
the birds themselves. We do the same thing, less elaborately and probably
more unconsciously, in our everyday uses of figures of speech and analogy. We
use expressions such as *eagle-eyed, craning one's neck, swanning around, wise
as an owl, a magpie* (hoarder), *gullible, cocksure, sniping, bill and coo, crow
over, puff up, strut, cluck, brood on, winging it, goose-step, rook,* and *cuckold.*
There are also verbs such as *duck* and *hawk,* where it is unclear whether the
bird was named after the action or vice versa. A number of other avian words
are effectively dead metaphors, where we may forget the connections with
birds altogether: *quail, grouse, peck, jinx, pigeon-hole, squabble, feather* (oars),
flocking (to the scene), *nest* (of tables), and *flight* (of refugees). Birds can help
explain and describe the human world by enlarging the range of expressions
and comparisons we can use. Shakespeare is said to have used more images
taken from birds than from any other source, excepting only the human
body.

These images can also work on a larger scale. We have seen from the exam-
ples of Aristophanes' *The Birds* and Farid ud-Din Attar's *The Conference of the
Birds* how birds can provide a model for a whole society or a spiritual quest.
One thinks of Chaucer's *Parliament of Fowls* in the same genre. Birds can
also affect how individual people picture their lives. The novelist Jonathan
Franzen wrote a moving and funny article in *The New Yorker* about how he

got the birding bug and how it interacted with, and gave him metaphors for, his agonised personal life at that time. He has been watching some nondescript waders roosting on a beach in Florida:

> Camped out amid high-rise condos and hotels, surveying the beach in postures of sleepy disgruntlement, with their heads scrunched down and their eyes half shut, they looked like a little band of misfits. . . . The well-adjusted throngs of collaborator birds in South Florida, both the trash pigeons and the trash grackles and the more stately but equally tame pelicans and cormorants, all struck me now as traitors. It was this motley band of modest peeps and plovers on the beach that reminded me of the human beings I loved best—the ones who didn't fit in. The birds may or may not have been capable of emotion, but the way they looked, beleaguered there, few in number, my outcast friends, was how I felt. I'd been told that it was bad to anthropomorphise, but I could no longer remember why. It was, in any case, anthropomorphic only to see yourself in other species, not to see them in yourself. To be hungry all the time, to be mad for sex, to not believe in global warming, to be shortsighted, to live without thought of your grandchildren, to spend half your life on personal grooming, to be perpetually on guard, to be compulsive, to be habit-bound, to be avid, to be unimpressed with humanity, to prefer your own kind: these were all ways of being like a bird. Later in the evening, in posh, necropolitan Naples, on a sidewalk outside a hotel whose elevator doors were decorated with huge blow-ups of cute children and the monosyllabic injunction "SMILE," I spotted two disaffected teenagers, two little chicks, in full Goth plumage, and I wished that I could introduce them to the brownish-gray misfits on the beach.

But perhaps the best-known use of a bird as an image of human life comes in an extended simile in Bede:

> When we compare the present life of man with that time of which we have no knowledge, it seems to me like the swift flight of a lone sparrow through the banqueting-hall where you sit in the winter months to dine with your thanes and counsellors. Inside there is a comforting fire to warm the room; outside, the wintry storms of snow and rain are raging. This sparrow flies swiftly in through one door of the hall, and out through another. While he is inside, he is safe from the winter storms; but after a few moments of comfort, he vanishes from sight into the darkness whence he came. Similarly, man appears on earth for a little

while, but we know nothing of what went before this life, and what follows. (Bede, *A History of the English Church and People*, 2.13)

• • • • •

I have been trying in this book to explore some of the different ways in which human beings react to birds and some of the reasons why they are attracted to them or find them meaningful. This has involved looking at topics such as the pleasures of discrimination and collection, at rarity value, at the physical impact of birds through their appearance and their songs, and at their significance in the dimensions of time and place. And that in turn has led naturally to thinking about what we ourselves make of all these experiences, perceptions, and associations—how we represent them both in the names and descriptions we use and in the symbols and images we construct. Birds turn out to be good messengers, if we can read the signals. This is largely an exercise in seeing similarities and differences, and in this last section we have been looking particularly at the help we can get from the special power of analogies and metaphors, which see similarities *through* differences. These devices work in both directions in this discourse about birds, both from us to them and from them to us. Analogies can help us see round corners, get a new perspective, go to the heart of things, and leapfrog over obstacles (all metaphors, of course), when more literal descriptions fail.

Sometimes the best way to say what something is, is to say what it is like. Like a bird, for example.

Envoi: "Stirred for a bird"

All the facts of natural history taken by themselves
have no value, but are barren, like a single sex.
But marry it to human history, and it is full of life.
Emerson, "Nature"

Shingle Street, 10 April 2008

I'm back where I began, my home patch. I head off on the familiar path towards the seawall in bright morning sunshine, alert for all the small changes
each day brings in an English spring. Actually, there are subtle changes here
every day and every season, but they seem more accelerated, vivid, and intense in spring. I feel my own senses heightened, flaring. There is a strong impression of activity and movement everywhere. I look and listen, feel the air,
and let myself become part of the place again. Birds are singing loudly all
round me—thrushes, robins, wrens, greenfinches, reed buntings, and above all
larks. Indeed, the air itself seems to be singing with larks this morning, almost
vibrating, as if the agent and the medium had merged. The sense of abundance
is exciting in itself, a pleasure we now enjoy less often in this country. I pass
the rough pasture where the short-eared owls hunt in winter. They have moved
on now but there is a kestrel eyeing the same strip of tussocky grass from a
telegraph pole. He glides off, stalls, hovers motionless, and drops to the ground
with closed wings, improbably fast, somehow outpacing gravity. Gerard Manley Hopkins catches the wonder of this in "The Windhover":

> My heart in hiding
> Stirred for a bird,—the achieve of, the mastery of the thing!

And the wonder can become a self-forgetful pleasure in regarding something so other and independent, as Iris Murdoch discovered:

> I am looking out of my window in an anxious and resentful state of
> mind, brooding perhaps on some damage done to my prestige. Then

suddenly I observe a hovering kestrel. In a moment everything is al-
tered. The brooding self with its hurt vanity has disappeared. There is
nothing now but kestrel.

That's a favourite perch for the kestrel and I always glance up at it. We have
been told by the authorities that we can get all these unsightly poles removed
and have the wires put underground, but one or two local people have objected on the grounds that the birds like using the poles and the wires. They
expect me to join them in defending the birds' interests. Well, not on that
front. The birds managed well enough before there were wires, I argue, and I
would prefer to reduce the human impact on this particular environment.
Birds are adaptable and use what they find. It's true of course that some birds
have taken great advantage from human constructions and we mark that in
their names. Here, for example, we are fortunate to have flourishing populations of house sparrows and house martins, barn swallows and barn owls. Indeed, I was responsible for installing a grand new barn owl box on the edge of
these fields, where they hunt every evening, only to find to my chagrin that
they still preferred a draughty old stable shed a mile away. Ironic, I felt, but
not necessarily inconsistent, on my part or theirs. Everything we do or don't
do affects the environment in some way; we make our choices and birds make
theirs. The collared doves are another case in point. I look to the seaward side
where the line of dwellings is poised on the shingle bank and the doves are
sitting on several of the TV aerials, bleating their songs interminably. I remember hearing that a popular name for the collared dove in German is *Fern-
sehtaube,* "television dove," and this prompts a little playful fantasising. We
believe their rapid expansion through Northern Europe from the 1950s onwards to be a population explosion into a vacant ecological niche, but perhaps
the niche was in part the endless horizon of TV aerials they could see stretch-
ing over affluent Western Europe? And perhaps we are about to create new
urban subspecies of "high-rise peregrine," "trash gull," and the poor deafened
"motorway kestrel" *(Falco t. tinnitus),* soon to be split from the rural "pole kestrel" *(Falco t. telegraphicus)?*

I move on past fields where the grass is grazed and the ground is still satu-
rated from March storms. There are oystercatchers displaying by the small
pools of standing water, a little party of birds all piping excitedly in chorus and
following one another around in small circles, heads lowered, bills parted. On
a fence post a redshank is displaying too, its wings half-opened and quivering,
but with the head and body held still, quite different from the usual jerky bobbing motions. And overhead lapwing are plunging and diving with those wonderful war-whoops. If I scan the pools I shall find one or two snipe by the

muddy margins and I should hear some of them "drumming" a bit further on, where the pasture reaches a dyke and then becomes real marsh. Redshank, lapwing, and snipe all breeding—goodness, that makes this area a wetland wader site of potential interest to conservation bodies. I had better not find a bittern as well or else we might be declared a Reserve! A Reserve is a delimited area, with an inside and an outside, separating the human from the wild, observer from object. A conservation dilemma for me. A bittern would be lovely, if only it weren't a flagship species.

I wouldn't mind a garganey, though—one of the birds I'm actively looking out for this morning. This is a lovely little duck, just a shade larger than a teal, and it is a summer visitor to eastern Britain in very small numbers. I hadn't thought of it before, but this must be the only species of wildfowl that is actually a summer visitor here (most duck, geese, and swans are winter visitors or residents). Indeed "summer teal" is one of its English folk names and also its official name in French *(sarcelle d'été)*. Garganey arrive early (sometimes even in March) and one could easily come prospecting around here. I fancy that this pattern of dykes and channels with boggy pools and a little open water might suit them rather well and I look out for them every year at about this time. The drake is easy to pick up from the conspicuous white stripes over its eyes, curving downwards and backwards and almost meeting behind the neck. The female is trickier to separate from teal, but there's a whitish spot near the base of the bill that stands out surprisingly well at a distance if you're looking for it. The name is something of a mystery to me. It is said that the name "garganey" is onomatopoeic (via the Italian *garganello*), and I have indeed heard females call in a sort of muted gargle, though the call of the drake is more of a dry rattle, like the sound made by running a wooden stick rapidly along a line of palings. But neither sex calls much in my experience, and it would therefore be rather surprising if the calls were the key distinguishing feature from which the name arose. The Latin specific name *querquedula* is also odd. You would think an invented name would have a more obvious meaning, though this one does at least suggest a quacking noise and might be onomatopoeic itself? Anyway, I don't find a garganey this April day (for about the tenth year in succession), but I shall go on expecting one each year.

Other water birds are just leaving rather than just arriving. It's nearly high tide, so there will be some waders roosting on a little shingle bank at the end of the spit in the channel, including, I hope, a grey plover. Yes, there are about ten dunlin there today, already in summer plumage with their trademark black bellies, huddled together with a couple of very smart turnstone in harlequin chestnut, black and white, and, indeed, one grey plover, still in sombre winter plumage. We only seem to see the grey plover's stunning summer colours of spangled silver, white, and jet-black (what effects from such a simple palette!) when they return in late summer from their brief breeding season on the Siberian tundra. There were some golden plover on the meadows this morning too, I noticed, as I walked up to the seawall. These goldies are the "dry" cousins of the grey, feeding in winter usually on farmland and grassland instead of on the estuarine mud. There were large flocks of them around last month but they are now quite advanced in their summer plumage and are heading for the hill country in northern England or Scotland. They too look gorgeous in breeding plumage, but their golden patterning also gives them remarkably good camouflage on the heather moorland of their breeding grounds and you usually pick them up only from their whistled calls. I'm reminded that plovers have the Latin generic name *Pluvialis*, literally "rain bird" (another seasonal marker), though it's uncertain whether the word "plover" originally comes from that rather than from their plaintive calls. Both grey and golden had the folk name "whistling plover" in Britain, but you know from the habitat that Burns must have had the goldie in mind in his line,

The deep-toned plover gray, wild whistling on the hill

To my left, on the landward side, there's a line of poplars with some scrubby bramble patches and sallows where the marsh adjoins some arable land. This woody cover is several hundred yards away, but I can hear lots of bird sound, including a green woodpecker calling (another "rain bird") and the explosive notes of a Cetti's warbler. The Cetti's arrived at this site only two years ago in their steady expansion through southern Britain but they now seem to be settled residents—and they are real residents, staying through the year, though very hard to find when they are not singing. Other warblers are just arriving for the summer. In the reed beds I can hear the first sedge warbler of the season (a day or two early this year), and in the copse beyond a blackcap and willow warbler. It's always nice to clock these species in at their due dates: blackcap on the third, I usually reckon, willow warbler on the fifth, sedge on the twelfth, and reed on about the twentieth. It does vary a bit with wind and weather, of course, and the dates have been getting earlier over the last twenty years, presumably as a result of climate change, but the duration of daylight hours is also a key factor in migration and that is unaffected by the weather.

The summer visitor I am really looking forward to, however, will be in the air, not in the bushes. It should be here any day now. I scan the shingle bank and the seawall ahead as far as I can see. There are some distant flutterings—meadow pipits, probably—and above and beyond them the bulkier shape of a skylark spiralling upwards. But I am looking for something sleeker, something quick and darting. In the event, I hear it before I see it, coming up fast behind me, that sweet but just slightly hoarse *sveet* call (or is it *uiveet?*). I whirl round to greet the first swallow of summer. I feel like punching the air, as it slides easily past. Back from Africa, the annual reassurance and promise, a symbol if ever there was one, as Ted Hughes says about the swifts returning in May:

> They've made it again,
> Which means the globe's still working, the Creation's
> Still waking refreshed, our summer's
> Still all to come . . .

I started this book with the swallows leaving Shingle Street in the autumn and I seem to have come full circle with their return. I have learned more about the swallows, and indeed about birds in general, in that time. I have also relived some experiences and pleasures, both mine and other people's. There is a famous quotation from T. S. Eliot about such journeys and rediscoveries:

> And the end of all our exploring
> Will be to arrive where we started
> And know the place for the first time.

I do feel that I have come to understand more, or at least that I am now confused in more interesting ways. Eliot's striking lines are much quoted, but what do they really mean? More, I think, than just saying that experience gives us new insights into the familiar. If you read back a bit he says:

> What we call the beginning is often the end
> And to make an end is to make a beginning.
> The end is where we start from.

And if you read right back to his original epigraph to *Four Quartets,* from which these lines come, there is an enigmatic quotation from Heraclitus (which Eliot austerely leaves in the Greek): "The way up and the way down is one and the same."

We think of these springtime changes as somehow forward-moving and progressive—the start of new life. But we also know that the circle of the year is continuous, without real beginnings and endings. So is it anthropomorphic— or do I now mean zoomorphic?—to talk of *growth* and *decay* in this way, one life-form projecting its own structures onto the cosmos? Isn't it just *process,* without purpose, point, or direction? Maybe so, but it would still be a process in which we are actively involved as agents and participants, perhaps the only participants able to reflect on it and to have our own deliberate purposes within it, even if we are only able to express them in human terms. Is that more a limitation than a privilege, though? We can embrace the world as we understand and experience it, interact with it and celebrate it, without demanding an ultimate meaning in return. That may require courage, irony, and modesty on the way, but it need not lead to desperation or a sense of futility.

Eliot himself is pessimistic. Interestingly, he uses a bird as the messenger, first inviting us to pursue the echoes of meaning in what he calls the "rose-garden," but then warning us to leave:

> Go, go, go, said the bird; human kind
> Cannot bear very much reality.

I'm not sure I share Eliot's mood or his solution, even if I understand them. Should we not at least try to have this both ways? At any rate, I want to be knowing and unsentimental about the swallow, as well as welcoming. He evidently didn't feel anything at all to see me. There was I, turning my sensations into perceptions; thinking of spring, thinking about the huge journey he had just made from Africa and about the hazards faced by such a fragile creature en route; wondering at the delicate control mechanisms that had brought him back to this exact place at this time; at his colouring, song, and flight; musing about representations of swallows in art, literature, music, and myth and what they might tell me; and then wandering off into personal associations and memories. He just swerved round me, calling. I was only a minor obstacle on the way, neither threatening nor welcoming. I didn't even get the "quiet *dewihlik* of distress" the reference books had led me to expect sometime. But why should this matter? After all, not all our relationships and concerns have to be fully reciprocal ones to be worthwhile. We can care about all manner of things and find different kinds of pleasure, stimulation, enrichment, and interest in them. We can lose ourselves and find ourselves in art, gardening, music, work, sport, travel, or science. In the case of the natural world, there is this further sense of affinity, certainly for many people a deep sense, and one that no doubt has its own evolutionary explanation in our biological history. We do feel a kind of belonging and recognition, because of ourselves, not despite ourselves.

There is scope here for many modes and levels of engagement—for study, curiosity, discovery, play, imagination, and affection. Wondering about birds is one way to explore and enjoy such things.

Appendix 1

Some Notable Lists: The Sumerians,
Thomas Jefferson, John Clare

See chapter 4, pages 83–89.

The Sumerian List

This list is derived from the monograph by Niek Veldhuis, *Religion, Literature, and Scholarship: The Sumerian Composition Nanshe and the Birds* (2004), and in particular from his summary on pages 209–305 and 331. There are more than a hundred different words for birds in the texts but some of them are just different forms of reference to what is clearly the same species and others cannot be reliably identified. Veldhuis believes the following thirty-one can be identified with some confidence (though where there are names in parentheses, those are my own suggestions about the likely species or subspecies).

The order here follows the alphabetical order of Veldhuis's Sumerian transliterations (which I have not reproduced).

Grey heron	Goose (greylag)
Wren	Stork (white)
Crow (hooded)	Magpie
Sparrow (house)	Harrier (marsh)
Partridge (see-see)	Vulture (griffon)
Black francolin	Swallow
Bittern	Falcon (saker)
Crane (common)	Buzzard (long-legged)
Grebe (great-crested)	Turtle dove
Gull (black-headed or	Rock dove
slender-billed)	Swan (mute)
Imperial eagle	Raven
Purple heron	Coot
Pigeon (wood)	Mallard
Sandgrouse (spotted or pin-tailed)	Ostrich (Syrian)
Little egret	Hoopoe

Thomas Jefferson's List

This list appears in *Notes on the State of Virginia* (1787) as part of chapter 6 on "Productions Mineral, Vegetable, and Animal." Virginia then comprised both of what are now the two states of Virginia and West Virginia. In his original list Jefferson gives the popular name and the Latin designations both of Linnaeus (1707–78) and of Mark Catesby (1682–1749), who was an English naturalist and explorer whose descriptions and illustrations Jefferson relies on closely.[1] I have omitted these Latin names (which have in any case sometimes changed since then) and have added the current popular name in parentheses where the name current in Jefferson's time may now be unfamiliar. I have followed Jefferson's sequence and included some of the alternative vernacular names he himself gave, separated by periods. His list falls into two parts: the first seems to be directly derived from Catesby's work (completed in 1747), and it is possible to identify most of the species names from that. It is an uncritical list in that it purports to be the birds of Virginia but probably follows Catesby in including species from "Colonial America" more generally; and it sometimes lists the same species more than once. The birds in the second list do not appear for the most part in Catesby and are more difficult to identify with certainty but I have attempted most of them, relying on early dictionaries of American English. Jefferson emerges from this as a much less careful or involved observer of birds than, say, Clare or Thoreau, though he does seem to have known and cared more about flowers and plants. His list of birds represents secondhand knowledge, poorly edited:

Tyrant. Field martin. (eastern kingbird)
Turkey buzzard (turkey vulture)
Bald eagle
Little hawk (American kestrel)
Pigeon hawk (merlin)
Forked tailed hawk (swallow-tailed kite)
Fishing hawk (osprey)
Little owl (screech owl)
Parrot of Carolina (Carolina parakeet, now extinct)
Blue jay

Baltimore bird (Baltimore oriole)
Bastard Baltimore (orchard oriole)
Purple jackdaw (common grackle)
Carolina cuckoo (yellow-billed cuckoo)
White bill woodpecker (ivory woodpecker)
Large red-crested woodpecker (pileated woodpecker)
Red-headed woodpecker
Gold-winged woodpecker (northern flicker)
Red-bellied woodpecker

[1] Though he can't stop himself saying, "His drawings are better as to form and attitude, than colouring, which is generally too high." Actually, they are not very accurate at all.

Smallest spotted woodpecker
  (downy)
Hairy woodpecker
Yellow-bellied woodpecker
  (sapsucker)
Nuthatch (white-breasted)
Small nuthatch (brown-headed)
Kingfisher (belted)
Pinecreeper (pine warbler)
Humming bird (ruby-throated)
Wild goose (Canada goose)
Buffel's head duck (bufflehead)
Little brown duck (female
  bufflehead)
White face teal (drake blue-winged
  teal)
Blue wing teal (blue-winged teal)
Summer duck (wood duck)
Blue wing shoveler (northern
  shoveler)
Round crested duck (hooded
  merganser)
Pied bill dopchick (pied-billed
  grebe)
Large crested heron (great blue
  heron)
Crested bittern (yellow-crowned
  night heron)
Blue heron (little blue heron)
Small bittern (green-backed heron)
Little white heron (little blue heron)
Brown bittern (yellow-crowned
  night heron)
Wood pelican (wood stork)
White curlew (white ibis)
Brown curlew (white ibis)
Chattering plover (killdeer)
Oyster Catcher (oystercatcher)
Soree (sora)
Wild turkey

American partridge (northern
  bobwhite)
Pheasant. Mountain partridge
Ground dove (common ground
  dove)
Pigeon of passage (passenger
  pigeon, now extinct)
Turtle. Turtle dove (mourning
  dove?)
Lark. Skylark (horned lark)
Field lark (eastern meadow lark)
Red-winged starling. Marsh
  blackbird
Fieldfare of Carolina (American
  robin)
Fox coloured thrush (brown
  thrasher)
Mocking bird (northern)
Little thrush (hermit thrush?)
Chatterer (bohemian waxwing)
Red bird. Virginia nightingale
  (cardinal)
Blue gros beak (blue grosbeak)
Snow bird (dark-eyed junco)
Rice bird (bobolink)
Painted finch (painted bunting)
Blue linnet (indigo bunting)
Little sparrow (Bachman's
  sparrow?)
Cowpen bird (brown-headed
  cowbird)
Towhe bird (eastern towhee)
American goldfinch. Lettuce bird
Purple finch
Crested flycatcher (great crested)
Summer red bird (summer tanager)
Red start (American redstart)
Cat bird (grey catbird)
Black cap flycatcher (eastern
  phoebe)

Little brown flycatcher (eastern wood-pewee)

Red-eyed flycatcher (red-eyed vireo)

Blue bird

Wren

Yellow-breasted chat

Crested titmouse (tufted titmouse)

Finch creeper (northern parula)

Yellow rump (yellow-rumped warbler)[1]

Hooded titmouse (hooded warbler)

Yellow-throated creeper (yellow-throated warbler)

Yellow titmouse (yellow warbler)

American swallow (chimney swift)

Purple martin. House martin

Goatsucker. Great bat (common nighthawk)

Whip-por Will

Besides these we have

Royston crow (American crow; a confusion of names with the British hooded crow)

Crane (whooping?)

House swallow (barn swallow)

Ground swallow (bank swallow)

Greatest grey eagle (immature bald eagle?)

Smaller turkey buzzard, with a feathered head

Greatest owl, or nighthawk (great grey owl?)

Wethawk, which feeds flying (nighthawk?)

Raven

Water pelican of the Mississippi, whose pouch holds a peck

Swan

Loon (common)

Cormorant

Duck and mallard

Widgeon

Sheldrach (canvasback)

Black head (scaup or shoveler)

Sprigtail (ruddyduck or pintail)

Didapper (pied-billed grebe)

Spoon-billed duck (shoveler)

Water-witch (grebe, possibly horned; or anhinga?)

Water-pheasant (pintail or merganser?)

Mow-bird (gull)

Blue Peter (gallinule, probably common)

Water wagtail (Louisiana waterthrush)

Yellow-legged snipe (lesser-yellowlegs?)

Squatting snipe (pectoral sandpiper?)

Small plover (snowy?)

Whistling plover (black-bellied plover)

Wood cock

Red bird, with black head, wings and tail (rose-breasted grosbeak, or cardinal again?)

And doubtless many others that have not yet been described and classed.

---

[1] A reminder for those who have a sentimental attachment to the name "myrtle warbler" that "yellow-rumped warbler" is in fact the "old" name.

John Clare's List

In the list that follows I have followed Fisher's sequence and his headings and fourfold division of the species according to the degree of confidence he had in the identification. I have put the modern names first and added Clare's names in parentheses where I think they have some local colour and interest in themselves.

Among the many interesting things about Clare's list are a few species absent from it. It is no surprise that little owl and red-legged partridge don't figure (both introduced later), but one might have expected tufted duck, pochard, lesser whitethroat, and one or two others?

Records of Reasonable Certainty

Great crested grebe	Pheasant	Cuckoo
Black-necked grebe (eared grebe)	Spotted crake (watercraik)	Barn owl (screech owl)
	Corncrake (landrail)	Tawny owl (brown owl)
Dabchick	Moorhen (waterhen)	Long-eared owl (horned
Cormorant	Coot	owl)
Heron	Lapwing (pewit)	Nightjar (fern-owl)
Bittern (butter-bump)	Ringed plover	Swift (sooty swallow)
Spoonbill	Golden plover	Kingfisher
Mallard	Snipe	Hoopoe
Teal	Woodcock	Green woodpecker
Wigeon	Curlew	Great spotted woodpecker
Shoveler	Black-tailed godwit	Lesser spotted woodpecker
Scoter	Common sandpiper	Wryneck
Greylag goose	Redshank	Skylark
White-fronted goose	Greenshank	Swallow
Pink-footed goose	Dunlin (purre)	House martin
Barnacle goose	Ruff	Sand martin
Canada goose	Avocet	Raven
Buzzard	Herring gull	Carrion crow
Sparrowhawk	Common gull (winter	Hooded crow (Royston
Kite (puddock)	gull)	crow)
Osprey	Black-headed gull	Rook
Hobby	Common tern	Jackdaw
Kestrel	Puffin	Magpie
Partridge	Stock dove	Jay
Quail	Wood pigeon (ring dove)	Great tit (blackcap)

Blue tit (bluecap)

Coal tit (small blackcap)

Long-tailed tit
  (bumbarrel)

Nuthatch

Treecreeper

Wren

Mistle thrush (mavis)[1]

Fieldfare

Song thrush (throstle)

Redwing

Ring ouzel

Blackbird

Wheatear

Stonechat

Redstart (firetail)

Nightingale

Robin

Grasshopper warbler
  (cricket bird)

Reed warbler

Sedge warbler

Blackcap

Whitethroat

Willow warbler
  (pettichap[2] or willow
  biter)

Chiffchaff (pettichap)

Goldcrest

Spotted flycatcher (Egypt
  bird)

Dunnock (hedge
  sparrow)

Tree pipit (wood lark)

Pied wagtail

Yellow wagtail

Waxwing (silk tail)

Starling

Hawfinch (gross beak)

Greenfinch

Goldfinch (red cap)

Linnet

Redpoll

Bullfinch

Crossbill

Chaffinch (pink)

Yellowhammer

Corn bunting (ground
  lark)

Reed bunting (fen-
  sparrow)

House sparrow

Tree sparrow (mountain
  sparrow)

Identification Unclear as between Similar Species

Goosander or red-breasted merganser [more probably the former inland]

Marsh or willow tit

Whooper or Bewick's swan (wild swan)

Hen or Montagu's harrier (moor harrier)

Uncertain Identifications

Slavonian grebe (black and white
  dobchick)

Brent goose

Rough-legged buzzard (hairy-
  legged falcon)

Goshawk

Peregrine (blue hawk)

Merlin

Water rail

Dotterel

Turnstone (red-legged sandpiper)

Knot

Stone curlew (Norfolk plover)

Great skua

Great black-backed gull

Lesser black-backed gull

Guillemot

Black guillemot

Turtle dove

Whinchat

[1] An alternative name also for the song thrush

[2] He uses the same name for the chiffchaff sometimes, but his descriptions of their nests and songs make it clear that he distinguishes them too.

Wood warbler
Meadow pipit (tit-lark)

Grey wagtail
Cirl bunting

Other References

Eagle (literary allusion)
Red grouse (Scottish species)
Peacock (literary allusion)

Appendix 2

Birds and Bonnets: A New York Hat Story

What follows is a transcript of the letter Frank Chapman sent to the journal *Forest and Stream* (see p. 86). It was published in the issue of 25 February 1886. Chapman confidently identifies 40 species of birds in the course of these two walks. One does wonder what effect he had on the seven hundred or more wearers of the hats, who must have been very closely observed for some of these identifications to be possible.

Birds and Bonnets

Editor, Forest and Stream

In view of the fact that the destruction of wildlife for millinery purposes is at present attracting general attention, the appended list of native birds seen on hats worn by ladies in the streets of New York, may be of interest. It is chiefly the result of two late afternoon walks through the uptown shopping districts, and, while very incomplete, still gives an idea of the species destroyed and the relative numbers of each.

Robin, four	Bobolink, one
Brown thrush, one	Meadow lark, two
Bluebird, three	Baltimore oriole, nine
Blackburnian warbler, one	Purple grackle, five
Blackpoll warbler, three	Bluejay, five
Wilson's black-capped flycatcher, three	Swallow-tailed flycatcher, one
	Kingbird, one
Scarlet tanager, three	Kingfisher, one
White-bellied swallow, one	Pileated woodpecker, one
Bohemian waxwing, one	Red-headed woodpecker, two
Waxwing, twenty-three	Golden-winged woodpecker, twenty-one
Great northern shrike, one	
Pine grosbeak, one	Acadian owl, one (the northern sawwhet)
Snow bunting, fifteen	
Tree sparrow, two	Carolina dove, one
White-throated sparrow, one	Pinnated grouse, one

Ruffed grouse, two	Virginia rail, one
Quail, sixteen	Laughing gull, one
Helmet quail, two	Common tern, twenty-one
Sanderling, five	Black tern, one
Big yellowlegs, one	Grebe, seven
Green heron, one	

It is evident that, in proportion to the number of hats seen, the list of birds given is very small; but in most cases mutilation rendered identification impossible.

Thus, while one afternoon 700 hats were counted and on them but 20 birds recognised, 542 were decorated (?) with feathers of some kind. Of the 158 remaining, 72 were worn by young or middle-aged ladies and 86 by ladies in mourning or elderly ladies, or—

Percentage of hats with feathers . . . 77%
Without feathers . . . 10%
Without feathers, worn by ladies in mourning or elderly ladies . . . 12%

Frank M. Chapman

Appendix 3

Nightingale Mysteries

The nightingale is such a bird of romance and fancy that it has gathered around itself more myths and legends than almost any other bird. Indeed so powerful is this process that the significance the bird now has for us may owe more to its literary and musical persona than to its actual characteristics. Keats's "immortal bird" seems to have become more defined by its associations than by itself, more symbol than substance. What is it in the bird that makes it so metaphorical? The song, of course, really is extraordinary; but there is also a sense of mystery about the contrast of its plain plumage,[1] the regularity of its seasonal appearances and reappearances, its favoured habitats in dense woodland cover, its nocturnal behaviour, and its great secretiveness. At any rate the bird generates fascination and uncertainty in equal measure, and I have found it more than usually difficult to establish beyond doubt some of the details of the anecdotes I have reported in chapter 6. A couple of examples may be worth citing here, which are too lengthy to fit into footnotes and too digressive even for my easily distracted text.

The first relates to Respighi, who, as I explained in the footnote on page 164, performed an early musical experiment in including some recordings of actual birdsong in a live concert. He nominated the specific gramophone recording of a nightingale he wanted to be used in his original score of *The Pines of Rome* (1924), but of course many other and better recordings have been used since. BBC Radio recently reviewed the best modern versions of this piece in its regular programme *CD Review* and selected the Seiji Ozawa / Boston Symphony Orchestra version on the Deutsche Grammophon label as the recommended choice. An alert friend heard the broadcast and told me that the nightingales in the third movement sounded rather odd, more like song thrushes in fact, but not quite right for them either. I duly listened to the repeat and I believe the bird featured is in fact a thrush nightingale, a quite different species, though very similar to the common nightingale to look at (see fig. 10 on p. 38). The thrush nightingale does indeed sound rather like a song thrush in some of its notes and sometimes even mimics thrushes as well as other birds (including

---

[1] A "sort of sooty ball," as the Owl unflatteringly puts it in the allegorical thirteenth-century poem *The Owl and the Nightingale*.

nightingales, confusingly). But Respighi's bird must have been the common European nightingale, *Luscinia megarhynchos,* which is common in Italy and the Mediterranean, while the thrush nightingale, *Luscinia luscinia,* is a bird of Central and Eastern Europe. The two species overlap in Germany and what may possibly have happened is that Deutsche Grammophon could have used some local German recording to dub in the song but picked the wrong species. I checked the von Karajan version (also on Deutsche Grammophon) and they seem to have made the same mistake, possibly with the very same birds. I have tried to follow this up both with Deutsche Grammophon and the BBC but that trail has petered out. I had more success with the Respighi Society, however, and got a very helpful response from Adriano, the conductor and great Respighi expert. He wasn't very interested in the species question but gave me full details about the original recording, which was a commercial 78 rpm disk on the RCA Victor label (catalogue number 64161) "made by a captive nightingale in the possession of Herr Reich of Bremen."[1] The quality of these old 78s is very poor, of course, so Adriano declares himself much in favour of modern live recordings and advises "So you had better forget about authenticity." He goes on to say that in one sense the modern recordings are *more* authentic:

> What is also important to consider about this fact is that the old recording was the singing of a CAPTIVE nightingale, which is totally against the natural atmosphere Respighi wants to give with his music! Today's recordings are surely made in free nature and the bird's song may sound more spontaneous.

But he ends with what seems a quite inconsistent thought (though, as it turns out, a suggestive one):

> An experiment to try would be one day to use a human bird imitator.

Could it then be that an "inauthentic" thrush nightingale or human mimic could produce a version that was musically better and more appropriate than a real nightingale? Would Respighi himself have cared about the difference? And should we in any case prefer effect over authenticity? All we do know is that the real nightingales at the Massenzio Basilica in Rome responded well to the recording:

> A poetic and meaningful event was stirred by *I pini di Roma.* When the recorded singing of the nightingale began, all the nightingales in the

[1] A recording of Herr Reich's bird is included on the British Trust for Ornithology's CD and this individual, at least, is a common nightingale (though Bremen is, intriguingly, just at the point where the ranges of the two species meet).

surrounding gardens began to sing, creating a striking impression on everyone in the audience. I wonder what the nightingale of *Pini* said to give impetus to such an expression of love among those birds that we hear singing so rarely.[1]

My second example comes from the episode of Beatrice Harrison and her nightingales (see pp. 178–80 in chapter 6). My account of this relies heavily on Richard Mabey's book and on Beatrice Harrison's own autobiography, but I have also listened to the BBC's original recordings of the event and to the CD *Nightingales: A Celebration* (produced by the British Trust for Ornithology, the BTO), which includes some of this historic material and various other wonderful nightingale recordings. It turns out to be quite difficult to reconcile all this material, though. Harrison clearly did arouse real nightingales with her playing in the woods of her home, and she describes the first occasion like this:

> As the nights began to feel warmer I had a sudden longing to go out into the woods surrounding the garden and play my cello and gaze on the beauty of it all as the moon peeped out through the trees. I sat on an old seat which surrounded an ivy-clad tree. I began to play, very lazily, all the melodies I loved best and to improvise on them. I began the *Chant hindou* by Rimsky-Korsakov and after playing for some time I stopped. Suddenly a glorious note echoed the notes of the cello. I then trilled up and down the instrument, up to the top and down again: the voice of the bird followed me in thirds! I had never heard such a bird's song before—to me it seemed a miracle. The sound did not appear to come from the high treetops but from nearer the ground; I could not see, I just played on and on.

Next day she asked her old gardener what the bird could have been:

> He nearly fell over with joy and delight. "Why it's that nightingale come back once more, after so long. Were you playing to him, Miss?" He had heard the cello in the wood. I nodded my head. "Why, then you have brought him back to these parts—don't ye let him go again."

So she repeated the performance every night and the famous live broadcast itself took place on Saturday, 19 May 1924. She started playing at about 9 PM but got no reaction until nearly two hours later:

> Suddenly, at about quarter to eleven on the night of 19th May 1924, the nightingale burst into song as I continued to play. His voice seemed to

[1] From Elsa Respighi's autobiography, *Fifty Years of a Life in Music, 1905–1955* (English translation, 1993), recalling the performance in Rome in the summer of 1939.

come from the Heavens. I think he liked the *Chant hindou* best for he blended with it so perfectly. I shall never forget his voice that night, or his trills, nor the way he followed the cello so blissfully. It was a miracle to have caught his song and to know that it was going, with the cello, to the ends of the earth. My excitement was intense. My greatest wish was accomplished!

The response was overwhelming. An estimated million people heard the broadcast and some even relayed it to friends by telephone. Beatrice herself was almost beatified:

The public, I must say, went completely mad over the nightingale, the experiment touched a chord in their love of music, nature and loveliness. I received thousands and thousands of letters: one old gentleman from New Zealand said he had left the old country when he was a boy and to hear the song of the nightingale again, out on a New Zealand farm, was a prayer answered. Many of the letters were just addressed to "The Lady of the Nightingales, England."

There were just two sceptics. One was the old gardener, who had changed his mind (and got his facts wrong):

"I loves your music, Miss," he said to me, "but I do wish it didn't attract them birds the way it do. They eats up all the fruit, something cruel."

The other surfaced some sixty years later. Darren Giddings wrote a very good programme note on "Birdsong and Music" for a concert celebrating spring, sponsored by the environmental charity Common Ground, and he mentions the Harrison story in the course of this. The organisers later received this letter from a correspondent:

I read with interest the references that Darren Giddings makes to Beatrice Harrison and the BBC recording of her playing the cello to a nightingale singing. However I fancy that this is not quite the case.

Whilst not doubting that Beatrice Harrison oft sat in her garden playing her beautiful music to the birds and occasionally their song and her music matched, what really happened in that garden in Surrey was that an extremely well known bird impressionist—Maude Gould, sometimes known as Madame Saberon—was contracted by the BBC as a "backup" to things not working. The trampling around of all the technical staff and all the heavy equipment scared any birds off and the recording is actually that of Maude Gould whistling to Ms Harrison's playing.

Maude Gould was my great grandmother. She whistled at concerts to the Royalty of the day and was in great demand—people laugh nowadays, but whistlers (or siffleurs as they were called) were in good demand on variety bills.

Ted Pittman, Sidcup, Kent, 23 June 2003

Now, the recording on the BTO CD is dated 3 May 1927. It is undoubtedly of a nightingale but must relate to one of her repeat performances in later years. The original BBC recording of the event on 19 May 1924 is quite different and now that I listen to it again, with this letter in mind, I do wonder if it is really a nightingale at all.

This is a very satisfactory state of uncertainty in which to leave the topic of nightingales.

Postscript

But I couldn't quite leave it there, of course. I eventually tracked down Mr. Pittman, after calling all the Pittmans in the Sidcup area telephone directory, and he confirmed the story. He also sent me a sheaf of newspaper clippings about the career of his great grandmother, who worked as a professional artist both before and after the First World War. She clearly was a famous and very impressive performer, a regular turn in variety halls, who also made various appearances before the Royal Family and in early BBC broadcasts, working under a number of stage names, including Sabaronne, Sabonoff, and Sobonoff. She ascribed her remarkable powers to an inherited condition that enabled her to whistle from her throat, not with her lips (as the other lady siffleuses of the day did). Her specialities were the thrush, the lark, . . . and the nightingale.

Her most demanding commission came from the last czar, Nicholas II, whose wife had come under the baneful influence of Rasputin and was in serious decline. The czarina was a deeply superstitious woman and came to believe that her only hope of recovery was to hear a nightingale sing in the palace gardens. The newspaper report goes on:

> Her physicians informed the Czar that if she could only hear the song of a nightingale she would most likely be cured by suggestion. The Czar of all the Russias, however, could not command a nightingale to sing, although he could send ten millions of men to their death by a word! The physicians were in despair, as the poor Czarina used to sit sobbing by her open window that looked on the garden waiting for the nightingale that never warbled his love song. One night, however, her hope was granted. From a leafy bower the full-voiced sweetness of the bird rang

out. The Czarina was in ecstasies and commenced to recover from that moment. It was not, however, a nightingale that she had heard, but Madame Sobonoff, whose wonderful mimicry had deceived her and all the members of the court who were not in on the secret.

Could the BBC engineers have brought her in as a backup in the same well-meaning way—they would have worked with her before, after all? Would Beatrice Harrison have known the difference? Would Lord Reith?

Surely an expert would know the difference, anyway? I sent copies of the original Beatrice Harrison recording independently to two specialists on birdsong (Peter Slater and Geoff Sample), who each analysed the recording and produced sonagrams to compare it with real nightingale song. Both agreed that it had curious structural and other features, but one of them concluded that it probably was a nightingale and one that it probably wasn't. I should have known this would happen. There is an eighth-century riddle poem that goes like this:

> I talk through my mouth with many tongues,
> Vary my tone, and often change
> The sound of my voice. I give loud cries,
> Keep my tune, make songs without ceasing.
> An old evening singer, I bring pleasure
> To people in towns. When I burst
> Into a storm of notes, they fall silent,
> Suddenly listening. Say what I am called
> Who like a mimic loudly mock
> A player's song, and announce to the world
> Many things that are welcome to men.

The title of this riddle and the "solution" to it are always given in anthologies of poetry as "Nightingale." But even here there turns out to be a mystery within the riddle. Anglo-Saxon scholars have in fact disagreed about the solution, on textual and linguistic grounds, and have made suggestions including not only nightingale but also jay, wood pigeon, jackdaw, chough, and a bell! Internal evidence suggests to the mere birder that some of these are ruled out by the description, though I suppose starling (which hasn't been mentioned, as far as I know) might also fit. This is a further happy note of confusion on which to end the nightingale enquiry.

Appendix 4

Some Australian Bird Names

These are further notes on the derivations of the popular names of the Australian birds discussed at the start of chapter 9, together with various other interesting Australian bird names.

Apostlebird: related to the chough and magpies; a highly social species, often seen in family groups, which were fancifully believed by the early settlers always to number 12, like Christ's apostles.

Bellbird (crested): one of the whistlers or shrike-thrushes; the name is onomatopoeic; Pizzey describes the territorial call of the male as "one of the most unusual and lovely sounds of inland and drier coastal districts . . . of fugitive and ventriloquial quality." There are also unrelated South American and New Zealand bellbirds.

Blue bonnet: a native parrot with blue forehead, cheeks, and throat (so not really a "bonnet").

Boatbill (yellow-breasted): a small flycatcher with a very broad bill shaped like the hull of a boat.

Boobook (southern): an owl with an onomatopoeic name (and an Aboriginal equivalent); the New Zealand name for the bird is morepork and supposedly derives from the same call.

Bowerbird (various): the bowerbirds and the related birds of paradise are confined to Australia and New Guinea; the elaborate "bowers" are constructed and decorated for purposes of courtship and display.

Bristlebird (various): related to scrub-wrens and grass-wrens; they all possess little bristles near the base of the bill; but the birds are shy and elusive, the bristles are indistinct in normal field conditions, and various other Australian species have such bristles too (so, all in all, not a great distinguishing feature).

Brolga: a crane, the name adapted from the Aboriginal *burralga;* also known as the "native companion" because it was often seen near Aboriginal communities.

Bronzewing (common, brush): pigeons with iridescent secondary wing feathers that appear bronze in certain lights.

Budgerigar: name derived from one of the many Aboriginal names for this species; it was originally called the "warbling grass parakeet" by Gould (1865), and other popular names are "love-bird," "shell parrot," and "zebra parrot."

Burdekin: popular name for the white-headed shelduck, so called after the River Burdekin in northeast Queensland, a noted location for the species.

Butcherbird: like various shrikes worldwide (which share the nickname), this species has the habit of impaling food items, such as lizards and frogs, on thorns in bushes or trees.

Cassowary: a giant flightless species, related to the emu; the name probably comes from the Malay *kasuari* (or possibly, according to Macdonald, from the Papuan *kasu wari* meaning "horned head").

Chowchilla: one of the "logrunners," birds of the forest floor, which are very noisy, especially at dawn and dusk; the name is onomatopoeic, as are the Aboriginal equivalents.

Cockatoo (various): from the Malay *kakatuwa*, which means "vice," a reference to the strength of the beak.

Corella (long-billed, little): derived from one of the many Aboriginal names for this species.

Cuckoo, channel-billed: obvious when seen.

Currawong (pied, grey, black): from one of the similar Aboriginal names; onomatopoeic in the case of the pied currawong (though not the other currawongs, who just got swept up into the same generic name).

Dollarbird: a roller with a large white spot visible on each wing in flight; the spots were said to look like Spanish silver dollars (it was named this well before Australia changed its currency from pounds to dollars).

Drongo, spangled: a Malagasy word; also Australian slang for a stupid person (from a famous racehorse that always finished last), which seems inappropriate in this case.

Emu: from the Portuguese word *ema* originally applied to the crane and later the ostrich.

Emu-wren (various): they have filamentous tail-feathers, which in just this respect resemble the feathers of the emu (though the emu is Australia's biggest bird at 1.5–1.8 metres and emu-wrens are one of the smallest at 120–200 millimetres, of which the tail is more than half).

Figbird: closely related to orioles; named after its principal food-item.

Friarbird (various): large honeyeaters with heads that are largely unfeathered and were thus thought to resemble the bald heads of friars; hence also the alternative name of "leatherheads."

Frogmouth (various): nocturnal species related to nightjars, with wide mouths said to be reminiscent of the mouths of frogs, which allow them to catch insects in flight at night.

Galah: originally the "rose-breasted cockatoo" but later given this name derived from one of the many Aboriginal names for this species.

Gang-gang: a cockatoo; the name is Aboriginal and imitative.

Gerygone (various): a genus of warblers; the name literally means "born of sound" (from the Greek).

Gibberbird: a desert chat, which inhabits arid inland environments known as gibber plains.

Hardhead: a duck in the pochard family, said by early collectors to be difficult to skin around the head when preparing specimens.

Honeyeater (various): honeyeaters probe flowers for the nectar, which is gathered by specially adapted, brush-tipped tongues. A large and diverse family, found also in New Guinea and the Pacific islands, many of whose members are at least partly insectivorous.

Jabiru: popular name for the black-necked stork; the name comes from a Brazilian language Tupi, via the Portuguese *jaburu* meaning "swollen," a reference to the thick neck. The name is also used as the generic scientific name and the common name for the even larger and more massive Latin American stork.

Jacky winter: the brown flycatcher, "a plain little bird of much charm" (Pizzey), called "Jacky" because of its small size and "winter" perhaps because it is one of the few birds singing throughout the year; other popular names are Peter Peter (from the call), Postboy, Postsitter, and Stumpbird (from the perches it uses when fly-catching).

Koel: a cuckoo, onomatopoeic.

Kookaburra (laughing, blue-winged): from one of the many similar Aboriginal names, which are also onomatopoeic. Both species are large arboreal kingfishers, the laughing kookaburra being mainly a southern bird (also known as the laughing jackass) and the blue-winged a northern one.

Letter-winged kite: named after the dark "M"- or "W"-shaped marking on its outspread wings.

Logrunner: related to the quail-thrushes; they inhabit the floor of rainforests, often scampering among fallen timber, including mossy logs.

Lyrebird (superb, Albert's): named after the shape of the tail; the outer tail-feathers are gently curved in the shape of the frame of a lyre while the other tail feathers are more filamentous, resembling its strings.

Malleefowl: one of the megapodes ("great feet"), which heaps up mounds of earth and decomposing vegetation in which to incubate its eggs; it lives in a habitat known as mallee, which is a type of semi-arid, open woodland with small trees.

Manucode, trumpet: in the same family as birds of paradise; the name comes from the Malay *manuk dewata* ("bird of the gods") via French.

Mistletoebird: the only Australian representative of the large Asian flower-pecker family; the name comes from its staple diet, for which it has a specially adapted alimentary system to deal with the stones (the Australian mistletoe-fruit is not the same as the European mistletoe).

Owl, powerful: no doubt true, but another case where the taxonomist seems to have run out of ideas.

Pardalote (various, including spotted, striated): from the Greek word that means "spotted" and presumably attached first to the spotted pardalote, with the other species named by association.

Pilotbird: a small ground-dweller of dense rainforest, named after its habit of feeding co-operatively with superb lyrebirds, often taking soil organisms exposed by their foraging activities in the leaf-litter, like pilot fish with sharks.

Pitta (various): stumpy ground-feeding birds of the forest floor; the name comes from Telegu (an Asian language) and means "young bird."

Plains-wanderer: a rare and rather mysterious bird with an evocative name; it has characteristics both of a true quail and a button-quail and occurs only on open native grasslands, but its status and numbers are uncertain.

Riflebird (various): in the same family as the birds of paradise; the name is of uncertain origin but may derive from a supposed similarity of the plumage to a military uniform.

Rosella (various): small parrots supposedly named after the settlement at Rose Hill (now a suburb of Sydney), where they were numerous in the early days of settlement; but this may be an etymological "urban myth."

Scrub-bird (various): "scrub" and "bush" are used to describe almost any natural habitat with shrubs and trees and so potentially refer to a wide range of possible habitats, but in practice scrub-birds prefer dense vegetation.

Silvereye or white-eye (pale, robust): named for their prominent white eye-ring; the iris is actually brown. There are related species elsewhere in Asia and the Pacific.

Sitella (various): a diminutive of the Greek word for nuthatch.

Spinifexbird: an Old World warbler named after the spiky grass that forms dense, impenetrable clumps in its preferred habitat in arid regions.

Tattler (wandering and grey): a migratory sandpiper; the name comes from the call (as in "tattle").

Thick-knee (bush and beach): stone curlews, whose generic scientific name *Burhinus* translates as "ox-nose"; the bull-headed appearance and the large

eyes are certainly better ID criteria than the size and shape of its knees,
though the British counterpart has the specific name *oedicnemus,* from
which the vernacular Australian name must come. It also has the popular,
onomatopoeic name of weeloo or willaroo, derived from Aboriginal names.

Wattlebird (various): large honeyeaters named after the fleshy wattle near the
base of the bill, which comes in different sizes: huge (in the yellow wattlebird), moderate (the red wattlebird), and nonexistent (the little wattlebird);
no connection with the widespread Australian trees and shrubs commonly
known as wattles.

Wompoo pigeon: the magnificent fruit pigeon of northeastern Australia; the
name is onomatopoeic and probably Aboriginal.

Reference Matter

Abbreviations

The following much-cited works are usually referred to by abbreviations after their first mention:

BB: Cocker, Mark, *Birds Britannica* (2005).
BWP: Cramp, Stanley, K. Simmons, and C. Perrins, *Handbook of Birds of Europe, the Middle East, and North Africa: Birds of the Western Palearctic,* 9 volumes (1977–94).

I also make repeated use of a few standard field guides and other reference works, whose full bibliographical details I do not repeat in each chapter. They are:

Brown, Andy, and Phil Grice, *Birds in England* (2005).
Fisher, James, *The Shell Bird Book* (1966).
Jonsson, Lars, *Birds of Europe* (1992).
Leahy, Christopher, *The Birdwatcher's Companion to North American Birdlife* (2004).
Moss, Stephen, *A Bird in the Bush: A Social History of Birdwatching* (2004).
Mullarney, Killian, Dan Zetterström, Lars Svensson, and Peter Grant, *The Collins Birdguide* (Swedish edition, 1999; first English edition, 2000).
Peterson, Roger Tory, *A Field Guide to the Birds* (1934).
Peterson, Roger Tory, Guy Mountfort, and P.A.D. Hollom, *The Field Guide to the Birds of Britain and Europe* (1954).
Sibley, David, *The Sibley Guide to Birds* (2000). Now divided into *Birds of Eastern North America* and *Birds of Western North America* (both 2003).

Notes, Sources, and Further Reading

Notes are divided by chapter, keyed to the page number and to a brief phrase from the text. Sources and further reading are also divided by chapter. They include fuller details of works cited in the text and some further reading for readers interested in pursuing the topic of each chapter and seeing what my own background reading was.

Chapter 1

NOTES
Page
[2] Leonardo on flight. See his notebook jottings in Irma A. Richter, ed., *The Notebooks of Leonardo da Vinci,* especially chap. 3. Freud picked up on this fascination with the kite in his psychosexual study of Leonardo, but unfortunately based his

interpretation on a mistranslation of the Italian word for kite *(nibbio)* as "vulture" and then proceeded to make connections between "vulture" and "mother" in Egyptian mythology (the figure of *mut*), and then to construct a series of heady hypotheses purporting to explain Leonardo's feelings about his mother and about women in general.

[2] Swallow flight speed. In fact, the usual flight speed is 8–11 metres per second when foraging, though migrating swallows average a little faster. See Angela Turner, *The Barn Swallow* (2006), pp. 28–29.

[6] "other interests." See, for example: Robert MacFarlane, *Mountains of the Mind* (2003), Bee Wilson, *The Hive* (2004), and the classic C.L.R. James, *Beyond the Boundary* (1963).

[7] John Clare. The quotation about Clare is from James Fisher in *The Shell Bird Book*, p. 192. Clare's own quotations come mainly from the anthology edited by Jonathan Bate, *John Clare: Selected Poems* (2003), which has a very good introduction, making the comparison with Keats; and there is a collection of the prose writings, edited by Margaret Grainger, *The Natural History Writings of John Clare* (1983).

[11] The British list. Fisher in *The Shell Bird Book* (chap. 2) charts the growth of the British list, and there is a comprehensive modern treatment in Peter Bircham, *A History of Ornithology* (2007).

[12] Quotation from D.I.M. Wallace, *Beguiled by Birds,* pp. 186–88.

[13] Quotation from Jeremy Hickman, "Tree Swallow on Scilly," *British Birds* 88 (1995): 381–84, reprinted in Adrian Pitches and Tim Cleeves, eds., *Birds New to Britain, 1980–2004* (2005).

[14] Variations in gull plumages. Theo Musse et al. "Identification Update: Moult Variability in 3rd Calendar-Year Lesser Black-Backed Gulls," *Birding World,* October 2005.

[18] The contributions of amateurs. See the presidential address by Ernst W. Mayr to the American Ornithologists' Union (1962). The same general point is made very winningly in another and very different presidential address, that by R. W. David to the Botanical Society of the British Isles, "Gentlemen and Players" (1980): "Not only are gentlemen and players still in the same game—they are on the same side." On the list of professions Mayr might have added to his list even at that time, see James Fisher's classic *Watching Birds* (1941), p. 11; and for an up-to-date survey, Stephen Moss's *A Bird in the Bush: A Social History of Birdwatching* (2004).

SOURCES AND FURTHER READING

Baden-Powell, Robert, *Scouting for Boys: A Handbook for Instruction in Good Citizenship* (1908).

Baker, J. A., *The Peregrine* (1967).

Bate, Jonathan, ed., *John Clare: Selected Poems* (2003).

Benson, S. Vere, *The Observer's Book of Birds* (1937).

Bircham, Peter, *A History of Ornithology* (2007).

Clare, John, "The Landrail" (from *The Midsummer Cushion,* 1835), "The Nightingale's Nest" (from *The Rural Muse,* 1832).

David, R. W., "Gentlemen and Players," 1980 presidential address to the Botanical Society of the British Isles, *Watsonia* 13 (1981): 173–79.

Davies, Nick, *Dunnock Behaviour and Social Evolution* (1995).

Fisher, James, *Watching Birds* (1941), and *The Shell Bird Book* (1966).

Grainger, Margaret, ed., *The Natural History Writings of John Clare* (1983).

Hickman, Jeremy, "Tree Swallow on Scilly." *British Birds* 88 (1995): 381–84.

Howard, Eliot, *A Waterhen's Worlds* (1940).

Jamie, Kathleen, *Findings* (2005).

Jeffries, Richard, "Hours of Spring" (1886), collected in *Field and Hedgerow* (1889).

Keats, John, "Ode to a Nightingale" (1820).

Kennedy, J. S., *The New Anthropomorphism* (1992).

Lopez, Barry, *Arctic Dreams* (1986).

Mabey, Richard, ed., *The Oxford Book of Nature Writing* (1985).

Mayr, Ernst W., "Presidential Address: The Role of Ornithological Research in Biology," *Proceedings of the XIII International Ornithological Congress* (1962).

Millington, Richard, *A Twitcher's Diary* (1981).

Morris, F. O., *A History of British Birds* (1853).

Musse, Theo, Mars Musse, Bert-Jan Luijendijk, and Ruud Alternburg, "Identification Update: Moult Variability in 3rd Calendar-Year Lesser Black-Backed Gulls," *Birding World*, October 2005.

Pitches, Adrian, and Tim Cleeves, eds., *Birds New to Britain, 1980-2004* (2005).

Richter, Irma A., ed., *The Notebooks of Leonardo da Vinci* (1952).

Ruskin, John, "The Relation of Wise Art to Wise Science," in *The Eagle's Nest* (1887).

Sandars, Edmund, *A Bird Book for the Pocket* (1927).

Turner, Angela, *The Barn Swallow* (2006).

Wallace, D.I.M., *Beguiled by Birds* (2004).

White, Gilbert, *The Natural History and Antiquities of Selborne* (1789).

Young, Andrew, "The Swallows," in *Speak to the Earth* (1939).

Chapter 2

NOTES

Page

[29] "crane dance." Edward Armstrong argued for a common source and motivation, and went even further in describing shared forms of dance and choreographies (*Bird Display and Behaviour*, chap. 15); see also Richard Mabey, *Nature Cure*, pp. 159–62.

[29] Crane quotations. Homer *Iliad* 3.3; Hesiod *Works and Days*, lines 448–51. See Peter Matthiessen, *The Birds of Heaven*, for many other quotations (including one case of mistaken identity, see note on p. 157).

[34] Robin aggression. See the classic work by David Lack, *The Life of the Robin* (1943), especially chap. 12, "Adventures with a Stuffed Robin." Lack also published a popular work on the very different literary and cultural image the robin enjoys, *Robin Redbreast* (1950), which has now been updated and enlarged by his son, Andrew Luck, under the title *Redbreast: The Robin in Life and Literature* (2008). See also E. A. Armstrong, *The Folklore of Birds* (1958), chap. 10, "Fire-birds."

[35] Grey and Roosevelt. Grey tells the story of their day out together, when Roosevelt impressed him a great deal with his knowledge of birds, in *Fallodon Papers* (1926), pp. 69–79. The anecdote is also recorded in Seton Gordon's biography, *Edward Grey of Fallodon and His Birds* (1937), p. 14; and in Roosevelt's own *Autobiography* (1946), pp. 322–26.

[36] Recordings of *The Lark Ascending*. Performances vary quite a bit, interestingly. Haitink and Susan Chang (EMI) take 13 minutes, 37 seconds; Marriner and Iona

Brown (Argo) take 16 minutes, 4 seconds. The bird itself can take longer, though the average has been estimated to be 2–2.5 minutes, with exceptional cases recorded at 57 and 68 minutes. See *BWP*, vol. 5, p. 196, which makes a further reference to a study by John Brackenbury in *Ibis* 120 (1978): 526–28 on the coordination of song production with syringeal and respiratory movements.

[37] Decline of the skylark. According to a recent census, a decline of more than 50 percent between 1980 and 2000 (see Brown and Grice, *Birds in England*, p. 453). On the culinary popularity of the skylark in the nineteenth century, see A. C. Smith, *Birds of Wiltshire* (1887), p. 183; and more generally on the woodlark and skylark, see Cocker, *BB*, pp. 308–12.

[37] Skylarks and the Nazis. The headline is quoted in *Bird Notes and News* 16, no. 4 (1934), and discussed in Helen Macdonald, "'What Makes You a Scientist Is the Way You Look at Things': Ornithology and the Observer, 1930–55."

[39] Blackcaps imitating nightingales. The British Library CD of *Bird Mimicry* (2006) includes a very convincing blackcap-nightingale, and John Clare's poem "The March Nightingale" may refer to the same phenomenon.

[43] Ostriches as big game. See further on these problems of classification the famous article by Ralph Bulmer, "Why Is the Cassowary Not a Bird?" *Man* 2 (1970): 5–25, and the discussion in chapter 9, pp. 251–52.

[44] Allen Lane and the name "Penguins." See J. Lewis, *Penguin Special*, p. 91.

[45] Owls in folklore. Edward Armstrong documents an extraordinary range of traditional beliefs and practices associated with owls worldwide (*The Folklore of Birds*, pp. 113–24), and Mark Cocker has an engaging selection of both literary and folk references in his introduction to the owls section in *BB*, pp. 281–85.

[46] Penguins and soft toys. On the importance of shape, see K. Taylor, *Puffins*, p. 138.

[46] Charisma in people. Max Weber developed the idea of charisma in social science, applying it to "natural leaders . . . who possessed specific physical and spiritual gifts which were regarded as supernatural, in the sense of not being available to everyone," though he noted that it was an "unstable kind of authority." See "The Nature of Charismatic Domination" in *Wirtschaft und Gesellschaft* (1922).

[47] Charisma in birds. I published an article, "Charisma or Just Charm?" in the magazine *Birdwatching* (May 2004), in which I proposed a personal list of ten charismatic British birds, which in turn led to a poll in the August 2004 issue. That produced a "top twenty" list, which included most of the birds I mention here: barn owl (the runaway winner), red kite, kingfisher, puffin, nightjar, lapwing, and raven. There is always a high degree of convergence when national polls of this kind are taken too.

[49] The Icarus fantasy. There is a detailed scholarly account of this and other "flying" motifs in European literature by Piero Boitani, *Winged Words: Flight in Poetry and History* (2007).

[49] Freud on dreams. See *The Interpretation of Dreams*, vol. 5 p. 394.

[50] The arrival of swifts. Ted Hughes, *Season Songs*, p. 33.

[51] Supercharismatic birds. For the "supercharismatics," see further chapter 5, pp. 127–37, for birds of outstanding natural beauty and Stephen Moss's "world" list of the hundred best in *Remarkable Birds*.

[52] "pilgrimage." Matthiessen, *Birds of Heaven*, p. 164, but perhaps one should not think of this in too exclusive a sense, since in another book he also talks of his

"pilgrimage" to see the emperor penguin "to simplify my self" (*End of the Earth*, p. 122).

[52] "epiphany." L. Nathan, *Diary of a Left-Handed Birdwatcher.*

SOURCES AND FURTHER READING

Armstrong, Edward A., *Bird Display and Behaviour,* second edition (1947), and *The Folklore of Birds* (1958).

Baker, J. A., *The Hill of Summer* (1969).

Boitani, Piero, *Winged Words: Flight in Poetry and History* (2007).

Brown, Andy, and Phil Grice, *Birds in England* (2005).

Browning, Robert, "Home Thoughts, from Abroad" (1845).

Clifford, S., and A. King, *England in Particular* (2006).

Freud, Sigmund, *The Interpretation of Dreams* (1909), volume 5 in *The Standard Edition* (Hogarth Press / Vintage).

Gordon, Seton, *Edward Grey of Fallodon and His Birds* (1937).

Grey, Edward, *Fallodon Papers* (1926) and *The Charm of Birds* (1927).

Hesiod, *Works and Days* (eighth century BC).

Homer, *Iliad* (about 700 BC).

Hughes, Ted, "Thrushes," in *Lupercal* (1960), and "Larks," in *Wodwo* (1967).

Lewis, Jeremy, *Penguin Special: The Life and Times of Allen Lane* (2005).

Mabey, Richard, *Nature Cure* (2005).

Macdonald, Helen, "'What Makes You a Scientist Is the Way You Look at Things': Ornithology and the Observer, 1930–55," *Studies in the History and Philosophy of Biological and Biomedical Sciences* 33 (2002): 53–77.

Matthiessen, Peter, *Birds of Heaven* (2002).

Meredith, George, "The Lark Ascending" (1881).

Moss, Stephen, "The Hit List," in *This Birding Life* (2006); and *Remarkable Birds* (2007).

Mynott, Jeremy, "Charisma or Just Charm?" *Birdwatching* (May 2004).

Nathan, Leonard, *Diary of a Left-Handed Birdwatcher* (1996).

Roosevelt, Theodore, *An Autobiography* (1946).

Shelley, Percy B., "To a Skylark" (1819).

Smith, A. C., *Birds of Wiltshire* (1887).

Taylor, K., *Puffins* (1993).

Weber, Max, "The Nature of Charismatic Domination," in *Wirtschaft und Gesellschaft* (1922), translated in W. G. Runciman, ed., *Max Weber: Selections in Translation* (1978).

Chapter 3

NOTES

Page

[55] "the standard field guide." This was *The Collins Bird Guide,* ed. Killian Mullarney, Lars Svensson, Dan Zetterström, and Peter Grant, first published in Swedish in 1999 and in English in 2000, which Peter Grant tragically did not live to see finally published (he died in 1990).

[56] "noticing differences." The emerging subfield of ethno-ornithology records a great deal of cultural data of this kind: see, for example, C. S. Majnep and Ralph Bulmer *Birds of My Kalam Country* (1977); S. Feld, *Sound and Sentiment: Birds, Weeping,*

Sentiment, and Song in Kaluli Expression (1982); Stephen R. Kellert and Edward O. Wilson, *The Biophilia Hypothesis* (1993); and the lavishly illustrated N. J. Collar, *Birds and People: Bonds in a Timeless Journey* (2007).

[59] Birds as individuals. There are of course many published accounts of ordinary people's recognition of and relationships with individual birds. One classic is Len Howard, *Birds as Individuals* (1952), which had an admiring preface from Julian Huxley recommending it to professional biologists.

[69] California skylark. The incident is referred to in David Sibley, *Birding Basics* (2002), p. 41.

[69] The ambiguity of images. Richard Gregory, *Eye and Brain* (1998), p. 205. This is the classic text on illusions and Gregory discusses most of the examples that follow.

[72] Arctic illusions. These and other examples are cited in Lopez, *Arctic Dreams*, p. 239.

[75] Constable as representational artist. There is a very good curator's note in the Christchurch Mansions Museum in Ipswich that makes this point about one of the museum's Constables.

[75] "peak-shifting." V. S. Ramachandran, *The Emerging Mind*, based on his 2003 Reith lectures.

[75] Robin aggression. See note on page 325.

[77] Aircraft recognition. See further T. Hamilton, *Identification: Friend or Foe* (1994); and, on the parallels in the language of description used in the two pursuits, Helen Macdonald, "'What Makes You a Scientist Is the Way You Look at Things': Ornithology and the Observer, 1930–55," especially pp. 66–67.

[77] Raptor ID. The raptor illustration above is taken from the Collins *Pocket Guide* of 1952 (ed. Fitter and Richardson), but the first really serious raptor guide was *The Flight Identification of European Raptors* (ed. Porter et al., 1976). No longer did one have to stare at pictures of huge and subtly patterned eagles sitting out on branches at close range to help one identify specks in the sky seen from below at ranges of up to a mile away.

SOURCES AND FURTHER READING

Collinson, Martin, "Shifting Sands: Taxonomic Changes in the World of the Field Ornithologist," *British Birds* 94 (January 2001): 2–27; and "A Written Constitution for Species-Level Taxonomy," *British Birds* 95 (August 2002): 370–71.

Darwin, Charles, *Origin of Species* (1859).

Doyle, Conan, "The Greek Interpreter," in *The Memoirs of Sherlock Holmes* (1894).

Fielding, Henry, *Joseph Andrews* (1742).

Fitter, R. S., and R.A.R. Richardson, *The Pocket Guide to British Birds* (1952).

Gregory, Richard, *Eye and Brain* (1998).

Hamilton, T., *Identification: Friend or Foe* (1994).

Hardy, G. H., *A Mathematician's Apology* (with an introduction by C. P. Snow, 1973).

Howard, Len, *Birds as Individuals* (1952).

Johnson, Samuel, *Rasselas* (1759).

Kastner, David, *A World of Watchers* (1986).

Kaufman, Ken, *Advanced Birding* (1990).

Knox, Alan G., "Order or Chaos: Taxonomy and the British List over the Last 100 Years," *British Birds* 100 (October 2007): 609–23.

Lack, David, *The Life of the Robin* (1943).

Lopez, Barry, *Arctic Dreams* (1986).

Macdonald, Helen, "'What Makes You a Scientist Is the Way You Look at Things': Ornithology and the Observer, 1930–55," *Studies in the History and Philosophy of Biological and Biomedical Sciences* 33 (2002): 53–77.

Maclean, Norman, et al. "Taxonomy for Birders: A Beginner's Guide to DNA and Species Problems," *British Birds* 98 (October 2005): 512–37.

Pope, Alexander, "To Lord Cobham," in *Epistles to Several Persons* (1734).

Porter, Richard, et al., *The Flight Identification of European Raptors* (1976).

Ramachandran, V. S., *The Emerging Mind* (2003).

Sibley, David, *Birding Basics* (2002).

Saville-Sneath, R. A., *Aircraft Recognition* (1941).

Snow, Philip, *The Design and Origin of Birds* (2006).

Stephansson, Vihjalmus, *My Life with the Eskimo* (1923).

Tolansky, S., *Optical Illusions* (1964).

Chapter 4

NOTES

Page

[80] "If you should happen after dark." Ogden Nash, "City Greenery," in *Everyone but Thee and Me* (Boston: Little Brown, 1962), p. 107.

[83] Lexical lists. These have given rise to a specialised scholarly industry with the splendid name of *Listenwissenschaft*. See Jack Goody, *Domestication of the Savage Mind* (1977), pp. 80–96; and in particular the comprehensive work by N. Veldhuis, *Religion, Literature, and Scholarship: The Sumerian Composition Nanse and the Birds* (2004).

[84] Lists in literature. There is a charming anthology of literary lists compiled by Francis Spufford under the title *Cabbages and Kings* (1989).

[85] Kinds of lists. Robert Belknap has many distinctions of this kind to make in the preface to his excellent book, *The List: The Uses and Pleasures of Cataloguing* (2004), and he goes on to produce a sort of typology of lists.

[86] Chapman's hat list. For more information on the fashion trade of the time, see Welker, *Birds and Men*, pp. 196–99.

[88] Thoreau on distinctions between thrushes. See *Journals*, 22 May 1852, 9 June 1852, and 10 May 1854.

[89] Clare's list. For estimates of the complete British list at the time, see Fisher, *The Shell Bird Book*, chap. 2, "The Naming of the Birds"; and Peter Bircham, *A History of Ornithology*, appendix. Fisher estimates that the British list stood at 214 in 1758, 229 in 1780, and 240 in 1800. White (note to p. 89) seems to have had a larger figure in mind in 1774.

[91] Collecting oneself. See Jean Baudrillard, *Le Système des objets* (1968), part of which is translated in Elsner and Cardinal, *The Cultures of Collecting* (1994), itself a very good source of anecdotes and theories about all this. See also Walter Benjamin, "Unpacking My Library," in *Illuminations*, ed. H. Arendt (first published in German in 1931); and Bronislaw Malinowski, *Argonauts of the Western Pacific* (epigraph to this chapter), talking about the *kula* rituals of the Trobriand islanders, who make great efforts to collect items of no apparent intrinsic value.

[93] Balfour on field excursions. From the preface to his account of a three-week excursion to two areas famous for their mountain flora, the Clova district and Ben Lawers. The report appeared in the *Edinburgh New Philosophical Journal* for July 1848 and is cited with approval by John Raven and Max Walters in their introduction to the New Naturalist volume on *Mountain Flowers* (1956).

[95] Ian Heslop. Quotation from Matthew Oates, "Extreme Butterfly Collecting," *British Wildlife*, February 2005. See also *The Aurelian Legacy* by Michael Salmon (2000) and *An Obsession with Butterflies* by Sharman Apt Russell (2003).

[96] "hunters of mammals." Turgenev has many lyrical descriptions of the pleasures of the chase in *A Sportsman's Notebook* (1852).

[97] Kenny Salway. In the BBC *Natural World* programme "Mississippi: Tales of the Last River Rat," broadcast 11 June 2006.

[101] Peterson and Alanbrooke. This and many other stories about the twitching fraternity are told by Mark Cocker in his entertaining anthropology *Birders: Tales of a Tribe* (2001). The Alanbrooke "pallid harrier" anecdote is in Alanbrooke's *War Diaries, 1939–45*, p. 374, and the diaries are interspersed with ornithological distractions of this kind.

[102] Phoebe Snetsinger. Her book *Birding on Borrowed Time* was published posthumously in 2003.

[102] Narratives of the year list. There are now even novelistic treatments of the same theme, as in Cris Freddi's *Pelican Blood* (2005), which includes some very realistic material.

[103] Hilda Quick and Scilly. See Hilda Quick, *Birds of the Scilly Isles* (1964), pp. 89–91. The blue-cheeked bee-eater turned out in the end to be the second record for Scilly and the United Kingdom when the mounted skin of a bird shot in Tresco in 1921 was later identified as being of this species.

[104] Asperger's syndrome. See the Web site of the Institute of Neurological Disorders of the U.S. National Institutes of Health, www.nih.gov/disorders/asperger/asperger.htm.

[105] Designated authorities. Like the American Birding Association (ABA) in the United States and the British Ornithologists' Union (BOU) in the United Kingdom, which have special committees and elaborate rules. You also get breakaway groups, impatient with the conservatism and slow procedures of the central authorities, that produce their own lists and criteria (which are usually more generous taxonomically).

SOURCES AND FURTHER READING

Alanbrooke, Field Marshall Lord (Alan Francis Brooke), *War Diaries, 1939–45*, ed. Alex Danchev and Daniel Todman (2001).

Allen, David Elliston, *The Naturalist in Britain: A Social History* (1976).

Barbellion, W.N.P., *Journal of a Disappointed Man* (1919).

Balfour, J. H., "Excursion to Clova and Ben Lawes," *Edinburgh New Philosophical Journal* (July 1848).

Baudrillard, Jean, *Le Système des objets* (1968).

Belknap, Robert, *The List: The Uses and Pleasures of Cataloguing* (2004).

Benjamin, Walter, "Unpacking my Library," in *Illuminations,* ed. H. Arendt (first published in German in 1931).

Bircham, Peter, *A History of Ornithology* (2007).

Chapman, Frank, "Birds and Bonnets," *Forest and Stream* (25 February 1886).

Clare, John, see under Fisher and Grainger.

Cocker, Mark, *Birders: Tales of a Tribe* (2001).

Cruickshank, Helen, ed., *Thoreau on Birds* (1964).

Dickens, Charles, *Bleak House* (1852–53).

Dooley, Sean, *The Big Twitch* (2006).

Elsner, John, and Roger Cardinal, *The Cultures of Collecting* (1994).

Fisher, James, "The Birds of John Clare," *A History of the Kettering and District Naturalists' Society and Field Club*, pp. 26–69 (Kettering 1956).

Fisher, James, and Roger Tory Peterson, *Wild America* (1955).

Fredi, Cris, *Pelican Blood* (2005).

Goody, Jack, *Domestication of the Savage Mind* (1977).

Grainger, Margaret, ed., *The Natural History Prose Writings of John Clare* (1983).

Hanlon, James, *UK 500: Birding in the Fast Lane* (2006).

Houlihan, Patrick, *The Birds of Ancient Egypt* (1986).

Jefferson, Thomas, *Notes on the State of Virginia* (1787), and *Garden Book* (1766–1824).

Koeppel, Dan, *To See Every Bird* (2005).

Liep, John, "Airborne *Kula*: The Appropriation of Birds by Danish Ornithologists," *Anthropology Today* 17, no. 5 (October 2001).

Malinowski, Bronislaw, *Argonauts of the Western Pacific* (1922).

Marren, Peter, *Britain's Rare Flowers* (1999).

Millington, Richard, *A Twitcher's Diary* (1981).

Moss, Stephen, *A Bird in the Bush: A Social History of Birdwatching* (2004).

Mynott, Jeremy, "The Scilly Season," *World of Birds* 2, no. 9 (August 1974).

Nabokov, Vladimir, *Speak Memory* (1966).

Oates, Matthew, "Extreme Butterfly Collecting," *British Wildlife*, February 2005.

Obmascik, Mark, *The Big Year* (2004).

Quick, Hilda, *Birds of the Scilly Isles* (1964).

Raven, John, and Max Walters, *Mountain Flowers* (1956).

Riley, Adrian, *Arrivals and Rivals* (2004).

Russell, Sharman Apt, *An Obsession with Butterflies* (2003).

Salmon, Michael, *The Aurelian Legacy* (2000).

Sanderson, R. F., "The Birds of Hyde Park and Kensington Gardens," in E. M. Nicholson, *Bird-Watching in London: A Historical Perspective* (1995).

Snetsinger, Phoebe, *Birding on Borrowed Time* (2003).

Spufford, Francis, ed., *Cabbages and Kings* (1989).

Thoreau, Henry D., *Journals* (1837–61) and "The Natural History of Massachusetts" (1842).

Veldhuis, Nick, *Religion, Literature, and Scholarship: The Sumerian Composition Nanse and the Birds* (2004).

Welker, Robert Henry, *Birds and Men: American Birds in Science, Art, Literature, and Conservation, 1800–1900* (1955).

Wilson, E. O., *The Future of Life* (2002).

Chapter 5

NOTES

Page

[111] "the smell of violets." Diane Ackerman, *A Natural History of the Senses*, pp. 9–10.

[113] The Lord Chamberlain's Office. For some of the documentary details, see N. de Jongh, *Politics, Prudery, and Perversions: The Censoring of the English Stage, 1901–1968;* and J. Johnston, *The Lord Chamberlain's Blue Pencil.*

[115] Ted Hughes's descriptions. Several of these are anthologised in the collection *Season Songs* (1972). See also my comments on flight on pp. 1–3 and 283–85.

[116] Sir Thomas Browne on the roller. "Notes on Certain Birds Found in Norfolk," in a letter to Dr. Christopher Merrett, 16 September 1668.

[117] "until we shall have need to eat them." Henry More, *An Antidote against Atheism,* cited by Keith Thomas in his magisterial survey *Man and the Natural World: Changing Attitudes in England, 1500–1800* (1983).

[119] Audubon on Bewick. Audubon liked to think of Bewick as "purely a son of nature" (*Ornithological Biography,* 1831).

[119] Bewick on working from nature. Thomas Bewick, *Memoir,* ed. I. Bain, p. 122. See also the excellent biography of Bewick by Jenny Uglow, *Nature's Engraver* (2006).

[120] Natural history in Britain in the nineteenth century. See Thomas, *Man and the Natural World,* pp. 269–87. And specifically on the Audubon subscriptions, see Welker, *Birds and Men,* pp. 68–69.

[122] Liljefors and French impressionism. In particular *Mallards, Evening* (1901) and *Goldfinches* (late 1880s), both of which suggest a Japanese influence too. See further Hammond, *Modern Wildlife Painting,* pp. 31–40.

[123] Recent British artists. There is an excellent survey of recent British artists by Alan Harris, himself a very successful illustrator, in *British Birds* 100 (May 2007).

[123] Roger Tory Peterson. See J. Devlin and G. Naismith, *The World of Roger Tory Peterson: An Authorised Biography,* and G. Mountfort's obituary in *British Birds* 89 (1996): 544–45. On Peterson's ambitions as an artist, see Devlin and Naismith, pp. 215–38.

[125] Jonsson, *Birds of Europe.* This was first published as such in 1992 but was developed from a series of guides by habitat that had been appearing since 1978. See also the wonderful collection of his other paintings and sketches in *Birds and Light* (2002).

[129] Darwin on female choice. The male critic was St. G. Milvert in *Quarterly Review* 131 (1871): 47–90. For a more modern sceptical note, see Louis J. Halle, *The Appreciation of Birds* (1989), especially chap. 8; but see also the ingenious Darwinian defences offered by Helena Cronin in *The Ant and the Peacock* (1991).

[130] "the Great Exhibition of 1851." For a fuller account of Gould's role in the Great Exhibition, see Isabella Tree's biography, *The Bird Man* (1991), chaps. 12 and 13; and Jonathan Elphick, *Birds: The Art of Ornithology* (2004), pp. 236–37.

[134] "David Attenborough's bird of choice." Interview in *The Observer,* 14 March 2004.

[141] "objective and subjective." Ruskin's warning comes at the start of his famous essay "Of the Pathetic Fallacy" in *Modern Painters,* vol. 3 (1856), which is a powerful assertion of the importance of Truth in poetic descriptions of nature. Subsequently, there was a surprising lack of serious work on the aesthetics of the natural world for most of the twentieth century, for reasons that are interesting in themselves; but this has now been at least partly remedied by publications such as R. Hepburn, *Wonder* (1984); S. Kemal and I. Gaskell, eds., *Landscape, Natural Beauty, and the Arts* (1980); M. Budd, *The Aesthetic Appreciation of Nature* (2002); and D. Cooper, *A Philosophy of Gardens* (2006).

[144] The biology of beauty. For a report from the front line, see Evan Thompson, *Colour Vision* (1995); and John Barrow, *The Artful Universe* (2006).

SOURCES AND FURTHER READING

Ackerman, Diane, *A Natural History of the Senses* (1990).

Attenborough, David, *Life of Birds* (1998).

Audubon, John James, *The Birds of America* (1927–38) and *Ornithological Biography* (1831).

Barrow, John, *The Artful Universe* (2006).

Bewick, Thomas, *A History of British Birds* (1797–1804), and *Memoir* (1862; ed. I. Bain, 1975).

Browne, Thomas, "Notes on Certain Birds Found in Norfolk," in a letter to Dr. Christopher Merrett, 16 September 1668.

Budd, M., *The Aesthetic Appreciation of Nature* (2002).

Cocker, Mark, *Birders: Tales of a Tribe* (2001).

Cooper, David, *A Philosophy of Gardens* (2006).

Couzens, Dominic, *Birds by Behaviour* (2003).

Cronin, Helena, *The Ant and the Peacock* (1991).

Darwin, Charles, *The Descent of Man* (1871).

Davies, N., *Dunnock Behaviour and Social Evolution* (1992).

de Jongh, N., *Politics, Prudery, and Perversions: The Censoring of the English Stage, 1901–1968* (2000).

Devlin, J., and G. Naismith, *The World of Roger Tory Peterson: An Authorised Biography* (1978).

Dickens, Charles, *Hard Times* (1854).

Elphick, Jonathan, *Birds: The Art of Ornithology* (2004).

Gould, John, *The Birds of Europe* (1832–37).

Halle, Louis J., *The Appreciation of Birds* (1989).

Hammond, Nicholas, *Modern Wildlife Painting* (1998).

Harris, Alan, "Bird Illustration in the Twentieth Century," *British Birds* 100 (May 2007): 266–79.

Hazlitt, William, "On the Love of the Country," *The Examiner*, November 1814.

Hepburn, Ronald, *Wonder* (1984).

Hudson, W. H., *The Naturalist in La Plata* (1895) and *Idle Days in Patagonia* (1917).

Hughes, Ted, *Season Songs* (1972).

Hume, Rob, et al., *Birds by Character: The Fieldguide to Jizz* (1990).

Johnston, J., *The Lord Chamberlain's Blue Pencil* (1990).

Jonsson, Lars, *Birds of Europe* (1992) and *Birds and Light* (2002).

Juniper, Tony, *Spix's Macaw* (2002).

Kemal, S., and I. Gaskell, eds., *Landscape, Natural Beauty, and the Arts* (1980).

Macfarlane, Robert, *Mountains of the Mind* (2005).

More, Henry, *An Antidote against Atheism* (1653).

Mountfort, Guy, "Obituary of Roger Tory Peterson," *British Birds* 89 (1996): 544–45.

Ruskin, John, "Of the Pathetic Fallacy," in *Modern Painters*, vol. 3 (1856).

Selous, Edmund, *Thought Transference (or What?) in Birds* (1931).

Skutch, Alexander F., *Origins of Nature's Beauty* (1992).

Thomas, Edward, "Haymaking," in *Collected Poems* (1920).

Thomas, Keith, *Man and the Natural World: Changing Attitudes in England, 1500–1800* (1983).

Thompson, Evan, *Colour Vision* (1995).

Tree, Isabella, *The Bird Man: The Extraordinary Story of John Gould* (1991).

Uglow, Jenny, *Nature's Engraver: A Life of Thomas Bewick* (2006).

Wallace, Alfred Russel, *The Malay Archipelago* (1869).

Welker, Robert Henry, Birds and Men: American Birds in Science, Art, Literature, and Conservation, 1800–1900 (1955).

Wilde, Oscar, "The Decay of Lying: An Observation" (1889).

Wordsworth, William, "Lines Composed a Few Miles above Tintern Abbey" (1798).

Chapter 6

NOTES

Page

[146] Time of first songs. See Catchpole and Slater, *Bird Song,* second edition (2008), pp. 128–35. My flip remark that they don't have much else they can do in the dark may in fact be part of the answer.

[149] Delbene's Gate of Hearing. From the didactic poem *Civitas Veri* (City of Truth) by the Florentine Bartolemeo Delbene, printed in 1609. See Louise Vinge, *The Five Senses: Studies in a Literary Tradition* (1975), for these and other examples of the priority often given to hearing in religious allegories.

[149] The senses in different cultures. See Classen, *Worlds of Sense* (1993), pp. 10 and 135.

[150] J. A. Baker, *The Hill of Summer* (1969), pp. 86–87, from chapter 8, "June: Midsummer."

[152] Memoirs of deafness. David Wright, *Deafness: A Personal Account,* second edition (1990), pp. 11–12; and Helen Keller, from a letter to Dr. J. Kerr Love, 31 March 1910.

[153] Birds and urban noise. See Catchpole and Slater, *Bird Song,* second edition (2008), pp. 101–4.

[155] Ted Parker. K. J. Zimmer, "Ted Parker Remembered," *Birding* 25, no. 6 (1993): 377–80. See also Don Stap, *Birdsong* (2005), pp. 106–7, and *A Parrot without a Name* (1990).

[156] Hollywood story. R. T. Peterson, "Bird Song on the Silver Screen," in *All Things Reconsidered,* ed. Bill Thompson III (2006).

[157] "Cranes" in John Clare. For his references to herons, see James Fisher, *The Birds of John Clare* (1956), p. 29.

[163] Transcriptions. You can find even longer and less usable transcriptions in the big reference works such as *BWP,* as Geoffrey Hawthorn did in his highly entertaining "Diary" article in the 2 November 1995 issue of the *London Review of Books,* an essay that begins as a review of *BWP* and becomes a more general rumination that I now see anticipates many of the themes of this book.

[165] Marcus Coates. See further www.picture-this.org.uk/current/marcus2.htm.

[167] Sound cartoons. A rather good system of graphic shorthand of this kind was first proposed by Aretas Saunders in his book *Guide to Bird Songs* (1935), as Sibley himself notes in *Birding Basics,* p. 71.

[169] Recordings of birdsong. Some of them come with their own excellent documentation and commentary, an outstanding example being the Geoff Sample CDs *Warbler Songs and Calls* (2003), which was what I used for my warbler homework before going to the Volga Delta.

[169] Field guide descriptions. All from Jonsson, except the sandwich tern and the wood warbler, which are from Collins.

[172] "Kant's question." Malcolm Budd takes the opposite line to Kant in *The Aesthetic Appreciation of Nature* (2002); see in particular p. 11, note 14. The Kant reference is *Critique of Judgement* (1790), section 42.

[174] The benefits of birdsong. See the U.K. Department for Environment, Transport and the Regions report "Achieving a Better Quality of Life" (2001); and Chris Watson of the Liverpool hospitals Sonicstream project, reported by Simon Jenkins (*Guardian*, 5 October 2007). The contents of the Golden Disk put on *Voyager 1* and *2* is described in Carl Sagan's *Murmurs of the Earth* (1992) and on the Web site http://re-lab.net/welcome.

[175] Thoreau on the wood thrush. Thoreau, *Journal*: first extract 17 May 1853, second extract 22 June 1853, from vol. 6 of the Princeton University Press edition, ed. Sattelmeyer et al. (2000).

[177] The panda's thumb. See Stephen Jay Gould, *The Panda's Thumb* (1980).

[177] Birdsong and music. See Darwin, *The Expression of the Emotions in Man and Animals* (1872); and, for a range of different views: Charles Hartshorne, *Born to Sing* (1973); Peter Slater and F.-B. Mâche in N. L. Wallin et al., eds., *The Origins of Music* (2000); David Rothenberg, *Why Birds Sing* (2005); and Don Stap, *Bird Song* (2005).

[178] Messiaen and Mâche. *Conversations with Olivier Messiaen*, ed. Claude Samuel (1976), chap. 4; and F.-B. Mâche, "The Necessity of and Problems with a Universal Musicology," in Wallin et al., eds., *The Origins of Music*. See also John Blacking, *How Musical Is Man?* (1973); John Barrow, *The Artful Universe* (1995); and S. Mithen, *The Singing Neanderthals* (2005).

[178] The Beatrice Harrison story. Richard Mabey tells the whole story very well in his *Book of Nightingales* (1993), including the sequel in 1942. There is a CD with some of these historic recordings, published by the British Trust for Ornithology under the title *Nightingales: A Celebration*. See also the original account in Beatrice Harrison, *The Cello and the Nightingale*, ed. P. Cleveland-Peck (1985); and, for some surprising complications, my appendix 3.

SOURCES AND FURTHER READING

Aristotle, *On Sense and Sensibilia* (about 350 BC).

Baker, J. A., *The Hill of Summer* (1969).

Blacking, John, *How Musical Is Man?* (1973).

Barrow John, *The Artful Universe* (1995).

Budd, Malcolm, *The Aesthetic Appreciation of Nature* (2002).

Catchpole, C. K., and P.J.B. Slater, *Bird Song: Biological Themes and Variations* (1995; second edition, 2008).

Classen, Constance, *Worlds of Sense* (1993).

Crystal, David, *As They Say in Zanzibar* (2006).

Darwin, Charles, *The Expression of the Emotions in Man and Animals* (1872).

Dawson W. Leon, *Birds of Ohio* (1902).

Delbene, Bartolemeo, *Civitas Veri* (1609).

Fisher, James, *The Birds of John Clare* (1956).

Golden Guide to Field Identification: Birds of North America (1966 edition).

Gould, Stephen Jay, *The Panda's Thumb* (1980).

Harrison, Beatrice, *The Cello and the Nightingale,* ed. P. Cleveland-Peck (1985).

Hartshorne, Charles, *Born to Sing* (1973).

Hawthorn, Geoffrey, "Diary," *London Review of Books,* 2 November 1995.

Hume, Rob, *Birds of Britain and Western Europe* (2002).

Kant, Immanuel, *Critique of Judgement* (1790).

Keller, Helen, letter to Dr. J. Kerr Love, 31 March 1910.

Mabey, Richard, *Book of Nightingales* (1993).

Mâche, F.-B., "The Necessity of and Problems with a Universal Musicology," in *The Origins of Music,* ed. N. L. Wallin et al. (2000).

Mithen S., *The Singing Neanderthals* (2005).

National Geographic Field Guide to the Birds of North America, fourth edition (2002).

Peterson, Roger Tory, "Bird Song on the Silver Screen," in *All Things Reconsidered,* ed. Bill Thompson III (2006).

Raddings, Phoebe, *The Open Cage* (2000).

Rothenberg, David, *Why Birds Sing* (2005).

Sample, Geoff, *Warbler Songs and Calls* (with CDs) (2003).

Samuel, Claude, ed., *Conversations with Olivier Messiaen* (1976).

Saunders, Aretas, *Guide to Bird Songs* (1935).

Sibley, David, *Birding Basics* (2002).

Stap, Don, *Birdsong* (2005) and *A Parrot without a Name* (1990).

Thoreau, Henry, *Journal,* Princeton University Press edition, ed. R. Sattelmeyer et al. (2000).

Vinge, Louise, *The Five Senses: Studies in a Literary Tradition* (1975).

Wallin, N. L., et al., eds., *The Origins of Music* (2000).

Wilson, A. K., "Synaesthesia," *The Alleynian* 86, no. 586 (October 1958): 248–49.

Wright, David, *Deafness: A Personal Account,* second edition (1990).

Zimmer, K. J., "Ted Parker Remembered," *Birding* 25, no. 6 (1993): 377–80.

Chapter 7

NOTES

Page

[185] "golden winged-warbler." See P. Doherty, "Golden-Winged Warbler: New to the Western Palearctic," *British Birds* 85 (1992): 595–600.

[192] "Kaluli people." S. Feld, *Sound and Sentiment: Birds, Weeping, Poetics, and Song in Kaluli Expression,* p. 61.

[193] Robins becoming redstarts. See Aristotle *Historia animalium* 9.632b28; and Pliny *Naturalis historia* 10.44.

[193] "bird navigation studies." *Bird Navigation* (1955) was the title of the book by one of the modern pioneers, Geoffrey Matthews. Banding of a systematic kind started in the United States in 1907 and in England in 1909, though Denmark (1899) and Germany (1904) preceded both of these.

[194] Liddington Hill. Stephen Edwards, "Just Going Up the Hill." The hill is Liddington Hill with Liddington Castle, the site of an Iron Age hill fort, at the western end, rising to 277 metres, one of Wiltshire's highest points.

[196] The Scilly cream-coloured courser. See *Isles of Scilly Bird and Natural History Review* (2004) for a full account.

[198] Lonsale Road patch. Originally the August 1996 "Birdwatch" column by Stephen Moss in *The Guardian,* and later included in his collection *This Birding Life* (2006), which has a whole section titled "My Local Patch." Lonsdale Road is in southwest London, alongside the southern bank of the Thames to the west of Hammersmith Bridge. You can see the local patches into which London is now broken down and the lists of the top London birders on www.editthis.info/londonbirders.

[200] James Fisher on "The Seafarer." See Fisher, *Shell Bird Book,* p. 43.

[201] Brontë on Bewick. Some of Brontë's text here is a direct quotation from the introduction to the second of the two volumes of Bewick's *History of British Birds,* which was published from 1797 in two parts, *Land Birds* and *Water Birds.* By the time of Bewick's death in 1828, *Land Birds* had already been through eight editions and *Water Birds* six.

[203] Sir Peter Scott. Lieutenant-Commander Peter Scott (as he then was), from a radio broadcast on Easter Day 1943, as reported in R. Harman, ed., *Countryside Mood* (1943), p. 5.

[203] *Tawny Pipit* film. This and other examples of the appropriation of nature for nationalistic purposes are discussed in David Matless, *Landscape and Englishness* (1998).

[204] Julian Huxley quotations. From Julian Huxley, *Bird-Watching and Bird Behaviour,* pp. 4–6. The book was derived from a series of six BBC radio broadcasts. The American "thrushes" mentioned are, with the confusing exception of the American robin, in quite different genera from the British ones.

[205] Birds mentioned in *Montaillou.* He refers to the pelican, magpie, and owl on page 458 of the Gallimard edition (1978), in chapter 9, "Le sentiment de la nature et du destin," which is in any case omitted in the English translation.

SOURCES AND FURTHER READING

Allen, David Elliston, *The Naturalist in Britain* (1976).

Aristotle, *Historia animalium* (about 344 BC).

Baldwin, Stanley, "Speech to the Annual Dinner of the Royal Society of St. George," 6 May 1924, reprinted in *On England* (1926).

Brontë, Charlotte, *Jane Eyre* (1847).

Cocker, Mark, *Tiger in the Sand* (2006) and *Crow Country* (2007).

Doherty, Paul, "Golden-Winged Warbler: New to the Western Palearctic," *British Birds* 85 (1992): 595–600.

Durrell, Lawrence, "Landscape and Character," in *Spirit of Place* (1969).

Edwards, Stephen, "Just Going Up the Hill," *Wiltshire Ornithological News,* Winter 2001/2.

Feld, Steven, *Sound and Sentiment: Birds, Weeping, Poetics, and Song in Kaluli Expression,* second edition (1990).

Fermor, Patrick Leigh, *Between the Woods and the Water* (1986).

Fisher, James, *Watching Birds* (1942) and *The Shell Bird Book* (1966).

Hoskins, W. G., *The Making of the English Landscape* (1955).

Huxley, Julian, *Bird-Watching and Bird Behaviour* (1941).

Irish anon., "The Coming of Winter" (ninth century), in *A Celtic Miscellany*, ed. K. H. Jackson (1951).

Keats, John, "Ode to Autumn" (1819).

Lawrence, D. H., "Whistling of Birds" (17 February 1917).

Le Roy Ladurie, Emmanuel, *Montaillou: Village occitan, de 1294 à 1324* (1978; English translation, 1980).

Lopez, Barry, *Arctic Dreams* (1986).

Mabey, Richard, *Gilbert White* (1986) and *Nature Cure* (2005).

Matless, David, *Landscape and Englishness* (1998).

Matthews, Geoffrey, *Bird Navigation* (1955).

Mayhead, Robin, *Understanding Literature* (1965).

Moss, Stephen, *This Birding Life* (2006).

Pliny, *Naturalis historia* (about AD 77).

Puccini, G., *Madame Butterfly* (1904).

The Seafarer (ninth century?), quoted in James Fisher, *The Shell Bird Book* (1966).

Sparks, Tim, et al., "Phenology in a Changing Climate," *Trans. Suffolk Nat. Hist. Soc.* 42 (2006): 6–14.

Scott, Peter, radio broadcast on Easter Day, 1943, as reported in R. Harman, ed., *Countryside Mood* (1943).

Shakespeare, William, *The Tempest* (ca. 1611).

Thoreau, W. H., *Journal* (17 April 1854) and *Walking* (1862).

Wordsworth, William, "I Wandered Lonely as a Cloud" (1802) and "The Solitary Reaper" (1807).

Chapter 8

NOTES

Page

[209] Old Hall rarities. See the excellent reviews in the *Essex Bird Reports* for 1984 (Mackenzie-Grieve) and 2005 (Paul Charlton).

[209] John Clare "out of his knowledge." Jonathan Bate, in the introduction to his edition, *John Clare: Selected Poems* (2003).

[210] The Great Storm. The National Trust forester is David Russell, quoted by Paul Evans, reporting twenty years on in *The Guardian* of 10 October 2007. See also R. J. Fuller et al., "Responses of Woodland Birds to Storms," in *Ecological Responses to the 1987 Great Storm in the Woods of South-east England*, ed. K. J. Kirby and G. P. Buckley (1994).

[211] Birds of the western front. "Saki," from *The Square Egg and Other Sketches* (1924).

[213] Loss of diversity. There is a wealth of polemical but well-documented literature on this, running from Rachel Carson's *Silent Spring* (1963) through to books like Graham Harvey's *Killing of the Countryside* (1997). The BTO meanwhile publishes sober (and sobering) scientific reports on the steep and worsening declines of farmland species such as skylarks, turtle doves, corn buntings, and grey partridge; the only winners seem to be wood pigeons, magpies, and collared doves (see Eaton et al., "The State of the UK's Birds," 2006). But at least "bird populations" are now one of the official indicators

in the U.K. Government Sustainable Development Strategy (see www.sustainable
-development.gov.uk/progress/national/20.htm), which is a coup for the lobbying organisations.

[213] Clare and ecological ideas. See Jonathan Bate, *The Song of the Earth,* especially
pp. 146–47 and 161–68; and the introduction to his edition, *John Clare: Selected Poems.*
See also John Barrell, *The Idea of Landscape and the Sense of Place, 1730–1840.*

[214] The idea of nature. Raymond Williams, "Ideas of Nature," reprinted in *Problems in Materialism and Culture: Selected Essays.* There is a huge literature on the different and changing meanings of terms like "nature." See in particular: W. Cronon, ed.,
Uncommon Ground: Toward Reinventing Nature (1995); David Matless, *Landscape and
Englishness* (1998); and Jonathan Bate, *The Song of the Earth* (2000).

[218] Trapping. See the remarkable book by S. Haddon-Riddoch, *Rural Reflections:
A Brief History of Traps, Trapmakers and Gamekeepers in Britain* (2007); and also Roger
Lovegrove, *Silent Fields: The Long Decline of a Nation's Wildlife* (2007).

[221] On the Royal Society debate, see Oliver Rackham, *Ancient Woodland,* pp.
329–30; and C. D. Preston, "Approaches to Native and Alien Species" (2002).

[223] The great bustard reintroduction. A good brief account of the history is given
in the comprehensive avifauna *Birds of Wiltshire,* ed. J. Ferguson Lees et al. (2007),
pp. 319–22.

[224] Audubon Society report. Report of 14 June 2007, reviewed in the *New York
Times,* 15 June 2007.

SOURCES AND FURTHER READING

Barnett, A. and R. Scruton, eds., *Town and Country* (1998).

Barrell, John, *The Idea of Landscape and the Sense of Place, 1730–1840* (1972).

Bate, Jonathan, *The Song of the Earth* (2000), *John Clare: A Biography* (2003), and (as
    editor) *John Clare: Selected Poems* (2003).

Brown, A. and P. Grice, *Birds in England* (2005).

Cater, Ian, et al., "The Role of Reintroductions in Conserving British Birds," *British
    Birds* 101 (January 2008): 2–25.

Clare, John, "The Lamentations of Round-Oak Waters" (1818), "The Moors" (mid-
    1820s), "The Lament of Swordy Well" (about 1830), and notes to *Autobiography* in
    Prose Writings, ed. J. A. Tibble and A. Tibble (1951).

Cronon, W., ed., *Uncommon Ground: Toward Reinventing Nature* (1995).

Eaton, M. A., et al., *The State of the UK's Birds in 2006,* a report for the Royal Society
    for the Protection of Birds, the British Trust for Ornithology, and the Wildfowl and
    Wetlands Trust (2007).

Essex Bird Report, reviews of the birds of Old Hall Marshes, 1984 (Colin Mackenzie-
    Grieve) and 2005 (Paul Charlton).

Evans, Paul, "Winds of Change," *The Guardian,* 10 October 2007.

Ferguson Lees, J., et al., eds., *Birds of Wiltshire* (2007).

Fuller, R. J., et al., "Responses of Woodland Birds to Storms," in *Ecological Responses to
    the 1987 Great Storm in the Woods of South-east England,* ed. K. J. Kirby and G. P.
    Buckley, *English Nature Science* 23 (1994).

Haddon-Riddoch, S., *Rural Reflections: A Brief History of Traps, Trapmakers, and
    Gamekeepers in Britain* (2007).

Hansard, Report on Proceedings in the House of Lords, Thursday, 23 March 2006.

Jones, Judith B., *The L. L. Bean Game and Fish Cookbook* (1983).

Lovegrove, Roger, *The Long Decline of a Nation's Wildlife* (2007).

Matless, David, *Landscape and Englishness* (1998).

Preston, C. D., "Approaches to Native and Alien Species," *Transactions of the Suffolk Natural History Society* 38 (2002): 37–48.

Rackham, Oliver, *Ancient Woodland* (1980).

"Saki" (Hector Hugh Munro), "Birds on the Western Front," in *The Square Egg and Other Sketches* (1924).

Shakespeare, William, *Henry IV, Part 1* (1596–97).

Wiggins, David, "Nature, Respect for Nature, and the Human Scale of Values," presidential address to the Aristotelian Society, 11 October 1999.

Williams, Bernard, "Must a Concern for the Environment Be Centred on Human Beings?" in *Making Sense of Humanity* (1995).

Williams, Raymond, "Ideas of Nature," in *Problems in Materialism and Culture: Selected Essays* (1980).

Chapter 9

NOTES

Page

[234] Anonymity. See John Mullan's book *Anonymity* for the various cases cited.

[234] The "right name." See David Figlio, "Why Barbie Says 'Math Is Hard,'" *Journal of Human Resources* (forthcoming).

[238] "ruff." See Potter and Sargent, *Pedigree*, pp. 132–33; and Greenoak, *British Birds*, pp. 92–93.

[241] People. The statistics and much of this information are drawn from the comprehensive survey by Bo Beolens and Michael Watkins, *Whose Bird* (2003). Philip Lutley Sclater was founder and first editor of *The Ibis*, the journal of the British Ornithologists' Union. William Swainson was a Liverpudlian who became an illustrator and author, settling in the end in New Zealand, where he was attorney general but continued to contribute to many American publications and had several American species named in his honour. Coenraad Temminck was a Dutchman with a tragopan and a cuckoo-shrike to his name, as well as the well-known stint.

[242] "woodchat shrike." See Potter and Sargent, *Pedigree*, p. 110.

[246] "North American." I say "North American" rather than "American" because Canada shares in and has contributed to some of these names. See W. L. McAtee, "Folk Etymology in North American Bird Names," *American Speech* 26, no. 2 (May 1951): 90–95.

[248] Guillemot name. See the accounts in Lockwood, *Oxford Book of Bird Names*, pp. 75–76; and Greenoak, *British Birds*, p. 112.

[251] Taxonomies of the Foré and Western ornithologists. The article by Diamond is in Kellert and Wilson, eds., *The Biophilia Hypothesis*, as is G. P. Nabhan and Sara St. Antoine, "The Loss of Floral and Faunal Story: The Extinction of Experience," on the North American Indians and their loss of both experience and a repertoire of language. See also the references in the note on "noticing differences" on p. 327.

[251] "celebrated article." R. Bulmer, "Why Is the Cassowary Not a Bird?" *Man* 2 (1970): 5–25. This example and more general questions about natural kinds are discussed in S. Atran, *Cognitive Foundations of Natural History: Towards an Anthropology of Sci-*

ence (1990); Rosch and Lloyd, *Cognition and Categorisation* (1978); and Ian Hacking, "Natural Kinds: Rosy Dawn, Scholastic Twilight" (2007).

[252] Australian grammatical genders. See Dixon, *The Languages of Australia* (1980) and *Where Have All the Adjectives Gone?* (1982).

[254] American vernacular names. There is a handy list of all these and many others in C. Leahy, ed., *The Birdwatcher's Companion to North American Birdlife.*

[255] Collective names. There are longer lists in sources such as *Brewer's Dictionary of Phrase and Fable,* and some helpful explanations in Potter and Sargent, *Pedigree,* especially pp. 47–51.

[256] Butterflies. There is a useful list of current and former names in Peter Marren, "The English Names of Butterflies," *British Wildlife,* August 2004, pp. 401–8.

[257] Language control. The complaints by Dryden, Defoe, Swift, and others are cited, along with other examples, in David Crystal, *Cambridge Encyclopedia of the English Language,* pp. 72–73.

[260] "sound symbolism." A phenomenon recognised by the linguist Otto Jespersen in the 1920s and later taken up by Edward Sapir and others. For a lot more possible examples and some sensible reservations, see Crystal, *Cambridge Encyclopedia of the English Language,* pp. 250–53.

[261] "names chosen by some native peoples." Brent Berlin, *Ethnobiological Classification.* See also Mithen, *The Singing Neanderthals,* pp. 170–71.

SOURCES AND FURTHER READING

Atran, S., *Cognitive Foundations of Natural History: Towards an Anthropology of Science* (1990).

Austin, J. L., "A Plea for Excuses," in *Philosophical Papers* (1961).

Beltetsky, L., *Birds of the World* (2006).

Beolens, B., and Michael Watkins, *Whose Bird* (2003).

Berlin, Brent, *Ethnobiological Classification* (1992).

Book of St. Albans (1486).

Brewer's Dictionary of Phrase and Fable, seventeenth edition (2005).

"The *British Birds* List of English Names for Western Palearctic Birds," in *British Birds* 97 (January 2004): 2–5.

Bulmer, Ralph, "Why Is the Cassowary Not a Bird?" *Man* 2 (1970): 5–25.

Carroll, Lewis, *Alice through the Looking-Glass* (1871).

Choate, E. A., *The Dictionary of American Bird Names,* new edition (1985).

Collar, N. J., *Birds and People: Bonds in a Timeless Journey* (2007).

Crystal, David, *Cambridge Encyclopedia of the English Language,* second edition (2003).

Defoe, Daniel, *An Essay upon Projects* (1697).

Diamond, Jared, "The New Guineans and Their Natural World," in *The Biophilia Hypothesis,* ed. Stephen R. Kellert and Edward O. Wilson (1993).

Dickens, Charles, *Great Expectations* (1861), chap. 42.

Dixon, R., *The Languages of Australia* (1980), *Where Have All the Adjectives Gone?* (1982), and *Australian Aboriginal Words in English* (1990).

Dooley, Sean, *The Big Twitch* (2005).

Dryden, John, *Defence of the Epilogue* (1672).

Figlio, David, "Why Barbie Says 'Math Is Hard,'" *Journal of Human Resources* (forthcoming).

Fortey, Richard, *Dry Store Room No. 1: The Secret Life of the Natural History Museum* (2008).

Greenoak, F., *British Birds: Their Folklore, Names, and Literature* (1997).

Hacking, Ian, "Natural Kinds: Rosy Dawn, Scholastic Twilight," in *Philosophy of Science,* ed. A. O'Hear (2007).

Hilty, Stephen L., *Birds of Venezuela,* second edition (2003).

Jennings, Paul, "Ware, Wye, Watford," reprinted in *The Jenguin Pennings* (1963).

Jobling, J., *A Dictionary of Scientific Bird Names* (1991).

Johnson, Samuel, *A Dictionary of the English Language* (1755).

Kellert, Stephen R., and Edward O. Wilson, eds., *The Biophilia Hypothesis* (1993).

Leahy, Christopher W., *Birdwatcher's Companion to North American Birdlife* (2005).

Lockwood, W. B., *The Oxford Book of Bird Names* (1984).

Macdonald, J. H., *Illustrated Dictionary of Australian Birds by Common Name* (1987).

Marren, Peter, "The English Names of Butterflies," *British Wildlife,* August 2004, pp. 401–8.

McAtee, W. L., "Folk Etymology in North American Bird Names," *American Speech* 26, no. 2 (May 1951): 90–95.

Mill, J. S., *System of Logic* (1843), from the "Early Draft," pp. 979–81, in volume 8 of the *Collected Works,* ed. John M. Robson (1974).

Mithen, S., *The Singing Neanderthals* (2005).

Monroe, B. L., and C. G. Sibley, *A World Checklist of Birds* (1993).

Mullan, John, *Anonymity* (2008).

Oxford English Dictionary, second edition (1989).

Plato, *Cratylus* (ca. 380 BC).

Potter, Stephen, and Laurens Sargent, *Pedigree: The Origins for Words from Nature* (1974).

Punch 57 (1869): 96.

Rosch, Eleanor, and Barbara Lloyd, *Cognition and Categorisation* (1978).

Swift, Jonathan, "A Proposal for Correcting, Improving, and Ascertaining the English Tongue" (1712).

Tennyson, Alfred, "The Princess" (1847).

vom Bruck, Gabriele, and Barbara Bodenhorn, *The Anthropology of Names and Naming* (2006).

Chapter 10

NOTES

Page

[265] Ravens. See Tate, *Flights of Fancy,* p. 113; Armstrong, *Folklore of Birds,* pp. 71–93; and Cocker, *BB,* pp. 423–28.

[266] Oracles. See the works by Bowden, Flacelière, and Wood in the list of sources and further readings. Bowden (p. 19) does at least discuss the possibility of intoxication by natural emissions of the gas ethylene. Other useful discussions are in Simon Price, "Delphi and Divination," in *Greek Religion and Society,* ed. Pat Easterling and John Muir (1970); and Catherine Morgan in *Athletes and Oracles* (1990).

[268] Aristophanes. Translations from Aristophanes are from the Penguin edition (1978). All other translations from the Greek in this chapter are my own.

[273] The two emperors Andronikos. See Donald Nicol, *The Last Centuries of Constantinople, 1261–1453,* second edition (1993), p. 170n10.

[276] "creation of an official seal." My source on the early discussions about the American eagle as a symbol of state is the article by Tom Evans in Stefferud, ed., *Birds in Our Lives.* The article by Shirley Briggs in the same volume deals with the later and generally less serious adoption of birds as state emblems in the United States.

[291] "other minds." See in the list of sources and further reading the works by Wittgenstein, Lévi-Strauss, Geertz, Sperber, Skorupski, and Nagel. On metaphors in science, unconscious and otherwise, see Boyd, "Metaphor and Theory Change."

SOURCES AND FURTHER READING

Aeschylus, *Agamemnon* (458 BC) and *Prometheus Bound* (ca. 456 BC).

Aesop, *Fables* (probably sixth century BC); the *Fables* and the *Life* are both included in translation in *Aesop without Morals,* ed. Lloyd W. Daly (1961).

Aristophanes, *The Birds* (414 BC).

Armstrong, Edward A., *The Folklore of Birds* (1958).

Arnott, W. Geoffrey, *Birds in the Ancient World from A to Z* (2007).

Attar, Farid ud-Din, *The Conference of the Birds* (early twelfth century), abridged edition, ed. R. Abdulla (2002).

Baker, J. A., *The Peregrine* (1967).

Bateson, Patrick, "Assessment of Pain in Animals," *Animal Behaviour* 42 (1991): 827–30; and "Choice, Preference and Selection," in *Interpretation and Explanation in Animal Behaviour,* ed. M. Bekoff and D. Jamieson (1990).

Bede, *A History of the English Church and People* (eighth century), translation by Leo Sherley-Price (1955).

Berger, John, "Why Look at Animals?" in *About Looking* (1980).

Bowden, Hugh, *Classical Athens and the Delphic Oracle* (2005).

Boyd, Richard, "Metaphor and Theory Change," in *Metaphor and Thought,* ed. Andrew Ortony, second ed. (1993).

Briggs, Geoffrey, *Civic and Corporate Heraldry* (1971).

Briggs, Shirley A., "Symbols of States," in *Birds in Our Lives,* ed. Alfred Stefferud (1966).

Collar, N. J., *Birds and People: Bonds in a Timeless Journey* (2007).

Douglas, Mary, *Purity and Danger* (1966; reissued with a new introduction, 2002).

Evans, Tom, "The Nation's Symbol," in *Birds in Our Lives,* ed. Alfred Stefferud (1966).

Evans-Pritchard, E. E., *Witchcraft, Oracles, and Magic among the Azande* (1937); abridged version, ed. Eva Gillies (1976).

Flacelière, R., *Greek Oracles* (1965).

Franklin, Benjamin, Letter to Sarah Bache, 26 January 1784, in the Library of America, *Benjamin Franklin* volume (1987).

Franzen, Jonathan, "My Bird Problem: Love, Grief and a Change in the Weather," *New Yorker,* 8 and 15 August 2005.

Geertz, Clifford, *The Interpretation of Cultures* (1973).

Gordon, Seton, *The Golden Eagle* (1955).

Graves, Robert, *The White Goddess* (1956).

Homer, *Iliad* and *Odyssey* (about 700 BC).

Kennedy, John S., *The New Anthropomorphism* (1992).

Kruuk, Hans, *Niko's Nature: The Life of Niko Tinbergen and His Science* (2004).

Levi, Peter, *The Hill of Kronos* (1981).

Lévi-Strauss, Claude, *Totemism* (1962).

Macdonald, Helen, "Covert Naturalists" (2005, unpublished).

Maclean, Adam, "The Birds in Alchemy," *Hermetic Journal* 5 (1979).

Machiavelli, Niccolò, *The Discourses* (1531).

Nagel, Thomas, "What Is It Like to Be a Bat?" in *Mortal Questions* (1979).

Nozedar, Adele, *The Secret Language of Birds* (2006).

Pausanias, *Guide to Greece* (about AD 170), translated in two volumes by Peter Levi (1971).

Pollard, John, *Birds in Greek Life and Myth* (1977).

Plutarch, "On the Cleverness of Animals," *Moralia* 12 (about AD 70).

Shakespeare, *Henry VI, Part III* (ca. 1595).

Skorupski, John, *Symbol and Theory* (1976).

Sperber, Dan, *Rethinking Symbolism* (1974).

Spurgeon, Caroline, *Shakespeare's Imagery* (1935).

Tate, Peter, *Flights of Fancy: Birds in Myth, Legend, and Superstition* (2007).

Taylor, Richard, *How to Read a Church* (2003).

Whitman, Walt, "The Dalliance of Eagles" (1880), included in *Leaves of Grass* (1881).

Wittgenstein, Ludwig, *Philosophical Investigations,* trans. G.E.M. Anscombe (1953).

Wood, Michael, *The Road to Delphi: The Life and Afterlife of Oracles* (2003).

Envoi

SOURCES AND FURTHER READING

Burns, Robert, "The Brigs of Ayr" (1786).

Eliot, T. S., "Burnt Norton" and "Little Gidding," from *Four Quartets* (1944).

Emerson, Ralph Waldo, "Nature" (1849).

Heraclitus, fragment 200, in *The Presocratic Philosophers,* by G. S. Kirk, J. E. Raven, and M. Schofield, second edition (1983).

Murdoch, Iris, *The Sovereignty of the Good* (1970).

Weitz, Morris, "T. S. Eliot: Time as a Mode of Salvation" (1952), reprinted in *T. S. Eliot: Four Quartets,* ed. B. Bergonzi (1969).

Wilson, Edward O., *Biophilia* (1984).

Appendices

NOTES

Page

[303] My suggestions about species. I have based these on the distributions in R. F. Porter et al., *Birds of the Middle East* (1996). Veldhuis dates most of these texts to the Old Babylonian period of about 1900–1600 BC. It is interesting to compare the list compiled by the U.S. soldier stationed in Baghdad in 2004–5 and published in his diary (Jonathan Trouern-Trend, *Birding Babylon: A Soldier's Journal from Iraq,* 2006), which was based on a daily blog that attracted thousands of readers on-line.

[304] "directly derived from Catesby's work." Catesby's list seems in turn to have been directly derived from John Lawson, whose catalogue of 129 birds in his *New*

Voyage to Carolina (1709) can properly be regarded as the first American list of birds. See Alan Feduccia, ed., *Catesby's Birds of Colonial America* (1985).

[307] John Clare's list. The manuscript is in Peterborough Museum (MS A46). It has been published with some excellent notes by James Fisher, but unfortunately this edition appeared in a rather recondite source, *A History of the Kettering and District Naturalists' Society and Field Club*, pp. 26–69 (Kettering 1956), and I am grateful to the Fisher family for giving me a copy. Other sources worth consulting are: Eric Robinson and Richard Fitter, eds., *John Clare's Birds* (1982), and Margaret Grainger, ed., *The Natural History Prose Writings of John Clare* (1983).

[312] The literary and musical persona of the nightingale. This is all very well documented and discussed in Richard Mabey's *The Book of Nightingales* (1997), originally published as *Whistling in the Dark* (1993).

[314] "Beatrice Harrison and her nightingales." Beatrice Harrison, *The Cello and the Nightingale*, ed. P. Cleveland Peck (1985). See also Mabey, *The Book of Nightingales*, pp. 109–14, and David Rothenberg, *Why Birds Sing*, pp. 142–43.

[317] "eighth-century riddle poem." The nightingale riddle is one of a group of Anglo-Saxon riddles in the *Exeter Book* (anon., probably eighth century). This version is cited in Richard Mabey, *The Book of Nightingales* (London: Sinclair-Stevenson, 1997), p. 41; and in Peggy Munsterberg, ed., *The Penguin Book of Bird Poetry* (London: Allen Lane, 1980), p. 105. The identity of the "solution" is discussed in Frederick Tupper, *The Riddles of the Exeter Book* (1910), and in Kevin Crossley-Holland, *The Exeter Riddle Book* (1979), both of these scholars favouring "jay."

[318] Australian bird names. The main published sources for these are the complete *Oxford English Dictionary*, second edition (1989), the *Australian National Dictionary* (1988, largely derived from the *OED*), R.M.W. Dixon et al., *Aboriginal Words in English* (1990), Graham Pizzey, *A Field Guide to the Birds of Australia* (1980), and J. H. Macdonald, *Illustrated Dictionary of Australian Birds by Common Name* (1987). I have also been much helped by a correspondence with John Peter, a senior editor of the *Handbook of Australian, New Zealand, and Antarctic Birds* (7 volumes, 1990–2006), which also contains information on the derivation of the scientific names.

Index of Birds

Extreme listers might like to know that there are entries for 683 species below (plus a few more for genera and families). I have not, however, indexed birds mentioned only in the lists in appendices 1, 2, and 4. I have generally used the British form of common names, with cross-references to North American names where needed.

General Index

Acknowledgements and Permissions

Plates
1. (a) National Archaeological Museum, Athens. Photo by Nimatallah/Art Resource, New York. (b) Dan Zetterström © Killian Mullarney, Lars Svensson, Dan Zetterström, and Peter J. Grant, *Collins Bird Guide: The Most Complete Guide to the Birds of Britain and Europe,* HarperCollins Publishers Ltd., 1999.
2. Ramiel Papish/Windsor Nature Discovery with inset from A&C Black Publishers © Jon Curson, David Quinn, and David Beadle, *New World Warblers,* Helm, 1994.
3. (a) Photo by Shootov Igor/Shutterstock. (b) and (c) photos by Bill Baston, www. billbaston.com.
4. Plates 1, 181, and 260 in John James Audubon, *The Birds of America* (1827–38). Images courtesy of the Academy of Natural Sciences, Ewell Sale Stewart Library.
5. (a) Thielska Galleriet, Stockholm. Photo by Tord Lund. (b) Photo by Nikolay Stepkin. (c) Plate 37 in John Gould, *The Birds of Europe,* vol. 1, printed by R. and J. E. Taylor. Image courtesy of the Academy of Natural Sciences, Ewell Sale Stewart Library.
6. (a) Photo by L. Kelly/Shutterstock. (b) A&C Black Publishers © Tony Juniper and Mike Parr, *Parrots: A Guide to Parrots of the World,* Helm, 2003. (c) Photos by Bill Jolly, www.abberton.org (variegated fairy-wren, red-backed fairy-wren); Graeme Chapman, graemechapman.com.au (superb fairy-wren, splendid fairy-wren).
7. (a) Royal Society for the Protection of Birds © Mike Langman. (b) Reproduced by kind permission of Sarah Adams. (c) Crabtree & Evelyn, 2007.
8. (b) Royal Mail © Kate Stephens/Royal Mail. Reproduced by kind permission of Royal Mail Group Ltd., all rights reserved.

Figures
1. Biblioteca Reale, Turin. Image courtesy SCALA/Art Resource, New York.
2. Edward Armstrong in *The Folklore of Birds,* reproduced in S. Reinach, *Répertoire des vases peints,* 1899.
3. In Eric Robinson and Richard Fitter, *John Clare's Birds,* Oxford University Press, 1982. Reproduced by kind permission of Robert Gillmor.
4. Dover Publications, Inc. © ed. Blanche Cirker, *1800 Woodcuts by Thomas Bewick and His School,* 1962.
5. Drawing © Richard Millington.
6. P. 189 in Edmund Sandars, *A Bird Book for the Pocket,* Oxford University Press, 1927.
7. (a) In S. Vere Benson, *The Observer's Book of British Birds,* 1937. Reproduced by permission of Frederick Warne and Co. (b) In Roger Tony Peterson, Guy Mountfort, and P.A.D. Hollom, *A Field Guide to the Birds of Britain and Europe,* 5E, 1993. Reprinted by permission of Houghton Mifflin Harcourt Publishing

Company. All rights reserved. (c) Dan Zetterström © Killian Mullarney, Lars Svensson, Dan Zetterström, and Peter J. Grant, *Collins Bird Guide: The Most Complete Guide to the Birds of Britain and Europe,* HarperCollins Publishers Ltd., 1999.

8. Photo by Nikolay Stepkin.
9. Oxford University Library Services.
10. Photos by Robin Chittenden.
11. Photo by Steve Bryant, www.stevebryantphotography.co.uk.
12. In D. Cottridge and K. Vinnicombe, *A Photographic Record of Rare Birds in Britain and Ireland,* Collins, 1996. Reproduced with kind permission of Peter E. Wheeler. Photo by Peter E. Wheeler.
14. Sir Peter Scott/Wildlife and Wetlands Trust. Reproduced by kind permission of Lady Scott.
15. Plate facing p. 745 in David Snow, Christopher M. Perrins, and Robert Gillmor, *Birds of the Western Palearctic,* concise edition, Oxford University Press, 1997. By permission of Oxford University Press.
16. (d) In Richard Gregory, *Eye and Brain,* Weidenfeld and Nicholson, Orion Publishing Group, 1966. Reprinted with permission.
17. In Alan Harris, Laurel Tucker, David Christie, and Keith Vinnicombe, *The Macmillan Field Guide to Bird Identification,* Pan Macmillan, 1989. Reprinted with kind permission of the artist.
18. Solo Syndication/Associated Newspapers Ltd.
19. In Roger Tory Peterson, Guy Mountfort, and P.A.D. Hollom, *A Field Guide to the Birds of Britain and Europe,* HarperCollins, 1954. reprinted by permission of HaperCollins Publishers Ltd. © Peterson, Mountford, Hollom 1954.
20. (a) In R. S. Fitter and R.A.R. Richardson, *The Pocket Guide to British Birds,* HarperCollins,1952. (b) P. 26 in T. Hamilton, *Identification: Friend or Foe* (1994). Courtesy the Imperial War Museum, London.
21. Image courtesy Hulton Archives/Getty Images.
22. Photo © Ed Alcock, 2008.
23. Plate 46 in Roger Tony Peterson, Guy Mountfort, and P.A.D. Hollom, *A Field Guide to the Birds of Britain and Europe,* 1993. Reprinted by permission of Houghton Mifflin Harcourt Publishing Company. All rights reserved.
24. In John Johnston, *The Lord Chamberlain's Blue Pencil,* Hodder & Stoughton Ltd., 1990.
25. (a) Reproduced in Jonathan Elphick, *Birds: The Art of Ornithology,* Scriptum Editions, 2004, © Natural History Museum, London. (b) In *The Birds of Europe,* 1992.
26. Dover Publications, Inc. © ed. Blanche Cirker, *1800 Woodcuts by Thomas Bewick and His School,* 1962.
27. Plate 219 in John James Audubon, *The Birds of America* (1827–38). Image courtesy of the Academy of Natural Sciences, Ewell Sale Stewart Library.
28. In Rob Hume and Peter Partington, *Birds by Character: A Field Guide to Jizz,* Pan Macmillan, 1990.
29. Lars Jonsson, p. 111 in *The Birds of Europe,* 1992; and in Dan Zetterström © Killian Mullarney, Lars Svensson, Dan Zetterström, and Peter J. Grant, *Collins*

Bird Guide: The Most Complete Guide to the Birds of Britain and Europe, HarperCollins Publishers Ltd., 1999.

30. Mary Evans Picture Library Ltd.

32. Photo "Sky Chase" by Manuel Presti.

33. Image courtesy of World Coin Gallery, www.worldcoingallery.com (fig. 33)

34. In Alfred Russel Wallace, *The Malay Archipelago,* 1869.

35. In *Civitas Veri,* 1609.

36. Reproduced in the Readers' Digest *Book of Birds,* 1969.

37. In *Misurgia universalis,* 1650.

38. Images courtesy Geoff Sample, www.wildsong.co.uk.

39. © 2002 by David Allen Sibley. Reprinted by permission of Alfred A. Knopf, a division of Random House, Inc.

40. Image courtesy Geoff Sample, www.wildsong.co.uk.

41. Photo by Topical Press Agency/Getty Images.

42. In P. J. Lanspeary, *The World of Birds on Stamps,* HH Sales Ltd, 1975.

43. *The Ship,* plate 5 in Thomas Bewick, *A History of British Birds,* volume 2, *Water Birds,* 1804. Dover Publications, Inc. © ed. Blanche Cirker, *1800 Woodcuts by Thomas Bewick and His School,* 1962.

44. Image courtesy Mike Howarth/The National Trust.

45. By permission of Lou Chapman and *The Denver Post,* for the 14 February 1987, edition of *The Denver Post.*

46. Reproduced in S. Haddon-Riddoch, *Rural Reflections: A Brief History of Traps, Trapmakers and Gamekeepers in Britain,* 2007.

47. The Great Bustard Group/Bryn Parry.

48. (a) In Graham Pizzey, Frank Knight, *The Field Guide to Birds of Australia* HarperCollins Publishers, Australia, 1997. Reproduced by permission. (b) and (c), pp. 240 and 546 in Thomas S. Schulenberg, Douglas F. Stotz, Daniel F. Lane, John P. O'Neill, and Theodore A. Parker III, *Birds of Peru,* Princeton University Press, 2007. Reproduced by permission.

49. In Steven L. Hilty, *The Birds of Venezuela,* Princeton University Press, 2003.

51. Photo © William Shepherd.

52. (a) Birdwatchers' guide in *Where to Watch Birds in Turkey, Greece and Cyprus,* Octopus Publishing Group,1996. Reprinted with permission. (b) In the *Green Guide Greece,* 1987. © Michelin et Cie, 2008, Authorisation no. GB0806001.

53. Albanian eagle courtesy of Cradel/Wikipedia. Mexican coat of arms, Egypt coat of arms, Russian Federation flag, courtesy of Wikipedia.

54. Reproduced in A. Stefferud, ed., *Birds in Our Lives,* 1966.

55. (a) Courtesy of Cornwall County Council. (b) Courtesy of Wiltshire County Council.

56. Dan Zetterström © Killian Mullarney, Lars Svensson, Dan Zetterström, and Peter J. Grant, *Collins Bird Guide: The Most Complete Guide to the Birds of Britain and Europe,* HarperCollins Publishers Ltd., 1999.

57. Time and Life Pictures/Getty Images. Photo by Nina Leen/Stringer.